To
New
Zealand

Saunders Coast

Whales

Mt. Rea

Mt. Grace
McKinley

EDSEL FORD RANGES

MARIE

BYRD

LAND

OUTH POLE

(U.S.)

A PLATE

ICE

ICE

The Antarctic Diary of Charles F. Passel

By Charles F. Passel
Edited by T. H. Baughman

Texas Tech University Press

This book was set in Garamond and printed on acid-free paper that meets the guidelines for permanence and durability of the Committee on Production Guidelines for Book Longevity of the Council on Library Resources.

Printed in the United States of America

Library of Congress Cataloging-in-Publication Data
Passel, Charles F.
    Ice : the Antarctic diary of Charles F. Passel / by Charles F. Passel ; edited by T. H. Baughman
       p.   cm.
    ISBN 0-89672-347-X (cloth : acid-free)
    1. Passel, Charles F.—Journeys. 2. Byrd Antarctic Expedition.
    3. Antarctica—Discovery and exploration—American.
    I. Baughman, T. H. II. Title.
G850 1939 .P38P38 1995
919.8′9—dc20   95-17180
                                           CIP

95 96 97 98 99 00 01 02 03 04 / 9 8 7 6 5 4 3 2 1

Texas Tech University Press
P. O. Box 41037
Lubbock, Texas 79409-1037 USA
   1-800-832-4042

I dedicate this writing to my wife, Alda, who is very much a part of this Antarctic Experience, and to my daughters Charlotte, Jane Ann, Martha

EDITOR'S PREFACE

How I envy the reader picking up this book for the first time: he or she is about to be transported back to Antarctica in the 1930s for an intimate portrait—as Oliver Cromwell might have suggested, warts and all—of life on Admiral Richard E. Byrd's 1939 expedition. *Ice: The Antarctic Diary of Charles F. Passel* is a valuable and interesting addition to Antarctic lore before the Second World War. Passel's simple, direct narrative captures the essence of Antarctic expedition life in the 1930s as few other accounts have, offering the reader an insight into daily routine and giving that person a genuine sense of being at West Base Unit, 1939-41.

Although at one point Passel was frustrated enough with the devastating cold and misery of the Antarctic clime to note of Antarctica that "they can give it all back to the Indians," the respect and fascination that the South Polar regions developed in the explorer overcame this frustration. Passel wrote every day, an essential aspect of journal keeping. Through his daily accounts, the reader joins in the transformation from distress at the conditions to admiration for the majesty of the continent and all it offers the scientist and adventurer.

Antarctic life in the 1930s was still a constant struggle against the elements. Simple tasks like getting up in the morning or going to bed in the evening took half an hour in the field; even at base camp life remained challenging. Preparing breakfast required the cook to begin by prying the frozen griddle loose from its moorings on the shelf. Transportation during the United States Antarctic Expedition of 1939 was in the transition phase between human and animal power to that of machines. Still, engines had to be heated with a blowtorch, oil froze during changes, and traction problems meant that one key tractor would only operate in reverse. All these vagaries related to the southern clime are brought to life in the terse, straightforward style of a young geologist drawn by the opportunities of making his mark on science.

Although technological advances eliminated some of the remoteness—radio kept trail parties in contact with the base and the men in touch with their families back home—the eminent danger of the Antarctic was still a part of expedition life in 1939. At one point, Passel arrived back at base camp after a harrowing tractor trip to support a field crew only to have the machine break down the next time it was used. Had it quit a day earlier, Passel would have been caught miles from his station.

Unlike many formal published accounts of other explorers that filter out the loneliness and isolation, the twenty-five-year-old Passel exhibited the real concerns a young man has so far from family and fiancée. Nothing makes the story more vivid or appealing than the realization that the girl he hoped would wait, did, and their marriage of fifty-four years began three weeks after Passel returned from the South Polar regions. Alda, while getting her master's degree at New York University and continuing her retail career, eagerly awaited word from her young explorer and the reader senses the tenderness of Passel's affection for her so far from his windblown Antarctic station.

The far off reaches of Antarctica first came to the attention of humans centuries ago, but Antarctica was not discovered officially until 1820-21 when within a few months of one another three separate expeditions, representing three different nations, spied the frozen wastes of the continent. Important preliminary investigations took place in the 1830s but only with the efforts of the 1840s did the formal exploration of Antarctica begin.

In that decade, three major expeditions were launched—Jules-Sebastian Dumont d'Urville (1740-1842) of France, Charles Wilkes (1798-1877) of the United States, and James Clark Ross (1800-62) of Great Britain. These major preliminary efforts were not pursued by subsequent expeditions for more than forty years. In 1874 the *Challenger* explored southern waters at high latitude but no landing was made on the continent.

The first undisputed landing on the Antarctic continent took place 23 January 1895 when Carsten E. Borchgrevink (1864-1934), a sailor on

H. J. Bull's *Antarctic* expedition, leaped ashore from the back of the boat to claim to be the first man on the last continent. Borchgrevink went on to lead an important pioneering expedition, the *Southern Cross* (1898-1900) to the Antarctic, which was the first to overwinter on the continent, while Adrien de Gerlache's *Belgica* expedition (1897-99) spent a bleak winter beset in the ice off the continent. Also in that decade the International Geographical Congress in 1895 passed a resolution noting that the exploration of Antarctica was the most pressing geographical problem in the world.

The Heroic Era (1901-22), roughly from the launching of the *Discovery* to the death of Sir Ernest Shackleton (1874-1922), has garnered the most attention from historians. Each of these endeavors contained stories of wonderful hardiness and adventure. Whether one considers the great bravery of Shackleton turning back from the pole rather than risk the lives of his men, the daring, superbly planned successful attempt on the pole in 1911 by Roald Amundsen (1872-1928), or the ill-fated attempt by Robert Falcon Scott (1868-1912) to reach that same southern extremity, few periods in modern history are so replete with great tales.

The 1920s and 1930s saw a change in the kinds and goals of expeditions. Small, private ones continued to be launched, but the Discovery Committee, which Great Britain sponsored, pointed to larger, governmental projects, beyond the scope of a single person to plan, to generate funds, and to execute. The first expedition (1928-30) of Richard E. Byrd (1888-1957) was a private one, as was his second (1933-35), and while containing such events as the first flight over the South Pole, emphasized science. As such, Byrd's three expeditions in the thirties formed a transitional phase.

Byrd's 1939 effort was significantly different from the first two as it was a government expedition, with Byrd with overall direction but assuming a much more minor role in daily affairs than in previous efforts. The United States Antarctic Service (1939-41) grew out of two separate plans for exploration, one by Byrd and the other by Richard B. Black (1902-92) and Finn Ronne (1899-1980). Franklin D. Roosevelt urged the two efforts be combined and funded by the federal government, thus heralding the emergence of big government expeditions.

Two bases were planned, East Base in Marguerite Bay under the command of Richard Black, and West Base under the command of Paul Siple (1908-68), formerly the Boy Scout who had accompanied Byrd in 1928.

World War Two already had begun in Europe and Hitler's Germany had launched the *Schwabenland* (1938-39) expedition to stake claims in the South Polar regions. To some degree the United States government was motivated to act similarly to claim land in Antarctica.

Passel takes the reader aboard the *North Star* with the United States Antarctic Service for a voyage of science and discovery to great white South. Al Wade, Passel's former professor at Miami University in Oxford, Ohio, chose him to join the expedition as the sedimentary paleontologist and soft rock geologist. Passel went to Boston to interview with Admiral Byrd and remained there to take charge of the supplies for the expedition. Larry Warner, also from Miami University, joined Passel later to be his assistant. Passel's account takes up the story when the expedition sailed from Boston 15 November 1939.

This edition reproduces the full text of the limited press run of the original publication. In addition, end notes supplement the manuscript with information to explain and illuminate the events of 1939-41. Economy demanded that the notes be limited; however, I have endeavored to provide sufficient explanation to enhance the enjoyment of reading Passel's diary. The reader should begin by determining how the notes are organized and how best to profit from them.

Antarcticans will be gratified that Texas Tech University Press has undertaken the publication of this material, making it available to a larger audience. In preparing this recension I enjoyed a wonderfully pleasant relationship with the editorial staff at Lubbock and express my thanks to them for honoring me with the opportunity of joining in this project.

I would also like to thank Katherine Immel for her assistance in the preparation of the editorial materials. My colleagues at Benedictine College, especially William P. Hyland, Georgia McGarry, and Rupert Pate, have been supportive at every stage. As with all my scholarly work, I wish to acknowledge my enormous debt to Richard L. and Judith Dieker Greaves and mention again how much I have appreciated their kindness and inspiration.

My greatest appreciation in this endeavor goes to Charles Passel who is the real hero of this tale. Return with him now to the world of Antarctica in the 1930s.

Atchison, Kansas
August 1994

FOREWORD
to the 1984 edition

I couldn't have been more surprised when a few months ago my father handed me an enormous stack of typed pages and informed me what it was and what my job was to do with it. I had my doubts. It was the first I had heard of it. But the acknowledgment of my "editorship" was already written so I agreed. What else could I do? The job turned out to be a total pleasure and a true privilege.

The pleasure was in the story itself, like the difference between turning the pages of an art history book and later having the opportunity to visit an art museum and really see the paintings themselves. I had known the story of the expedition for almost as long as I can remember for seeing my father's "slides of the Antarctic" many times, which I always looked forward to and enjoyed. Now I feel as though I have really been there, as nearly as possible, because I have seen the details and colors through my father's eyes.

The privilege was simply to have a glimpse of my own father before I knew him, the person I know as my father as a person, who is also a person besides my father. And I am very grateful for that rare privilege.

The editing job itself, I might add, turned out to be easy, although it did take a little time. It was a simple matter of proofreading, not my forte, clearing up two or three scrambled sentences and relocating a few commas. Vicky Pierce, who typed the final copy, was an invaluable help to me both in her expert skills and in her enthusiasm and genuine enjoyment of the writing.

I don't know how or why my father came up with the idea to keep a journal during the expedition, but I am glad he did and I am very glad to have it now.

Charlotte Passel
Escondido, California
April 1984

ACKNOWLEDGMENTS

It gives me pleasure to honor the memory of Dr. Paul Siple and Dr. F. Alton Wade with this writing, and to acknowledge my old comrade and fellow geologist Larry Warner.

I am most indebted to my daughter, Charlotte Passel, who has painstakingly edited this work and has supervised its printing.

The Scientific Staff
of the U.S. Antarctic Service Expedition 1939 1941,
Rear Admiral Richard E. Byrd, Commanding Officer

Snow Cruiser Unit

F. Alton Wade, senior scientist, geol. . . . . Al, F. Alton, Doc

West Base Unit

Paul A. Siple, base leader, geographer . . . . Paul
Leonard M. Berlin, cadastral engineer . . . . Klondicke, Len
Arnold Court, meteorologist . . . .
Roy G. Fitzsimmons, magnetician, sei . . . . Fitz
Russel G. Frazier, medical officer . . . . Doc., Doc. F
Earnest E. Lockhart, physiologist . . . . Earl
Charles F. Passel, geologist . . . . "C"
Jack E. Perkins, biologist . . . . Perk
Lawrence A. Warner, geologist . . . . Larry
Murray A. Wiener, auroral observer . . . . Murray

Snow Cruiser Unit

Felix Ferranto . . . . Phil
Clyde W. Griffith . . . . Grif
Theodore Petras . . . . Pete

West Base

Loran Wells . . . . Joe
Adam Asman . . . . Sgt, Nib, Nibble
Clay W. Bailey . . . . Clay
Vernon D. Boyd . . . . Buck
Jack Bursey . . . . Jack B.
Raymond Butler . . . . Ray, Zeke
Louis Colombo . . . . Toney
Malcolm C. Douglass . . . . Malc, Doug
Walter R. Giles . . . . Walt
Harold P. Gilmore . . . . Gil
Orville Gray . . . . Pappy G.

1939

Sailed at 6:00 o'clock a.m. this morning. A few people were down to see us off. I received farewell telegrams from the Fattig's and Bob. Al, Wade, Palmer, Warner and myself were snapped by photographers as four from Miami University. We spent about two or three hours outside the harbor setting the compass. Finally the pilot boat pulled alongside and we headed for Philadelphia. Beautiful day, sea just right for a landlubber. We spent most of the morning getting squared around, lashing things down, etc. During the afternoon, I looked over my dogs—nine in all, Eskimos and Malamutes, seven are black and white, and two pure white. A fine bunch of dogs— Kotik the lead dog is especially smart.

Tonight after dinner Al, Larry and myself went to Al's cabin, broke out West Base records and had sort of a jam session. Dr. Frazier dropped in a little later. It is now 9:00 o'clock and it is getting a little rough.

November 16

About 7:00 o'clock in the morning, ate a hearty breakfast. Had a meeting at nine o'clock. Charlie the Mate gave us a little talk on fire and what was expected of us, a little gab feast so to speak. Spent the morning lashing canvas to the deck railing as much of our equipment will have to remain on deck. Tried to finish some of my paperwork but did not have much success. Sea is fairly rough today. The *Star* is taking spray over her bow and ever so often the cruiser gets her share. None of the fellows have missed any meals, *yet*, but if this weather keeps up I imagine there will be a few empty places. Tonight after dinner played bridge with Doc Geyer (ship Doctor), Commander Schlossbach (Ike), the chief Engineer. Doc and I got kind of taken. We are now probably (10:30) somewhere off the coast of Delaware, looking for a lighthouse boat where we change our course and head north (?) toward Delaware Bay where we will anchor till morning—then we will proceed to Philadelphia.

November 17

Harbor Pilot came aboard about seven o'clock a.m., and we started the trip up the Delaware. We passed several foreign ships, mostly Finn and Norwegian. Most of the fellows loafed around back aft shooting the bull, stopping dog fights, etc. We arrived at the Navy yard about 2:00 o'clock. Quite a few people were on hand, reporters and the most important, my folks. We had some trouble landing the line on one of the tugs (port) which broke and we crashed into it, smashing it between us and the dock. The *Star* swung her bow and hitting the dock put several deep nicks on the port side. I was very glad to see my folks, and after helping unload the dogs I got cleaned up and we went to their hotel, ate and sat in the lobby waiting for Howard. He arrived about 9:00 o'clock and we all went to the room and had a kind of family reunion. Was very nice. I got back to the ship around midnight.

November 18

Worked during the morning trying to find something to do. There are so many WPA fellows, Navy yard employees on hand that we fellows of the expedition are having a tough time finding work. However, I did water my dogs and answer a bunch of questions concerning them, thus completing a very strenuous morning. The *Condor* was loaded back aft during the morning and she takes up about all the aft well deck. My folks and Howard came aboard around noon and we ate lunch down below. Our table consisted of we four, Dr. Frazier, Finn Ronnie, Commander Schlossbach, Don Hilton and Larry Warner. After lunch Ray Butler, Dick Moulton and myself posed for a cigarette advertisement—Camel, took several group pictures with dogs, then some close-ups, each fellow having a huskie. Of course we all said we would walk a mile for a Camel. We each received a carton of Camels which will come in very handy for trading purposes. The folks left for Indianapolis on the five o'clock train. Howard and I ate downtown, met Larry, and we all

2

went to see the Marx Brothers in "The Circus." Got to the ship about midnight.

November 19

Received a telegram last night from Alda saying to meet her at the Broad Street Station at 10:45 a.m. She certainly looked very sweet and attractive. We ate dinner at Childs on Chestnut. After dinner we came out here to the Navy Yard. I showed her around on the ship and we had a little gathering in Cabin #8—Al, Larry, Gilmore, Alda, Jane and myself. Time seems to pass very fast because it seemed that we were together such a short time. We had a light supper at Lofts and Alda caught the eight o'clock train for New York.

November 20

Today was more or less just hanging around. Tried to clean our cabin and get squared around. Wrote Alda a nice sugar report. After lunch Gil, Larry and I went to town. Got my clarinet fixed, we tramped around town, looked Wanamakers over, played a $1050 radio and was told politely but firmly to keep hands off. We all looked like bums, it's a wonder we were not locked up. During the evening we had an orchestra practice which consisted of my clarinet, a couple of tambourines and some toy horns and harmonicas. It was quite a session with Larry, Pappy Reese, Ennis Helm, Moe Morency, Bob Steele, Sgt. Asman, Doc Frazier and Malcolm Douglass.

November 21

It had been breathed that we were going to sail at noon so all hands ran around taking care of various odds and ends. The Beechcraft was loaded up beside the Snow Cruiser. She is certainly a trim ship. We loaded all the dogs, which is an awkward job. We had a couple of planks but they didn't like the idea. Quite a few people were aboard, wives, sisters, daughters and friends. There was the usual assembly of photographers and newsmen running around taking pictures of all the big shots. It started to snow about 11:00 o'clock a.m., which will certainly be appreciated for sailing. We finally got started at 3:00 o'clock, just two hours late. There were only a few people to see us off besides the fellows' wives and friends, and they were mostly gobs and men working around the yard. The weather was rather bad, foggy and wet. It makes it pretty hard

3

since we have to make the trip down the river which is a crooked one. After a final salute from our tug we all pulled ourselves from the railing and started the job of making things seaworthy, which was quite a job. After dinner we got a little bridge game started, Doc Geyer, myself, the Commander (Ike) and Moe. Doc and I kind of took the boys over + 35. It is now 9:00 o'clock p.m. and the ship seems to be rolling a little and there is some hail and snow. A good night to stand watch.

Wednesday, November 22

After breakfast worked awhile on deck, lashing down. We stopped last night about eleven o'clock and dropped anchor inside Delaware breakwater. Was fairly rough outside, so Capt. Lysted thought it better that we get squared around before we hit open seas. About 10:00 o'clock in the morning had a smallpox vaccination, also a typhoid (first) shot. The shot seemed to have ill effects on me as I spent the rest of the day in my bunk. I was not seasick-sick at my stomach, but just seemed weak. Toward morning I felt a little better and did eat an apple. During the evening meal I tossed out pipes "Yellowball" donated to the expedition, to all of the members and the crew. I went to sleep about 6:00 o'clock and woke up at midnight, took a walk around deck and turned in for good. Was beautiful that night, moon and a little warmer. Sea not so rough.

Thursday, November 23

Roosevelt Thanksgiving, only we didn't have to acknowledge it on the high seas, and we didn't because too many fellows were a little under the weather and also there are a few Republicans on board. Felt like myself today, ate a light lunch and breakfast. Sky a little cloudy but water warm, about 78° and is very blue. Tell we are nearing the gulf stream because there is much seaweed present. Not much doing today except moved about 24 of the dogs up to the fo'c's'le deck. Played a little bridge and loafed around. The weather is getting warmer and I imagine that by tomorrow night we will be squawking about the heat. Our position at noon was lat. 33° 92′ 00″ N., long. 74° 39′ 00″ W. Distance to Christobal 1,599 miles. Just before lunch we saw a few porpoise and one small sailfish. The day before there were quite a few laying around the bow. Spent the evening with Paul, Al, and Larry looking over some rock specimens from the continent Antarctic. After dinner Paul called a meeting of men on the ice party. He gave a short general talk along with Al and

Dick Black. We are going to have school six nights a week to get us acquainted with the Antarctic. We are to take different subjects, Al is going to talk the next few nights on the Antarctic continent rocks, etc. It is now 11:30 p.m. and the ship seems to be rolling and pitching a little more, the night however seems beautiful, moon is partially out.

Friday, November 24

Has been a beautiful day, sea fairly calm and the water very blue. Spent most of the morning doing my washing, all of about ten or eleven pieces. Paul broke out some sextants and I have been practicing on one. We have started to make dog sleds, have to make about 25 in all, plus four tractor sleds which are about six feet wide. The ship is so crowded now that there is hardly room to move, so the sleds are being made on topside, much to the disgust and dislike of the Captain. I took a few pictures around the ship—Larry doing his washing, Ray Butler holding one of the pups and several of the dogs were fanging at each other. There are several that just stand by the hour and growl at one another. Doc Wade talked tonight on the continent Antarctic—was very interesting. After the meeting Larry and myself went to Paul and Al's cabin and spent the rest of the evening looking over some rocks that were brought back from the last expedition. The general idea was to acquaint Larry and me with the various rocks, and to give us an idea what to pick up, etc. Of course the whole thing ended up in a big bull session. At 9:00 o'clock every evening there is a lunch prepared for the members of the expedition; in other words, from nine to ten the chow hounds gather for a nightly feast. Sighted a ship but was too far off for us to tell what she was.

Saturday, November 25

Has been a beauty all day, sea has been fairly calm and the water is very blue. Coach Schlossbach had the first team putting up awnings over the poop deck and over the focs'le deck to protect the dogs from the heat. We sighted San Salvadore about noon, the (port) island certainly looked inviting, nice white beaches and shady trees. With the aid of glasses we were able to see very well, although we were approximately four miles from shore. A little later we passed another island called Rumkey, which was fairly small. Our position at noon was lat. 24° 37′, long. 74° 35′, 973 miles to Christobal. Had class again tonight and Dr. Poulter gave us the dope on the snow cruiser. The discussion had lasted some time, as everybody had his particular pet question to ask the doctor—some were very silly and we had a good time. Sighted a ship about 8:00 o'clock in the evening, evidently a passenger ship because she was all lighted up. We could not make out what nation she was, she came up from the east and seemed to be gaining on us rapidly.

Sunday, November 26

Sunday, and we did not have church because we couldn't get anyone to be the pastor. Spent the morning working on the port deck cleaning it up so there will be room to build dog sleds. On the port side aft the salon deck seems to be the only space not really used. Every other nook and corner is crowded, either with dogs or some sort of equipment. We took on some additional underwear at Philly, so to save space, Paul, Al and myself issued it, putting the box below. Davis, who had the dog watch this morning, reported that our ship of last night passed us and is now out of sight. She was a United Fruit vessel. Also about 6:00 o'clock a.m. a destroyer pulled along side and gave us the once over. Davis said that her Commander carried on quite a conversation (blinker) with our mate. Probably asking who we were and so forth.

We had our Thanksgiving dinner today which consisted of turkey, cranberry sauce, mashed potatoes, biscuits and about everything else from soup to nuts. Just as we of the second shift were getting started on our dessert (pumpkin pie with whipped cream) the fire bell rang—we all jumped up, ran for our life preservers and returned to our posts, then a couple of blasts from the ship's whistle rushed us all topside to our respective lifeboats. Well, all I can say is that I think they could have picked a better time for a fire drill other than during a Thanksgiving dinner. The boat I was in is commanded by the second mate John, and Al. Wade is in charge of the expedition members therein. Boat #3 is on the starboard side aft. During the afternoon most of the fellows took sun baths. Also a Navy plane flew over us several times—I am glad that our American flag is very much in evidence. Our position at noon was lat. 19° 40', long. 74° 18', distance from Christobal being 715 miles.

Tonight we had school class 400 and Dr. Paul A. Siple talked—gave a lecture on "Life, Both Plant and Animal" of Antarctic. I took some good notes, very interesting. Have been pretty busy learning international code—how to send and how to receive. It's a beautiful night, moon very full. I have been writing Alda every day—I certainly miss her.

Monday, November 27

Breakfast at 7:30—bacon and eggs, raspberries, coffee and Smuckers Apple Butter. I am sorry now that I did not write Smuck a poop sheet and ask him about his preserves—they gave us ten cases of apple butter and we might just as well have a few of strawberry, raspberry, etc. I forgot about their making anything other than apple butter.

Went down to see Doc Frazier this morning—I sprained my back about the middle of September, but it was much better till this morning. I guess I can't lift as much as I thought; anyway, the box did not budge but my back did. Doc strapped it up for me and it feels much better. During the afternoon I finished a twenty-page letter to Alda. I have been writing her every day. She still promises that she will wait and I kinda think she will. Noon distance was approximately 415 miles from Christobal. We are making very good time having a nice swell behind us. We had class tonight, Dick Black gave a talk on the history of exploration of the Antarctic. Was very interesting. Malcolm Douglass asked his usual number of silly questions. After class Larry and I had a little bull session about what it's all about. He had just been signed over to the dogs and is going to drive my team. I am to drive the International. It is a beautiful night, moon and the continuous rolling which none of us like. Missed 9:00 o'clock chow—must be slipping.

Tuesday, November 28

Woke up to a beautiful day—the water is very blue, white caps, foamy above, and our friend the roll. Not much work was done today as all of us are keyed up for Panama. Our position at noon was 160 miles from Christobal, so we will arrive there sometime Wednesday morning. Took a nap this afternoon. Doc Geyer gave a little talk tonight, medical talk warning us about Panama. His talk was very vivid and explanatory. Of course the whole thing ended with much foolishness and wisecracking but it made me stop and think. Afterwards Larry and I decided to keep on a straight and narrow and not take any chances. Tonight I completed my list of letters including Bob, and the folks. I also added a few lines to Alda's letter. It will probably cost a fortune to send it. Have to get to bed early tonight as I am going on watch with Doc Wade at four o'clock a.m. Another moonlight night and a wonderful breeze. Paul's toothache is no better and the medicine only makes him groggy.

Wednesday, November 29, 30

Up at 3:45 a.m., met Sarg Asman coming from the fo'c's'le head, meaning that Doc had already released him. We were in the breakwaters of Christobal and could see the lights very plainly; we were only about a half-mile from the city. We dropped anchor about 4:15 a.m., most of the crew was up and some of the expedition members, O'Connor, Helm, Steele, Doc Wade and myself. A tanker was anchored off the starboard bow, a fairly large ship. After we anchored Doc and I went aft to the social hall; I crawled up on a few bags of laundry and took a nap—Doc went the rounds, looked at the dogs and finally he too sank in a chair and dozed off—a couple of fine watchmen. By 5:00 o'clock all the dog men were up, cleaning and arranging the dogs so that the lines could be used going through the canal. About 6:00 o'clock the pilot boat came alongside, also a laundry boat which Paul, Dr. Poulter, Petras, Carroll and McCoy took ashore. Also a banana boat came alongside and when he passed up his wares, Coach Schlossbach, Steele and myself rushed our purchases to our bunks. It consisted of two cans of pecan brittle, one for both Steele and myself, also a box of stogies for the coach. The funny part was that the banana boat got tied alongside and we were all ready to pass the bananas aboard when our boat started and it then became impossible to take them on, and O'Conner was in the other boat and had quite a leap to make to ours. The banana boat followed alongside for a while, then turned back. We started through the canal about 6:15 and following us was a Coast Guard boat, a small banana boat, and a freighter. Going through the first locks was very interesting—four mules pulled us along, two before and two afterwards. When the pilot boat came out, another boat came out also with about twelve hands aboard; they were to handle the lines. On either side of the locks were soldiers, Panamanians and a few misfits. The Snow Cruiser was the first interest, then the dogs. The pilot boat brought aboard mail and I did surprisingly well, six letters—two from Mary, two from the folks, one Eastman Kodak and one package of developed films. I can't understand why I did not get a letter from Alda—I certainly hope that I get one at New Zealand. We anchored in Lake Gatum about eight o'clock and were

8

not scheduled to leave there till 11:00 o'clock, the reason being that at one set of locks they had only one-way traffic, due to repair; hence we had to wait our turn. This was after going through. We spent the time at the Gatum locks buying and bartering with the natives who came aboard. They had odds and ends, from handkerchiefs to stamps. I bought a few cards and a handkerchief with the American and Panama flags embroidered on it. It is supposed to be silk but is probably rayon. About half of the fellows went swimming in the lake and it was reported that the water was fine. Dick Moulton threw one of the dogs overboard and it had quite a swim, although scared half out of its wits. All of the fellows were in very good spirits and we all loafed around and shot the bull. Sig Sundt, the steward, put a few slugs in the Vic. I wrote a card to Katherine Hedrick (Newby), George Minnas and Dick Graves. We started again, probably at 11:00 o'clock. Lake Gatum is a very beautiful lake, largest artificial lake next to Boulder Dam. The trip through the canal was very delightful. We passed several ships and got the most kick out of the British cruiser, evidently going home after being on patrol in tropical waters. The men's uniforms consisted of white shorts and blouses, several had beards. Also we passed a "Limey" freighter, painted a dirty gray; she tipped her flag, we likewise.

It was interesting to note that the bedrock in one part of the canal (sides) was tipping at a pretty good angle toward the canal proper, hence explaining the trouble they have been having with landslides. Also we saw a couple of good faults.

The foliage along the way was very interesting, banana trees, coconut trees, and palm trees (of some variety) and someone pointed out orchids. We had quite a gathering at the port rail—Doc Wade, Doc Geyer, the Chief, myself, etc.

We next went through Pedro Minguel locks and the pictures which I took of the locks turned out very well. I took several of Gatum Lake, but I over-exposed since I thought I had Plus X, but was actually using Agfa Super Pan.

Of special interest were the large derricks (two) used to lift ships, etc.—probably have a capacity of 200 tons or better. Also we all remarked about the Canal from Colon to the Pacific side.

Our last look before reaching Balboa was Mira Flores and we arrived at Balboa about 3:30 in the afternoon. We docked at pier 15—I immediately got cleaned up and Al and I went into Balboa, our first stop being the post office where I mailed my letters. The one to Alda weighed so much that it cost me $.60. When we left and started to walk into town a taxi pulled alongside and wanted to know if we were going into town, meaning Panama City—well we stalled him off till after the post office. Our next stop was the Eastman film Kodak store where I left my roll of film. Doc suggested that we go to old Panama so we dickered with the driver and got a $2.00-an-hour rate. The ride we had was very enjoyable—we went to every section of the city. In old Panama we saw the church ruins, burned by Henry Morgan, some of them being 300 years old. The thing which was rather odd was the use of so many kinds of sandstone with a layer of what seemed to be brick. We couldn't decide whether or not the bricks were used recently for repair purposes.

The interesting part of the drive was in seeing how the living conditions varied in different sections of the city. In going through the part called Harlem, the streets were narrow and rooms, very small with a kind of folding door opening right on the street, would house from ten to fourteen people. There seemed to be no privacy at all. Went in the resident-district, we found beautiful homes, Spanish-type and very modern apartment buildings. Coming from old Panama we saw several nice villas with beautiful gardens, high walls and a kind of colonial-type house. We got back to the downtown district about six in the evening and were riding along watching the crowd when Al yelled at some fellows passing by and it turned out to be Capt. Lysted, Mr. Black, Finn Ronnie and Pride Clark. They had not eaten, so they climbed in the cab and we went to a very enjoyable place called the Balboa Gardens. Our table was on the veranda and we had a very nice dinner out under the stars. Just as we were getting ready to leave, the Capt. saw Clay Bailey and the Admiral come in but disappear, so we all hunted them up and found them at the bar. The Admiral shook hands with all of us and bought us a drink and offered (or wanted to know) if we would join them for dinner. Sadly we had had ours. However, we made arrangements to meet them at a place called "Happy Heaven." Before leaving the Gardens we wrote several cards furnished by the management. I wrote one to the folks and Alda.

After that we started to walk into town which was a matter of three or four blocks. When we got on the main drag, expedition fellows popped out right and left and all appeared to be having a fairly good time. Our group went to a place called Kelly's owned by a person called Mary Lee Kelly, whom I later met—that is the reason why I changed the lady part.

She seemed to have a crush on the Commander, which was a holdover from the last expedition. She kept giving drinks on the house, we thought, but at the end of the evening she presented the Chief with a nice little bill for about $25.00. It kind of burned us up. All of the fellows were there, even the Admiral and the Capt. of the ship. Kelly furnished, or had some girls there to dance with, about four girls for about fifty fellows or so. I never did get around to dancing with any of them, although they seemed to be very nice. Warner, Al Wade and myself sat at our table. Charles S. had introduced himself to two blondes and a man sitting at one of the tables, so he introduced me and I danced with one of them whose name was Miss McCartly from Colorado, the other girl being Miss Beasly; the man was Dr. Chavis of the Balboa, a Panama City hospital—he being a very noted surgeon. They invited me to sit with them, which I did, and soon half of the expedition had gathered around. I spent about all of the evening after that talking to Dr. Chavis. They left about 1:00 o'clock and Miss Beasly invited Larry and me to visit her the next day at her dress shop. Al Wade had quite a time leading the orchestra. First he started leading various ones in the "nickelodeon" until finally as the evening progressed he led the Kelly orchestra, which consisted of natives. They have a very nice and decent floor show at Kelly's, which surprised me very much. The whole thing broke up about 4:00 o'clock in the morning and we piled in a cab and went to the ship. Doc Wade, Larry, Gutenko, the coach, and myself. When we got to the ship we found that the Commander was locked out of his cabin so he spent a rather bad night atop some boxes on the deck. The rest of us had a little session reviewing how much fun we had and what a clean innocent evening we all had.

Thursday morning 7:00 o'clock seemed to come around very quick-like. Some of the fellows ate a hearty breakfast, others did not, while others gave up and stayed in bed. However, most of us were up as we had two carts of bamboo to take aboard—poles about 20' to 30' long. They are to be cut in 3' lengths and slit into small poles to hold trail flags. We finished this job about 10:30, then Larry and I cleaned up a bit and headed for Panama City. I wanted to get my film and also we wanted to look around the town in the daylight. We took a taxi to the Kodak store, we started to walk around, looking in store windows, etc. Then happening to think that Miss Beasly's dress store was in this vicinity, 6B, we stopped and inquired of a native policeman, but he could not comprehend English. So after stopping several persons on the street, he managed to find an old man who knew some English. After much difficulty he directed us, and in short while we were at 6B, Miss Beasly was inside and was very glad to see us, also Miss McCartly who had spent the night with Miss Beasly. She introduced us to her dressmaker who was a Panamanian girl, and very attractive—she did all of the altering, etc. Also there was a Negro who washed windows and cleaned up in general. He was a Jamaican and understood very little English. He was certainly a homely fellow and she called him "Sonny Boy," and what a lad he was—he scared me. After spending a little time there talking, Larry and I went back to the ship, but finding we did not sail till three o'clock, decided to go into Balboa for lunch. We ate at a place called the Veranda Club or something like that. We really stuffed ourselves having about two or three dishes of ice cream with a little apple pie under it. We then loafed around the commissary but could not even buy tobacco because we had to have some sort of tickets and had to be a canal employee.

We got back to the ship in plenty of time and there was quite a crowd gathered, also the Army band. It was a beautiful day, the Admiral's flag was flying, the band playing, everyone was in good spirits. We all hung over the rail and tossed apples at the girls. It must have been a holiday or something because the deck was loaded with school kids. The Admiral finally came aboard and we got underway about 4:30, a little late as usual. As we pulled out to sea, several ships gave us a salute and a light cruiser followed us out giving us the 13-gun salute for the Admiral. It was quite a thrill to be on an Admiral flagship. So we started out on our long trip across the Pacific and it was true to its name, not a ripple on it, just a gentle swell. There was quite a bit of congestion on board, everything was very unship-like and to top it, some of the boys, little Moe and the rest of the soldiers made some potent punch which they had been passing around since noon so I can firmly say that all were in good spirits. It was funny seeing little Moe run around asking everyone if they would like some tea.

Friday, December 1

We are about twenty hours out of Panama. It's hard to conceive being 26 to 30 days at sea without sight of land. Our position at noon today was lat. 5° 44' N., long. 81° 30', our distance from Balboa being 269.3 miles. During the morning Larry, Al, Paul, and myself cleared the port deck of our equipment (various odds and ends) so the dog department could have the space for sled construction. We put quite a bit of the stuff in the mid-ship shower which has been turned off since we have been using salt water. However, real water is turned on from 7:30 to 8:30 in the morning, 11:30 to 12:30 noon and 4:30 to 5:30 at night and drinking water is available at all times in the social hall. Doc Geyer cut my hair today, and did a very good job—a burr head. In fact, some of the other fellows like it so well that the Doc is quite busy now. After the haircut I took my first seawater shower and it isn't so hot, felt very sticky after it. Tonight the shellbacks had a meeting as we pollywogs had one also—our watchword being "be prepared." Ever since we left Panama more and more has been said about passing the Equator and the shellbacks have been making themselves known. There has been much joking and razzing back and forth. After dinner tonight I got my third typhoid shot. We have been busy all day cutting trail flagpoles out of the bamboo sled we took on at Panama. The first team under Coach Schlossbach has been working hard. Some of the fellows working up on the fo'c's'le deck were Sgt. Asman, Steele, Warner, Court, the Coach, and myself and Moe. Their role consists of sawing the large pole in 3-foot lengths, then splitting them into small poles about ¼- to ½-inch thick. I don't think any of the fellows escaped cut hands as not only are the knives sharp, but the bamboo also. The Admiral has so far kept pretty much to himself, although he does come down from topside every now and then. He had the captain's cabin which is starboard topside.

Saturday, December 2

Rain and sea pretty choppy, so is a good sign we must be heading toward the line. Had a terrible storm last night, and we took much water over the side. The first team tried to cut bamboo on the fo'c's'le deck this morning but it was such a wet job that the coach called time out. I went to my bunk about 10:30 this morning and stayed the rest of the day. The typhoid shot finally caught up with me. I slept and rested, took things kind of easy. I went down to eat tonight but the pork or chili did not appeal to me so I had a dish of applesauce and turned in.

Woke up at 7:00 o'clock tonight and Gilmore informed me that they were having some of the Neptune Ceremony tonight at 7:30, so I got aboard. We pollywogs went on top the Snow Cruiser and awaited the arrival of Davy Jones and promptly at 7:30 a blast from the ship and Charlie the Mate dressed as Davy Jones appeared along with the shellbacks, then each of we pollywogs were in turn handed a summons (The Black Spot). We read the charges before the group amid much shouting, hissing, and comments of better pollywogs and shellbacks. When Roger Horthorne received his summons, the shellback police were ordered to seize him. But all the pollywogs seemed to think differently and we had quite a tussle which lasted a few minutes, till the railings gave way and we were all in danger of really getting hurt. The whole thing ended in good fun, and we all more or less were ready for the crossing of the Equator—the ceremony being called for 9:30 a.m.

It rained off and on all day and it looks like it is going to rain all night.

Sunday, December 3

Got up this morning at 7:00 o'clock feeling very much better although my arm was still a little sore. Had a light breakfast in spite of the initiation, which was due at 9:30 a.m. and all of the shellbacks said that it was going to be plenty tough, so eat heartily. After breakfast all of the pollywogs sat around the social hall like we may be doomed men. And we might, but such affairs never start on time and this one was true to form, so we started around 10:00 o'clock. My name was called about tenth and I went topside, was blindfolded and then taken before the judge who read my charge (which was my charge the night before)—then he passed sentence which was "I recommend this man be thrown to the sharks." Then I was taken before King Neptune and the Queen, had to kneel before them and got a few swats, then I had to go up a few steps, arise the "Royal Baby" (Al Wade) then I visited the "Royal Doctor" who gave me a pill of some kind (which I did not swallow), then I went to the "Royal Dentist" who squirted more awful red stuff in my mouth and the "Royal Barber" who lathered me up quite well with soap, then shaved me with a wooden straight razor. Then I got a shampoo with more ugly green stuff—the barber put it on with a three inch paint brush. After the shampoo, during which I had to sit on a small tin can, I was told to fold my arms and was given a push and worse, in other words it varied with the person. Some got hung, the rope being cut into and patched with a piece of tape—then when the chair was pulled out from under the fellow his weight broke the rope. Quite effective when blindfolded. The men who took part in the initiation are as follows:

14

King—John, Second Mate
Queen—Fred Dustin
Royal Baby—Doc Wade
Royal Doctor—Doc Geyer
Royal Dentist—Barber
Royal Barber—Vernon Boyd

There were several there which I did not know, as their costume could have been most anything.

After I went through the initiation I went below, got my camera and watched some of the other fellows go through, and took a few pictures.

We crossed the equator about 6:15 a.m. During the afternoon Larry and I did a big washing and loafed around. After dinner we had the "Glory Hole" band practice. The "Glory Hole" is the name the fellows have to apply to the post storage, the fellows being Asman, Steele, Morency, Schlossbach, O'Conner, Pappy Reese, Helm, Joe Wells and Arnold Court. Practice was not quite well underway when Paul came down after me as the Admiral was holding a meeting with the scientific staff concerning a big "poop sheet" from the president which stated that we all had to turn in our diary, specimens, data, etc.—naturally we raised a big smell about the whole thing, hence the meeting. The Admiral assured us that he would look into the matter. Larry and I have decided that if nothing is done about the thing that we will get off at Dunedin as there would be no incentive for our going as we would want the material to work up for our Ph.D. work.

After the meeting was over we had a little jam session in the social hall, then Larry and I retired to our cabin and were just plain shooting the breeze when Al came in and we had a nice chat about everything. Got to bed about 12:00 o'clock, wind blowing, fairly cool, sea rough. Our position at noon being lat. 0° 26′ 3″ S., long. 87° 15′ 2″ W., distance from Balboa 759 miles, distance to Dunedin 3,722 miles.

Monday, December 4

Breakfast at 7:30—we are having cereal now with powdered milk, which is very good. It is really surprising the variety of food that we have aboard. Almost every meal we have a choice of two meats—beef or pork, ham or chicken, and we have a very good mixture of vegetables.

However at present we are eating bananas as fast as we can. It seems that we were given so many bunches and so we have to hurry and eat them before they spoil. That's the way it is, we either have too much of one thing or not enough, or not at all. We have been having bananas in every way, shape and form for the past week. The same with the apples given to us by the Admiral's brother. Each fellow aboard has eaten at least ten to fourteen per day, besides we have applesauce, baked apples, fried apples, apples in salad, stewed apples and the rest just plain apples.

This morning I worked with the first team on the fo'c's'le deck splitting bamboo. Our ultimate aim is to split 10,000 separate poles and the number up-to-date is 6,000. During the afternoon I worked in Paul's cabin filing—I worked for about two hours then gave up as it was hot in there and I get sleepy; besides I really didn't feel like working, so turned in my bunk and took a nap.

I had the first shift tonight, as I went on watch from six to eight. Was rather nice up at the fo'c's'le head, rather windy but the sunset and sky was beautiful. Ever since we crossed the equator we have had miserable weather, damp, cool, and very windy, however the nights are very nice.

After watch I came back to the cabin and the fellows across the way were having kind of a spread. Davis, Perkins, and Lobell are the inmates of cabin six, but whenever there is any food around the boys gather, so there was Doc Wade and Doc Geyer, myself and Warner. Our feast tonight consisted of peanuts, peanut butter, cheese and crackers. I think they are called Neslits. We had gotten pretty well underway when the Admiral appeared on the scene looking for Gilmore, but he stopped long enough for a bite to eat.

Tuesday, December 5

Another rather chilly day, wind blowing, and a hazy sun. During the morning I wrote letters to my various friends at Chantangua to put on the U.S.S. *Bear*.

It is remarkable how time flies aboard the ship—I had no sooner written the letters when chow bell rang. After lunch Larry and I gathered in the cabin for a pipe. He feels the same way that I do, as we get farther from home, our dear ones, friends and civilization, I know that I can't help but think about it all. Especially Alda and my folks. I hope they are all well, and that Alda will be waiting.

Last night I sent my folks and her a telegram from the ship by another connection. I hope that they answer soon. Worked some

1. Etched portrait of Admiral Byrd by Walter Tittle.

2. First stop in the Pacific.

3. *North Star* anchored off Rapa Island.

4. Huskies aboard ship. Each dog had its own dog crate.

5. Dogs were everywhere.

6. First sight of ice floes after leaving New Zealand.

7. Large iceberg and heavier concentration of ice.

8. The early sailing ships had trouble getting through the ice pack which surrounds the Antarctic.

9. The Ross shelf ice. This mass of ice rises 100 to 150 feet above the water.

10 & 11. Icebergs.

12. The *North Star* headed into the ice in the Bay of Whales. This ice is approximately seven feet thick and breaks out each summer to form the ice pack.

13. The *Bear of Oakland* headed into the ice.

14. Our tent home on top of the Ross shelf ice. We lived here while we were unloading the ships.

more on bamboo this afternoon and we finally reached the 10,000 mark. I am glad that job is over. Clay Bailey spoke in class tonight on "Radio Communication." It was very interesting and gave us an idea what part we play in the whole setup. Went down to the 9:00 o'clock supper and stayed the whole hour, and had some very good honey and peanut butter. Al Wade, McCoy, Court, Warner, Gilmore, Carroll, Dick Black, Asman, Morency (the chow hounds), were all present. Our position noon today was lat. 5° 41′ 31″ S., long. 94° S. 1′ 4″ W., and we were 1,317.6 miles from Panama.

Wednesday, December 6

Spent the morning working on sleds with Larry, Don Hilton, Jack Richardson. We fellows bind the frame while Boyd, Doc Geyer and Ronnie bind on the top slate. The rawhide is very tough to work with and my hands are pretty sore. Worked on sleds during the afternoon till 3:00, then looked over the talk I am to give tomorrow night. It is more or less a book review that is about the Southern Cross Expedition under the leadership of E. E. Borchgievick. I certainly hope that I give it all right.

It is very cloudy tonight and looks like we are running into a storm. We can't seem to get out of the cloudy belt as we have been in it ever since the equator. Also it is very chilly and windy.

Our position noon today was lat. 8° 07′ 2″ S., long. 98° 18′ 9″ W. and we are 1,595.9 miles from Balboa.

Court talked at the scientific meeting on the Meteorological Program for West Base.

Thursday, December 7

Another day, that's about all. Seventh day out of Balboa—our position lat. ° 07.1′ S., long. 102° 373.3′ W.—1,886.1 miles from Balboa. Average speed noon to noon, 11.99 knots. Worked on sleds all morning and afternoon. Hilton, Richardson, Warner and myself have been working together. There is always quite a bit of bull-spreading as we work, but that's to be expected.

We have been having the same cloudy weather, but the sea is very still, and calm. Every evening about 5:30 or 6:00 o'clock it becomes very cloudy and looks like there is going to be a storm, yet around about 9:00 o'clock it clears up and then the stars come out. I can't quite get over the beautiful clouds, they seem to just float along the horizon and when the sun sets, the twilight lingers and the clouds are silhouetted against the sky. I have never noticed such a variety of clouds or such a conglomeration of shapes and sizes and colors. It is really inspiring to sit and watch and look at the clouds —we do it by the hours.

Tonight Capt. Lysted showed us some moving pictures of trips to Alaska on the U.S.S. *Boxer*, which is a 125-ft. motor and sail ship used by the Dept. of Interior in Alaska for telegrams and supplies, etc., to the U.S. schools. The pictures were very interesting and we all enjoyed them very much.

Was rather cool tonight and a very good night to sleep.

Friday, December 8

The eighth day out of Balboa and it's like all the others. The water is very blue and the day is perfect, gentle breeze and a slight swell, winds have helped us some. Our position noon today was lat. 13° 28′ 8″ S., long. 106° 51′ 5″ W., 2,173.6 miles from Balboa. Noon to noon we did 287.5 miles, average speed 11.86 knots. Spent practically all day reviewing Borchgievick's Southern Cross Expedition which I talked on tonight. It was more or less of a book review and I think that it went off fairly well. Jack Perkins reviewed the Belgic and Ross expedition. I went on "watch" at 8:00 o'clock—from 8:00 to 12:00. Doc Frazier and I were the "eyes and ears" of the ship. I would stay an hour at the fo'c's'le head and keep a weather eye on things. We changed around every hour. It was really wonderful up forward, stars were out, nice breeze and the phosphorescent Protozoa were very much in evidence.

When I came in off watch at midnight there was a big tall bull session going on in Cabin #8. Doc Frazier who also just came off watch was there, also Al Wade, Larry, Gilmore. The whole thing broke up about 1:00 o'clock.

Saturday, December 9

Our position today at noon was at lat. ° 53′ 5″ S., long. 111° 3′ W., being 2,462.5 miles from Balboa. Noon-to-noon run was 288.9 miles.

The boys played a good joke on Doc Lockhart—who it seems bit on the "mail buoy." About 9:00 o'clock this morning some of the fellows ran and got Lockhart telling him that the buoy was in sight, in fact it could be seen on the horizon. Now the boys had been talking the thing up the last couple of days and had told Lockhart that we would pass the buoy today—so he spent all last evening writing letters to deposit in the mail buoy. Anyway at the call this morning Lockhart rushed below, got his letters and there he stood at the fo'c's'le head, letters in one hand, searching the horizon with his glasses looking for the "mail buoy." He took the whole thing pretty good. I guess he had at least written a dozen letters.

Finn Ronne got his finger quite a cut this morning—clear to the bone. Also V. Boyd came very close to getting his eye put out in making our sleds. It is necessary to use a wood bit. One of the fellows was using the ratchet, and in putting it down, he just missed Boyd's eye, hitting him in the temple. Boyd was kneeling by the sled talking to Ronne. It certainly was a narrow escape. I was down to Doc Frazier's again to have my back strapped.

P. A. Siple talked tonight on climate, giving a very interesting lecture. After the lecture I read some from Cushman. I have been doing quite a bit of reviewing lately on forams. Took in the 9:00 o'clock chow and the usual fellows were present. They have been having some pretty good honey which goes very well with peanut butter. I don't think that Al Wade, Warner and myself have missed the 9:00 o'clock chow yet. He happily announced that the last stock of bananas was out to ripen and that we had eaten the last box of grapes. For some time, ever since Panama, we have been having a run on bananas, and I think that we are all getting tired of them. I know I am.

Sunday, December 10

Woke up this morning at 7:30 and since today was Sunday we had French fried bread—we only get that on special occasions. Spent all morning shooting the sun with Sextant—Larry, Paul, Al Wade and myself. They are giving Larry and me a little instruction. We took about ten to fifteen shots then Paul gave us the dope on how to figure the latitude. It is very interesting. We took a moon shot and determined our latitude position as 18° 06.5′ S. and after more firing we found that we were a little off, about forty-five miles. I don't suppose the ship's navigators are off, so I guess it is us. We had our chicken for dinner today, with all the trimmings—was very good. I slept half of the afternoon, then Sig Gutenko and Arnold Court dropped in and we kind of talked things over. My two roommates slept away the afternoon also. After supper tonight I played the clarinet, Al came in and I played over a few old tunes. Later Don Hilton, Jack Richardson, (his violin), Bob Steele and Charles S. dropped in and we had quite a music night. Vernon Boyd took a picture of the bunch. Went down to 9:00 o'clock chow, the baker had just baked some very good potato bread, which was very good with honey and peanut butter.

It was a perfect day today, nice and sunshiny, same beautiful clouds. It is getting hot again, but not sticky as it has been since crossing the equator. We expect to get to Dunedin in about two weeks, and we are supposed to stop at Pitcairn Island this coming Thursday.

Our position noon today was lat. 18° 05.03′ S., long. 115″ 24.7′ W., noon-to-noon running 279.5, average speed 11.52 knots.

Monday, December 11

Did not sleep very well last night as the flies were pretty bad and it was so hot—at least ninety degrees as we had the fan going wide open, but still no relief. Yesterday some of the fellows saw about five whales, off our port side, by the time I came up from below I missed them. Little Moe has been made a member of the ship's crew so to speak—he is now quartermaster and stands a watch along with the rest. Al Wade, Larry and myself worked all day on some snow measurers which are sticks about 240 centimeters long; on one side they have inches and the other, centimeters. These will be divided and placed at each base, used to measure the snowfall or drift. They have to be read twice a day. There are to be sixteen in all and we were one-quarter finished. We had our old swell with us again today—Pacific swell—and it certainly has given us a push. It was hot today, being about ninety-six degrees. There were quite a few clouds in the sky and the water was its usual blue. This evening during dinner Kotik my lead dog got in a fight, tore quite a piece out of his tongue. There were about two other dog fights today—in this hot weather they become more nervous. To-night at school Finn Ronne talked on "Sleds, Dogs and Travel in Antarctic." He gave a very interesting talk, although it was rather hard to understand him at times. Larry is on watch 12:00 to 4:00, he has gone to bed now. Gil is out roaming around somewhere on the ship—probably shooting the breeze someplace. Our position today noon, lat. 20° 15.8′ S., long. 119° 44.6′ W., noon-to-noon run was 279.2 miles, speed 11.514.

Tuesday, December 12

This time tomorrow night we will be stopped at Pitcairn Island. I think the plan is to stay there one whole day. Was very hot last night and I slept very lightly, waking when Larry came in off watch.

This morning Al, Larry and myself worked on our snow measurers again, finishing about half of them. It is rather slow work as we have to mark off our scales. During lunch Larry and I challenged Al and Doc Poulter to an ice cream eating contest when we get to Dunedin. We are not so worried about Al but the Doc looms upon the horizon as a dark horse which will bear watching.

This afternoon Larry and I both slept till 4:00 o'clock then I went up forward and helped Warner and Hilton feed the dogs. Those two fellows take care of twenty-four dogs."!!!" I got a telegram from Alda this morning which will make this a very special day—in fact, the best. One of the radio men brought it around at 7:00 o'clock this morning, I was just getting up—that is really starting the day off right. "!!!"

Yesterday Roger Hawthorn ran off some envelopes on the mimeograph, which had on them a cut of Pitcairn Island, the ship's latitude and longitude, etc. Each one was issued ten envelopes which we will be able to mail or have postmarked at the island. They will be quite nice to have. All of the fellows are a little excited about the island and I am no exception. I suppose that I will be as glad as the next to get my feet on good old "terra firma."

Gilmore is sound asleep and Larry just finished a "Navy Bath"— which merely means out of the bowl, in about a cupful of water.

It has been clouding up since lunch and has started to rain— probably just a tropical downpour, which will be over in a few minutes. Dick Black talked tonight on two expeditions, Lincoln Ellsworth and Sir Hubert Wilkins.

Wednesday, December 13–14

Was on watch last night from midnight to 4:00 this morning. It was very nice up on the fo'c's'le head, cool and very clear. At certain times the stars would show through. I saw the Southern Cross very plainly. I spent all morning in bed and most of the afternoon as I had not slept any the night before. We sighted Pitcairn Island about 5:30 in the afternoon—dead ahead. At that time I was up forward helping Larry and Don Hilton feed the dogs. I have been chopping up the horse meat (canned) for them the last couple of nights. There was quite a bit of excitement as we drew near the island, and by 8:00 o'clock we were signaling the radio man on the island, asking where the best place to anchor, how deep the water, etc., and they wanted to know if we were an American ship as they had been expecting the *City of Glasco* the last couple of days and thought that we were she. About 8:30 or 8:45 we dropped anchor and in the meantime various shore parties were designated, I being in Gilmore's party along with Larry, Jack Perkins, and Malcolm Douglass. Also the islanders had started out from shore with two boats and arrived alongside about the time we had finished anchor procedures. They immediately poured over the side, up the "gang way," and we all got our first glance of the descendants of the survivors of the *Bounty*. Never have I seen such a strange, sorrowful, forlorn group of persons as came aboard that night—there they were, odds and ends of clothing, various array of headwear, every last one barefooted and each one carrying one or two large baskets containing fruit or souvenirs of some type or another. Their clothing, in case of the men, consisted of shirts, some faded-out blue work shirts, while others wore old shirts without the collars. The pants were everything from old cast-down suit pants to dungarees, in some cases brand new ones from New Zealand or New York. They were rather uniform in that they were wearing light shirts and fairly dark pants. Each man had a knife, which looked like a garden knife, held in place in its sheath around the waist by leather, string, or a piece of rope. The hats were either old felt of various colors or homemade straws of different designs and patterns. The women and young girls wore printed, colored ginghams with hats, when worn, of straw and a wide brim. They wore in some cases native flowers which would consist of seed beads, and I did notice a few gold wedding bands. Immediately upon coming aboard they started to do business, selling, barter and trade, any way to sell their wares or to get the things necessary to them. Of the small items they were especially interested in and needed, were matches, razor blades and flashlight batteries. They were really hard up because since the war, ships have not been landing on the island and one of the fellows said that we were the first ship for a long time. I guess our stopping was a "godsend" to them. After getting to talk to these people and getting more or less acquainted with them, I can truthfully say that I have never met a more friendly or generous group, and they were very polite, speaking perfect English, except in cases when they got excited or wanted to hurriedly say something to a fellow islander. Then they would speak "pig English," which was impossible to understand. At first we thought that it was a native tongue of some kind, but they said that they spoke only English. At 9:00 o'clock we had our regular "9:00 o'clock" chow and quite a few of the Pitcairn people joined us and it was a reward in itself to see them so glad and excited over a mere piece of bread. We happened to have crab last night and that was when their eyes really popped.

The souvenirs which they had to sell and trade were very nice and the fellows bought them up and traded for them with the keenness of a son of "Weiner." I bought and bartered for several nice pieces of work, wood carving done by a fellow named Fred Christian, the fifth descendant of Fletcher Christian. He does beautiful work, and after a little "finagling" around I got a very nice pipe rack, beautifully carved, with the history of the bounty, also a fish and a trick jewel box. I also traded two bars of soap for a cane made of coconut wood, orange wood and some other wood. Its handle screwed into a very nice piece of wood.

About 10:30 they started to leave the ship, so we fellows that wanted to go ashore hopped in. They really had some boats, eight oars on either side and thirty-five feet long. It was impossible to determine the exact capacity as one of the fellows said that "they hold as many as we can get in." Anyway I think we had at least seventy-five persons in our boat. Gilmore, Larry, Perkins, Douglass and myself were in one boat. The crew was composed of a "lookout man" and a coxswain. The boat was so crowded that the men could hardly row—we were literally "packed like sardines." That is one night I will never forget, it was very dark, only a few stars out, thus the only light was that from the ship, being the large searchlight which for a short time was flashed against the cliffs. And there we were heading toward shore, tremendous breakers and swells; plus an overcrowded boat. As we got close to shore, heading for their boat dock landing, huge grotesque rocks loomed on either side of us and we seemed to be lost among them as we rode an extra-large wave ashore, grounding us on the beach. After we had all pulled the boats up to the boat houses, we started the long walk up to the village.

While on the ship, during the process of barter and trade, Gilmore had become acquainted with a fellow by the name of Warren, whom he had in the cabin. We were talking about going ashore and sleeping on the beach, so Mr. Warren invited us to stay at his house. So he rode in the same boat as we did, and upon landing we hiked up a very steep hill to the village and to his cottage which was on the far side of town. It was quite a sight to look back halfway up the hill and see the long line of lights of the procession working its way along the side of the cliff. We got to Warren's house about

11:30, met his wife and two children, a boy and a girl, Wiles and Charlott, and after talking till 1:30 we finally turned in. Warren was a very interesting conversationalist and told us of his experiences while working in Tahiti, also of some of the history of the island. It seems that his grandfather married Christian's daughter. Larry and I slept on a couch in the front room. The house was furnished rather sparsely, the front room containing a table, a pump organ, a homemade cot or couch, and a few chairs. No rug on any of the floors. Our room had a bed and a dresser, the mattress being (I think) filled with straw or grass (of some sort); nevertheless, it was hard. However, everything seemed very clean. Mrs. Warren got her best sheets for us, which were spotlessly clean. I woke up about 6:00 o'clock after hearing the women talking in the kitchen, which was the adjoining room, so I woke Larry and we hauled out. Mr. Warren with a very cheery "good morning" said he hoped he did not disturb us, but he had been up since 4:00 o'clock and had tramped to the other side of the island to shoot chickens. (He kept his in a certain place on the island, as did the others.) Next he brought us soap, towel, and water, and by that time Gilmore had gotten up and we had breakfast which consisted of native coffee and crackers. After our farewells we headed down the path to the boathouse. The islanders took us back to the *North Star*. As soon as we were sure all hands were accounted for, we lifted the anchor and got underway.

Friday, December 15

Underway again—beautiful day, sea calm except for swell. I helped Roger Hawthorn separate the Pitcairn envelopes in the morning till Paul came in and told me that I was to go to bed— Doc Frazier's orders because of my back. So to bed I went. And since I was going to be on the sick list Doc decided to move Dick Moulton in with me as he also has a bad back. It seems that while we were at Gatum Lake, he went in swimming and while diving off the top side, he chipped a vertebra, so he has been in bed now for the last ten days. His back is pretty bad, and there is some chance that he might not be able to stay down. However, Doc is doing his best and they are going to take X-rays at Dunedin. Larry has been nurse for us and has been bringing our meals. Gilmore moved to where they wear pajamas so he says, and where a man can stand up straight and throw out his chest. Since our cabin has been the clinic, it has been the eating place for all aboard and Doc says if

24

the fellows don't quit hanging around he will have to post visitor's hours. Tonight Doc gave us a rubdown. My back is hot and sore as a boil.

Woke up to a rainy day—sea calm except for swell. Doc came in about 7:00 o'clock and took our order for breakfast. Have been doing quite a bit of reading and have started Schuchbert and Dunbart II Historical—I thought now would be a good time to do a little reviewing. So between eating, sleeping, reading and writing to Alda, and writing in my diary, I seem to have a pretty busy day. Oh yes, and keeping up with the various sessions which congregate in the room. I did not get to hear last night's mail bag however, but Larry told me my folks' message. Then I made up my Christmas telegrams and sent the folks and Alda a message which will go out tonight—I hope they answer promptly. Doc Frazier gave me another rubdown tonight and I can hardly move. Dick feels a little better tonight. Larry has gone on watch, 8:00 to 12:00.

We stopped at Rapa Island around noon today. I got up and took a peek at the island about fifteen minutes before we dropped anchor and it looked very beautiful, very rugged country, high peaks, being a volcanic island. Jack Perkins took pictures for me as did Larry who took duplicates while on the island. A boat came out, rowed by the natives, one acting as coxswain, and the governor —a magistrate of the island—a French viscount. It appears that he murdered three men in Paris, but since his family had power and money they made it possible for him to spend his life sentence on Rapa Island. The natives were Polynesian and besides Frenchmen there were also two Japs and a half-cracked American who had been on the island for twenty years. The Japs and he ran stores, but the farmers were running him out of business—underselling him. So cut-rate competition runs strong even in the South Sea islands. After Doc Frazier went ashore I got up and sat out on the deck for a while till my back started to ache, then I turned in again. The island from all reports was very dirty, chickens, pigs and people all living under one roof. And the only enjoyment the fellows got was tramping around the hills and peaks. The natives had quite a bunch of horses (100), cattle and goats. Doc gave me another rubdown and my back feels better. I forgot to say that we anchored in the old crater of the volcano—entering through a narrow channel, and the water in the crater was extremely deep, approximately eighty feet. We got underway about 6:00 o'clock and while leaving the harbor ran aground just slightly, but enough so that we could hear the scraping of the rocks and coral. It was very interesting, and we were surprised to find out that we were the first ship to stop there in a year and that they knew nothing of the war.

Monday, December 18

Doc Frazier woke us up about 7:00 o'clock bringing our breakfast. I spent most of the morning reading, taking a little nap before lunch. Did not feel hungry so had only a bowl of soup and a cup of hot tea. Tried to sleep during the afternoon, but could not because of the noise going on outside. Seems that the aviation crew is working on the skis for the Barkley-Grow making them lighter, which means that they have to tear them apart and rebuild them. The dog men have been in and out all day consulting with Dick Moulton, as they are moving the dogs and since he cannot be up he has to direct things from bed. He is feeling much better today and I think that Doc is going to cut out the growth along his spine in the next day or two—it's not a growth as much as it is a bag of liquid of some sort, or an abscess. Doc did not come in to give us the once-over; I imagine that he is busy elsewhere. Larry brought Dick and me a bite to eat about 9:30, tea and biscuits.

Tuesday, December 19

Doc woke us up about 7:00 o'clock and took our order for breakfast. Dick feels a lot better, in fact he wanted to get up and tear around; but of course Doc put the quietos to that. We both slept all morning, Doc coming in around 11:30 with a corset for me to wear, meaning that I could get up for meals as long as I wore the corset. Joe Wells the sailmaker made it out of heavy canvas, with leather pieces to go between my legs to keep the thing in place, since the strain is around the vicinity of the sacrum. After putting on my corset, I went down to lunch but could not stay up too long, as my back began to ache. The Admiral dropped in on us during the afternoon, asking how we felt, etc. He has been in about every day—I think that is a nice gesture. I slept most of the afternoon waking up several times because of the noise. Some of the fellows are working on the airplane skis. McCoy, Vernon Boyd, Fred Dustin and Collier have been doing the work. The Admiral has been spending considerable time with them. Some of the fellows spotted the first albatross. I went down to eat dinner, and had spaghetti and two pieces of hot mince pie which was very good. We have had exceptionally good weather, sea being very calm, no waves, only the ever-present swell which at times causes us to pitch and roll some. Doc came in and gave me a rubdown and my back feels much better.

Wednesday, December 20

Was awakened this morning about 6:00 o'clock by Doc Frazier coming into the cabin to operate on Moulton. He had with him all sorts of paraphernalia, from scissors and knives to tape and cotton. Then Doc Guyer came in loaded down and between the two of them they really fixed Dick up, drained his back. He slept all morning and tonight feels one hundred percent better. Doc thinks that he will be up and around in a couple of days. Spent most of the day reading *The Good Earth* and sleeping. I can't seem to get enough sleep. I got up for all meals today and after dinner sat out on the deck for a while watching the albatross which had been following the ship all day. They are probably the closest thing to perpetual motion that we will ever see. They are in motion constantly, yet they very seldom move or flap their wings, they just glide, taking advantage of the wind, air currents, coming so close to the top of the waves that we swear every time that they will go awash. At full speed they would glide clear around the ship, and Davis said that they could reach a speed of forty miles per hour. I sent my Christmas telegrams tonight, my folks, Alda, Bob Fattig, Howard, Mrs. Rose, the Weisheits, Doc Wolford and Scheidler. I hope they all get them in time. We are going to have our Christmas aboard the ship on the twenty-fourth, Christmas Eve, since we cross the international date line; probably on that date between the next day will be the twenty-sixth and we lose out on Christmas. I am getting pretty anxious to open packages. After Dick's operation, Larry put a sign on the door "Hospital—Stay the Hell Out" by orders of Doc Frazier, so all during the day we have had fellows sticking their heads in to find out what the score was. The Admiral looked in, as did Paul A. Doc came in to change Dick's bandages after class and Larry was here, so we had a small bull session with various ones joining in through the windows. Then Doc gave me a good rubdown and we all turned in. The sea was getting quite rough, white caps and we dipped some water over the aft well deck. Little Ellis is becoming

more acquainted with the fellows and now he is continually underfoot and was all over the ship. He has gotten over his seasickness
and is now quite a playful lad of four.

The days certainly are flying by—it's hard to believe that Christmas is only four days off. It's really a shame that we will not be at
Dunedin so we can spend Christmas ashore. Doc Frazier as usual
started the day off by coming in to bring Dick's breakfast—I have
been getting up to eat lately. Doc also changed the bandages and
made Dick comfortable. I spent all morning writing letters, since
we are only five days from Dunedin. I am just starting to write my
letters. I have been writing Alda every day so she is all set. It has
been rough all day, fairly heavy seas and we are taking much water
over the aft well deck and poop. She has been more rolling than
anything else, I imagine about ninety degrees, just enough to make
it uncomfortable. It's hard to walk or do anything else. The fellows
have been pretty busy all day making things more secure. Most of
the dog sleds have been fastened to the awning supports up forward
and the majority of the tractor sleds have been stacked on top of
the snow cruiser. There are thirty-six dog sleds and twelve tractors.
I am having quite a hard time writing; being in bed I roll back and
forth with the slightest movement of the ship. During the afternoon
I read two chapters of Schuchert & Dunbar, Silurian and Devonian.
It seems like I learn more every time I read that book—I learn something new. Dick has been having quite a time eating in bed and
tonight he lost control of a piece of chocolate pie and it went sliding
down his chest. We had a very good meal tonight being steak. After
dinner I sat on deck while watching the shearwaters, a bird resem-
bling the albatross, only smaller, and similar in that it glides close to
the surface of the water. When I came back to the cabin, Douglas
was talking to Dick so I joined in and soon Perkins arrived, then
Warner and finally one by one Doc Frazier, Earl Lockhart, and Doc
Wade drifted in till we had quite a gathering and the makings of a
good bull session, which finally broke up at 10:00 o'clock. Butler
and Richardson could not get in so had to stand in the doorway
and at the window—Gilmore came up later. It's so nice and peaceful now, like the passing of a storm.

Didn't sleep a wink last night, it stormed, rained, the wind blew, and to top it all off the dogs howled all night long. Besides, we rolled back and forth—in fact it was a fairly heavy sea. The poor dogs must have been scared half to death, as they hate water anyway, then to have the waves send sprays over them, I guess it was too much. The storm lasted all day getting worse along toward late afternoon. We did not do much pitching as we had an eastern sea and the bow acted as a pivot. The waves back aft would come right up to the poop deck and would swamp the aft well deck. The dogs back aft were certainly a miserable bunch; they couldn't sit down because they would be sitting in water about six to eight inches deep, and they couldn't stand up because the deck was much too slick. So they did a little of each and all managed to stay aboard—they were a forlorn howling bunch of critters. Larry came in after taking out our wastebaskets and said that if he tossed stuff over the port side, it blew back, and he tried the starboard and he got it back in the face. And he even rolled up forward and back aft and got the same results. By that time he gave up, the wind was not acting according to "hoyle." I stayed in bed most of the day except for meals, but it was too hard for me to keep my balance because of my back. I did however try to take Dick's tray down. Well, I stepped out of our cabin door and proceeded to dump the whole business right in the hall, broke only four out of six dishes.

Davis (Bring Em Back Alive) talked tonight on the above subject. He gave a very nice and interesting talk, taking us to all parts of the world, wild animal hunting. We hunted cobras in India, lions in Africa, and Birds of Paradise in small islands of India. His work must be very fascinating. The Washington Zoo has animals from practically every region and country in the world but the Antarctic, so Dave is going to try the impossible and bring back a few penguins. After the talk I got back in bed and Don Hilton dropped in for a while, followed by Doc Frazier, so we talked things over for quite a while. By then the sea had let up a little and it was not too much of an effort to stay in bed. The old "salts" aboard said that it was not much of a storm, but I noticed that they did not ask for more. About every fourth time a wave would slap up on the "salon" deck, so with the rain and the spray we had a fairly damp day. Almost finished reading *Hell Beyond The Seas* by Aage Krarup Nielse, telling of his experiences at Devil's Island and French Guiana —very interesting book and makes one wonder whether the world really is civilized and just. We are now approximately 1,200 miles from Dunedin—they have failed to keep us posted on mileage etc., so my record is not complete. I guess I will never make a sailor as I am certainly tired of seeing nothing but water.

Sunday, December 23

It hasn't been bad today; no sun, but the sea has let up considerably. I slept all morning—I just can't seem to get enough sleep. Got up for lunch and worked with Gilmore for a while on clothing divisions. I couldn't resist it any longer, I opened my Christmas packages this afternoon. I was certainly glad to see the molasses, peanut butter, and cherries, but I will equally enjoy the rest, especially the candy and fruitcake. When I showed Larry, he and I both decided that mother knew best, especially what her son would want most, miles from home. I could not have gotten a thing that I would have liked better. Tonight when I went for dinner I was surprised to find that the salon was all decorated with Christmas trimmings, and that there was a nice fireplace put up, and the whole thing done up in fine style. All of the fellows on the ship the day before had to draw a name, being some other member of the group to give a Christmas present to, so I drew Vernon Boyd. But so far I cannot think or find anything to give him. Vernon talked tonight at school on "Tractor Transportation," he is a very interesting speaker, very humorous. He told me that I had been definitely picked to drive the little International tractor, so that means I was one of the tractor departments. We had a big bull session tonight, Gilmore, Warren, Jack Richardson, Dick Moulton and myself, the topic of conversation was the "dog men having to work down in the galley." We have quite a time around here, everyone has his pet gripes and it seems that all the boys have to come to cabin #8 to air their views. Dick has to rest quite a bit—the Doc said that he could stay up a little longer every day.

Sunday, December 24

"MERRY CHRISTMAS" to the lads on the U.S. Antarctic Expedition. It is Christmas day because we crossed the international date line this morning so tomorrow will be the twenty-sixth. Spent all morning playing the clarinet—Christmas carols and hymns, also watching Gilmore open his package. All of the fellows were in a good mood, everyone wishing everyone else a very Merry Christmas. We had a very light lunch as we were to have our big meal at night. About 4:00 o'clock everyone gathered in the social hall and Sig (the steward) served punch (that's what he called it). I drank about half a glass and started to get dizzy and some of the fellows were getting a little high, so you can imagine. We spent the time till dinner putting slugs in the nickelodeon. Dinner was served at 6:00 o'clock and what a meal. Sig did very well in setting the table—it looked very nice and the food was wonderful. To start out with we had a shrimp cocktail, then consomme, followed by turkey, with all the trimmings—in other words we had everything from soup to nuts and to top it off we had a nice piece of hot mince pie. Frankly, I was so full I could hardly climb the stairs to go top side to the salon deck, and I barely made a chair before I gave out. At 8:00 o'clock we had a play—"Tragedy of Rapa Island," played by Gilmore, Moe, Warner, Dustin and McCoy. Dick Black was the master of ceremonies rather than director. I don't know when I laughed so hard; my sides still ache. Moe was the Viscount and Gilmore was his wife or a native dancer. McCoy was a prospector. The whole theme of the play was based on different incidents, a takeoff on happenings en route. One especially funny one was a tale of the Admiral getting kicked (this happened some time ago). One of the fellows mistook the Admiral for someone else coming around the corner and placed a nice number twelve in the seat of his pants—well, they had the same effect in play. One of the fellows was leaning over picking up something and Dustin slapped him on the buckett with a rag club, the fellow looked up surprised and Dustin said, "Pardon me, I thought you were the Admiral." The old man really got a kick out of that. There were also some other good ones.

After the play, Santa (Little Moe) passed out our Christmas presents. I got a nice pipe and cleaners from some friend. I wish I could find out who it is so that I could thank him. The gifts were of various assortments ranging from a bar of "Lifebuoy soap" to cigarettes, socks and cigars. Little Ellis was really taken care of. One of the crew, a Bill Lee, made him a model of the "North Star." Everyone gave him some toy or another. Mother had a couple of toys in my package so I wrapped them up for him. Tex Helm made him a cowboy suit. For the past week the boys have been telling him about cowboys, etc., so that he would appreciate it. He was afraid of Santa at first, being the first time he had ever seen him, but after a while he would walk up when his name was called and thank him. He certainly is a cute little kid, four years old and smart as a whip. Doc Wade gave him a little toy train that his mother had put in his box. Little Moe played the part of Santa very well and kept us all laughing throughout the evening. Quite a few of the gifts were very clever and one poem which Arnold Court gave the Admiral was exceptionally good. I hope to get a copy. Jack Richardson and Paul Siple; Paul designed it and Jack inked it in, made a large Christmas card showing the *North Star* and *Bear* entering the ice, etc., and all of the fellows signed it. Then Moe presented it to the Admiral who gave a little speech showing his appreciation, saying that when any of us visit him, and that we would all be welcome, we would find this scroll right over his desk. Later in the evening he was in Dave's room, I happened in and he shook hands with me thanking me for my part in signing it saying that that little gift would mean more to him than anything in the world. After all of the gifts were passed out we sang several carols hence completing a very wonderful evening. However, there were still a few things missing—my folks, naturally, as this was the first Christmas spent away from home. I would have liked to have been with Alda over the holidays. I hope both of them get my Christmas message. I sent Aunt Nellie one Friday, she will get it a little late for Christmas but before the New Year, so that will be all right. The sea was very calm today, the usual swell but outside of that not a ripple. There have been quite a few of the "wandering" albatross following the ship. The other day I counted about a dozen. There has been some problem concerning oil in New Zealand. We are not sure where we can get it and have not been able to get any word from Dunedin, so they think it might be possible to have to stop at Wellington, to have oil tested also to see if we can get the oil at the right price. The war might have some effect on the whole matter. The oil that was bought at Panama was such a poor quality that they are afraid that it will ruin the engines. They could not get the right mixture, so all of the fellows are trying to find out where we really are going to dock. About the only way one can find out anything on this ship is through the "grapevine," which works very well. Went to bed fairly late last night, so am pretty tired tonight.

Tuesday, December 26

Here we are up to the twenty-sixth already—passed up the twenty-fifth like it was nothing. When I got out of the bunk this morning Perkins was yelling "land ho!" Sure enough there was land, New Zealand off the starboard bow. Boy it certainly looked good. I spent part of the morning writing letters, then Larry and I went back to the storage, borrowed Helm's portable darkroom and loaded some film cartridge. After lunch we brought the things up to the cabin and I loaded some for Douglas, then Larry and I decided to polish off the roll that Doc Wolford gave us. We got about twenty and one-half cartridges out of his roll, which was about right. Tonight the Admiral called a meeting and gave us the lowdown. It seems that we are stopping at Wellington to find out about the oil, and if they cannot supply us then we will move on to Dunedin. If they can, then we will be there for three days, then Dunedin for about one. The tough part about it is since the main New Zealand communication has been cut off, our radio men have tried to get them but no luck. Hence, our visit. Larry, Dick and I wrote letters part of the evening then Vernon Boyd dropped in and before we knew it we had a "bull session." I took my first fresh water shower since Panama tonight, it certainly was a treat. I have taken so many spit baths in the bowl that I begin to feel like a canary. Larry has gone up to the social hall to read, Dick is below reading, so I think I will turn in as we dock at Wellington at 6:00 o'clock in the morning and I have to be up and ready. Beautiful moon tonight.

Wednesday thru Saturday, December 28-30

1940

Wednesday, January 3

Out at five o'clock this morning as the custom official wanted to take muster of all hands. It was rather wild that early in the morning—we find the most ungodly hours to sail. Six o'clock in the morning is just too early. There were a few people down to see us, most of them newly-made acquaintances of the crew or members of the expedition. There were a group of Maoris on hand. Some of the crew met them the night before and from the looks of the whole mob they had been out on an all-night binge. The Maoris however gave us a few native dances, and say, it was very good. The second time we have ever sailed on time, for at 6:00 o'clock sharp we were underway. Mrs. Black came down from the states to see Dick one last time, she was on hand for sailing. Right after we got underway I went into my bunk and did not wake up until noon. I had caught a cold from someone there and I was feeling pretty punk, so stayed in bed the rest of the day. It has been very rough all day, this old tub does more rolling and pitching. I can say that I don't enjoy such weather. Don and Larry moved all of the dogs from up forward to the port salon deck which means they are right outside our window. We were shipping so much water over the fo'c's'le head that the poor dogs had quite a time keeping on all fours. Now all Larry has to do is stick his head out the window and yell at the mutts and they quiet down in a hurry.

It's good to be underway again. Taking in all of these ports is nice enough but it's been a slow drag from Boston. Over six weeks and I, for one, want to get down on the ice and get settled.

Still farther south and it's getting a little colder. I am thankful for an end to that hot weather. It's all right if you like it but it makes me feel lazy. I have not been worth a plug nickel all the way across the Pacific. Last night Dunedin played our special request program which lasted for an hour and a half. They got it on the snow cruiser radio using the loudspeaker system in the social hall. I had two numbers requested and they played both of them. The first thing was "Moonlight Serenade" for Alda, that being her favorite, hence our song, and "Wishing," which was a second choice. I know I have been doing enough wishing, hoping and praying that everything will be all right at home, that Alda will wait for me.

It's rather hard to write sitting up in bed. I sleep rolling back and forth. The sea is still rough and half of the fellows are down and out. I certainly am fortunate to be in bed with a cold or else I would probably be here from some other cause. What a ship—first she will roll, then pitch, then she seems to hesitate, stop in midair, then pitch and roll at the same time. It is almost impossible to ever stand up. Last night I woke up hearing Larry utter a few choice words; everything from the glass shelf over the sink had slid off and one heavy can of tooth powder hit him square on the head. All through the night things dropped from seemingly "nowhere" and we have spent most of the day picking things up from nooks and corners. I guess the other fellows have had the same trouble, because in almost all of the cabins the floors are covered with debris. We have been running at about three/quarter speed so have not been making our usual good time. The Admiral got a wire from the *Bear* and she is in the ice but is far to the east. If things work out right we should meet and go through pack together. Al Wade, Larry, Gil and myself had a rather executive bull session earlier in the evening. Talked on about every topic imaginable, from geology to the trip here. We did reach the decision, however, that the Captain is some sort of a heel and Gil elaborated on the subject some, giving us several incidents which helped strengthen our already well-formed opinion. The outstanding happening was in the case of broadcasting last night. The Captain's name was not mentioned, so he, this morning, hopped all over Roger Hawthorn asking him what was the big idea, saying, "All you hear around here is Expedition and etc.—you'd think there was not even a Captain aboard." He certainly was burned up, and I know that none of the expedition members respect him because as a Captain he is a wash-out. He is so busy getting his picture taken and getting publicity that he hasn't time for anything else. He certainly is one disliked man. Also, in the case of our Pitcairn Island cache, the Captain was sore because his picture and name was not on the cut, so he hopped on Roger for that. Poor Roger has to take it, but I know that he didn't like it. So to bed—asleep.

Friday, January 5

Another day. It has been light since about 2:30 this morning and I woke up about then with the sun shining brightly right in my face. It is really something around here. Stays light till 10:00 every night, so we never know really when to get to bed, then the day starts so early. Stayed in bed all day trying to get rid of my cold and I still am glad that I had it, because if I had been up I know I would have been seasick. Sad life. The sea was still rough and we have been rolling and rolling around, sometimes on course and sometimes off. Then last night the snow cruiser fellows had quite a scare—the thing moved about an inch or so, and the whole bunch cleared out, all but Doc Poulter who stayed on waiting for it to move some more. Just to be sure, he was not going to leave the ship till all hope was abandoned—a true captain and leader. However, all is well now; she is secure now they took up about an inch and a half in the chain winch to hold her tight. It is still getting colder and we should be seeing icebergs in the next day or two. We had quite a bull session in cabin #8 tonight, it seems to be the gathering place. Doc Wade comes in after dinner, then they all seem to gather. Al, Larry, Doc Frazier, Gilmore and myself talked things over pro and con. Although there is really nothing accomplished at such sessions they are quite fun. Otto, the engineer, came in today and turned on the heat, filling the radiator, etc., so I guess it's going to get cold in earnest.

Saturday, January 6

I woke up this morning feeling like a million, so got up for breakfast—the first food in three days except for some candy that Robin sent to Larry. Al, Gilmore and I enjoyed it very much. After breakfast Paul suggested that it was calm enough to break in the aft hold and get out the clothing to be issued for unloading, so he got the boys of the first team and opened the hatch. Then I went down with my "poop" sheets and we started to work. We got out shirts #100, heavy pants, socks, ski boots, mushing boots, etc. It was an all-morning job and it took the rest of the day to distribute the issue. Al, Paul, Gilmore, Warner, and myself set up a store, so to speak, in the social hall and as the fellows would go down the line they would receive their clothing. Naturally there was the usual squawking about sizes, fellows with size six feet having to wear size eleven mushing boots, ten being the smallest unless it was the fellow with five and five and one-half foot. It was quite an inspiration to hear the fellows so contented with what we provided.

There is only one fellow aboard this ship who I really like to issue clothing to. Ask him what size he wears, he'll ask what you got, then you will say coat size forty-four, forty-six, forty-eight, then he'll say just what I take. Yes, Clay Bailey is tops all around. It's the same with shoes or anything, he doesn't care—they all fit him. We also issued the sheep-lined coats which were given to the Admiral. They were given to certain fellows for use on deck watch, also we loaned the crew a dozen. There has certainly been a mixup about the crew's winter clothing. Capt. Lysted had commented all along that we were not going to furnish them clothing; now, there has been quite a feeling amongst the crew because of that. Lysted knew it in Boston and he still told the crew that they did not have to have their own clothing. Now, I know they do not work in Alaska in their underwear and I don't think it is fair for us to have to clothe them out of our supply because after all we have only enough to go around for the ice party. The whole problem was brought before the Admiral at Dunedin and it was decided to buy them just the bare necessities. Boy, the Admiral was burned up about the whole thing and I don't blame him. We had steak for dinner tonight and it was really good, steak and fried potatoes. Well, it took up the rest of the evening to repack the clothing, which is to be for the fellows on the *Bear*. By that time it was 11:00 o'clock and still light, and by then I was rather tired so turned in. Oh! Yes, we also got our sleeping bags and Larry decided to use his last night. He even cracked out a clean pair of pajamas for the occasion. It's really pathetic to see our cabin now with all of the added clothing, etc. The mushing boots alone are so large that they have to be hung from the wall; as for the sleeping bags they are at the foot of our bunks. The rest of the stuff is neatly packed away under the mattress. Such is life in a two-by-four cabin, a home for three.

Sunday, January 7

Was up and at them bright and early this morning—7:00 o'clock. Pappy Reece started the day off right by giving me a telegram from the folks. I can't understand why they did not get my Christmas message. I suppose and hope that they got it after they sent this last wire. If not, it must have gotten lost in the mail or something. Also I have not heard from Alda lately, I hope that she is not ill or that something is wrong. I sent both her and the folks one today. I hope they get them. Clay Bailey says that he has not had much luck in contacting the fellows in the states; and then we were laid up in dock for about five days while at New Zealand, so that put them behind schedule. We still have not sighted ice, but the Admiral says or bets we will in the next twelve hours. I spent the morning writing letters, getting a few ready for the *Bear*. Larry has been working steady all day trying to pack his gear and here it is 9:00 o'clock in the evening and he is still going strong. Of course he was delayed a couple of times because of bull sessions but outside of that no interference except for the Admiral who dropped in this afternoon looking for a couple of math sharks. We sicked him on Eric Clark, it was really a close call. We did, however, spend some time working on the problem which had to do with the coefficient of friction in regards to the size of skis for his plane. Eric just dropped in and after a gabfest we decided that there was no difference in the friction of the two; which after all was very simple. Gilmore came in and reported bits from a meeting which he attended all afternoon, some of the bigwigs. He told Larry and myself that we were to be quartered together down there, also that I definitely was assigned to the tractor department, while Larry has a "poop sheet" job which does not suit him very much, and I don't blame him after my experience in Boston. I am on watch from 12:00 midnight to 4:00, so hope to get a little sleep before then. We saw a very large school of dolphins, largest Paul said he had ever seen on either trip before. We are down around 61° latitude, and are not supposed to see any albatross. I have not heard reports today, but for the last two days about ten to twelve have been following us.

Monday, January 8

I stood watch last night from 12:00 to 4:00, it was quite cold standing up on the fo'c's'le head and was light all the time. Yes! we have seen our last darkness for about two or so months. Since I was on watch last night I slept all morning, working all afternoon

38

packing my things and getting all squared around. That was some job and took till late in the evening. We sighted our first iceberg this afternoon about 3:30, it was a beautiful sight. Throughout the course of the afternoon we saw two more, but none as large as the first. It was a pretty sight to see all of the fellows disappear then all run up forward with their cameras. They have nicknamed this the "U.S. Antarctic Photographic Expedition" because everyone and his brother has a camera. It certainly was sweet of Alda to give me mine. I don't know what I would have done without it. I started reading *The Tumult After the Shouting* by Parrott, very good story. Since we are traveling right down the 180th Meridian, Sig, the steward, announced before noon meal that on the port side of the dining salon it was Sunday. Hence, anyone sitting there would have chicken, and those sitting on the other would have hash since it was Monday. It was pretty witty of him, but incidentally, we all had bread. It's still rather hard to get used to the continual light. Half of the fellows do not know when to go to bed. They all sit around waiting for it to get dark; hence there is always a crowd in the social hall. I have been getting in my bunk to read till finally I fall asleep.

Tuesday, January 9

Well, looks like we have lost another day as we are now west of 18°, hence it is still Monday, but at home it is Tuesday. We started to run into packs of ice this morning, at first just scattered pieces of ice till now. At 10:00 p.m. we are having quite a time making our way through. We are really in the pack and the old ship is smashing her way through, riding up on the ice and crashing it with her weight. We are running at about half speed, stopping ever so often or speeding up as we get a little clear space. Right at present there is ice pack all around us, we are barely creeping along. We saw three seals during the day, two crab eaters and one weddell, also a few penguins floated by on chunks of ice. It is still getting colder, being now about twenty-five degrees above zero. At least most of the fellows are beginning to get out their long drawers. I cracked mine out the other day and put them on, size forty-two around the waist, but with the aid of safety pins I managed to keep them in tack. I hope they shrink just a little; however, it doesn't matter because I cut and am now using the drawstring (pajamas) style on them which worked very nicely. Water ration has been cut down now and the faucets are on only twice a day, in the morning and at night. Then only for an hour. I haven't had a bath for so long—it will be wonderful to get back home where one can soak and soak. I have been taking quite a few pictures today and yesterday, and if I have any luck at all they should turn out fairly well. At least I hope so.

Tuesday, January 9

It seems funny having two January 9th's, but after all, we had two Thanksgivings and no Christmas day, so I guess that really there is nothing too strange in this world we live in. Had a hard time getting up this morning as I still can't quite get accustomed to the idea of no darkness. I was up until 1:00 o'clock last night and I just didn't seem to get sleepy. I hope that when we start unloading I will be so sleepy that when my twelve hours are up I will fall right to sleep. I spent all morning writing letters in the social hall. As usual, there were quite a few of the fellows around there, some writing, others working trail flags, and Joe Wells the tailor was busy at his sewing. And as usual there was a lot of bull flying around. Doc Geyer and Lobell were right in the center of it. I didn't really get much done since far be it for me not to enter into things. Early in the morning we passed through the barrier into clear ocean, but around 1:00 o'clock we ran into more pack ice. We saw several more huge icebergs, one in particular must have been eighty to one hundred feet high. It was a beautiful thing and of course as we passed it all of the cameras went into play. Wednesday, Finn Ronne and I divided the McElwin ski boots and Paul gave Larry and me a pair. They certainly are fine boots, costing about $25.00 a pair. Each base only got fifteen, these are trail boots; while the Bass boots are not so good they are going to be used by the rest of the fellows.

Wednesday, January 10

Last night we had a meeting and Paul talked about the unloading program telling us of our various assignments and giving us tips as to how to wear our clothing and cautioning us about wearing sunglasses, taking our sleeping bags with us at all times, and never wandering around alone—always in pairs. As I learned, I was signed up to drive the little red tractor which has been named "Dolly," and Pappy Reese will be the other driver. I have the P.M. run which means from noon to midnight, while Pappy has the A.M. I am going to change the tractor name to "Alda," secretly of course,

40

cause the fellows would make fun of me. Still, I don't think Alda would appreciate a tractor named after her. After the meeting I went into Carroll's cabin and developed a roll of films, didn't turn out very good. I really wanted to develop one so I could see how I was doing. The negatives were all nice and sharp but I do such dumb things, like letting the flap of the case get in front of the lens, or else forgetting to remember whether or not I turned the film after I took a shot. But all in all, they are turning out pretty good. I will never be able to thank Alda enough for giving me the camera —it certainly was sweet of her. I couldn't get along without it. I slept through breakfast, just didn't have the nerve to get up. Finn Ronne came in about 5:30 this morning, waking Larry, telling him that they had to move the dogs from up forward as waves and spray were coming over the side and the poor dogs were getting soaked and were freezing to death. So old Larry bales out bringing the howling pack back on the salon deck, placing two of them right under our window. I am pretty busy this morning, once I got up, breaking out some clothing for the Admiral and summer mukluk for the dog drivers. The Admiral needed some heavy socks for flying. After lunch I turned in to take a nap, Al woke me up at 4:45. I would have slept through evening chow. It is now midnight, I still can't get used to the light, still am not sleepy. I went up and talked a while with Clay and he thinks that he will be able to get my message through to Alda and the folks. I certainly hope so because they will both be worried. Finished up a few more letters tonight, am about caught up. We are due to arrive at the barrier around noon tomorrow. It is possible now to get what is called the "barrier blink," that is light from the barrier. The *Bear* is about two hundred miles east of us and will probably get to the Bay of Whales a little after we do. It will certainly be some sight to see her breeze in—full sail. We finally got our certificates for crossing the equator. The Captain just signed them then I got the Admiral to sign mine. That will look pretty nice framed and in my den (if I ever have one).

Thursday, January 11

Woke up this morning, the barrier staring me in the face. What a sight—I will never forget it—my home for the next year, ice and snow. We went eastward along the barrier looking for the Bay of Whales which we turned into about 9:00 o'clock. But there was no place to tie up because it was frozen in with pressure ice, we couldn't get up to the barrier itself. Paul said it would probably be two weeks before the Bay cleared itself of the ice. So we headed eastward again to Kainan Bay, finding there a barrier low enough to land, and in order to test the ice we hit her head-on, causing quite a jolt. In fact, we hit her much harder than was counted on. Some sort of mixup over the command. However, there was no damage done (at least noticeable). I later talked to the Chief Engineer and he said that that was no way to treat a ship and that even at that it didn't do her any good; after all, 3,500 tons is pretty heavy and we were making about half speed, although the prop was going reverse but not soon enough to slow us down. All we did to the ice was take a little chunk. However, they seemed not satisfied so we still headed eastward to Okuma Bay where Paul originally wanted to come. It was really beautiful, but the barrier was way too high, eighty to one hundred feet, hence it was impossible to tie up there. The main objective in selecting a place to tie up is one where the snow cruiser can be unloaded all right. So we headed out to sea again and followed the barrier again, and this time back toward Kainan Bay since it was the only place within reason. It is impossible to describe the barrier ice and it is of utmost interest why the bays are present in it. We took sounding at Okuma Bay and they found it to be sixty-four fathoms.

It is now midnight and I just came off watch. We have started our twelve-on-and-twelve-off arrangement, and since I have the P.M. I had to work till now. We did not have to do much since it was the first watch, except unlash a few things prior to our tie-up at Kainan Bay. We are still underway and Larry just reported that we missed the opening of the bay and have turned around and are now heading back east.

Friday, January 12
Didn't sleep very well last night, too much excitement I guess. I woke up about 8:00 o'clock in the morning after getting to sleep about 2:00 A.M. There was much going on this morning. Paul, Vernon and Ike Schlossbach left the ship when we first hit the ice in Kainan Bay, that being around 2:30 A.M.—purpose being to plan site for west base, Paul saying that he would be back in four hours. So by 8:00 o'clock no word of them, the Admiral said to send out a party to look for them. Black, Ronne and Dick Moulton took off with Dick's dog team and provisions for the dogs plus tents and sleeping bags. It seemed that there had been some mixup in orders or intentions—anyway Paul asked Black to follow immediately

with a dog team, but evidently Dick forgot or something—mostly something. Anyway, there was quite a stink about the whole thing. Here Paul and his party all the time were waiting for the follow-up party which just wasn't out. Of course, we who were not on the ice did not know but what something was wrong with Paul, hence the Admiral's orders. It was really a beautiful sight to see Dick's dogs start out. First of all he put out his lead dog, Snowball, then the rest of the team, and not one of them budged or raised cain. Snowball kept the line taut, and when Dick gave the word they all started out as one. It was really a pretty thing to see a well-trained team. Ronne and Black were on skis, Ronne in lead setting trail flags, then Dick Moulton with the dogs, followed by Black. It was beginning to snow, "blizzard," and there was quite a swell in the bay, so we had to back out because the ice was breaking up, wind increasing in velocity. After we got back out from the ice we stood by and tooted the whistle every eighteen minutes and Clay Bailey contacted them every fifteen minutes with radio trail set. It was sometime before we saw them again and when we did both parties were together; but there was such a swell, the sea so choppy, that it was impossible for us to land. Hence it was suggested that the ice party take off toward Little America as we were again going to try the Bay of Whales, but Black said they would have a hard time making it as it would be a two-and-one-half-day journey, unknown trail, besides six men in a small tent, only a small supply of food and one injured dog. Besides, the blizzard was getting worse. So the Admiral was called and it was decided that the ice party stand by and wait till the weather let up. So they pitched their tent and we stood by. Finally around 4:00 o'clock in the afternoon the weather let up and the seas calmed down, so after a council of war it was decided to risk taking them aboard. It had been impossible to get them by radio for the last three or four hours, so we used the ship's whistle to arouse them, heading the ship toward the spot where we wanted to take them aboard. They hurriedly broke camp and we came down to the edge of the ice and headed in, nose rammed in the ice. We raised all of the equipment and dogs by use of hand winch. It was funny to see the dogs come up—naturally hitched on by their harnesses. They came up with their tail first, sideways or any old way. The poor devils really have to take it, and they do without a whimper. After all were aboard we put out to sea headed west along the barrier for the Bay of Whales.

We arrived there about 10:00 o'clock and Paul, Al and Dr. Poulter went on shore to look over the lay of the land and to decide on a landing place for the cruiser. After they came back a war council was held and it was decided to stay. So being on watch till 12:00 midnight, we fellows went ashore and started to dig holes for the dead men (timbers to tie the ship to the ice). While we were doing this, several penguins called on us and we had quite a time catching them. They would sauce us, absolutely defy us to get them, and when we would get too close they would flop over on their bellies and with the aid of their flippers and wings would scoot along at a very swift pace. It was a lot of fun catching them, just like a football game. They certainly knew all of the tricks. We threw them back in the bay a couple of times, and before we could take a step away they would be back at our feet. They are very fast swimmers, and when they come out of the water they jump out going about three feet high, lighting almost anywhere usually, even on their noses' beaks. Our shift did not get all the dead men put in, luckily we did get one completed when the midnight relief came on.

Saturday, January 13

Got up about 11:00 this morning and took a few pictures. This bay was rightfully named because about twelve to fifteen whales had been swimming around the ship all morning. I took some pictures of them, however I doubt if they will turn out. Went on watch at noon and Don Hilton and I drove Jack Bursey's dog team, with King as lead dog. We had a terrible time. I have never seen a more stubborn dog than King. We would yell "yak" and he wouldn't budge and the rest of the team would run over him, which would end up in a dog fight. Then we would have to wade in and use the whip on them. That, however, didn't seem to phase King because if we were lucky enough to start him, when we wanted to stop him (yelling "whoa" wouldn't do the trick), we would have to run him into something. Then Don would get off the sled or else if we happened to have a load he would leave his place at the "G" pole I was on, and go ahead to go and really talk it over with him. Finally, however, King began to pull in line and he would heed the commands fairly readily. Since it was the first they had been driven, we made only five trips from the ship to the first "cache," and they were really tired. Naturally they would be because they were soft. Jack Richardson had quite a time. He said he rode on all parts of the sled trying to stop his dogs, control them; he even rode underneath and with the sled upside down. On the return trips we would ride in order to hold the dogs back a little. Don and I fed our team about 9:00 tonight, seal meat. We had quite a time cutting the stuff up—and did it ever smell. We spent the rest of the evening working by the ship, taking barrels of fuel off the sling. It certainly is a good feeling when midnight comes around and the relief comes on.

Sunday, January 14

The little red tractor was taken out on the A.M. watch so I drove her on my watch. It was really funny because she will go only in reverse. She digs right down going forward and gets no place fast, but in reverse with the drive front she goes fine. It isn't bad driving her that way, except from the stiff neck angle. Right now mine is so stiff from trying to look out the rear window seeing where I was to go. Sgt. Asman worked with me and we hauled stores from the ship to the top of the barrier, being run by the ship's winch. The tractor sleds are loaded and tied to this rope and pulled to the top where Sarg and I would hitch on and take it to the cache. The weather so far has been fine, not too cold, just right. I have been running with the windshield open on the tractor and the fellows working on the caches are stripped to the waist, some being in their undershirts. The *Bear* came in this morning about 9:30 or so. I asked Doc Frazier to wake me when he came in as I wanted to take some pictures. He, however, was way up top on the barrier level and did not take pictures himself. But luckily I happened to hear someone yell "here comes the *Bear*" so I woke up and took my share. She looked pretty loaded down, the Barkly-Grow on the aft part of the ship and dogs stuck in every corner. It was really a sensation to see another ship in the waters. I shall never forget the sight, the feeling that I guess possessed every one of us—all eager to see our fellow men, to talk to them, to see if letters from home could be had, some to see old friends or acquaintances. A morning long to remember—was fortunate in the mail situation—one from home, and the Bible which Mother sent that I was to get in Panama. I thought our bunch on the *Star* looked tough and hard, but I think the fellows on the *Bear* beat us by a hair. Their beards were just a bit longer, however, we run a close second. I haven't washed for the last three days or so, since the water is turned on when I am asleep. I manage to wash my hands just a little but as far as a good going-over with soap and water, etc., it can't be had. I am getting pretty good however, in that when I go to bed I get a glass of water (from the drinking fountain) and in it I can clean my teeth and splash my face and hands, and still have enough left to drink.

Monday, January 15

Today was a big day in the life of one Doc Poulter—for on this day about 8:00 o'clock P.M. the Doc drove off in the snow cruiser amid shouts and yells of encouragement from all hands. They spent all afternoon getting her lined up and putting the ramp up to the ship, made of heavy timber with sixty foot telephone poles as supports. But all of this was not enough to hold the tremendous weight of the snow cruiser. She started down, getting halfway before the timber broke and the only thing that saved her was a drum of oil which happened to be sitting under the ramp. The left side broke through and the left front wheel stopped, hit the barrel, and at the same time Doc Poulter gave her the gun and she got a new hold, but still breaking the timber as she crashed down. Even though she was breaking and cracking the wood, the added speed saw her down and when she hit the snow the Doc kept right on going for about a mile. The back wheels spun around, due to the lack of weight, because of the removal of the tail and tires. The front wheels took hold and pulled her right along. A success. Later I saw Doc Poulter and it was worth the whole trip just to see his face. The Admiral rode down the ramp on top of the cruiser and when she first crashed through he almost took a flying leap. Petras just hung on for dear life to the winch back of the control room. I think it was really wonderful the way Doc Poulter had enough presence of mind to act fast, to do the right thing at the right time—most men would have lost their heads and probably jumped, but not the Doc. He just hung on and gave her the oil. To our surprise, as she left the ship she trailed a bluish-brown cloud of smoke. Doc probably had her wide open. He at one time said that he wouldn't stop this side of "Little America." The Doc had a trail set for Elmer Bolling Bit which is about four miles west and south from here, along the pressure ice. Al Wade was on deck, as was Ferranto. The whole gang worked hard and we were all glad to see the cruiser work so well. Toward the end of the watch I got together with Dorsey and he and I tried to straighten out the clothing proposition. He moved a whole box of west base clothing to east base men on the *Bear*, hence rather complicating things. One thing is certain and that is there is not going to be quite enough clothing to go around. There

46

are about sixty-four men and only clothing for sixty. This expedition started out with twenty-two men per base, now there are thirty at each base, plus the cruiser. It's quite a mess. However, I imagine all will be taken care of.

Tuesday, January 16

Another day and fairly mild, sun has been shining brightly and we have been able to strip down pretty much. It is actually hot in the tractor cab. Did the usual thing today hauling sleds from the line to the main caches. Still going strong in reverse, still have the same stiff neck. They broke out the ordinance tractor on the last shift, but she stopped dead halfway up the barrier—dirty gas lines. Sarg Asman got the west base tank out of the hold. I tried pulling him with "Dolly" but it could not be done. He finally got her started, hit it top speed right over the barrier with the Admiral riding on top. The Sarg got stuck up on top, pretty far back in the fresh snow, so I went up to assist. We dug and dug, shoveled more snow than I had ever dreamed could exist, till finally we had the tank dug out. So I put a tow line on and I pulled and he helped me. Well, the outcome was that I didn't move, he did since he was going in reverse, he couldn't see me, climbed right on Dolly's radiator. I yelled and did everything else, but that didn't help matters any—I thought I was a goner. He would have climbed right on over me but luckily he stopped after the first jolt. He thought that since he was moving I was probably pulling him. Well he dug me out and I swear that is the last time I will ever help anyone, especially when "Dolly" is a three-and-a-half-tonner and small, and the tank is large, around nine tons. Moe had been working on the "Doodle Bug" and he finally got her going again and decided to try to bring her up on the barrier. Well, right at the top of the hill happens to be a nice crevasse, just before one reaches the barrier coming from the bay ice. We built a bridge of one description or another over the crevasse, but when the tank went over it tore up, caving in some of the ice and making the thing really dangerous to cross. Moe decided to take the Army ordinance tractor down along the bay ice, coming up a little further, right near the first cache. So he wanted me to help him—sucker me—so I went over to the top of the barrier and pulled him (with help) up to the crevasse which at that point didn't show. We built a plank bridge over the thing and were all ready to go. Just then Boyd came along to take charge. After Moe and I had eased the tractor up this far without mishap, he decided to take her over the crevasse. So he got in and gave me the signal and I started to pull. Well, there was nothing to pull because he was already rolling right away. So, when he got over the planks he gave me the signal to stop, which I did, he stopped also, which was a mistake because the bottom dropped out of everything and there was Boyd, tractor and all, in the crevasse. If he had only kept going everything would have been all right. My first experience with dropping a tractor into a crevasse—which isn't any fun. If it had been just a little larger, it would have been "goodbye Boyd."

For the last couple of days cracks have been appearing, running the complete length of the bay ice and to the east of us along the barrier. About 10:00 o'clock P.M. she started to groan and creak, it had been just warm enough during the day—the weight of the cruiser the day before, plus a current and wind from the east caused it to crack. We got the call for all hands, and worked frantically to clear the ice. Luckily it is a policy to always carry away anything as soon as it is unloaded from the ship, so there was really not much around except some heavy timber used in the snow cruiser ramp. Since the Admiral always says wood just doesn't grow down here, we naturally try to save all we can, so we hauled all of it up to the barrier. We no sooner got the last tractor sled of wood up when she broke—the east barrier first, then our bay ice. Naturally we fellows working on the barrier were stranded from the ship, it was getting colder and our watch was about up, besides, half of us did not have our sleeping bags on the beach. It was a beautiful sight to see the ships tied up to a floating cake of ice with large hunks, pieces of the barrier, floating alongside. There was nothing we could do, we were stuck, so we decided to start hauling up bamboo, dog crates, etc., which had been dropped beyond the cache. Since one never knows when the bay ice will go, it's better to always drag things to the barriers. By midnight we were tired, hungry and ready to be relieved. By this time due to the good wind, the bay was clearing herself of ice. The broken ice moved toward the west to the pressure ice, leaving our part clear water. The *Star* had been circling the bay several times, evidently standing by to land again. Finally, I guess the Captain was satisfied because he nosed her in and they threw over the ladder, and I will say that we didn't lose any time getting aboard to chow. I don't remember ever eating so much, and I noticed that none of the fellows merely picked at their food. I was certainly ready for bed.

48

It was much colder today and much wind, causing the snow to drift, a blizzard effect. The trail which I had packed down between the cache and line was covered up, and when I got to one place I couldn't see the other. Have had quite a bit of trouble with the pedals on the tractor, they are all on one shaft and they get iced up, hence, not only are they hard to work, but when, for instance, I step on the clutch, the other pedals work also. I drove more with my hands on the pedals than with my feet because when I would finally get a pedal down, I would have to pull it back out by hand. If I wanted to turn half around, I would spin around a couple of times before I could get the darn thing stopped. One trip coming back from the cache I was riding along minding my own business when the front end of the tractor disappeared—I had fallen in a hole made by the tank. I worked for about an hour, digging a trench clear around the continent Antarctica before I was finally able to get "Dolly" out. The thing that made it so tough was due to the fact that the tank is as wide as "Dolly" is long, hence I was wedged in and had to start digging before I could ever budge. The Barkly-Grow was taken up for a test hop the other day with the Admiral aboard, Snow as pilot. They got off all right, but at about one hundred and fifty feet the motor stopped, and by that time they were over the pressure ice. There was only one alternative, land, which Snow did—landed on ice with pontoons. No one was hurt and the plane was not damaged. The *Bear* cast off her lines and went after the Grow, taking her aboard. Boyd and Moe got the ordinance tractor out of the crevasse—dug her out. That is, dug under her so that she would settle down from a thirty degree angle to about five degrees, so by using the winch on the red tractor with the tank as a dead man she came out very easily and was not damaged in the slightest. The last part of my watch I unloaded in the aft hold with Paul, Dick Black and Joe Healey. We worked to get the furs accessible for division. We got through about 12:00 o'clock, hence I had an hour to myself which surprised me so much that I simply wasted it when I had planned to write letters.

Up again 11:30 on the dot. It is really torture to get out of bed nowadays. It seems that I can never get enough sleep. Larry and I both are so dead tired by the time our twelve hours are up that it is all we can do to keep awake long enough to eat, which is really something. Started out the day by putting the finishing touches to holes dug for deadmen. Since we moved the ship because of the ice breaking, it was necessary to move the line which is now connected to the aft capstan, bringing the other end of the line almost one hundred yards from the cache. It seems rather silly to me to have to haul from the line to the cache—it seems to me that the haul should be longer because in the case of the dogs a mile or so would be just the thing for them, whereas a short distance gives them opportunity to get tangled. Unloading progressed pretty slow today as the aft capstan is not strong enough to pull up tractor sleds, hence we used all dog sleds, the dog teams picking them up at the top of the barrier. I helped them with the tractor by dragging a sort of road back. Then to spell them I would haul over dog sleds, which is not so hot because they get in the tractor tracks and tend to tip over. I lost two sleds that way which would mean that I would have to hop out and reload. It was pretty cold today, being ten degrees above with a pretty fair wind. When there was a slack time in the unloading we would try to huddle on the lee side of one of the cache piles, but it didn't do any good. The wind hunts one up where he is. There was no getting around it, we were all just cold.

The snow cruiser is still over at Elmer Bolling Bight and I haven't seen Al since its departure a couple days ago, I suppose that he was so engrossed in his cooking that he won't get over here till he runs out of food. Joe Healey took some supplies over to them the other day and said he got there just in time for a steak dinner, so they must be doing all right with Chef Wade at the stove. The cruiser will stay at the Bight till she gets her two spare tires which Doc Poulter is going to put on the front, making pin wheels on the front giving the thing more load surface since the front end is heavier and Doc plans to use the front wheels for power.

Friday, January 19

Just finished twelve pretty fair hours of work. The weather is perfect, being up to eighteen degrees and no wind plus a very hot sun. My face fairly burns, it is so sore, probably from the sun and wind combined. The boys worked in the aft hold sending up barrels of fuel during the morning. They came up pretty fast and it left me busy hauling from the line to the fuel cache. I would have time to make just one complete trip before another sled would get up to the barrier. A funny thing happened today, I needed gas so went over to gas up and the barrel the pump was in was empty. So I

50

changed to another one—filled her up. Little Moe brought the "Doodle Bug" over and gassed up also. Well! It turned out that we had used kerosene and "Dolly" sounded like a coal burner the rest of the day. It was alright because the engine in "Dolly" is built to burn a mixture of gas and kerosene, and Moe evidently did not get enough to harm him because he made the trip to the snow cruiser with the other tire OK. But when he got back he filled the tank up again with kerosene and this time there was not enough gas in the tank to counteract. So the "Jitter Bug" just wouldn't run. She just sat and sputtered, so Moe had to drain the tank and start all over again. I was lucky because I could burn the kerosene providing the engine is kept hot enough. While Moe was at the cruiser he heard the mail bag and told me that I got a letter but didn't or couldn't remember who it was from. Anyway, they wanted to hear from me —letters. I know it can't be the folks or Alda because I wrote them. Paul and Dick Black went out today to pick a campsite and found a good place about two and a half miles inland, so that won't be so bad hauling. Can make the run in about an hour or so. Work stopped an hour early tonight since they moved the ship so as to be able to work the forward hold the next watch. The aft hold is completely empty. Sig Gutenko dug a nice icebox up on the barrier to keep his meat—a regular igloo.

Saturday, January 20

It's really funny around here—no one knows what day it is or even the date. The only reason I know is because of this journal, and I am not really sure. We work twelve hours then sleep twelve hours—our day is occupied thoroughly. In other words, we go by watches whether we are working or sleeping. Our watch today (P.M.) we moved the housing sections. The boys really turned out the cargo and it kept Sarg Asman and myself busy hauling from the line. He used the ordinance tractor. Moe had driven it, but so far had not done any work with it except run back and forth to the snow cruiser. So Sarg got mad and decided to run it himself and put it to some good use. It certainly worked fine and we could not have gotten along without it. The whole trouble with Steele and Moe is that they gun her too much and since she has fairly new treads she digs in. But the Sarg kind of eases her along and she does the work fine. The only trouble with the thing is that she has no top windshield and it is a cold job driving her. I relieved Sarg during the afternoon, he drove "Dolly." I didn't have any trouble with the

"Jitter Bug" and hauled everything in sight. The barrier to the east of us has been breaking, and cakes and bergs of ice have been floating by the ship, more or less jamming up the mouth of the bay. Several times the Capt. thought we would have to move the ship but the wind being from the south kept the ice from hitting against the ship. The current in the bay flows from the east to the west, hence circulates all of the ice into the bay from the east, around the bay, and then out at the west.

Sunday, January 21

It seemed funny getting up at 11:30 to a chicken dinner, I can't quite get used to getting up to a heavy meal instead of breakfast. The bay was full of ice again today, scraping and cracking against the ship. The barrier east of us must really be caving in. Worked both tractors today and spent most of the day hauling oil from between decks for the cruiser. We finished up between decks tonight and the next shift will work in the lower hold unloading coal. Am certainly glad that we did not have to start in on it—I hope only that they finish up. Had quite a talk with Jack Bursey, he is a pretty nice fellow. We talked the thing over pro and con but really didn't decide anything. At the same time we were watching one of the fellows was chasing a crab eater seal with a rifle. Burned us both up because the fellow missed him a couple of times—wholesale murder. Besides that, the fellow didn't stop to gut the animal, just left it laying hence not doing the meat any too good. We have quite a gang working up top the barrier—Moe, Warner, Colombo, Lockhart and Court as the muscle men. They do the unloading. Sarg and I drive the tractor and Jack Bursey has been handling the flags which control the sleds coming up on the line. Was pretty cold up here today, toward the end of the shift reading a low of five degrees above, and riding out in the open in the "Jitter Bug" is no picnic.

I divided the Bass ski boots today and what do I find but that "@#%$" Ronne had opened up the boxes and issued all but one of the size ten to east base men. Hence such fellows as Sig and Sarg who have small feet, five and one-half and six, have to wear eleven or maybe even twelve. Ronne and I just aren't going to get along and I am very glad that he is going to east base. Another thing, he has the ski and ski pole affair all screwed up, which does not help matters any. I know one thing—if I ever serve on another expedition, I am going to be an Admiral or at least a transportation engineer like Ronne, and do nothing. He skis around during our watch hour like he is an "over-seer" when he ought to be working like the rest of us, like Black, Siple. While I am on the subject I might as well mention another thing Ronne did—just a stubborn Norwegian, he can't be told—he insists on bringing his dog team down along the line toward the sleds coming up. Well, it so happened that a sled was coming up loaded down with one of the condor's wings and what did Ronne do but run the dogs, sled and all, through the wing. McCoy was so mad he could have torn Finn up with ease. It was no one's fault but Ronne's because the whole gang told him. After all, I don't care how good a dog driver is, one can't tell what a team might do. I guess Finn means well, but! Al Wade and Doc Poulter came in from the cruiser to pack, etc. We kidded them about coming for a square meal. Doc Wade said I got a letter from Alda over at the mail bag and the important part was "I love you." But I can't understand what she meant about my not writing, because I have mailed letters every chance I got and will continue to do so. The *Bear* has not returned yet and Court said that the Admiral had not made his flight yet but would start tomorrow.

Monday, January 22

Not a chance of the Admiral making his flight today as it was the coldest, most miserable day that we have had—zero temperatures, plus a wind of about twenty-five to thirty miles per hour. In other words, a blizzard. It was bad driving today, couldn't see more than fifty feet or so, and there was no horizon at all. It's a good thing that we had the dark objects of the cache to go by or it would have been too bad. On the last shift Pappy Reece broke the window in "Dolly" and I had a fair sized blizzard in the cab. However, I just finished cutting a piece of plywood which I will put in tomorrow. We put the top on the "Jitter Bug," but that didn't help much except keep the wind off. The fellows didn't do much work last night, as the line broke, hence, we got our share of the cold today. So all of my wishing and praying were in vain. The gang that works on the ship and near her always stops at three and nine for coffee. Well, before today we upon the barrier wondered what was causing the delay. They wouldn't let us know, so today we stopped at three and nine and went over to the cook's tent and had our coffee. It was a life saver. There were seven of us working up above—Warner, Colombo, Lockhart, Bursey, Asman, Butler and myself. Colombo has a full beard and he looks funny when he gets all icicled up, and the rest of us I guess look about as bad. Today was the kind of day which makes a fellow want to give up—throw in the towel and sign his resignation. It's odd, but on such days all the talk is of home, what we will do when we get back with our loved ones.

Tuesday, January 23

Finally we got the last of the coal out of the lower hold and I personally pronounced the ship unloaded. What a relief. Today was certainly a red letter day for us. Just eleven days of work, she's riding high now. I would hate to make the trip up to Valpo, the *Star* will bounce around like a piece of cork. Paul has set up a tent city back at the base and dog teams have been working cache, hauling food and necessary supplies to start with. Sig Gutenko will go out next and start cooking, as the ship will probably leave in the next day or so. We had a bit of bad luck. One of the sailors, Lamberson, was riding on the hook, shifted and fell clear to the lower hod, lighting on his back—a drop of about twenty-five feet. His condition at present is pretty serious. No bones broken, but internal injuries. Doc Geyer might have to operate just to see how his innards were affected. A wire from the Admiral saying that he wanted to stay away a couple more days, but Dick Black wired of the accident urging return so that the Doc on the *Bear* could help Doc Geyer. They are awaiting the Admiral's answer. He made his flight. How successful it was we don't know, but since the flying weather is good here and since he made one flight, he probably will want to make another. The *Bear* is about one hundred and fifty miles east of us. It's hard to say what will happen in the next twenty-four hours. So if I am going to get off before the *North Star* sails, I had better get packing. We were kind of short handed today, since the dog drivers were working cache. Just Colombo and Warner unloaded, Sarg and myself worked the tractor, and Lockhart at the line. It was pretty tough going, mainly because it was cool all the way through.

Just finished packing, didn't know I had so much junk. The things that take up so much room are my big mushing boots, ski boots, sheep lined coat, etc. Everything had to be put in boxes except what is going on my back tomorrow. The shift as of now are unloading oil drums from the forward well deck—oil for the *Bear*. So it looks like the *Star* is going to sail before the *Bear* arrives. My eyes hurt and ached like mad tonight. It's probably from wearing the dark glasses. It's impossible to go without them, the glare

54

is terrible. I guess the light from the sun coming in from around the glasses has something to do with it. I will certainly be glad when we get a little darkness—this continuous sunlight is maddening. There is some difference, though, being that it is usually cloudy around midnight, hazy and much colder, which helps break up the sequence of light.

Wednesday, Thursday, Friday, January 24, 25, 26

The unbelievable happened today. The *Star* sailed—Yes, and only one-half hour late. The Captain set the time for 5:00 o'clock and she actually got away at 5:30. It was certainly a shock to most of us, and we hurried pell-mell all around trying to collect gear and have it put ashore. It was quite effective, quite impressive as our home for the past twelve weeks moved out of the bay, out to open sea, bobbing over the waves as she was riding high—empty. I would hate to make the trip because she's going to be a rough one. Of course all the cameras were in full use and when she was finally out of sight (from cameras) we all turned to, upon the barrier getting things ready to go back to the base. I was on watch so I rounded up "Dolly" while O'Conner and Wells loaded up a sled with lumber, then loaded two sleds of personal gear and I started the back-first trip over the trail. About half of the fellows hopped on to hitchhike and away we went.

It was a hard trip as it was pretty windy, the fellows on the sleds had it bad because they had no protection. It took us an hour and a half to make the trip and when we got there they had just finished putting up the cook tent and were working on the stoves. We then put up four army tents for sleeping quarters, putting large tarps on the floor, and issuing mats to put under the sleeping bags. Meantime, Sig had fixed some soup and coffee which certainly hit the spot. By that time it was about midnight so all the fellows turned in. Paul put me on the night shift with Court so we started back to the cache for a load of snow sills. We both rode in the cab of the tractor. It was quite crowded, but that helped keep us warm. We had quite a conversation en route about the little gals back home. It seems that Court has a little lady waiting for him and is going to get married pronto on return. So we had each other's interest at heart. We loaded the sills, about thirty weighing sixty-five pounds each, got two dog sleds tied together and put on a load of food. Still not thinking we had enough, we put on two barrels of tractor gas on a dog sled, which was our mistake. About halfway back she tipped over and the sleds with food on them separated and dumped. However, our load of lumber did stay intact and that was something. We put back the food but couldn't put back the barrels, the trouble being the tractor leaves a high place between treads and the dog sled, being too narrow, runs along with one runner in the tractor track and one on the high place. And when we hit a rough spot—that's the end.

That trip just about finished us, but after a little coffee, we took heart, unloaded and started out again. More sills plus a deck load of odds and ends, boxes of bread, some weather beams, equipment and clothing. Since by then it was chow time, we woke up Pappy Reece and Sarge who had turned in after the ship sailed. They naturally wanted to know what day it was, what month—it was really funny. They were certainly in a daze. We got to the camp about 11:00 o'clock A.M., and I was really tired. All the way along, my head kept bobbing and several times I even dozed off. One nice thing about a tractor, though, she plugs right along regardless, and during naps she doesn't get off the trail too much. After a little chow I turned in for the day (I thought), but was I ever fooled. It's almost an impossibility to sleep with dog teams all around the tent —"Gee, haw, yak, go ahead now, you @#$%¢&." That's all I heard for the two hours I tried to sleep. I finally decided to put up a small officer's tent more distance from the main camp. By that time it was 6:00 o'clock in the evening, but since Sarge had so much sleep he said he would take one more trip, so I turned in till 9:00 o'clock. Gil woke us up, just curious. He saw the tent so he wanted to know who was in it. It took about "umpteen" minutes to get up enough nerve to get out of my sleeping bag, and since I was new at the thing I set up and talked with Gil for a while till it finally dawned on me that it was damn cold, so I dressed in nothing flat. Court learned from my experiences so he dressed in his sleeping bag. We ate a bite and started out, taking two empty tractor sleds with us. Sarge had started a new trail cross country so we decided to try it. We made it in one hour, just thirty-five minutes under the old trail. Well, our load was lumber and we just about gave out after half a load. It's no fun loading tractor sleds. We had to stop about every so often to rest. Both of us were plenty disgusted—the whole thing, not enough sleep. However, we did finally get them both loaded and started back. It was pretty foggy and there was a fog bow, first I had ever seen. Also, Court pointed out the moon, which was full. It was hardly visible, but it was there alright. We got into camp about 3:30 A.M., went into the cook tent, started a fire, woke up Sig and had a little cocoa and cookies. That is our job of the night crew, tending the fire and waking Sig. We were too tired to make another trip so I stayed and helped Sig get breakfast ready. We have breakfast at 6:00, lunch at 12:00, and supper at 6:00. To thaw things out, Sig has to start about three hours before meal time. I made the toast, and odd jobs. After breakfast I turned in and slept till 5:30 in the afternoon, ready to get out again. But it so happened that Vernon decided to take me off the night shift so I could work on clothing and help Warner keep the supplies straight as they come up from the cache. Pappy Reece was to take the tractor. I helped Sig with the evening meal, and what a meal, braised beef, squash, mashed potatoes and soup. And afterward, washing the dishes. It is now 11:00 o'clock Friday night and time to turn in. It's hard to keep track of days, and whether it's morning, noon or night, and ever since the ship sailed I have been especially mixed up.

Saturday, January 27

I got up this morning at 5:00 o'clock to help Sig with breakfast. I handled the toast end of the ordeal. After breakfast I went over to the clothing cache just to be sure all of the boxes had come up from below. Warner and I took care of the dog sleds as they came in. Sarg made two trips, one in the morning and another in the afternoon, loaded down with roofing floor panels and lumber. Chuck O'Conner and the boys had laid the floor of the bunkhouse and put up half of the wall panels. I imagine that in another five days the house will be up, and I certainly will be glad. Living in tents is all right, but it's cold business. Their only protection is keeping the wind out. We have no heat in the sleeping quarters, only in the cook tent. I am getting so I can crawl into my sleeping bag in nothing flat, dragging my socks and everything else in after me. The tough part though is getting up in the morning, which is done in less than nothing flat, making a dash for the cook tent. It is getting colder and the wind is increasing. It promises to be a hard, cold night, trying to keep warm.

Sunday, January 28

The Sabbath, and all should rest. But we were up at 6:00 o'clock and worked all day. The house has two-thirds of the walls up and it looks like we will be ready to move in soon. (I hope.) Warner and I put a floor in the cook tent. The heat from the stove had sunk the snow floor so that it was hollow in the middle, and Sig had to walk uphill to get to his stove. It was quite a job because we had to lift the stove while the noon meal was cooking. We got it done all right and now the fellows want to hold a dance because the floor is as nice as ever. We used floor panels. Chuck O'Conner about went crazy. We spent most of the day unloading dog sleds and the tractor. I am glad that Sarge made only two trips a day because when he comes in he is always loaded down with floor and roof panels which weigh about five hundred to six hundred pounds, or at least barrels of fuel which are almost as heavy. Paul and Doc Frazier furnished our "lavatory" today. They dug about twelve feet, taking out about seven hundred cubic feet of snow, cutting the snow blocks and making walks out of the blocks. It is quite an elaborate affair, being about sixty-five yards from our bunk house. I went down to the lower cache with Jack Bursey on his sled. We made the trip back in about a half hour, his team is part wolf and really gets right along.

Monday, Tuesday, Wednesday, Thursday,
January 29, 30, 31, and February 1

I stayed up too late last night and had a hard time getting up this morning. The bunkhouse is coming right along, all of the wall panels have gone up and the false floor has been put in place. It certainly will be fine living in a house, having a bunk to ourselves, a place where we can keep things—kind of a place one can call his own. All of the fellows have been working pretty hard so as to get the house done. The mainstays on the job, however, are head man Chuck O'Connor, then comes the Coach, Ike Schlossbach, Joe Wells, Leonard Berlin, and Tony Colombo. Warner and I have been working in the vicinity of the house, so anytime there is any lifting to do we are drafted in. When we hear the Coach yell "Mac" then we come a-running. That is something new—he calls everyone working on the job "Mac" now. Ike is quite a character. Larry and I tried all morning to think of the German for knife, so at noon chow we inquired around. No one seemed to know till Ike spoke up and said "Messer." We about fell over dead. I knew he was a darn good navigator, but I guess he is a German student as well. He certainly is full of surprises. This is his fifth expedition and he says after this one he is going to wait around till the next one.

The *Bear* came in early Tuesday morning so I took the first dog teams, the "Moulton Express," down to the bay ice so that I could see Dorsey and straighten out a little clothing problem. It seems that he issued a box of west base clothing to east base men, which would never do. However, while he was out cruising around, while the Admiral was making his flights, Dorsey then replaced the box which included some extra clothing. We spent almost all day opening the boxes and dividing the clothing. Also the Admiral was given some cigars, so I had to get our share for west base, plus some Wrigley's chewing gum, which was also a gift to the Admiral. I think Dorsey and I were very fair in our dealings, I know I am satisfied. I got half of the cigars and gum and we divided the clothing four/two. The darn bases have increased in size such that it is hard to keep all of the clothing straight. I ate lunch on the *Bear* in the crew's mess— and what a mess. The fellows do not have plates, etc., but eat out of a tray which is partitioned off. The chow was good, but I was spoiled since on the *Star* we had waiters, tablecloths, and even centerpieces sometimes. The Admiral called me in that afternoon and wanted to know why his rescue party was not outfitted with a trail tent, clothing, etc. I told him that was all on the *Star*, and said to myself if Ronne had not been so busy taking things that did not belong to him, the *Bear* would have been taken care of, since it was Ronne's job. He is certainly in the doghouse with everyone around here. First he got the wrong kind of dog harnesses, ones with leather collars which choke the dogs and cause them to wheeze, instead of a breast harness. Also, he got the wrong kind of ski bindings and had the wrong kind of clamps put on our ski shoes. Outside of that he did all right. I imagine that he is the most disliked man on the expedition, either base. Oh, yes! I forgot he also made a mess of the sleds. They have all fallen apart and are a mess. He certainly flopped as a transportation engineer, and I imagine the Admiral will talk it over with him when they get together.

Wednesday night after chow I was writing Alda a letter to be put on the *Bear* when Al Wade dropped in. We talked a while and I gave him another wire or message to send to her. He asked about a dog team to use so that he could start bringing up his gear. It so happened that Berlin's team had not been used but Dick Moulton had planned to use them on Thursday since his team was pretty tired. Dick has been working them every day hauling heavy barrels of fuel. He hauls two sleds with four barrels loaded on. His dogs were pretty tired and getting fairly stubborn. However, the tractor was not in use that night so I told Al that I would hitch up and take the bus down. Larry also said he would go along. We got started about 9:00 o'clock or so, picking Al up at the cruiser. Warner and

59

I rode in the cab together down to the cruiser. Two won't fit ordinarily, but with a couple of boards propped up on the arm rests we managed to squeeze in. It kept us warm, but I was so high that I couldn't see where I was going, so I steered by looking out the side window. We took quite a load back, got a large tarp, some fuel, then we rounded off with science equipment. When we got back to the cruiser we unloaded and Griffith in the meantime had fixed us a steak dinner. Here it was 3:00 in the morning, the cruiser gang was eating their dinner, while I haven't decided what Larry and I were eating. I suppose one could call it a mid-night lunch. We had quite a bull session. It did us all good. We Miamians kind of talked things over. Warner and I got back to camp about 4:30, turned in, and 6:00 o'clock came around too soon.

Thursday, and the *Bear* is scheduled to sail so I had to round up a few more things for the Admiral's rescue party. Paul and I spent about an hour digging around in boxes, getting such things as windproof pajamas, byrd cloth, blanket boots and various odds and ends. Moulton had to take some dogs down to go on the *Bear*, so we loaded all of our stuff on, plus a crate of puppies and some aviation equipment. We had three dog sleds loaded and ten dogs to pull it. It so happened that the dogs were puppies and were plenty wild. Well, we got along all right till we got to the edge of the barrier to go down to the bay ice. The crevasse had been getting a little larger till there were some places a drop of five feet. Well Dick thought that he was going over a low place but, incidentally, he didn't. All the sleds cracked up, I flew off, and nine dogs and every darn sled ran over me. I am still sore. I hit on the middle of my back. It took us about a half an hour to get things untangled. Dick took the dogs on down and we man-handled the stuff to the ship. I took all of the clothing down to the Admiral's quarters. He looked everything over, OK'd it, then we chatted for a while. He said that he thought we had the finest bunch of men he had ever seen on any expedition. It kind of made me feel good. He wished me luck during the winter and hoped that I had success in my work.

Just as I was leaving the ship, Dorsey called me saying that he had found some more gear to divide, so we went down into the hold and spent the next hour or so dividing bars of steel and odds and ends such as wood screws and hinges. So I lugged those off the ship and put them on a dog sled to haul up. I then went back to say goodbye to Hollie Richardson. It was a shame that Hollie had to return to the states. Doc Frazier said that he had ulcers of the stomach and advised him to return. Hollie was one fine fellow. He is going to try to come back next year as relief crew. Also he hopes that he can work on sleds for next year. Hope that if this thing goes on for the next couple of years that he gets Ronne's job. I finally finished my goodbye's and left the *Bear*, and since the tractor was not loaded I decided to walk back to camp. The *Bear* was due to leave at noon but up till the time I left at 2:00 o'clock she was still tied up to the bay ice. Some of the sailors were filling large canvas bags with snow for fresh water. While on the *Bear* I stopped in the officer's ward room and had a chat with Capt. Cruisen over a cup of coffee. I got back to camp around 3:30 and fixed a cup of cocoa. Pappy Reese was in the cooktent so we shot the bull till dinner time. He was standing by the radio keeping touch with the cruiser and *Bear*. The Admiral at noon called in Paul and Al, hence a big conference. That was the reason why the *Bear* was delayed. I have not heard the outcome of the thing, but I know that it had to do with the cruiser and the policy of the west base—a final conference.

The *Bear* finally sailed at 4:30 and we all were certainly glad. She threw everything in sort of a confusion, mainly since the Admiral was causing such a commotion wanting this and that for the rescue party. He had Dustin looking after things for him and he had a poop sheet a mile long. I worked on it for a while and cut it down some and Paul did the rest. They wanted a trail tent, a whole section. We only have eight or ten and if we would give up one it would cut down our operations, so I suggested to Paul to try to sell them on the idea of using an officer's wall tent. At first they did not like the idea, but finally decided to take it. It was the small one that Court and I put up for day sleeping. But when I got put on day shift, Pappy Reece moved in with Court. Well, we tried to take down the tent while they were sleeping; imagine their surprise to wake up when the thing fell on them. They were kind of angry. I don't know what I do to deserve some things, but now Paul made me official trail food divider—what a job. Lockhart worked out the rations so all I have to do is hunt the stuff up and weigh it.

Friday, February 2

Worked all day today on trail food and I still don't like it. I spent some time down at the cache digging around in the food pile. It seemed that every box I wanted was on the bottom of the pile, so Dick Moulton and I moved about every box in the cache. Dick at the time was driving thirteen dogs and hauling three sleds so we only had to make about two trips and we had all of the stuff up. We found several boxes that had been poached, Planters Peanuts. Moulton said he thought he knew who was responsible for it; Dyer, a surveyor from east base, had offered some of the fellows peanuts out of a can, the very same can that we had. It looked kind of bad. It was too bad that Dyer had already left because Paul was plenty angry about the whole thing. He said at one of the meetings on the *Star* that if anyone ever poached cargo and was caught, it would be his return ticket right back on the *Star*. I can't imagine anyone lousy enough to open boxes and steal, especially since food and everything is so important.

We have had good weather all along and the fellows have the roof half finished. They are working right along because they are anxious to get the thing finished. Walked over to the snow cruiser late in the afternoon to listen to the mail bag programs. Quite a few of the fellows were there, Gilmore, Fitzsimmon, Bursey and Richardson. I got a wonderful one from Alda. Boy, that certainly makes me feel good. I sent her another message. Phil has certainly been nice, sending all of my wires for me. I also received one from Bob Fattig and the folks. I am glad that Bob has settled down and is enjoying his work. That was the first program that I had ever heard first hand. Always either Al had given me the message, or Bailey. It certainly was a thrill to hear a letter from home, will be glad when we are wintered in and can hear them regularly. After chow I walked back to the cruiser and took the boys some gum and matches. The Beechcraft made a flight, an altitude hop 8,000 feet. Al took up the cosmic ray outfit. I was sitting with Phil in the radio room and we were transmitting the program to Al and Petras. They said that they heard the program perfect at 8,000 feet.

Saturday, February 3

It's getting more difficult to get up day by day. I used to get up about tenth, Doc Frazier first and Butler last. Now even Butler beats me up. Warner does not do much better, he gets up just before I do. How the bull flows in the early morning. Every fellow has his two bits worth to contribute to the cause, and never have I heard so much squawking and singing. But by the time breakfast is over the boys feel a little better, then comes the job of getting to work. Most of the dog teams manage to be on the way by 7:30 or 8:00 o'clock. I have been working in the cook tent sacking peanuts, powdered milk, milk chocolate, etc., for the trail. Paul expects to make a flight with the Condor tomorrow, but by the looks of the weather now there will not even be any work, let alone a flight. It's nothing less than a small blizzard, about twenty-three mile per hour wind and cold as hell. Boyd called off the tractor shift as it looked too bad out. He didn't want to take a chance with the men getting lost. Last night after I got back from the cruiser I dropped in the cook tent and as usual there was a big bull session going on. Paul made some ice cream and we all stood around the fire and ate chocolate ice cream. To make the cream all one has to do is make a chocolate paste then step outside the tent, hunt up a nice drift, fill up the cup then stir to taste. It tastes pretty good, something like a frozen custard.

Boyd had up to now prided himself on telling tall stories till Butler got started. Now Vernon hides his head in shame and admits that he is licked. Butler is quite a fellow. He and Perkins have been on the seal hunting detail ever since the *Star* sailed. They certainly are a sight, blood from head to foot. Often they kill the seals and load them onto the sleds, then hop on the sleds and sit on the seals coming in. Killing seals certainly is a gruesome job and I am glad that I do not have to have anything to do with it. Butler looks exactly like Lem in Esquire cartoons, long, lanky, skinny with a beard, plus his pointed face and southern accent—he certainly looks the part. We have the same boys who gather in the cook tent for nightly sessions and Butler is a mainstay, also Moulton who is a regular old night owl, and Boyd, who has never missed. Most of the supplies from the lower cache have been moved up to the camp. The dog teams moved most of the smaller things while the tractor has been working steadily on lumber and gas and oil drums.

Sunday, February 4

The Sabbath again today but I guess Paul and the rest have forgotten that it is supposed to be a day of rest. A beautiful day, sun was out and no wind. What a difference from last night. The Condor's flight was scheduled for today and I worked all morning trying to get flight rations finished up. Petras also was to make a flight. They both took off for test hops, then for some reason Paul called the Condor's flight off. Probably a few more minor adjustments to make. As for the Beechcraft, I don't think it made a flight. The house is coming along fine, the roof is all up but two panels and the gables. The fellows have had wonderful luck and the weather on the whole has been with them.

Monday, February 5

The whole camp got up late today as Sig's alarm clock froze up. We did not have breakfast till 8:00 o'clock. Boy, was it ever cold in the tent. It took all the courage I could muster to get out of the "sack." A sleeping bag is a wonderful thing, but they are sometimes rather hard to get along with. First, they are tough to get into. Once in, they seem to heat up in a jiffy, but then the really hard part is getting out in the morning. After work though they are the only place one can go to get warm. That is one reason why the fellows turn in so early. I broke out the ski boots today, just to take kind of an inventory. Paul thinks that it would be a good idea to check over all of the clothing. Yesterday Al borrowed Berlin's team with Navy as lead dog. The team hadn't been used since unloading, so were full of the old Nick. When Al left camp he left a little before he was ready, hence he lost his glasses, cap and whip and wasn't much interested right then enough to stop and retrieve them. I guess they ran all the way to the cache. Well, they broke away from him down at the cache and made a beeline for the snow cruiser where they proceeded to kill three penguins. An outlaw team if there ever was one. There are three blacks in the team which cause all the trouble. When Al got to the cruiser the dogs were asleep, so he kicked them up and they all moved but one. "Doc," who was dead, must have been dragged along when they broke away. Al certainly felt bad about the whole thing. It has been getting colder right along. Sunday night the lowest temperature recorded was four degrees below. The night before it was four degrees above.

Tuesday, February 6

Last night was one of the meanest nights we have had. It was just freezing in the cook tent and when we washed dishes the plates and cups would freeze up as fast as they were washed. Sig had a hard time serving the meal as every plate he would pick up would have a crust of ice on it. There wasn't any bull session last night after chow. The fellows all lit for their sleeping bags. Court recorded a thirty-one mile per hour wind, and this morning when we woke up it was blowing so badly that the fellows did not go down to the cache. Sarge Asman made a trip but he took a fellow with him to help load. In the first place, most of us did not get up until 10:00 o'clock. Sig as usual got up around 5:00 o'clock in order to thaw out food for breakfast. But he decided not to serve till 9:00

15. The *Bear of Oakland* and dog team used to unload the ship.

16. Dog team hauling a snow cruiser tire.

17. Unloading the Beechcraft.

18. The snow cruiser being unloaded.

19. Halfway down the ramp the snow cruiser broke through.

20. We were lucky the snow cruiser did not break through the ice.

21. Starting to build our winter quarters.

22. The building consisted of living quarters, scientific building, and machine shop.

23. The cook Sigmund Gutenko baking bread—a Navy cook.

24. On Sundays we were on our own—the cook's day of rest. From left, Clay Bailey, Larry Warner, Murray Weiner, Ike Schlossbach and our doctor Russell Frazier.

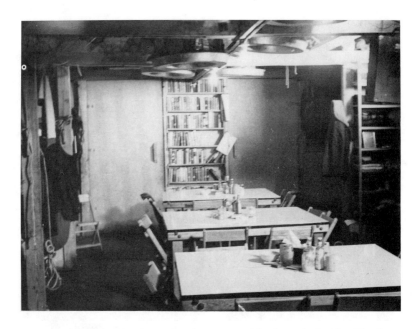

25. Living quarters, with tables down the center and bunks on both sides. The doors lead to the kitchen.

26. A typical bunk, a mattress with a sleeping bag on top.

27. Celebrating the completion of the buildings. The metal cages shown above are for drying cloths.

28. At the Antarctic movie house. We saw *Dodge City* about twenty times.

29. Taking readings for outside temperatures and wind during the development of the wind chill factor experiments. From left, Malcolm Douglas and the author.

30. Proof that the face can freeze in 45 seconds with a sixteen-mile-per-hour wind and −26.6 degrees temperature.

because of the weather. The inside of our tent was a sight, most of the fellows were drifted over with snow. Jack Bursey had about a three foot drift over him. I luckily had plugged up some of the holes over my sleeping bag so I wasn't completely snowed under. Sig said that when he woke up there was a foot of snow in the cook tent. Since we had breakfast so late we did not have our noon meal till 3:30. I helped Sig get things ready to serve. The hardest part is cutting frozen bread, almost have to take a cleaver to it. I went to cut it, it went fine until I got to the center then it was just like hitting rock. And to make things worse, all of the outside crumbled away. We had to serve the bread in a large bowl. Right after chow we moved the kitchen to the new house. We were afraid to continue cooking in the tent because we'd had two fires where the stovepipe went through the tent. If Sig hadn't kept his head and made a direct hit with a scoop full of water, the whole camp would have gone. So just as soon as the stove was put in and squared around, it was impossible to keep Sig out. The roof and the exterior frame of the house is all completed. As for the inside, the floors are laid and Chuck and his gang have started to put up the bunks. This is really going to be some dwelling when she is all finished, and the fellows are tugging at the bit to move in.

Wednesday, February 7

The temperature dropped to nine below last night. My feet are still cold. Usually the sleeping bag warms up in a hurry but it failed me last night. I took off my undershirt and wrapped my feet up in that, but that didn't even do any good. It just made me cold in two places. Al Wade and the cruiser have been going to move up to camp the last couple of nights. The blizzard stopped them the night before, but last night they got underway and this morning they were coming up alongside the tractor trail. Doc said later on that she went along alright. I am glad that they made the move to combine the cruiser with the rest of the group. I know that Paul is. If the aviation gang now will only get a little cooperation in their spirit everything will be "Jake." So far they haven't done a thing to really help the camp along. Like today they took the Condor up for a test flight, lasting for about forty-five minutes, and that completed their day's activities, spending the rest of the afternoon in their tents drinking coffee and just loafing in general. The rest of us are working like dogs to get the houses set up and things in shape for winter. The thing that burns me up, and Sig and a few others, is that they are the first ones into chow and always about a half hour early.

I guess I am the general flunky around here. I have done a little of everything today. I worked in the morning on trail rations. I kind of took over the old cook tent and set up a sort of grocery store. It makes a pretty good set up because I don't have to put stuff away before chow; hence, I was losing about an hour before each meal doing that. Clay Bailey dropped in and out all through the morning and we talked it over and played through a bunch of various records. After lunch I went over to the Condor and checked over rations that I had put in the day before. Then got out Sig's dressing table and meat block. I guess I am supposed to help him get settled, so I imagine I will spend the next couple of days opening boxes of "G" gear. Last night Warner, Butler and I had a rather extended bull session in the old cook tent, the topic of conversation being subjects for a Ph.D. dissertation, and also the disadvantages of staying in two years.

Thursday, February 8

Sig overslept again this morning, breakfast was not ready till 10:30. The funny part about it was that he had three alarm clocks set on a table. He didn't even stir, but slept through all of them. They rang till they ran down. The trouble is once the night shift has been laid off there has been no one to wake Sig. The whole camp depends on the cook when he oversleeps. I might say that we are never angry at him for being late because we can all use the sleep. We had our first hotcakes this morning and they were really a treat. I guess Sig was so ashamed of himself that he thought he would redeem himself. Well, he succeeded. Doc Frazier is going to sleep in the house tonight to see that Sig gets up in time. The inside of the house is coming right along. Most of the bunks have been put in, looks like we will be able to move in Sunday. Right after breakfast Paul informed me that he intended to make his long put off flight, and that he wanted the rest of the rations put up. I already had four in the Condor and he wanted a total of eight. So I spent most of the time before lunch, which was to be at 2:00, weighing and sacking food. Butler decided that since it was such a short time till lunch that he and Perkins would wait till after the meal before going sealing. Butler offered to help me, which just about saved the day. Between us we finished and had the rations

66

packed in the plane by chow time. But that wasn't all Paul thought of. There were a million and one things that would be needed for the flight, such as furs, socks, senna grass, innersoles and odds and ends. I ran around like a chicken with his head off for about two hours getting things ready. The aviation gang had one motor running but the other one just wouldn't start. It is now 10:30 P.M. and they are still trying to get that one engine started. It seems that nothing is wrong with the thing except that they can't heat it up enough. They have tent affairs over the engine, but Pappy Gray, the mechanic, says that it is colder in the tent than outside. Mac McCoy just came in and said that the engine is hotter than they have ever had it and they are going to give her another try. This is the third time that Paul has attempted to make his flight. He still thinks that they will make it because Paul still has faith in that old saying "the third time is charm." The weather has been perfect all day and at present there isn't a cloud in the sky. So as soon as they get the one engine going I imagine they will take off. It seems funny though, getting to go on a photographic hop at midnight or so. Warner is going along to help Paul with readings. Sarg Asman came in with his usual heavy load, so after helping him throw off the oil barrels we took the tractor and the snow scoop and cleaned out a trail by the house because they plan to carry coal tomorrow. Just before our evening meal I went out and worked in Sig's cache for a while. I opened boxes till I was blue in the face looking for his rotary can opener, but gave out with five more boxes to go. He has been using his cleaver ever since we have been camping out. Al Wade made a flight to Rockefeller toward the north to Alexander Mountains, and then back to the Rockefeller's. Al said that he can't wait to get back with his geology hammer. A true geologist. Time 11:45 P.M., just observed sun dogs with a partial halo—quite a phenomenon, very beautiful.

Friday, February 9

Just as I crawled in the sleeping bag last night the Condor took off. After fourteen hours of engine heating and general messing around they finally did take off. Warner had been waiting around all day and when the time finally arrived, no Warner. He was over in the tent getting ready for bed. It was cold again last night. The temperature dropped to five below. I still haven't figured out how to work the hook on my sleeping bag. There is a draft coming from somewhere. There is a kind of scarf arrangement which I haven't figured out yet. Joe Wells says not to worry because I have twelve months to go and that I ought to have the thing whipped by then. The Condor got back this morning by 8:30 A.M. They had quite a flight—crossed over the Rockefeller Mountains to the Edsel Ford, then followed the Admiral's flight route northeast for about an hour or so. They crossed over unnamed mountains and saw an enormous mountain peak east and north about the same distance the Rockefellers are from Edsel Ford range. They flew all told about one thousand miles. Mac said that after leaving Edsel Ford they flew over a very high plateau. He was flying at eight thousand feet and he said that he imagined that he was only two thousand five hundred feet above it. I talked to Warner later and he said, "Don't ever let anyone tell you that there are not plenty of mountains in this man's country." He said that he noticed much dark rock which he thought might be sediments. Sounds a little encouraging. It has been kind of chilly all day, very windy. Toward late afternoon it started to get a little cloudy, and at present is snowing. Temperature being about ten degrees above. I worked inside all day trying to build a cupboard arrangement for Sig. It at least ought to hold up as I have made the frames out of two by four's. We had steak tonight for chow, which was really a treat. A few of us went over to the snow cruiser for the 7:00 o'clock rebroadcast of the mail bag program, which comes from the west coast. It was too stormy and noisy however, so we had no luck. The cruiser has the only mirror available so every time we go over there we take a peek. I scare myself—I haven't had a bath for over six weeks, since we left Wellington. Our whole outfit would make a first class hobo camp look like a Sunday School gathering or something. I just talked to Court and he explained a little more clearly the sun dog business of last night, called a twenty-two degree part halo, caused by refraction of light through small ice particles in the air. Under the sun was the sun pillar and under each arm of the partial halo was the sun dogs. It is now 10:00 o'clock and I just finished cleaning and sweeping the galley. Some of the fellows have moved into their bunks. Warner, Fitz' and mine are not finished. Such is luck.

Saturday, February 10

Slept rather late this morning, till 8:30. Mother Douglass who usually does the honors in the morning as an alarm clock snuck out without saying boo!!! I guess his feelings were hurt the other morning when Chuck O'Conner gave him a tongue lashing. Malcom started his early morning spiel about the sun shining and that it wouldn't be any easier to get up five minutes later, etc. Chuck stuck his head out of his sleeping bag and told Smokey why in the hell he didn't shut up and tend to his own business instead of waking everyone up? Mack's Scotch temper flared up and he informed Chuck that it was expedition business and he was carrying it out. It was for the welfare of the expedition to see that all hands now are up for breakfast and he was carrying it out, and so as to start the day's work. It was really comical. I knew one of the fellows would blow up sooner or later. Malcom really takes a beating, especially from Clay Bailey who kids the life out of him. He is responsible for Mack's various nicknames, Suchos, Smokey, Stover, Mother, and his favorite topic is Doug's past being a Scout, Scout executive and camp leader. Also, every time Clay sees Mac writing he yells over to him, "Dear Diary." Doug is doing alright, though. He has his team working fine and makes as many trips as the rest. He is now driving nine dogs, training them. He carries a small shilelagh with him, which happens to be a piece of hose, and whenever he wants to administer a slight bit of punishment he pulls out the shilelagh and gently taps the unfortunate victim on the schnozer. It has really worked wonders. When Doug yells "down," the whole team drops, just as if a lever was released. Old Spot, his lead dog, will not even blink an eyelid unless Mac gives the word. Some of the drivers say that when Doug is on the trail he sings various camp songs and talks to his dogs. I guess to keep up their morale. He also calls them all lads or says "pull all together fellows, come on boys." Doug's all right though, and has surprised the whole bunch and is doing his share and more. After breakfast I worked on my pantry. It's really going to be a masterpiece when it's finished. Paul informed me that I was to do "mess duty" for the time being "officially," as I have been helping Sig anyway, besides doing my own work. It seems that yesterday the fellows down at the cache did not get enough to eat. Well, Sig was down at the cache all morning, so when he got back he fixed some soup and sent the fellows at the cache their share. We all had soup but evidently they thought they were gypped or something. They had worked hard and after all, soup is not enough for the type of work we have all been doing, but it was just one of those things. Anyway, Gil talked to Paul saying that possibly he needed help. Hence my assignment. Now, however, I am supposed to do nothing but work in the galley. Sig and I had a little mishap right after lunch. We got a wind backfire and the result was soot all over the place. Well, I had to wash everything in the place. I spent the afternoon cracking out chinaware, and the remarkable thing was that none of it was broken, after eleven thousand miles or so and innumerable handlings. When I think of people back home in the states moving from one street to the next and finding this or that broken, usually the handle off that rare tea cup, I wonder. So far we have had nothing turn up damaged. Maybe we are just lucky. It is now 10:30 P.M. and all of the fellows have moved into the house but Doug, Fitz and myself. I am too tired to move my gear. Mal'c loves the refreshing breeze and Fitz just hasn't thought about it one way or another. A few of the fellows are working around hammering, sawing, getting their bunks fixed while others are trying to sleep, complaining about non-union workers. Just one big happy family. They can't say much though, because Paul is one of the workers. Sig is working in the galley, getting ready for the house warming tomorrow, turkey with trimmings and, best of all, strawberry pie.

Sunday, February 11

Official house warming day, and a camp holiday for some people. However, I was up by 7:00 to help Sig. I made the rounds of the food caches, collecting odds and ends necessary for a holiday dinner. Cranberry flakes, tomato juice, mixed nuts, shelled walnuts and an extra large pan, or pans, for the turkeys. Then all of the new dishes had to be washed. Oh! yes, I forgot the occasion even called for candy and raisins. Raisins are precious as we only have fifty pounds. Asman helped us, mixed up the ice cream and helped me set the tables for the first time. Yes, we even ate off the tables! Chuck rushed them through because after all, one can't eat turkey on the floor. We ate around 2:00 o'clock in the afternoon, Nib and I served. He said I was the head waiter because I poured the coffee. He tried but missed a couple of cups, so he got demoted to just plain waiter. The fellows really put away the food, but I don't wonder because it was really good. I know, because I was official taster. The dressing was wonderful. In fact, everything was perfect. After dinner most of the fellows turned in, mainly because they could do nothing else. A case of overeating. Of course, there were all the dishes to do, so I put up a general alarm and behold, I got wonderful results. Gilmore, Malcom, Dick Moulton, Lem Butler, and Larry. We did them up in no time. The only trouble is there is no place to put them. I'll just have to finish the shelves tomorrow.

I went over to the tent and brought my gear over here to the house so I am now sitting in my bunk. I have the upper, Fitz the lower, and Larry the middle. We will have it pretty nice as soon as we get a few shelves put in. Phil just came in with some messages. I got one from Alda and Doc Wolford.

Monday, February 12

Sig woke me at 7:00 sharp to set the table for breakfast. I really slept last night—first night in my new home. I never realized that Simmons "Beauty Rest" mattresses could be so soft. I could have slept for a week. We all stayed up last night to see our first movie picture at the "Antarctic State Theater," which means we moved all of the tables outside and fixed rows in the bunkhouse. Shirley and Petras got out the projector and sound apparatus earlier in the evening, but they had trouble with the sound mechanism. We have been getting our current from the cruiser, but since Ferranto was scheduled up to 10:00 o'clock, we had to wait till then. So when he finally gives us the word, being about 10:30 and we were all keyed up to see Bob Burns in "Arkansas Traveler," it is impossible to imagine the disappointment when Shirley finally announced that they couldn't get the sound going. Just then Ferranto came in and he looked the thing over till finally between them they got things under control. But by then it was so late that Paul thought it best to show it tonight. The Beechcraft took off at noon so I spent most of the morning putting in extra gear since Paul was to go along, and I before had put only enough gear and rations for two men. During the afternoon all hands in camp turned to and helped put up the roofing tarp. That was really a job, an eight hundred pound tarp. So it was dark inside for about two hours till Chuck cut through the skylight. It so happened that at that time Vernon was working on the snow hopper in the galley, putting a large drip plate under the whole thing. An engineering job to lift the thing up, so Sig and I were called in as consultants. So there we were working in the semi-darkness. We had one door open, cold as hell because the fire had to be put out before we could even touch the hopper. To lift the thing we jacked it up on three jacks, and balanced it tediously while we pushed the pan under. When it was finished we were all so proud, so happy, that we forgot about chow time, the time then being about 6:00 o'clock and the dog drivers were starting to come in. It was impossible to have a heavy meal, so kippered herring, crackers and cheese were the menu. We ran out of bread the night before. Sig has not been able to bake any because we haven't found the yeast. The fellows liked the meal alright and didn't crab because there was no hot food—which is unusual.

Tuesday, February 13

Sig overslept again, so we did not have breakfast till 10:00 o'clock. The show was a big success last night, we all enjoyed it. The sound was very good, exceptionally good for a portable machine. The trouble around here though, whenever we have a big night, stay up late, we always suffer the next day and usually get a late start which throws the whole day off. The dog teams finished up hauling from the cache and today made two trips down to the pressure ice to haul in seals. Butler and Perkins have been plugging right along, averaging about eleven per day. They did have an exceptionally good day the other day and killed twenty-three. I haven't heard officially, but through the grapevine it seems that Fitz and Wiener are going to be moved out to base camp, probably around the twenty-first of the month. No preparation had been started yet, but they will start soon. I understand that all good teams will participate, plus the tractor. Nib will have to have a relief driver so maybe I will fit in there.

Friday, February 14

Valentine's Day. I sent Alda a wire, I hope that she *will* be my Valentine. I hope she got it in time, I know that she will like getting a "Valentine." I just got weighed on the Doc's foot scales and weigh exactly one hundred and eighty pounds in my "long johns" and my undershirt. That is the most I have ever weighed. I guess this climate agrees with me or something. Nib made some ice cream last night and I popped some corn. We didn't have to yell twice for the rest of the bunch to come and get it. Sig woke us up at 5:30 this morning, he would have to wake up on time. I think I will hide his alarm clock or something. Thank goodness I have two more days of mess duty. I spent fourteen hours in the galley yesterday washing dishes and helping Sig with the meals. Paul should have two fellows washing dishes and serving because it's too much work for one man. I walked over to the cruiser and had a little chat with Al. Asked him about staying two years and he advised me not to stay because of school, etc. He gave me a flashlight which will really come in handy during the winter nights. Sig and I had quite a time with Ike today. He decided that the galley needs some shelves, that he did not like the way the galley looked. So he proceeded to build them. Well, one really has to know Ike to appreciate his shelf building. Anything is alright with him just so long as it works or serves its purpose. So he proceeded to make shelves out of old box lids and odds and ends of scrap lumber. Sig and I about split our sides watching him work. I will admit that he is a man of action and he goes at a thing helter-skelter, just like a whirlwind, and out of the center is a misshapen piece of work. The funniest thing he ever did was, at the time they were building bunks and getting ready to move in, Chuck and the other carpenter had the coach's bunk filled with tools so when he came in to put his mattress in, there were the tools. So what did the Commander do but build an extension up over his bunk and put his mattress on it, the tools being underneath. Kind of a stilted affair. He said hell, they wouldn't move the tools.

Thursday, February 15

Got up at 5:00 o'clock this morning and it was cold as hell in the bunkhouse. It had dropped to freezing—someone had gone to bed and left the doors open. Sig said that the eggs and everything were frozen and that breakfast would be a little late. The silverware was so cold that it burned my hands. I finally wore a pair of gloves while setting the table. I later found out that Paul was the one who left the place wide open for a reason. When he went to bed around 1:00 o'clock it was so smoky that he said he couldn't see from one end of the room to the other. So he kind of aired out the place. We have been having some trouble with the galley range throwing out smoke. They made one mistake in building the stovepipe. It is curved in instead of going straight out, which has an effect on the draft and cold air. When there is no wind the fire will hardly burn and sometimes we get a wind blow back, which sends smoke and soot all over the place. Chuck has cussed out the designer of the house several times. He still can see no reason why they did not send the stack straight up and through the house. Yesterday at noon Ike decided to do the dishes. He said that he could do them in fifteen minutes. Well, he did, but I had to do them all over again. What a mess. He would wash three plates at a time and the only one getting any attention at all would be the top one.

Sig woke me up at 6:00 o'clock. He had been up fairly early, since 4:30, but had been busy mixing batter for corn fritters and baking biscuits. We really had a real breakfast except there were too many dishes to wash. We had corn fritters, tomato juice, prunes and coffee. Today was my last day, and was I ever glad. The only meal I like is noon because then we only have soup which means only one bowl. Went over to the cruiser at 4:00 o'clock to listen to the mail bag programs with Malcolm, Bursey, Richardson, Warner, Gilmore and Weiner. I got a letter from Alda, Mother and Dad, Howard and Bob. It is certainly wonderful to be able to have those letters come in. They really help a lot. We had supper one hour late tonight so that the fellows could listen to the programs. Vernon had his radio tuned in and they really heard the station clearer than we did at the cruiser. After supper I played my clarinet for the first time, had quite a lot of fun. Larry, Lockhart and Fitz named tunes and we had selections both classical and modern, as well as songs of the good old days.

It was really a wonderful feeling not to have to get up and set the table. Pappy Reese relieved me. I didn't do much of anything during the morning, just issued some scarves, worked on my poop sheet and then walked over to the snow cruiser with combs and brushes for the outfit. After lunch I took the tractor over as Sarg wanted to work on the tank, try to get it started. He wanted to try heating the motor to see if he could get the right temperature to start her. Larry, Earl, Sarge and myself went down to the cache. Colombo was to go but the weather cleared up a little for flying so he had to go out with Pappy Gray, heating the Condor motors. It has been cloudy for the past week and Paul has been wanting to take another flight, so when the sun did finally shine through and the sky cleared up a little the aviation crew hopped to it and started to get ready to fly. But just as they had the engines heated to start, it clouded up again and Paul called the flight off. Court had been making balloon runs to get upper air currents and none of his reports were favorable for flying. We made two trips from the cache hauling cruiser diesel oil, twenty barrels to a load. And there is nothing more back breaking than trying to move four hundred and fifty pound barrels over the snow and onto the sled. They are just heavy enough to be hard to handle. We had our second show tonight, were very fortunate in that Phil didn't have a schedule till now, being 11:00 o'clock, which meant we could show the picture earlier, around 7:30. The picture was "Wings Over The Navy," which I had seen in Oxford. I enjoyed seeing it again. It really helps us to relax, to get our minds off the oil barrels which are sure to come on the morrow.

Sunday, February 18

Semi-holiday today, didn't get up till 9:00 o'clock. Nib woke me so I could go down with him to get the tank. Tony was up also. We went out to start the tractor, she wouldn't budge. All three of us stood on the crank and did finally manage to turn her a little. We worked for a solid hour, each one taking a turn. Breakfast was at 10:30 so we stopped to eat. It was just what we needed because after we got a little food under our belt we went out and worked for another hour, finally getting her started. Before we were through we had about ten fellows helping us crank. It was down to fifteen below last night, and that didn't help matters any. Nib even used a Van Prague heater on it, but that seemed to make her all the stiffer. We finally got underway at noon, and Warner, Lockhart and I made three trips before supper. Tony and Nib stayed down to work on the tank. The barrier has really changed since I was down there last. All of the bay ice had broken out and now large pieces of the barrier were breaking off. The bay was full of ice and bergs, the most beautiful part of the Antarctic. There is not much left down on the barrier, some of Court's hydrogen bottles, snow cruiser supplies and the cruiser diesel oil which we had been working on. After supper we made another trip finishing up the diesel oil. Nib and Tony had the tank running so I hitched up "Dolly" and helped them get out of the drift which Steel had left her in. The bottom of the tank was frozen in solid, but by pulling together we managed to jerk her loose. Nib made it back to the base in twelve minutes. It took me thirty minutes with the tractor. Nib made ice cream, raspberry and orange. He is quite apt at the art. The trouble is there is never enough left for seconds.

Monday, February 19

Pappy Reese woke me this morning setting the table. I swear he must see how much noise he can make. I think that he holds the plates up about a foot and drops them, and as for the spoons I know he stands at one end of the table and just throws them. Sarge worked on the tank so I went out to start the tractor, and after fifteen minutes of cranking she started with a roar. It must not have been very cold last night. It was four degrees below at 10:00 o'clock. We unloaded that last load we brought in last night, then I took the tractor over for Nib and Pappy Gray to work on her. They took off the pan, fixed a leak in it, new spark plugs and everything. They worked on her all day. I made some grape jelly for lunch, which merely means boil water, throw in some grape powder and some sugar. It was very good and the fellows of the table where I eat had gotten two bowls full. I sit at the bum's table, which consists of Nib, Joe Wells, Chuck O'Conner, Pappy Grey and Pappy Reese (when he is not serving). After lunch Earl and I worked in my clothing cache, moving the boxes in close to the house. We worked at it all afternoon, but what slowed us up was that I would come across things that I wanted to issue. They haven't enough room to move now, so most of them put the extra clothing, etc., under their mattress or else put it at the foot of their bunks.

Tuesday, February 20

Went over to the cruiser last night with a couple of telegrams for Alda, folks and Bob. Phil was in the radio room with the door closed. I did not bother him and started away when Al came out, we shot the bull for a while. He took my message for me. Warner and I worked off and on all day in the clothing and small stores cache, putting the boxes in close to the house so as to build our tunnels. Just before noon Nib came up from the barrier with a load of floor panels and roof panels. We helped unload the sled, Chuck and the boys have finished laying the floor and foundation for the machinist's building and are half finished with the science building. They are going to keep both going at the same time. Our bunkhouse is now pretty liveable. Our heat stove is up and the ventilators are complete and in place. Now Chuck is working on the roof, putting in the third window glass in our skylights. I finally found the mirrors and issued them. Also Nib had been after me to issue the sheep lined slippers so I dug them out. Tonight after chow Jack Richardson and I had a little music. He has some classical stuff, two part, Minute Melody in F, Serenade, etc. It really sounded good —clarinet and violin. We just got warmed up when Sarg announced that the ice cream was ready and to come and get it. He made vanilla and he really outdid himself because it was fine. I think that I ate a quart myself and I know Larry did. A funny thing just happened. McCoy asked when the sun first started to dip. No one knew, so we looked it up and found that it was definitely last night, and we didn't even know it. It has been getting darker every night but since it has been cloudy during the day, it's hard to tell the difference. Or also I guess we just didn't notice. There has been some color, though, at night, noticed about a week ago. A real sunset.

Wednesday, February 21

Was supposed to go down with the boys to the cache but as it was kind of a blizzard and my clothing cache was beginning to drift over I decided to stay and work on it. It was cold work, windy and quite a bit of shoveling to do. However, by supper time I got the whole business lined up as a form for a tunnel along the south side of the house. It certainly was a relief to finish up. It really isn't done yet, but half of the battle is over by just having the boxes lined up. Now Larry and I will have to cover with tarp and secure. It was so bad out that the fellows did not go out after seals but stayed over in the old cook tent to work on their sleds repairing and making pemican for dog food. They have to boil seal fat meat and mix with Gaines dog food into a cake weighing about two and one-half pounds, which is for one dog per day. Boy, that seal blubber smells —it has an odor all of its own. I don't envy Dick having to prepare the stuff. But weather didn't stop Sarg though. He, Larry, Earl and Tony made their usual trips to the cache. They brought back a couple of good loads of panels, etc. We had seal meat for supper. Not bad, Sig fixes it up so it tastes pretty good. We call it Antartic veal. The success of the whole thing is not getting any fat in it, cutting thin and washing all of the blood out. Looks a faint red or pink and like any other steak. McCoy is a pretty funny fellow, humorous. He is trying to start a union of some kind, or else a club, and his rates and fees are fifty cents. No one seems to want to join but he keeps trying. His latest is a lodge ("The Mystic Knight of the Penguin"). Well, the inside of this place is getting more crowded with gear as time goes on. Vernon and Mac are across from us and their cubicle looks like a machine shop, drill press, motor driven saw and the movie camera and projector. Mac says that if anyone has anything to stow away, there is still a little room in his bunk.

Thursday, February 22

Washington's birthday—a holiday to some, but not down here. Washington probably wouldn't claim this country here anyway, probably never heard of it. We had breakfast a little late about noon, so we were late in getting started down to the cache. I drove the tractor and we took the short cut trail. The weather was kind of bad, windy, no sun, yet there seemed to be a glare and it was impossible to distinguish the horizon. In fact, couldn't even see the trail but I started out on what I thought was the trail, but after about a quarter of a mile we ran into soft snow, so I knew we had missed it. To make matters worse, we got bogged down and had to go the rest of the way in reverse with Nib and Tony walking ahead breaking trail. We don't have the short cut worked out and the only thing to go by is the old snow cruiser cache from before they moved up here, which is on the other side of the "Bight." I steered by that but when we got down in the "Bight" and I couldn't see the cache, that's when things went haywire. We loaded on all of the rest of the panels and lumber, about ten tons in all. We pulled in about 2:00 o'clock, late for chow, but we really made up for lost time. After we ate, all hands turned to and helped us unload the sleds. Five of us loaded and about fifteen unloaded. Just don't seem right, but that's the way things work. I'll swear that only half of the fellows around here are working. I don't know where they hang out, but they certainly keep scarce. We only made the one trip, Sarge wanted to grease the tractor. I planned to work in my cache but took a few pictures instead. Perk took a seal alive and was trying to weigh him so that took me from my work also. A young Weddell seal weighing about two hundred and seventy-five pounds.

Friday, February 23

Last night I did a small washing (very small), one pair of socks which I started to wash two weeks ago, which I had soaking in water out in the old cook tent. It used to be water, but when I went out to bring in the bucket they were frozen solid. It took me about an hour or so to thaw them out. A couple of nights ago Larry and I went on a shelf building spree. It so happened that while we were out during the day, Vernon and Shirley decided that at the end of Larry's bunk was a good place to put the movie projector, hence getting it out of the way. So what did they do but board up almost half of our cubicle and build shelves, etc., to hold the camera and accessories. It really improved things, but we had to raise hell just on general principles. So Larry and I decided to do the things up right by building shelves by our bunks for books, etc. During the morning we made a trip down to the barrier to pick up old wing crates to be used for garage and blubber house. Boy, they were really heavy. Five of us strained and tugged to load the sleds. The sides were about twenty feet long and eight feet or so wide and we had to lift them and flop them over. We would get them so high, then we would be stuck, couldn't lift any higher and afraid to drop them. Every time we would try to lift a little higher, get a new bite, we would lose ground. I personally have never been so tired, done so much lifting. Everything seemed to go wrong on the afternoon trip. We picked up the base of the crate which must have weighed a ton or more, luckily it was more or less on runners so we dragged it along, but not being satisfied we stopped and loaded on one hundred bottles of Court's hydrogen. Well, "Dolly" took the load all right till we hit a little hole, soft snow, then she just kind of stuck. That was just about one hundred yards before we would have been on hard surface, the main trail. We worked an hour or so trying to break that sled (crate base) loose, but she wouldn't budge. All that would happen would be the tractor digs in deeper. We pulled from every direction and angle, but no luck. So we went over, got the other crate base and pulled alongside and unloaded twenty-five of the hydrogen bottles, did a little digging, and out she came. I went halfway in reverse, but the load was pulling the tractor to one side, so tried going ahead and it worked fine in low. Had to feel my way along the trail as we hadn't quite centered it yet. I was really tired after that haul. My ears rang, head ached. I was just about ready to throw in the sponge. The hard, tough part about it was that I never knew when I would run off the trail and bog down in soft snow.

Saturday, February 24

Tractor started right up this morning. We made two trips to the cache, one in the morning and one in the afternoon. The whole bunch of us, Tony, Larry, Earl, Sarg and myself made the morning run. We dug out and loaded on the rest of the hydrogen bottles, took down the tent, dug up a few stray cruiser boxes and put on the last crate, the smallest of the lot, the Beechcraft wing crate. We tried to take everything up at one time. The large Condor crate was loaded down with hydrogen bottles, plus scrap lumber, etc., and one small sled holding thirty hydrogen bottles and another with this Beechcraft crate with a few hydrogen bottles thrown in. That would have been some load, but we couldn't budge it. The tractor has the power but we couldn't get the traction. Once we got a load started, throw her in low and that's all that is necessary—she will grind away all day. So we just dragged up the large crate to base and after lunch Earl and I went down after the other two sleds. We didn't have a sled up here for Earl to ride on so we both rode down in the cab; a couple of boards laid on the seat fixed us up. A little crowded, but comfortable (not as crowded as Court and myself). On the way down we ran off the trail a couple of times but it was of no serious consequence as all we had to do was throw her in reverse and we would climb right back on the trail. When we got down to the cache site we rode around just to check to see if we left anything and take a last look at this bay. We made good time coming back, all the way in high, Earl riding the last sled. When we got in we would have celebrated by cracking open a pint, if we had the pint. The last load—what a relief.

Sunday, February 25

Went to the show last night. All Larry and I had to do was sit in our cubicle, perfect seats. The feature picture and only one was "Angels With Dirty Faces." I have seen every picture so far but you couldn't keep me away. It's hard to see only one showing a week, after being used to seeing three or four a week. But, after all, it's one of the things I gave up to come down here. It's really hard to realize how much one misses little luxuries, conveniences which we have known all of our lives. Such as being able to run to the drug store for a bar of candy, etc. We have had one issue of candy and that was last night.

Sig slept in this morning and Doc Frazier did the honors—pancakes—and it was very good, too. The best part being we didn't have to get up till 10:00 o'clock. It "warn't a fitten day," as Joe Wells would say, blizzard, snowing, so we all stayed in and did little jobs around. I rolled some film and finished unpacking my box, then helped Vernon work on some skis, putting rubber padding to protect the wood from the rubbing of the shoe. We ate supper fairly late, around 8:00 o'clock, then loafed around till bed time. Vernon has been getting the states on his radio, so at 2:30 we listened to the "Hour of Charm"—9:30 in New York City, seven hours difference. We got the regular Sunday night program. His radio certainly helps. We've heard Lowell Thomas a couple of times and get news from London quite frequently.

Boy! What a blizzard. It snowed all night and the wind howled especially loud through the ventilators. It's a good feeling to be inside, warm, comfortable, laughing at the elements. Went out this morning and could hardly walk for the drifts, sank in several times up to my waist. Started up "Dolly." The Sarge, Vernon and I used the scoop, cleared several paths around. "Dolly" waded right through the drifts. Shirley took pictures with the Harvester people's camera, also some for the expedition. Had quite a job digging out my clothing cache. Even though it was in close to the house and covered with a tarp, the snow managed to sneak in. I also built a nice shelf along the house to put the furs on. After chow Sarge wanted me to drive the tractor, take a trail run with a sled that he fixed up. It has an airplane ski attached between the runners. The theory is that the ski will take weight off the runners and keep them from plowing along—keep the front of the sled up. We loaded her down with fuel, gas, ten barrels and took off. She worked fine so when we got back Sarge started to work on the other sled. We helped Clay put up a couple of his antenna poles—quite a job to keep them from bowing in the middle or breaking off entirely.

Wasn't so bad out today, although we haven't really seen the sun for better than two weeks or so. We got a scare a couple of nights ago. It started to clear up a little, so Paul decided to take off at midnight. Pappy Gray and Giles went out and started to warm up the motors, but within an hour she closed in again. Mac says he isn't going to speak to Court till he brings him some flying weather. The favorite expression around here is, "Why, the weather is so lousy that even the Skuagulls are grounded." Mac still tries, though, he is always going out to look at the weather. Paul hopes to get in one more flight before the winter night, but if this weather keeps up—I doubt it. Got a message from Bob saying Camel's using my picture in a cigarette ad. That's a laugh, a non-smoker walking a mile for a Camel. Spent all day working on clothing, issued wool breeches, coats number five hundred and one, union suits number eight hundred and fifty-five, fur gloves (mitts) and Sigs mukluks. If I ever come on one other expedition I hope I never have to have anything to do with supplies. I have never seen such a bunch, they are all afraid that someone is getting more than the other. One of the special issue hounds is Giles. If any of the other fellows shows up with something new on, he immediately runs to me and wants to know if I issued anything. It burns me up, but I suppose that's human nature or something.

Wednesday, February 28

Up at 7:00 and on the ball. Paul told me last night that the tractor was to leave Friday and that he was planning to go along. Nib, him and me. I worked today checking over clothing and issued socks, mitts, and mitt liners. I still have some trail clothing to issue before we start. The wind started up around 9:00 o'clock and it's been bad all day. Everything is drifting over again. I did manage to get the tarp secured over my cache and did a little patching job with cardboard, etc. Boy, the snow and wind against my face really burned. My beard got all full of ice and snow. I suppose it would cut worse, though, if I were clean-shaven. It is now midnight and the wind is still howling. Two blizzards in three days. Paul had a meeting tonight with the fellows going on the trail. He gave us a few pointers as to what to do and what not to do. One important thing being never let ice start to form in our sleeping bags. To prevent this, in the morning when one gets up he should air the bag in order to let moisture escape. Also never wear moist clothing to bed, because it will freeze up. I had a run-in with several of the fellows because they started getting a few things together for themselves, then when I went to make an issue things were missing. So I kind of read 'em off. The thing that sets things off were the fur sleeping bags. Each fellow to go on the trail is to have one, so a couple of the fellows kind of snatched theirs and hid them out.

Thursday, February 29

Another day gone by and still the tractor is not quite ready to leave for Advance base. We did get a breakthrough about 10:00 this morning. The weather started to clear up a bit and by noon there was hardly a cloud in the sky. The sun was shining, it was actually warm. Paul and Mac consulted Court who had taken a balloon run and it was decided to get set for flight. By 1:30 both engines of the Condor were tuned up and they took off at 2:00 o'clock—flight "C" for 78° 28′ lat. and 164″ long., southwestern 83° 30′ lat. and 175° east, turned southeasterly along Queen Maude 85° lat., 165° long. W., northeasterly 84° lat., 150° long. (Paul, Al, Mac, Shirley and Giles composed the flight crew). Turn west of north and head for

Little America and then home. I took several pictures in the morning, trying to get shadows formed by drifts. The fellows finished putting up the machinist's building and the three generators are in their place. In fact, they were moved in before the last wall was put up because they are a little large to go through the door. Pappy Reese and Vernon worked late Monday night and all of Tuesday getting the generators and diesel engine in working order, and during the evening meal the lights went on. Everyone cheered. It's still hard to realize how much little things mean to us. At home we turn lights off and on like they were nothing, but here we all had a part in making it possible—work, and plenty of it. An accomplishment by all of us. Then too, we have been using candles long enough, which added to the joy of getting lights. Larry and I are extremely happy now because we almost burned the place a couple of times. We couldn't quite get used to having a candle around, hence we were always knocking it down. Then too, it was rather hard to do any reading by candlelight so since we have had lights most of the fellows have been staying up all hours of the night reading. I worked in the clothing cache again today, issuing fur parkas to trail party— windproof fur caps, inner soles and extra duffle bags. We all turned to this afternoon and helped put up the tarp on the machinist building. It's been getting colder and the temperature is now twelve degrees below, and here we are just about ready to start on the trail.

Friday, March 1

This is the coldest first of March I have ever had the pleasure of experiencing. It has been ten degrees below during the day and last night the temperature reduced to a new low of twenty degrees below. We are still getting ready for the trail. The tractor was due to leave today but since the flight did not get back till around 2:00 o'clock this morning, Paul decided to leave Saturday morning sometime. That was alright with Nib and me because we wanted to hear the mail bag anyway. Puttered around in the cache today getting out such things as tooth brushes, powder, mouthwash and odds and ends for the fellows to take to the outpost. They have pestered me to death. None of them could get together on what they wanted and when they did, they would think of things one by one. Paul announced the third fellow the other night, Jack Perkins. Well, I wish them all luck. We had movies tonight, a day early because we are leaving tomorrow. Saw "They Made Me A Criminal," which I had seen for the third time. It will be just my luck to show one that I haven't seen while we are gone. Tonight I packed my duffle bag for the trail. Nib, Paul and I have quite a setup. They took one of the sleds and built a bungalow, so they call it. We will sleep and eat in it. So three sleds make up the train. Two payloads, one with our domiciles. We have quite an arrangement for sticking in trail flags. Whoever is driving the tractor will watch the time and when we are at the right mileage for a flag to be placed he will pull a string which will rattle some cans back in the caboose, and the fellow on watch there will lift up a small door, reach out and stick the flag. The third member of the party will sleep. I also worked with Earl for a while tonight finishing up the trail rations. He took over the job since I was busy with clothing.

We had a beautiful sunset tonight—about the only time we see the sun since it has always been behind clouds. Funniest thing, my toes have been hurting for the past week or so. I thought it was a corn or something but today I noticed they were puffed up a little, saw Doc, and he said they had been frost bitten. I remember now when it happened. That last tractor trip, both my hands and feet got cold as hell. I could hardly walk when I got out of the cab. Oh, well, such is life at Antarctica.

Saturday, March 2

Were to leave today but the wind started to blow a little and by noon we had a more or less blizzard on our hands, wind velocity being about thirty miles per hour and temperature around zero. Since it would be hard to see the flags Paul decided it would be better to wait till the wind dies a little, so we are standing by. Worked all day putting odds and ends in the caboose, last minute thoughts of Paul's. It's now 11:00 o'clock and the blizzard is still going strong. Just got back from a trip to the Palace, fell down a couple of times, flat in drifts. One of the fellows thought that he had a fairly safe course set to the Palace. Well, I tried it, but he crossed me up. Personally, I think the drifts were a little deeper the way he sent me.

Sunday, March 3

Got up this morning around 9:00 o'clock and the weather had improved so that Paul decided that we would make an attempt to get underway. So at 11:00 o'clock we tried to take off amid the encouragement and good cheer from the bunch. All were on hand, equipped with cameras—Shirley had movie cameras. It was a big event. Nib started out driving, going in reverse, but we couldn't budge the load—two loaded sleds and one caboose—the trouble being the tank had plowed up around camp here and the tractor just dug in. So after a couple attempts we took one sled out to the trail at a time. Klondike had, the day previously, lined us up for a mile. After we got all of the sleds out to the trail we couldn't line the three sleds up, and in our effort dumped the gas drums off the first sled, also breaking one of the runners on the second sled. We tried to jerk the second sled in line from the side and in doing that pulled the runner off. The hell of it is, as soon as one stops a sled around here, or anything else for that matter, it freezes tight. That was what made the drums so hard to handle. Well, Paul was determined to continue on the trip so we took the gas sled and caboose and started out, our ultimate aim to get ten miles out. Paul and I rode in the parlor car for the first mile, while Nib could see the flags. Since the bungalow extended a little over the width of the sled, hindering Nib from lining himself up with the flags in the rear, we had to get out and keep him on his course.

Our original plan was for the man driving to keep in a straight line by watching the flags just placed, being able to see three flags back, at intervals of one-tenth of a mile, and the other two of us would go in the caboose, one sleeping and the other watching the distance meter and putting flags out at the turn of every one-tenth of a mile. This could be done by merely lifting up a trap door in the side walling. Well, since Nib couldn't see the flags, our system went haywire. Also, to make matters worse, we ran into bad weather—fog. It must have been fog because even though there was some wind (about thirteen miles per hour) there did not seem to be particles of snow or ice blowing, stinging our faces, yet visibility was zero, getting so bad that we could see only two flags back, then eventually just one and lucky to see it.

Paul had to walk back a couple of times just to make sure that we were on a straight course, in line with the flags. One time he found that we were about one-tenth of a mile off to the left. Finally it got so bad, at times, when we couldn't even see one flag behind us. So after talking it over, it was decided to stop at five miles and get rid of the gas and our extra rations, making a five-mile beacon along the trail. The beacon would be handy for either this fall dog team operations or tractor work next spring. But poor visibility was not the only thing which we had to put up with. As long as there is snow and a tractor, the inevitable is bound to happen—just plain old stuck, bogged down. Seven times in five miles. The process of one stuck was simple, merely doing a little shoveling, unhitch the front sled, pull up the second, then hitch up both and slam into it. And usually (or sometimes) we got out the first try. The thing which made it so bad was the drift, it was just like riding a surfboard, bucking the waves. Paul said that he had never seen such sastruga. The tractor would strain to climb the sastruga, then in going down the other side would bog down. We were all glad when we reached the five miles. We got everything cached in no time and while Nib and I gassed up and checked the oil Paul fixed some pemmican and coffee—our first meal since morning. We were not in any particular hurry so sat around the primus stove and shot the bull for awhile. That caboose arrangement would be the way to travel in this country as it was really very comfortable and one stove heated it up very quickly, and even without one it was fairly comfortable. We had furs on the floor, which helped a lot. I was to drive back, so after we cleaned up the gear I put on my furs and we started back. I had to open the rear window in order to see out. For the first half-mile or so everything went fine as Paul had the flags a little closer, but after that I couldn't see from one flag to the next. It was a funny feeling after passing one flag, then it would become invisible and I wouldn't be able to see the next one for at least two or three minutes (getting sleepy). Those were really anxious moments for me because it is so easy to get off the course, especially when one can't see anything. Sometimes I would find the flag dead ahead, and others off to one side. And several times I caught a glimpse of the flag just in time. A perfect Antarctic white, no horizons or anything, but we got through alright without stopping. I envied Paul and Nib snug as a bug in a rug back in the caboose. We got into camp about 11:30 and did those buildings ever look good to me. I couldn't get out of the cab and into the house fast enough. Both Paul and Nib congratulated me. They pictured themselves having to go ahead and find the trail. Well, I think that takes care of advance base. We tried, did our best, but it would take a month to get out to the mountains at the rate we were going, and with dragging only one sled it would be apparent to make at least four trips. Paul felt badly about it and suggested we not give the verdict to Fitz till he broke it to him kind of easy-like. I even froze my right nostril a couple of times just to really be in the spirit of the thing.

86

Boy! I hated to get up this morning. That little trip yesterday kind of wiped me out. Didn't do much of anything today except unload the tractor caboose—brought in my personal gear and some of Paul's. Paul was over at the cruiser last night after we came in, had a little conference with Al. And today he told Fitz, Murray and Perk that the outpost was out. He didn't tell them right out but kind of broke it to them easy, smoothing over the whole thing. So I imagine that Larry and I will have to put up with Fitz for the rest of the year. I had quite a time during the afternoon getting back all of the extra clothing, etc., that I'd issued to the outpost boys. They kind of hated to part with the extra gear, but it would never have done to have them showing up with more clothing than the rest.

After supper, Larry, Gil, Earl, Fitz and I went skiing—an initial appearance for Larry and me, but the rest had been a couple of times so in our minds were little less than professionals, experts. We headed west from camp and kept going till we lost sight of Clay's radio antenna poles then we started back. Visibility was very poor, seemed to be foggy. We broke one law of Antarctic, that being we did not keep camp in sight, and that we did not follow a well-marked trail. The going seemed pretty rough to me, same old sastruga which isn't exactly ideal for skiing, especially for a beginner. However, I felt rather proud as I fell only once and then I didn't really fall, but merely eased down. I have one complaint to make and that is I think that these skis are a little too thin, they look like a couple of toothpicks around—a little awkward, but effective. Very simple to do, just lift the right foot, letting the ski stand straight, vertical, then let it fall in the direction you want to go (if your knee isn't pulled out of joint, or at least twisted out of shape) then lift the left foot and place beside the right. Very simple.

We got back to camp alright, although several times we thought we had missed it. I still say that there is no more grateful sight than our camp building looming up out of the invisible, the white haze. I enjoyed the skiing very much and now that the ice is broken I imagine that I will go a lot.

The fellows are almost finished with the construction of the science house. The machinist building is not quite completed as to ventilation, etc., but that can be done later on, the main job is getting the building up. The men in the house gang have been doing fine work and have stuck to their jobs in weather which really hasn't been an incentive to work. Working with a hammer and nails, saw, etc., is really no fun, especially in zero or so weather with about an eighteen- or twenty-mile wind blowing. Since the advance base project has been called off, Paul has put all of the fellows to work getting caches fixed and tunnels dug—getting ready for the winter nights. The preparation for the little mountain jaunt took quite a number of the fellows away from camp work. That is, the dog drivers were making dog pemmican, Fitz and Weiner were getting their supplies together, while Earl was working on man food and I on clothing and small stores. Hence about half (fifteen) of the camp was occupied in the preparation for this undertaking, so when they came back to work on camp jobs, things began to happen. A tunnel was cut from the front door to the palace which will be covered with tunnel tarp. All of the galley cache was brought in and put in place, as was Gil's candy, gum, etc. We also dug out the housing cache and Dick Moulton and I took his dog team and hauled canned goods from the cache over to the galley door. We took a few cases of each item which are to go in Sig's cupboards.

Wednesday, March 6

It seems like it is more difficult for me to get out of bed every morning. It seems like I am almost unconscious. I hear the breakfast gong, even wake up while the table is being set, but just don't seem to be able to snap out of it. Dick and I worked this morning on the canned goods for the cupboards. We took all of the cans out of the cases and stacked them on shelves. Reminded me of my grocery store days. We paid special attention to such delicacies as fruit salad, peaches, etc. We saw that Sig was also well stocked with desserts. Al feels much better today and Paul said he would be up and around probably tomorrow. He has been sick for the last couple of days with strep throat infection—had at one time a temperature of one hundred and two degrees. I guess he felt pretty lousy. Paul called me in this afternoon and sprung the Siple and Wade theory on me. Paul originated the thing and Al is going to help him with it. It seems that while looking at the globe of the world it dawned on Paul that a line of stress might have something to do with the alignment of mountains of different continents. He got the idea on the last flight upon seeing the direction of a group of mountains which they flew over—thus he studied the globe. It's amazing how the thing seems to line up, such as the case of one stress line on the east coast of North America, the U.S. Appalachian

Mountains, starting from Alabama along to Newfoundland and across the Atlantic southern part of Ireland down to the Red Sea. It looks perfect if only the geology will hold it up. Every place we looked on the map we seemed to see more examples. Al borrowed my historical geology and is going to work on the problem. I think the whole thing will prove interesting. It really seems so simple that I am afraid that there is some catch somewhere. Perk just came in from the Palace and reports that it is fifteen degrees below there, which does not help matters any. So it must be twenty-five degrees below outside. The boys finished the tunnel from the house out to the Palace. It's covered and everything looks fine—did a good job on it. Chuck and his bunch have just two more roof panels to put on the science building. It will be a relief to have that finished because it's getting pretty cold to be working on roofs, etc. Arnold just came in from reading the thermometer outside and the temperature at midnight was twenty-six and nine-tenths degrees below. Saw the first star tonight according to the Almanac. Arnold and Paul were to see the stars on the night of March 6. Of course, it has been cloudy nights for the past week, so we will never really know.

Thursday, March 7

Can't understand why we are getting up so early these days— 7:00 o'clock every morning. It just doesn't seem right, especially when we don't usually get in bed till around 12:00 or 1:00 o'clock. Late to bed and early to rise just doesn't make sense—it at least doesn't make one healthy. I don't know about wealthy, and as for wise. . . . During the morning Dick and I hauled some snow and cleaned up between the science building and machine shop prior to putting in the food cache. We used Dick's team. They were really full of pep as they have not been used for some time. Dick drove, naturally, all the way. My job was to try to keep the boxes, both full and empty, on the sled. The tough part was the return with the empties. We dumped the snow a short distance away from the buildings. Well, Dick would notify Snowball, his lead dog, that we were ready to go and the two wheel dogs, Mukluk and General, would throw, literally jump-fight to get started. Well, you can imagine how nine dogs can take an empty sled. A roller coaster will be tame after today. There are enough drifts around camp to make things interesting. I stood, rode the runner, holding our two crates on. One time however, the sled gave a sudden jerk. We almost tipped over—lost the two boxes but I jumped, throwing myself across them. I guess I didn't look before I leaped because I landed right on a nail. Did a kind of puncture job on my thigh. I went in and Doc Frazier fixed me up. It's sore as a boot tonight. Doc says he thinks I will live.

In the afternoon I drove the tractor dragging the Condor crate parts alongside of the machinery building. Nib is going to make a garage. It was pretty cold today, twenty-four degrees below. It's hard to realize it's that cold. We all worked right along, though. Our one aim is to get camp all set for the winter night. We all figure that it isn't cold now, at least to what it's going to be, so we work. Court says that we can expect thirty degrees to forty degrees below any day now. Tonight a couple of the fellows started a "let's have a show" movement, and lo and behold, it worked. The feature picture was "Rose of Washington Square." Very good, some say it was the best we have had so far. I guess it was Alice Faye. Gil made out a little "poop sheet" saying, "Movies if dishes done by 9:00 o'clock." Well, there was so much help in the kitchen that it was almost impossible to even get near the sink. Not that I tried.

Friday, March 8

Funny thing, nobody woke me this morning. So I didn't budge till 9:00 o'clock, and I was one of the first ones up. It just wasn't fittin' out so everyone slept in. I guess the wind started up around midnight, building up in speed till it had reached thirty miles per hour. The whole place was drifted over. Had to shovel to get to the Palace, this end in front of the house has not been covered, hence the wind drift had a merry time blowing, filling up the tunnel. We all went to the kitchen and fixed our own breakfast, such as it was —toast, coffee and jelly. After that I crawled back in my bunk and snoozed till noon. Since it didn't look like we were going to have anything to eat for a while, I did a washing—underwear, socks, etc. Quite a job—I guess because everything was so dirty. At 3:00 o'clock we had a sort of lunch, buckwheat cakes, having our big meal at 7:00. The wind let up a little, so afterward all hands went out and did a little snow shoveling. Personally I don't think I ever shoveled so much snow. It really seemed like a hopeless job because after all, when it is all said and done, there is still snow, and plenty of it. We then extended our tunnel system by adding the housing cache. Then we put up the tarp in front of the house. It is getting darker every night. It's a good thing that we have lights in the tunnels, there's no telling what might happen. From the looks of this thing we are going to have a very interesting system of tunnels and I would hate to get lost, as I imagine that one could wander around in them for days and really never get any place.

Saturday, March 9

Surprised myself by waking up at 7:00 o'clock. I guess the long sleep the other day kind of fixed me up. Dick and I started to work again on moving in the food cache. Of course at first we had to do a little snow shoveling as the blizzard of yesterday filled, drifting the place over again. We hadn't been at it long before Larry turned over the rest of the fellows to us, then we became bosses. About 10:30, Ray (Zeke) Butler came out and said that Paul wanted to see Larry and myself. We went into his office or whatever you want to call it, expecting anything. Well, we got it. Seemed like the weather looked promising for a photographic hop and that we should move to be ready to take off in an hour. It took us about that long to get into our furs. It certainly is a hot job dressing, so many pairs of socks, fur pants, fur parka, a couple of shirts and a jacket. Oh, yes, and fur mitts and cap. And by that time one feels about like quitting. It really seems funny—sweating, with furs on. The flight consisted of Pilot McCoy, Co. Walt Giles, Photographer Chas. Shirley, P.A. Siple, Larry, Perk, and myself. After a few pictures all around we took off at 1459. We had quite a bumpy takeoff as the sastruga isn't what one would call exactly smooth. It took me a little time to get oriented after we lost sight of camp. The flight E was to be simply a local hop, purpose to photograph the Bay of Whales, pressure ice, and the barrier to see changes of shape taken place the last ten years since the last map was drawn. We headed west circling around the edge of the barrier at an altitude of six thousand feet, flying over Roosevelt Island. I took some pictures of the pressure ice which I hope will turn out. It was a beautiful day, clear out with very low clouds over the bay and over Roosevelt Island. Camp certainly looked insignificant, just a couple of ink spots on a blanket of white. At first I thought it was a couple of seals, but later recognized Bolling Bight. It certainly takes a flight to really let one know where he is. At first I was not exactly sure of our location, but after today's flight I know. And now that I know, I'm not too sure that I like it. We are only a short distance from the barrier on the east and north, while on the south there seems to be pressure ice and quite a number of bights. On the west there is nothing but crevasses, bights and pressure ice. We then flew east back over camp, following along the barrier over the spot where we had first landed, could see rather plainly the few empty barrels which we had left there. Then we changed course and flew south and a little west, passing over the tractor cache that Paul, Nib and I had taken out a few days previously, touching Roosevelt Island, then back over Little America II. I couldn't quite make it out, but Paul said that was where it was. We then flew out over the bay, which was a beautiful sight—pancake ice, angular pieces and some frozen solid. Gaining altitude of ten thousand feet, Shirley took some vertical shots of the camp. Then we headed back toward Little America II, where we saw the Beechcraft. Shirley wanted to take some pictures of the craft in relation to the site of Little America II. So we lost altitude and I made out the poles which were still standing, twelve in all. Then we headed back to camp with the Beechcraft flying alongside. When we got over camp, Shirley took some more pictures of the Beechcraft. We circled around camp a couple of times, then landed.

A perfect landing, but once we got down it was rough riding, we all had to hang on. Since this was the first flight for the Condor, Paul left word that Mac could take up some of the others for a short hop. So when we pulled in, there were seven or so waiting, Nib, Joe Walls, Vernon, Gutenko, O'Conner, etc. We were up for three-and-a-half hours. Paul also pointed out Amundson's camp, but I am not sure whether I saw it or not. Also, we were able to see Rockefeller Mountains a hundred miles to the east. From six to ten thousand feet the sastruga looked like little ripples—but what a different story upon landing.

We had our regular Saturday night movie last night—a very good picture, "Young Abe Lincoln."

Sunday, March 10

Woke up this morning about 9:00 o'clock and she was really blowing out. I thought something was up since we were not awakened at the usual hour. As soon as I awoke I knew that the weather was not fittin', as the wind and our ventilators make quite a combination—she literally howls. We had breakfast about 11:00 o'clock, buckwheat cakes, which were quite a treat. There was nothing to do except climb back in the bunk to take it easy. I did take a tour inspection just to see if all was intact. We did a pretty good job as the tunnels leak only in a couple of places. I read a little geology, then started a novel by Warnick Weeping, called "Folly Islands."

92

We had dinner about 5:00 o'clock, read and loafed all evening. The days seem to fly by even when loafing, so I guess the winter night will not be so bad.

Paul's records have been very much in use—all classical—and if I do nothing else I am going to learn a few names. I know the tunes, but darn if I can remember the names. During the winter night will be a good chance to get caught up on a few things.

I got a message from Alda Saturday night. That was certainly a godsend, as I was beginning to get worried after not hearing from her over the mail bag program. I hope that she doesn't miss again. If she only knew how much hearing from her means to me.

Gil broke out the games the other day and little groups of fellows have been segregated about the room playing checkers, A'cy Ducey, Chess, Monopoly, etc. Helps pass time.

Wind velocity tonight is about twenty-nine and temperature around six degrees above, barometer dropping fairly steadily till around twenty-nine and twenty-two one hundreds.

Monday, March 11

Another late arising, still blowing out, velocity about thirty-five miles and temperature sixteen degrees above. Al said that he had quite a time coming from the cruiser. Visibility so poor he could not make out buildings till halfway along, the distance to the cruiser being about two hundred yards. Most of all, the caches not tunneled in are drifted over, which promises much shoveling. I only hope that we can find everything. Didn't do much of anything but sleep and read. The only fellows beside the cruiser gang who ventured out were the dog drivers, who naturally had to feed their teams. Paul got word from the Admiral today concerning East Base. They are having a pretty bad time of it, can't find a place to anchor in Margurite Bay because of shoals and ice, impossible to land. Can't seem to find site for camp. The Admiral seems to think that it is a hopeless task because of strong wind, bad swells and rough water.

Tuesday, March 12

It seems to be a habit with me waking up at 9:00 o'clock because it happened again today. However, the only reason I wasn't up by 7:00 is because the whole camp slept in. Although the wind has lost some of its fierceness, its howl is still registered at twenty-five miles per hour. We had breakfast at 10:30, then a few of us got ambitious and brought in snow blocks for the snow melter. It's the first I was out since the blizzard started and things were really drifted over. The food cache is completely covered and those boxes were stacked at least six or seven feet high. To get to the door at the north end of the machinist building Vernon had to tunnel in as it was drifted clear up to the roof of the building. It was quite a simple job to cut blocks for the snow melter, merely had to cut them out of the drift along the side of the machinist building. In fact, the Condor cases, foundation or flooring for the garage, were completely covered. Now that I think of it, I wondered why Nib was so anxious to get the snow melter filled. By doing it he got all of the drift cleared away from the garage and all he had to do was saw out the blocks. I guess he isn't so dumb. Since it was still blowing a little we came in and Nib, Fitz, Earl, Mac and myself started a game of Monopoly, but we didn't get to finish as the weather cleared up enough so that we could see. The wind ceased blowing so that it would be possible to shovel fast enough to get a little ahead of the drift which, to say the least, seemed to be encouraging.

Nib and I went out to start the tractor. I still can't figure out how one little tractor had so much snow in it. We had to take a shovel to the cab. Incidentally, I forgot to close the doors and when we opened the hood we found ice formed where the exhaust pipe comes down, as well as plenty of snow. Nib turned the crank about half a dozen times and she started right up—ice, snow and all. I guess the engine wouldn't feel right unless there was at least a little snow in the plugs, etc. Pappy Gray and I took "Dolly" out to the gas cache to fill her up. It seemed funny running right over the cache. At that place the drift was about four feet, which completely covered the barrels. Anyway, they made a good road.

We had lunch at 3:00 o'clock and when I say lunch, I really mean lunch. We had cake and coffee. Hardly a fit meal for working men. We did feel better when we found we were going to have steak at 6:00 o'clock. Spent the rest of the afternoon running "Dolly." Earl and I formed an evacuation company which consisted of "Dolly" and scoop, Earl worked the scoop. He made quite a showing after three hours' work—clearing a couple of paths and almost finished cleaning out all of the drifts between the houses. It looks like a WPA project around here—about ten or twelve fellows leaning on snow shovels watching the tractor work. Larry and Dick worked on the framework for the large tarp which is to go between the three buildings. It is about seventy-five feet by forty-five feet, and I am afraid that it is going to be a mess trying to put it up.

It is now 11:00 o'clock and a hot game of Monopoly is going on, it's dwindled down to Nib, Mac and Gil. None of them seem to be ahead, but by the noise and number of hecklers standing around it must be close.

Wednesday, March 13

They certainly pulled a fast one on us this morning—woke us up at 6:00 o'clock and breakfast was at 7:00, which meant we were out and at it about 7:30. I went out and started the tractor first thing, then Earl and I started to work on the rest of the drift between the buildings. All activities today have been centered around the food cache and radio cache. It took Earl and me all morning to clear the drift, while Dick Moulton and Perkins, with Dick's team, hauled in radio boxes which were made into pillars alongside of the science building. It was quite a busy place around here. Paul had about ten fellows working with him. They would all help with the scoop because one or two men couldn't hold her down when she was taking a bite. Then when Earl and I went to dump the load, the rest would either pile boxes or shovel snow. The weather started out pretty good, fairly warm but no sun. By noon it started to snow a little and the wind picked up. After lunch Nib, Earl, Doc Frazier, Pappy Grey and myself started to haul food which goes in between the buildings alongside of two radio caches. It was quite a job because we had to dig out everything. By about 2:00 or 3:00 o'clock the wind started to blow a little more and we had the workings of a blizzard. It was hell working out in it. The wind, ice, and snow cut our faces and it was so dark that we couldn't wear our glasses, which didn't help matters any. Today just wasn't my day, I guess. I had a tough time with the tractor fighting the drifts, and a couple of times it almost tipped over. I'll say one thing for that little red tractor, it certainly can take it. I really put it through drifts, pulling heavy loads. She didn't whimper once and I ran her for ten hours straight. Just as we were getting ready to quit tonight, it got a little brighter. The wind let up and there was actually a little blue sky to the north. An Antarctic blizzard disappeared, one could actually see it going to the south. When I came in tonight I don't think I ever remembered being so wet, cold and just plain miserable. I was wet clear through. What hurt me most was having to put on clean underwear when my other wasn't quite dirty—oh, well, such is life. After dinner I helped with the dishes so that we could have the show a little earlier, "The Awful Truth." The fellows really enjoyed it—laughed all the way through it.

It is now 11:00 o'clock and I am lying in my bunk and am completely fagged out. My legs especially ache, probably from working the pedals in the tractor. Well, to bed because tomorrow will be a big day. We hope to finish bringing in the food and plan to get the big tarp up. I certainly hope that it doesn't blow again tonight. It's really heartbreaking to get a place all cleaned, shoveled free from snow, then wake up the next morning and find it all filled in and covered up.

Thursday, March 14

Not much to say tonight except that I am plenty tired. Just about every muscle in my body is sore. It was that three-day layoff that did it, unless I am just getting old and can't take it.

I worked on that tractor all day with Shirley, Earl, Nib and Doc Frazier, Paul and Pappy worked with us in the morning. We cleared up the food cache, which is certainly one big relief. The tarp had been put in place between the buildings, supported by pillars of food. That is, we covered everything that we have brought in so far, and it's a good thing because the wind has started to blow tonight—twenty-eight miles per hour at present. I think my biceps are the sorest muscles, since the food boxes range from twenty pounds up to sixty pounds. Earl and I kind of throw them, which works alright as we do not have to bend over so many times, but that extra spark needed to do the throwing is kind of trying on one's already-tired muscles. I feel kind of like my second or third day out for spring football practice.

All hands turned in this afternoon to put up the one side of the garage, which is merely a crate side. When that was in place, Nib and Joe Wells worked putting up supports for the tarp roof. Around 4:30 this afternoon, Earl and I took the tractor and went out after that ill-fated tractor sled with the broken runner. It was drifted over, but "Dolly" pulled it right out. About 1:00 o'clock this afternoon it actually started to rain, and the windows on the tractor were all iced up. I tried to take a few shots around camp but am afraid that they will not turn out, because just as I was going strong I noticed a film of ice over the lens, which I think does not induce good photography. When I came in tonight for dinner I was wet, my

96

underwear, etc., but my windproof was a sheet of ice. Clay Bailey and his radio men have almost finished the antenna system for receiving and Chuck is working on tables, etc., for the radio room in the science building. Clay says that he will probably be on the air in a week, if not sooner.

Friday, March 15

Woke up late this morning, had breakfast at 9:30—another blizzard. They seem to be rather regular nowadays. Wind velocity thirty-six and temperature twenty-nine degrees above. Last night about midnight I took a walk around camp and the wind had started to blow, but no drifts as it was too warm. This morning the temperature lowered a little so that the wind could pick up particles of snow. In fact, it was literally impossible to see one's hand before one's face. Didn't do much today but sleep and read. I certainly needed the rest.

As usual there was a big Monopoly game started. That seems to be a refuge for one's thoughts or something. Heard the mail bag program starting at 4:30 our time. Got messages from the folks and Alda, Bob and Lois and Ruth Siple. It certainly is good to hear from home, from people you love, and from friends. It gives us all something to look forward to every two weeks. The mail bag plays an important part in our life here and the fellows all gather around the radio about 4:15, just to be sure. The station went off the air for about a half an hour. If there ever was a half hour suspense, that was it, and everyone cheered when she finally came on again. It was at least 2:30 their time before they had finished reading all of the letters.

Saturday, March 16

Things were not drifted over so badly after our little blizzard, although it took us all morning to clear out between the buildings— the part not yet covered by the tarp. Fairly warm out today but no sun, seemed more or less foggy. Snowed off and on most of the day. Arnold just came in from his midnight observation saying that the temperature is twenty-six degrees and wind northwest at nineteen miles per hour.

I drove the tractor all day, in the morning working with the scoop, and in the afternoon Nib, Earl, Pappy Grey, Doc Frazier and myself dug out the lube oil cache, also Nib's tractor cache, and hauled them in. The oil boxes were stacked back of the machinist building as pillars. Nib put the tractor parts and equipment in front near the entrance of the garage. When I went out this morning to start the tractor I was greeted by a most picturesque sight—there little "Dolly" stood covered with about a foot of snow, on the hood and roof, as well as inside. It was a major operation, an undertaking to clean the snow out from the cab. I swear I will never leave the door open again. Changed the oil, also putting in a little castor oil and valve oil. She started right up. Took several pictures around camp. About 5:00 o'clock, all hands knocked off work for coffee, then Paul announced that we would work till we had the rest of the tarp up. It took us till 8:00 o'clock to finish up. I worked on the roof with Jack (H. H.), Fitz and Dick. We pulled the tarp up nailing it down, etc. (that is, the small strips prior to putting up the large tarp), then that little one which weighs about five hundred pounds took about all hands to take care of it, especially since the wind had to be taken into consideration. It always starts blowing at the right time to mess things up. Well, she can blow now because the tarps are up and all that is left outside is some lumber and the science cache. Yes sir, I almost hope she blows all day tomorrow. It will be such a relief to know that for once we are prepared and that there will not be a shoveling job to be done after.

Sunday, March 17

Kind of a holiday today. Up at 8:00 o'clock, breakfast, then we all took off for L. A. (Old Little America). Fitz and I went with Jack (H. H.) with his team. Seven teams went and Paul assigned various fellows to different teams. We had some trouble getting started. Jack had the team all hitched and Fitz and I were loading some sleeping bags on the sled, just in case, when all of a sudden the dogs took off, knocking down Jack, spilling the sleeping bags, and started down the trail. Jack started out after them but that was hopeless and yelling did not do any good. It was lucky that Dick Moulton and his gang who had just started were only about half a mile or so out so that they were able to stop the team. I imagine that they would have kept going till they dropped, or at least till they caught up with Bursey's team. Well, Larry and I started to ski so that when Jack finally got back he did not have to come all the way back. Butler picked up the sleeping bags. The whole thing is the dogs have not been working, but have had plenty to eat, so naturally they were rather full of pep. Jack said that he thought the reason they started was because we were talking about taking some pic-

98

tures and Jack said "All right," which in dog language means "get along doggies," and they did. A pure and simple case of misunderstanding.

It was really fun going over. We all skied but since none of us are what one would call experts, we hedged by hanging onto the sled. We consoled ourselves by saying that it was necessary to hold the dogs down. It was a trip of five miles and three tenths, making it in about an hour and a half. We raced a couple of teams and without bragging too much I might say that we passed them flying. By the time we got there, Berlin, and the group with him had started to dig to find the building. Lon had used a map and transit to locate the approximate location. The first building we got into was the radio building and stock room adjoining. It's remarkable how well the shack was preserved but the tunnel leading from it was caved in. Those fellows must have left in a hurry or else Ellsworth and some of the others ransacked the place. Anyway, the inside was a mess—odds and ends of gear all over the place. Clay and Pappy Reese got some valuable radio equipment while the rest of us found bits of this and that, things each thought they could use. There was everything from old mushing boots to books and blankets. I got a couple of books, mainly for souvenir purposes because they had a "Byrd Antarctic Expedition" stamp in them.

I guess when we got through, the place really looked like a cyclone had hit it. We then started digging again, this time to enter the science building and mess hall. We were lucky because we dug in the vestibule right between the two. The fellows really swarmed the place looking for loot. I found some notebooks, paper, paper clips. The science building was partly caved in and all of the buildings had a musty damp smell. The tunnels here were pretty good and we were able to travel by crawling, worming our way on our stomachs to the mess hall, on to the cowbarn, the Admiral's quarters, etc. The mess hall was literally a "mess," and we had to crawl through it on all fours. The tunnels were full of the most beautiful icicles. The food tunnel seemed to have more food than we have now—coffee, Smuckers apple butter, jams, jellies and tobacco. We are going to take the tractor one of these days and really make a haul. The Admiral's quarters was a prospective place to plunder, but it proved to be a disappointment. There were a few books, but none of them belonged to him. I found a stray can of Planters peanuts and in the radio shack we found some chocolate candy which was very good. We had quite a feast eating everything from figs and dates to candy which Gill brought along. One of the prize takes of the trip was a few dishes used by the expedition, and I was very fortunate to get one. They were scarce, but Tony found one for me, in the cow barn of all places. They have pictures of the *Bear*, the *New York*, the *William Horlick*, and a dog. Mine is a partitioned plate. Several of the fellows have offered me ten dollars for it, but I think I'll keep it.

We left Little America about 4:30, and up till then the weather had been pretty good—no sun but not very cold, but on the way back visibility got poor—an Antarctic white. Larry decided to ski ahead so Paul hung on with Fitz and me. When we got back to camp there was the house all decorated in green and the table was set with green napkins and St. Patrick's Day favors. We had dinner about 8:00 o'clock, chicken. While at Little America, Vernon tried to find the tractor which Ellsworth dropped in a crevasse, but had to leave before locating it. However, he thinks that next time he can find it. Nib, who stayed at camp, heated up the tank and drove it into the garage. A wonderful day, I shall never forget it. Very interesting to visit the site and dwellings of the previous Byrd Expeditions.

Monday, March 18

It just wouldn't blizzard today. It did try, though, so I will give it some credit. I will admit that I did want to stay in my bunk today of all days, as I was plenty tired. Too much skiing, I guess. However, we did get a late start—about 10:00 A.M. I started the tractor and Nib and I brought in some twelve by three's for the garage floor. The tank broke through in a couple of places so Nib sorta got worried. The tractor isn't heavy enough for that, but she does chew up the planks pretty badly. After we spiked the boards in place we cleaned up the garage and shoveled all the snow out. I then drove "Dolly" in and really gave her the once over. Cleaned all of the snow out of the cab; in fact, I had to use an ice pick around the pedals and doors. I then checked the oil and gassed up. It was quite warm in the garage as we had two Von Pragues going full blast. It really sounded more or less like a boiler working, as the blower torches issue forth a roar as well as an equal terrific amount of heat. We used one in the old cook tent to heat, or rather melt, snow and it was impossible to work anywhere in that part of the tent, and usually it's necessary to open the tent flaps. We were supposed to haul in lumber this afternoon but they had not decided where they were going to put it. So I worked in my clothing cache, straightening things around and taking inventory, which I am afraid is going to be more or less of an ordeal.

They had a big Monopoly game again tonight. Nib is really getting good at the game, he won with flying colors. I read and finished "Christmas Holiday" by Somerset Maugham—very fine book, well written. Maugham does such a fine job in the portrayal of Simon. Phil brought over quite a few messages and I was fortunate enough to get one from Alda. I can't understand why she hasn't gotten my Valparaiso letters. I hope that Davis remembered to mail them.

Tuesday, March 19

Sig still seems to have trouble getting up and he always blames it on his alarm clock, says it stopped. I wonder. We had breakfast at 8:00. I do wish that we could be a little consistent about our meals. Today, 8:00, 1:00, and 7:00. The trouble is around here if you get hungry you get cold, and if you are already tired, it's hardly a pleasant combination. I expected to drive the tractor today so warmed it up, but found that Paul, Larry and the fellows working with them were digging out the panels, etc., for the extra outpost building which is going to be used as an annex to the science building. Larry, Paul, Al Butler, Berlin and myself will be situated there. They seemed to have all of the help they needed, so I went out and helped Dick M. dig the main dog tunnel which is to be one hundred feet long, extending from the Palace west and a little north. He and Jack Richardson has just started so they welcomed additional help. Pretty soon Zeke and Shirley arrived on the scene and the work began in earnest. I don't know whose idea it was but Dick started at one end of the tunnel site, Jack and I at the other, and the rest in the middle. Building tunnels is rather a simple process, being done by merely taking an ice saw and cutting out blocks of snow. We were not able to use the snow in the first few feet as it was pretty soft, but around six feet down it was compact enough to make nice blocks. These were placed three high along the edge, which made a total depth of nine feet.

The job was a cold one and about 3:00 P.M. the wind started to blow, so Dick and I decided that it would be a good idea to put the tarp over temporarily during the night, to at least keep the drift out of the sections we had already dug. By that time we had dug all of the tunnel but about fifteen feet. It is fairly easy to combat cold, but wind is another thing. I thought my face would fall off, and several times my right nostril started to get numb. We anticipated having trouble with the tarp, but we merely unrolled it the length of the tunnel and picked up one end, let the wind blow it over, then took another bite. For once the wind helped instead of hindering. I was certainly glad when we had the whole thing battened down, and when we all went in the stove certainly felt good. I got warmed up a bit so went out and found that the fellows were working on lumber. So I worked till chow time helping stack the lumber on racks along the garage. We had a little accident. It seems that one of the two by four superstructures in the rack couldn't stand the gaff and split away, causing pieces of lumber to fall on poor Nib's head. Lucky he had on his helmet or I imagine that it would have been severe. As it was, he got rather a bad bump.

Wednesday, March 20

Life is so cruel. I don't know why we have to get up every morning to work. It certainly would feel good to sleep in some morning, really sleep in with no noise. I don't know why everyone has to make it their business whether I get up or not. They won't even let one sleep through breakfast, and I was trying so hard to do that very thing, especially after I glimpsed at the chipped beef without toast sitting on the table. Larry and I have a big discussion every morning to decide whether or not we should get up. Larry is almost as bad as I am. I mean, well, my heart is in my work, but even then I just can't get up. My bones just won't move—and as for muscles, they gave out way back in Boston. Enough of that—I imagine one can gather from the above that I am just plain tired. Worked all day out in the main dog tunnel. Dick, Malcolm, Jack and I are the mainstays. That tunnel is really the pride and joy of our existence. For one thing, it is nice and deep and there is one thing certain— there will be no danger of anyone bumping heads as it is an average of nine feet deep and the walls are of solid barrier snow, one of which is at least seven feet. Then we have snow blocks up to support the tarp, which adds on a couple of feet. About 10:00 o'clock Dick and Vernon took off to L.A. to look for the tractor. A beautiful sunshiny day was the cause of such a quick decision. It cleared up in almost nothing flat. The sky was a clear blue with no clouds except for low stratus to the west and south. When Dick left we were without a boss, so he made me the head man and we carried on. It was colder today, being thirteen degrees below zero during the day, reaching a minimum at 6:00 o'clock of twenty degrees below. My beard was all full of ice and my shoes were frozen stiff. Yet working out, shoveling or cutting snow, was actually a hot job. I (excuse) sweat like a horse and was forced to remove some of my clothing till I was working only in my undershirt and a windproof parka. The only place I really noticed the cold was naturally my face and my wrists. I will have to get busy and make a face mask and some wristlets.

Had our Wednesday night show with full attendance, "Only Angels Have Wings." I saw it in Dunedin, a very good picture. Court just came in from his midnight round. It is now twenty-seven degrees below and time to turn out the lights and go to sleep.

Thursday, March 21

I could repeat how difficult it is to get up these mornings, but I won't. There is one salvation and that is I am not the only one who hates to arise. Larry and Fitz also feel the same way I do. Fitz says that when he wakes in the morning he is in a stupor, unconscious. His eyes are open, he's awake, yet he can't move a muscle. He says it seems like he is nailed to the bunk. The whole thing is, I think, that when we turn in we are so completely fatigued that we sleep so soundly and are completely relaxed, that it takes some time to regain ourselves, to get our hearts to pick up to a normal beat. (Sounds screwy.) I know that today we worked all day shoveling snow, keeping up a pretty hot pace. Naturally, the heart speeds up to meet the demand of such energy. Well, we can keep that up all day (being tired at night, naturally) but if we stop for coffee or something, there is a tremendous let down and it is terribly hard to get going again and one has a "washed out" feeling.

It was a beautiful day today, sky clear blue with low clouds to the west. The sun was shining brightly, although very low in the horizon. The temperature ranged from minus ten degrees to minus thirty degrees. We completed the main dog tunnel and started excavating a place for the blubber house and chop house. They are going to be at the far end of the tunnel and necessitate digging a hole twelve feet by twenty-four, and eight feet deep. We used "Dolly" and the scoop this morning till it was impossible because of danger of caving in tunnel sides. We had a good gang working with us, Dick, Larry, Jack, Zeke and myself. Malcolm and Perk worked in the tunnel putting on the finishing touches. We got half of the snow or better out but had to stop and rig up a tarp. That's what makes work here so damnable hard—we can't leave things open because of the chance or possibility of a blizzard, and it means we have to stop an hour early to batten down. Any way you look at it, shoveling is hard work. It kind of gets you in the shoulders and back. It is now 11:30 P.M. and most of the fellows have turned in. It is pretty hot in the building till Court opens the door—then sleep. A beautiful sunset, most gorgeous I have ever seen, almost crimson with orange yellow sky to the north, clouds to the south.

Friday, March 22

Blizzard today. This morning the wind velocity was nineteen miles; now at midnight it is thirty-eight miles. Everyone worked today, either in the buildings or in the tunnels. Dick and I worked on the tunnel leading to the Palace, putting up supports and a tarp door leading to the Palace. We leveled the floor of the tunnel, purely a selfish reason since we are both rather tall and at times are apt to do a little head bumping. There is nothing more discouraging than hitting the roof of a tunnel which has icicles hanging, or snow. It always goes down one's back. We also dug some fancy steps, we thought they would make it a little easier to walk. We have been cussed out several times by fellows who have either slipped and fallen or else stepped down the steps landing in the soft snow at the bottom—filling slippers. I did a little work in the clothing cache putting up bamboo poles to help support the drifts. Nib made some strawberry ice cream tonight—was very good.

Just talked to Phil and he says that he has been unable to contact WLMC, which means that the folks and Alda will not get Easter messages in time. He says the band is completely dead. He has, however, been able to receive from WLMC but he has been sending blind.

Saturday, March 23

Same old breakfast but with a little grapefruit which tasted very good. Worked out at dog town, as Dick calls it. Finished up the hole for the blubber and chop house. It's really more than a hole, though, as it is fifty feet by forty-eight feet and at least twelve feet deep. And I might mention that a tolerable amount of snow has to come out of such an excavation. Coach helped us in the afternoon, seven of us all told—Dick, Larry, Jack (H), Zeke, Malc, Coach and myself. We worked at a terrific pace till all of us were sweating. I had stripped down to my undershirt, no hat, and the perspiration was literally rolling off my face. I don't think that I ever worked so hard and fast, and I don't suppose I will ever shovel as much snow, at least till we start digging in the Condor. Oh yes, and when we get her out in the spring. (Something to look forward to.) I swear that the Coach will kill any man who tries to keep up with him. He works like a fiend and keeps the rest of us going. And to think they say he isn't half the man he used to be. I'd hate to have even tried to keep up with him then. After we finished, Dick, Larry and I went over and got the five pups and brought them over to the main dog tunnel and turned them loose. They will be there the time being for exercise till we get their tunnel dug. We only have about one thousand feet more to go, since there are eight dog teams and each one gets a tunnel.

We had our Saturday night show, "Brother Rat." Saw it in Indianapolis at the Circle Theater. Got a message from Alda—very sweet.

Sunday, March 24

Up at 6:00 o'clock this morning. Big Easter holiday, some took off for L.A. Frazier got up and prepared breakfast for us. Nib, Pappy, Chuck, Toney (Tony), Shirley, Doc and myself went in the tractor. Dick, Arnold and Vernon took Dick's dog team. We pulled out of here about 8:30 after having some trouble with the tractor. The darn governor freezes and it takes some time to thaw it out. That thing has caused more grief and trouble. If we pull the throttle half way back when we put "Dolly" up for the night, it will freeze that way. Then when starting it in the morning the motor runs faster. If the throttle isn't pulled back at all then the governor remains shut and the motor will not be accelerated enough to even start. After a half dozen tries there is nothing to do except get out the Von Prague and go to work. Well, this morning the throttle was pulled about one-fourth inch back so we at least got her started, but it took ages for the water to heat up enough to thaw out the governor. Finally we got underway, tractor going in reverse, one sled and the caboose. I drove. It was fairly cold out, being ten degrees, fairly cloudy and hazy, also a little fog. But I was able to see one and sometimes two flags ahead. We followed the trail we took last Sunday. I have never seen such a crooked trail. If I hadn't cut corners a little and straightened out some, we would have still been en route. None of us had watches, but I think we covered the six miles in about two and a half hours. Dick and the other fellows were already there. We lost no time in our hunt for canned fruit, jellies and preserves. Nib and Chuck worked on that angle while Pappy R. headed for the radio shack to find a few things needed. Doc Frazier went to the science building and started looting while Toney and I took in the Admiral's old quarters. That darn Toney really can find things. He hadn't been there five minutes before he had found a bowl. How we missed it last week I don't know. I do know at least a half a dozen of us hunted in there and I don't see how it was missed. I still think Toney planted it. He also found some expedition stamps, which he gave me. We didn't stay long at L.A. because Sig was having a big Easter meal for us and we were to be back at 4:00 o'clock. It didn't take long for the boys to load their plunder which ranged from old lanterns, chairs, tobacco and light wiring, to food. Decided to take a short cut and not follow the trail, but cut across country going in a straight line from Old L.A. to present L.A. We headed out well but ended up almost in the pressure ice. I had seen the camp several times but we went down in a valley and I lost sight of it and took, or rather mistook, some pressure ice for our camp. Visibility was very poor, and besides it was getting late afternoon. My heart dropped down in my shoes when I finally came to, realized that I was going the wrong direction, more west than northeast. I finally got squared around and maybe you don't think that little dark spot, camp, was a joyous welcome sight. We got in about 5:30 to a wonderful turkey dinner, dressing and all, with cherry pie for dessert.

Later on in the evening we had strawberry shortcake and coffee. Birdseye strawberries, and were they ever good. Just to enter into the spirit of things, I passed out cigars. A happy Easter. Temperature coming back was minus fifteen degrees.

Monday, March 25

Up at 9:00 o'clock, and believe it or not, one of the Antartic blizzards. Yes, we get one about every two days. The wind velocity was around twenty-eight or thirty, which was pretty bad. It was impossible to see "the nose on your face," so much drift. It was fairly warm out, about eight degrees above. The trouble with this country is when it is warm enough to work comfortably there has to be a wind, which at first blows gently, just enough to freeze your face, increasing till another blizzard is on hand. Spent most of the day in my bunk, reading and sleeping. Did take time out long enough to make a pipe holder. Quite a piece of art—made of plywood and copper tubing. I thoroughly enjoy these days, resting, listening to good music, reading an excellent book. Right now I am brushing up on my German, also trying to improve my vocabulary, which I might say can stand working over. Been getting to bed about midnight every night—getting my eight hours of rest.

Tuesday, March 26

Perfect out today. At least no wind, and the sun was shining brightly. Worked this morning along the south side of the science building—digging, shoveling snow, clearing a place for Court's balloon release, which is about sixteen by sixteen. The whole gang was on the job as Paul called on us fellows working on Dog Town to help. It was actually hot while working and we all stripped down to our undershirts. Next we worked on the other side of the building digging, clearing away the drift prior to bringing the science cache which consists of one-third Court's, one-fourth Perk's, and one-fourth Earl's. Larry and I have one small box.

After lunch Dick, Coach, Doug and I got the main hauling sled and started to move science boxes. Paul and Larry were on the receiving end. I don't think I ever did so much pulling and tugging in my whole life. I certainly take my hat off to the dogs—it's really remarkable, wonderful how they can pull such heavy loads. There we were, five or six supposedly strong men, and several times we had to throw off boxes because we couldn't budge the load. It got cold later in the afternoon and by 6:00 o'clock had reached minus twenty-one degrees. It was hell working then, as by that time we had brought in all of the cache and were nailing up the superstructure which is to hold up the tarp. I was using the saw and my hand got so cold that I had a hard time opening it to release my grip. Paul saved my nose several times this afternoon. He would say "The tip of your nose is a little white." Then I would work on it for a few minutes, restoring it to its normal color, which happens to be a wind burned, sun burned, chapped red. We had hoped to get the tarp up tonight but we got so cold, dinner overtook us, and besides it was getting a little dark. We just decided to take a chance on a blizzard. Paul thinks it is too cold for one, but contemplates that we will have one day after tomorrow. Some of the fellows are playing a football game. Gil and Perk are the players, but Mac, Coach, Earl, Pappy and Jack (H) are officials and hecklers.

Wednesday, March 27

Beautiful day but I can't quite understand why all such days have to be so darn cold. When we got up this morning it was minus thirty-three and seven tenths degrees, dropping off to minus twenty-five degrees for most of the day. We worked outside but had to come in often to get warm, to thaw out. Most of the fellows had trouble with their nose and face. Jack Bursey got a pretty bad case of frostbite on the left side of his face. Dick and Larry finished covering the science cache, while most of the other fellows worked on Vernon's cache, digging it out and bringing the boxes in along side the machinist building. I did a little work out in my clothing cache, putting up some more bamboo supports and getting squared around in general. I started a long-put-off inventory and did manage to get four boxes completed. I don't know why I am putting up so many supports as there is hardly any drift on my side. The wind seems to pick up the snow and blow it over the roof onto the tarp covering the food cache. There is quite a high, deep drift there. I did manage to get down to the rugs, so now each cubicle has a nice small rug, ever so inconspicuous on the floor. They really do seem to cheer the place up, add a little color, but one has to look twice in order to ever see them. Checked up on the electric razor situation and find that there are enough to go around. That takes care of what might have been a pretty ticklish situation. It is impossible around here to give one fellow something without the others getting equal.

Pappy Reece has done wonders with the radio room in the science building. It is complete to the last shelf. Clay and he had the receivers on last night, worked perfectly. Clay, Walt and Jack (B) finished the outside work yesterday, which just about brings the radio gang up to date. They are ready to go on the air any time. It was really some job to put up all of the poles, wire, etc. I know Clay is thankful to see that part of the work is finished. Had our show tonight—"I Am The Law." Full attendance, with Gil holding bank night—as usual, candy. Had quite a bull session tonight after the theater, Earl, Larry, Murray, Fitz and myself. The topics of conversation changed so swiftly that it would be impossible to jot them down and remember them all. I moved Alda's picture tonight to a position of advantage. She is on the shelf right by my bunk, while my folk's pictures are on the other shelf. It makes it cozy and home like. I always feel happy, rested and secure when I am up in my bunk. It is now 12:00 midnight and time for bed.

108

Wiener just finished his week of mess duty and Charles (S) beat the pan this morning awaking us at 7:45 on the dot—breakfast at 8:00 o'clock. Since all of the caches are in, there are only two major jobs, one being Dog Town and the other, digging in the planes. So after breakfast, Dick, H. H., Ray, Malcolm, Coach and myself started to dig a tunnel for Klondike's team. These have to be about ninety-six feet long, as the dogs have six foot chains which give them ample room for exercise, etc. We put each crate twelve feet apart, staggering them. The whole job looked hopeless to me. It was cold (minus ten degrees), windy and snowing, and five men to dig almost one thousand feet of tunnel, besides digging in the crates as we planned to set them in the wall. Well, I did something I very seldom do. I went to Paul asking for more help, saying that if it was to be an "all hands" job that we should have more men, since it would be fairly certain that we should have to work on the plane. The dog men take a beating anyway, having to help with everyone's work around here besides having to do their own.

It's really getting too cold to have the dogs outside. I think they should have been taken care of before a few other things. Well, my plea brought some action because after lunch we had some recruits—Doc Frazier, Pappy G, Larry, Earl, Sarge, Griff and Pete. So we decided to start another one, and by quitting time showed so much progress that we will be able to do two tomorrow. Griff and Pete will finish the two by digging in the crates, having put in place five. Also, Dick, who is securing the tarp, will continue as the roof is not quite finished. But the hard part of it is over, the digging. Just think, only seven more to go. It was very nasty out all day, especially this afternoon. My face got bitten a couple of times. In fact, I think my right cheek froze. As for my nose, the tip of it was white all the time. One of the fellows was always yelling for me to rub my nose, that it was turning. While we are out working we watch each other's faces, and if we see one getting a little white, we pat the fellow, and he immediately administers rubbing to the offended member or part of his face. It's quite a sport. My face is so sore now, burns like fire, and my nose has started to peel.

What a disappointment—tonight we were not able to get the mail bag program. We all look forward to Fridays. Every other one means that we are contacted from home, our loved ones. I know that Alda would have written me, as well as the folks and Bob. I hope that they repeat the program next Friday. They predicted this calm which has been noticed here for the past two weeks. Magnetic storms have certainly affected the band. I talked to Phil and he said that it would probably clear, open up in three or four days. He has sixty messages to send, an accumulation of two weeks. Clay's radio station went into commission today, but he couldn't officially report "on the air" because he couldn't contact Washington. They tried for an hour or so to get the mail bag program, but not a peep. He did get some Limey station, but that didn't help us any. Someone overslept this morning because Sig was late in serving breakfast—9:00 o'clock, with half the morning gone. Larry said that he didn't think there was much use putting on his shoes and going out to work because it wouldn't be long till lunch. But no one gave him any encouragement so after breakfast we were all at it, working in the tunnels in Dog Town.

Sarge, Coach and I finished digging the tunnel we were working on. Then Dick and I put on the roof, covered it with tarp. We then drove in stakes in front of the crates so that the dogs would not be able to pull them loose, tear them out of the wall. If they would ever get loose it would be too bad. A lot of damage can be done. Last expedition a dog pulled the crate out, got loose and killed three dogs. Well, we just weren't taking any chances. We brought in Berlin's team—what a bunch of mules. Old Navy, Al's dog, is lead, then Prince, Dick, Tuffy, etc. They are really a bunch of scrappers. If one of his dogs were to get loose in the tunnel there would certainly be first degree murder, or at least attempt to kill. Between them, Prince and Blackie have licked every dog on the team. I wonder when they will meet. Well, we are getting our blizzard for the week. Right now it is blowing like mad. It was warm today up to around 3:00 o'clock, and when Dick and I were bringing over Berlin's team I froze my hands—had the chains wrapped around them to hold back the dogs, cutting off circulation. Certainly was painful. If Zeke hadn't come to my rescue I think my hands would have fallen off. Took me at least an hour to revive them, now they burn like fury. The temperature has ranged from minus ten degrees to minus fifteen degrees all day.

Saturday, March 30
I don't think anyone could possibly predict weather down here. Last night when I turned in it was a perfect night, cold, clear and no

wind. But this morning a forty-five mile wind greets us. A real blizzard, worst one we have had. The tarp over the food tunnel really took a beating, the wind tore it loose in one place. The science cache was half full of snow. The tarp came loose at this end. It's really a wonder we didn't lose at least one of our roofs. I guess lady luck was certainly with us. I am glad I took pains with my cache. I took a look at it this morning, tight as a drum. It was so nasty out that Paul and Dick thought it best to bring the rest of the dogs in. So Dick, Larry, Jack B. and myself went out after them. The rest of the dog men prepared a place, or rather places, to put them. Well, it was no picnic. We had to use a rope so that we wouldn't get lost from each other. We looked over all of the teams, deciding to take Dick's since none of them were in immediate danger, none of them were drifted under. It's really no fun working out in such weather, and we had to chop with an axe, dig and pull to get the tethering line and stake loose. It was fairly simple to move them once they were free, taking all nine at once, one of us at the head, two spaced out along the line, one of us at the end of the line. From there on all we had to do was let the dogs pull us along. Sometimes they got a little too tangled up, but on the whole we didn't have any real trouble. Going back toward the building we had to face the wind. By the time we got back with the first team my face was a sheet of ice, my left eyelid was frozen shut, due to the ice on my eyelash. My beard (which, incidentally, I shaved off today) was frozen to the bottom neckpiece of my parka hood. Then the minute we got in, the ice would melt, my eye would open up, and we went out again, only six more to get.

The Coach helped us for a little while. It was really funny. He stumbled coming back and was dragged aways. Later in the house he told us that they must have been a very good pulling team to drag him along. Well, it's hard to imagine seven dog teams in our none too wide tunnels. They are everywhere, strung out from the front door clear back through the Palace to Dog Town, then one team is chained along the tunnel to the housing cache, the science cache and a whole string of dogs runs from the door of the science building to the machinist building. Every place one wants to go he has to run a gauntlet of dogs and one has to watch his step because if he doesn't step on a dog, which is likely, he might get snapped at. And oh, yes, the smell is going to be none too pleasant. But, if anyone could see the dogs they would feel well repaid for any inconvenience because never have I seen such a happy lot, not a peep out of them. They are so happy to be in out of the wind and I don't blame them. I know that I feel much happier now that they are in.

The first thing this morning I had to go down to Bursey's tunnel to get the axe (he brought his team in last night). Well, his tunnel was not quite completed so he had a few leaks and the place was really drifted in. Most of the dogs could get in and out of their crates all right but King, the lead dog, was snowed in. All that was out was his head. I dug him out and cleaned it so he could go in and out of his crate. He certainly was happy. I was well repaid for my very small effort, just to watch him. He was one very happy dog. After we got all of the dogs in and I had thawed out a little, for some reason I got started on my clarinet, cleaning it and putting on some new pads, etc. What a mess. I took it all apart and had keys and spring strewn all over the place. I felt pretty proud because I got it all back together again, and it plays. Today, big Saturday, and baths are in order. I took one and even washed all my dirty clothes. Used the washing machine for the first time, not bad. Saw "Dodge City" for the third time, gets better every time. Wind died down by supper time but has now started to blow again.

Sunday, March 31

Today being Sunday and a day of rest, we did not get up till 10:00 o'clock. It's been a long, lazy day, chicken dinner at 3:00 o'clock. Cleaned the cubicle this morning, took my sleeping bag out for an airing, also packed my extra clothing in my duffle bag and put outside. Decided to give out the electric razors today. Why today? I don't know, but anyway most of the fellows are now proud owners of a Remington or Rand razor. I had quite a time deciding who should get which, and to make it a little easier I opened each box and took out the price tags, which were $7.50 and $14.75, and I know that if the fellows saw the difference in prices there really would be hell to pay. And since we have twenty of the Rands and only fifteen of the Remingtons, and thirty-three men, well you can imagine. After dinner everyone sat around, smoked, shot the bull or played games ranging from Monopoly to Sorry to Bridge. Ike, Larry, Murray and I played Contract Bridge. Ike knows the game pretty well, so I should profit by being his partner. Incidentally, we took them. We had a buffet supper about 8:00 o'clock, then I got mixed up in a "quizbook." Several of us were trying our luck. By guessing on some, I did fairly well. The wind let up a little during the day, but is acting up again.

Who would have ever thought I would be here on April Fools
Day 1940? I still can't believe it. Al got a message from Doc Wolford saying that there would be a pretty good chance of my getting
a scholarship or fellowship at L.A. State. I hope so. I would like to
do my Ph.D. work there and who knows, because of this experience, etc., I might be able to get a fairly substantial stipend. Just
another one of those days, blizzard. Wind velocity at 8:00 o'clock
A.M. was forty-five miles, which isn't a very gentle breeze. And we
would have to fill the snow melter! The starboard side takes it one
week and the port side the next week. In the first place we had
quite a time trying to decide which of our two tunnel exits to go
out of—they were neither one too inviting. But it had to be done, so
Coach, Dick and I went out. I happened to have the saw so I had
the misfortune to be elected "block sawer" which merely meant
that I couldn't walk in with snow but had to stay out and take it,
and I might mention that it was no fun. It was almost impossible
to stand up, the wind being very persistent. The snow flakes and ice
were almost unbearable, like a thousand pins and needles piercing
my face. I had to keep my eyes closed most of the time to protect
from the penetrating wind-driven ice. But when I would have to
open them to start a new series of blocks, it seemed that all of the
snow would concentrate there. I can assure you that I didn't open
them very often. It was a Godsend when Fitz finally told me that
we had enough and for me to get in and thaw my face. It was a
mass of ice. My eyes have bothered me all day—a dull ache. Doc
Frazier just now put some salve in them and they feel better. The
wind velocity at 11:00 o'clock A.M. was fifty-two miles per hour. I
didn't venture out during the afternoon. Instead, Larry, Coach, Griff
and myself played Bridge. Ike and I had two thousand to the good
when we stopped. It is now midnight and although the wind has
let up some (twenty-five miles) it is still giving a good account of
itself. Fitz just came in from a walk around and said that the whole
camp is surrounded by seven foot drifts, that it's possible to walk
right up on the roof over the food tunnels. Poor Nib will really have
to do some digging if he wants to use the tractor when and if things
ever clear up.

Woke up to a beautiful day. Sun was shining, sky clear, temperature around zero and wind velocity about eight or ten miles per

hour. Right after breakfast I hurried out and took a few pictures around camp. The old cook tent was half blown down and one of the tents used as sleeping quarters seemed to have a very dangerous lean to it. I suppose that another good storm will finish it. It so happened that Gray, one of H.H.'s dogs which had just recently been bred, was in the old cook tent. She didn't seem to enjoy her predicament and I imagine that she was quite panic stricken during the blizzard. Dick discovered the tent last night when he made the rounds to see if the dogs were all okay. Nib and I cleaned out all of the snow in Jack B's tunnel. It took the two of us all morning and we really worked. There is nothing that tires one out any more than shoveling snow. Since we had only one opening we had to relay it along, which meant we handled every shovelful about eight or ten times, besides trying to keep from hitting the dogs. I guess that they are just naturally inquisitive and they wouldn't stay in their crates for anything. We did find, however, that by letting a shovelful fall where it may, which means on a dog's back, they soon took to their kennels, at least for as long as we were working. But if we should happen to stop to talk, lean on the shovel a little (which happened very seldom!!), out they would pop again until another shovelful would send them to safety. Our biggest offender was Pat, and nothing could convince her that she should get out of the way. So finally we took pity and quit throwing snow on her. Just like a female, I guess—either a little too curious or else just stubborn. Or maybe it's just the wolf in her. Most of Jack's dogs are part wolf, so maybe that is where Pat got her strain of curiosity. Dopey could almost pass as a timber wolf, I think he is almost all wolf. King, the lead dog, is just plain dog, I think. He is strawberry in color. He, by the way, bit my hand while we were in Philly. I do not trust him any too far, but we got along all right today.

Speaking of bites, Coach got bit yesterday while we were carrying snow blocks, but it couldn't be helped. He stepped on the dog, Mickey, one of H.H.'s dogs, and the dog bit him on the leg. Ike said that it was the first time that he had ever been bitten by a dog and what burned him up was that Mickey didn't give him time to say he was sorry. It was hard walking through the tunnels where the dogs are tied, especially after coming in with glasses all iced up or else blinded by the ice or snow. They took the dogs back outside today, which is one relief. I hope that it doesn't blizzard again till at least we get the last tunnel dug, because dogs are a little messy. It was comical though to see them, to see their beds. They made beds out of almost anything they could get to. Rusty, one of Zeke's dogs, had pulled down a bag of charcoal and curled around on top of it. Others managed to find paper, pieces of plank, etc., anything just so that it kept them off the snow.

After lunch I went out and worked on dog tunnel number three, which is of different structure than the other two mainly because we were running out of bamboo used to build the tarp roof. This tunnel is about eighteen to twenty-four inches across the top slanting down, and in about two feet where it widens out to four feet or so to the floor. By such a construction we can use any scrap lumber, odds and ends of bamboo, and one three foot strip of tarp to cover it. This type is a little harder to cut out, to dig, but it's just a case of "have to." Murray has been working nights now, observing Aurora. Tonight he sent Perkins to tell us to come out and see it, but by the time we got out, it was gone. However, it was an extremely beautiful night, clear, stars out and on the west the array of color of the sunset was still visible even though it was 10:00 o'clock.

Wednesday, April 3

I have been so completely tired the last couple of days that I am afraid that I have lost my enthusiasm for Antarctica, the Expedition. I am so darn fed up of work—shoveling snow, manual labor, day after day. And by the looks of things it will be at least another three weeks before we are really "wintered in." If only Paul would make these last two jobs "all hands" then we could all do a little of our own work, have a little time to ourselves. As it stands now everyone seems to be doing his own work which leaves about five to eight men free for work in the tunnels. I was under the impression that digging dog tunnels was to be "all hands," but when the work actually started "all hands" certainly disappeared, vanished in other words, kept scarce. But I guess it's a little late in the game now to mind because it's been that way all along since Boston, about six of us did all of the work. The whole thing is kind of one sided as only a few will really get something out of this expedition. I could write a book on the subject and since I am tired and sleepy I had better not get started now, I'll save it for the winter night. Finished dog tunnel number three and Malcolm's dogs are now installed, happy with their new home. We also have tunnel number four well under way and should finish it tomorrow. I don't suppose I should really feel badly as we only have five more to go, then dig in the planes and we are all done. There is really nothing to it. The show tonight was "Torchy Blane in China Town." What a flop. Well, one thing, we have seen it and it is certain (unanimously) that it will not be called back, at least not on popular demand.

Thursday, April 4

I am afraid this is going to be sweet and short as it is late and I am tired—what a perfect combination. I can never seem to get to bed before midnight or later. The bad part about it though is getting up in the morning. My evenings are really very full. By the time I finish studying Twenhofel, reading some such books as "Discovery, Beyond the Roaring Frontier," etc., writing in my journal (I prefer to call it a journal), play Bridge, shoot the bull and raid the galley, well, it's getting late. Got quite a lot of work done, finished tunnel number four and have number five practically completed. We put Perk's team in number four along with two of Vernon's dogs which were shedding their coats, and one of Ray's, who was a little thin, probably due to the cold weather. I got so darn mad today I couldn't see straight. It just burns me up to see any dumb animal mistreated or neglected, not cared for. Perk's lead dog, Tosk, looked bad and his whole team is thin. Perk has certainly been remiss in his duty. Well, as usual, when I get burned up about something I act, so I went to Paul and talked the whole thing over with him. He said that he had noticed the team. He said that there was no excuse for such cruelty. What he is going to do about it I don't know. Afterward I felt kind of badly about running to him, but darn it, he is so engrossed with his own work he hardly knows that anything else exists. I am really surprised at Perk. He seemed a rather nice fellow. I didn't think it was possible for anyone to be so inhumane, brutal. I can't understand why something hadn't been done about it. It stands to reason that Perk is no "dog driver" and that he hasn't got "dog sense," especially when he says that as far as he is concerned they could be dog meat. Dick says it's a damned shame and that he knows Tosk is a good lead dog because he has driven him before— so it must be Perk.

Friday, April 5

Hoped and prayed last night for a blizzard for today (minus twenty-three degrees). Got one, but as luck would have it, it was just a mediocre one, not bad enough to keep us inside. Hence, we finished tunnels number five and number six. Boy, just three more to go and one of these will be a short one for the five pups. At that, it was rather nasty working out today, the wind was blowing fairly hard, about eighteen or so, just enough to drift a little. And when one was working topside of the tunnel he really took a beating on his face. I had to duck in the tunnel a couple of times because my face started to freeze. We put Murray's team in number five. He has seven dogs, a good team with the exception of two dogs which are thin. They look overly thin because they are shedding their coats. I think that Murray is taking proper care of his team, feeding them enough. We had a big gang out working today—ten men, Phil had joined us. Since West Base radio has gone into commission, Snow Cruiser radio is out. Phil and Clay have had some sort of squabble and the outcome is Phil is out, his radio decommissioned, dead. I guess the two interfere with each other, static, etc., although Phil says that Clay just doesn't want to share time with him. Phil said today that he would like to be an operator over here if they would let him, but evidently they won't or something. It seems a shame but I suppose something will work out and all concerned will be satisfied. Evidently Clay has good reasons because I know that he would play square. Anyway Phil really worked today, first real physical work he has done since he has been down here. Also he said that it's the first day that he has had three meals. His appetite has picked up already. Got a message from Alda tonight wishing me a happy birthday. I forgot all about my birthday. She said she hadn't heard from me for over four weeks and was worried. Gosh I hope that she gets the message that I sent yesterday. Played Bridge tonight with Ike, Larry and Murray. Ike and I cleaned them again. Either my Bridge game has improved or else it's just Ike's influence.

Saturday, April 6

Today was a repetition of yesterday, just enough wind to make it uncomfortable yet the temperature was only at zero or a few degrees below. We certainly made progress, finished tunnel number seven and also a short tunnel thirty feet long to house the puppies. We put Butler's team in number 7, which leaves only two teams, one belonging to H.H. and the other being Dick's. Besides those tunnels, the boys dug number eight which is practically done. It kept Dick and me busy breaking up boxes, old crates, etc., for cover to be used as supports which hold the tarp. It takes about three hours to cover a tunnel, and I might say we don't waste any time. We have sort of worked up a system. After spacing the pieces of boards and blocks about two feet apart all along the tunnel, we then cut two strips of tarp and put those in place. Then we go along each side putting large blocks of snow on the edge of the tarp and also along the middle where the two tarps overlap. After that we shovel loose snow and smaller chunks along the sides and on the middle, completely covering the tarp. It is necessary to use larger blocks because we tried at first to use loose snow but found that the wind would move it almost as fast as we could shovel. And even if we did get a little ahead, during the course of the night it was sure to do damage and we would find the whole tarp bare and the edges exposed. It certainly is a good feeling to know that we have one more tunnel to go as it won't take long to finish number 8, and there are only four more crates to go in it.

The show tonight was a rather spoiled "Dark Victory," which is a fine picture, but the effect was disturbed, bungled due to the fact, first, that one whole reel was missing. Besides that, right at the most impressive part of the picture Clay's voice poured out of the loudspeaker—he was calling Boston, as he had scheduled with his wife. Well, there was nothing for us to do but wait. After the show we had a small bull session—Butler, Perk, Larry, Fitz, Earl and myself, had quite an enlightening conversation, subjects or topics mostly centered around those good old days—college.

Sunday, April 7

Twelve hours of heavenly sleep. I don't think that I even moved, and what woke me at 11:30 I still don't know. The place was as quiet as a graveyard, except for whispered voices from the galley, which I was not conscious of till I had been awake some few minutes. But I think the smell of bacon frying finally moved me to action. From the looks of the scene in the galley I knew it was Sunday and that Sig was not about. There was Doc Frazier working the stove with Toney (Tony) as his assistant, with three or four fellows standing around eating or waiting for seconds. Fried bread and bacon. The only variety we get in the mornings are the days that Sig is absent. Doc is a good cook, and to show him my appreciation I ate five pieces of bread. Oh yes, we had plums, of which I had two bowls full, unheard of when Sig rules the galley. That is one reason why I like to see Sundays come around, besides sleeping in, we eat royally, with Doc's ever "plenty more, boys, come and get it, all you can eat." After breakfast got back in my bunk and read, rested, and even slept some more, just plain lazy. This was the kind of day to be idle, remain inactive, because at noon the temperature was minus thirty-five degrees and now at midnight it is minus fifty-one degrees.

Earlier in the evening I was lying on my bunk deeply absorbed in "Beyond The Roaring Frontier," when Vernon came in and excitedly informed me that Clay had an Indianapolis amateur radio operator, so I jumped down and tore over to the radio shack. Clay gave me the phone, I took it and said "hello," of all the dumb things. Well, after some seconds I got squared around and the fellows got quieted down. Whenever one tries to carry on a private conversation there are always ten or twelve fellows hanging around the shack and I guess that "hello" kind of struck them funny, and I guess it was kind of sad. I gave the amateur our phone number, folks' name, etc., and lo and behold, a few minutes later he came back with a message from them. It was 2:30 A.M. at home and Dad probably answered the phone. I bet they were surprised. The operator (I will have to look him up in the amateur book) said that my father answered but that he could hear my mother's voice beside him. They were both fine and had sent me a birthday message. I will probably get it tomorrow night. It was a shame that I couldn't talk to them directly, but the fellow did not have a telephone connection. I swear it was just like a long distance call, I couldn't think what to say, but the whole thing was so sudden like. I hope to contact them again soon and talk to them, maybe with a little thought I will be able to talk sensibly.

Monday, April 8

Someone slipped up this morning as breakfast was an hour late, 9:00 o'clock, which meant that we did not get out to the tunnels till 10:30. Before I went out I got some of the fellows some mitts, innersoles, etc. Boy, it was hard to work today, very difficult to breathe, and with the least exercise, just walking out, I found that I was inclined to breathe hard. The temperature was thirty-five and six tenths degrees below zero and what work we did was slow. That is, we couldn't keep up the pace because if we worked too fast and got to breathing too hard or fast, panting, there would be a pain in the chest and there was always the danger of getting frosted lungs. Personally I didn't take any chances. But anyway Dick and I finished covering tunnel number eight, and spent the rest of the time shoveling off the roof of the hole dug for the blubber and chop house site, which had more or less covered in since we had only a temporary roof on it in the first place. The Coach, Larry and the fellows working with them almost completed digging the last tunnel, number nine, it will probably take a couple of hours in the morning to finish it up.

Tuesday, April 9

Who would ever have thought that I would be spending my twenty-fifth birthday down on continent Antarctic—West Base, Little America. It's hard to believe, but I guess it's true because I just finished talking again, indirectly, to the folks, and I also received a birthday message greeting from them, which was really fine. Talking home is getting to be a daily thing with me. Last night and here again tonight, and besides they are to be at Cliff's opera house on Sunday and I will be able to talk to them personally. After two times at the "phone" I find I am becoming a little more composed but my voice still seems a little forced or strained. Some of the fellows here have been talking to their wives, girls, etc., and here dad and mother have been listening in for at least two hours.

We finished our last tunnel today, number nine, which makes me so happy I would almost like to go out on a binge. Now all that is left to do is dig in those infernal planes, the Condor and the Beechcraft. I understand that it is to be an all hands job. If it isn't, or if as many show up as did for the dog tunnel work, I don't imagine that we will get done before total darkness, the Antarctic winter night, is on us. However, I will wait and see before I really condemn any good intentions. I do know, though, that since it has been getting colder, less and less of the fellows have been showing up for outside work. It all boils down that the same six or so do all of the work—the rest hide out. Well, anyway, I will know more after tomorrow.

Wednesday thru Sunday, April 10-14

Well, I will take back anything I said yesterday or last night because Paul really got the boys on the job. With the exception of the cook and Clay, all hands turned out. Clay had been working getting ready for the Saturday night broadcast and since he did most of his work during the wee hours of the morning—well, that was excused.

Even the snow cruiser gang was on hand, but that's explainable because Pete would, I suppose, like to get help with covering the Beechcraft. Well, Wednesday, Thursday and Friday was just one

120

big nightmare—up at 6:00, breakfast, then out in the cold for nine or ten hours. We would come in at 10:00 and 3:00 for coffee. As luck would have it, the temperature would have to be around forty-five and fifty-three degrees below, which doesn't exactly add to the beauty of things.

It was really a fairly simple task to cover the Condor, because after all she is only about an eighty-two foot wing spread and eighteen feet from the ski to top wing, sixty feet from nose to tail—in fact, nothing to it, and some fellows said shucks, it will only take one day. Well, here it is Sunday and the job isn't finished yet. Chuck and the carpenters are still working on the structure to hold the tarp roof, however, we finished building the walls Friday. The building consists of walls made of snow blocks, and it's quite a job to build such walls eighteen or twenty feet high and have them at all steady. So to get around that, we made them four blocks thick. Those walls will stand forever.

Well, I don't know how I got mixed up in this whole thing but anyway I started to lay the blocks for the wall to go around the tail. Nib was cutting, and Joe, Chuck, Toney and the rest were bringing me blocks. It's not quite clear what happened, but I guess that my wall was a little off the bias, because when I got up the sixteen feet and was trying to take a block from Toney, some how my feet got a little twisted up. I started to fall and made a grab for the wall, which was the wrong thing to do—the whole thing came down. I threw my shovel about thirty feet and came down out of there in a hurry with about a dozen blocks right at my heels. Oh, well, all in a day's work. It didn't take long to rebuild it and you can bet that it was as straight as a die.

The work would not have been so bad except for the cold. The same procedure every time I go out—first the right side of my nose starts to turn white, then the left side, my right cheek follows, also the left, and lastly my chin. By that time I give up and make a bee-line for camp. It's useless to try to rub the frost out, I have tried it. It just prolongs it a little, besides, you freeze your hand and can't get it back into your mitt, so you have to go in anyway. So what's the use? Right now the right side of my nose is one nice blister and sore as a boil. But about everyone in camp got bit.

Friday while some of the fellows were putting the finishing touches to the Condor the rest of us worked on the Beechcraft. Child's play. We had the four walls up by noon. Since we only had to go up from seven feet to ten feet we only used single thicknesses.

121

After lunch we covered the Beechcraft and part of the Condor (that is, the wings). Chuck and the fellows hadn't finished putting the upright around the tail. At 4:00 sharp we all went in and got ready to listen to the mail bag program. I got a message from mother and dad, Alda, and Bob—they never fail me. I look forward to hearing from them.

Since we worked like mad to get the planes dug under, Paul said we could have a holiday both Saturday and Sunday, which was a life saver. The fellows were really tired and everyone did a good job, worked hard. So Saturday it isn't any wonder that the majority of us slept till 10:00 or so. In fact, about 9:00 o'clock this place was like a morgue. Oh, yes, except for an occasional snore or mumble of some character or another—the sleep of the righteous. I needn't say that I was among those late sleepers, that's to be taken for granted —I got up at 11:30. Didn't do much during the day but clean up, took my sleeping bag out, brushed it, swept up in the cubicle. General all-around house cleaning, and read a little.

Finished reading "Magnificent Obsession" by Douglas, which I think was one of the finest novels I have ever read. One wouldn't exactly call it a novel, as the plot is not cut and dried as most novels. It's more or less like the man's inner thoughts coming forth—his ideas. We saw "Confession of a Nazi Spy" which was a fairly stirring picture. I know that afterward there were little groups scattered all over the place discussing spies in the U.S., the war, etc. Some were arguing. Oh yes, and Wednesday night we had Charles Boyer in "Love Affair," which will certainly be on our list for reshowing. I had seen it several times before and I still like it.

Sunday we all slept late again. Breakfast, when we got up, consisted of whatever we could find. I finally mustered up enough courage or something to get up at 11:00 o'clock, ate, and went out to the machine shop to do a washing and take a bath. I really did a large washing, consisting of my dress shirts, soiled dungaree pants, P.J.'s, socks, etc. I didn't finish till 3:00 o'clock, almost was late for dinner. Talked to dad and mother, it was good to hear their voices. I am so glad that they are both well. I guess I haven't quite mastered this thing yet, talking over the radio, but I hope to be able to say all that I want to say. I still feel rather funny having so many fellows around.

We all over slept this morning, getting up at 8:30, breakfast at 9:30. First job of the day was to fill the snow melter. It hadn't been filled since we started on the airplanes. In fact, the bunk house hadn't been swept for three days and we even ran out of drinking water—everyone was just too tired to care. I worked with Pappy Reece today, hence becoming an electrician's assistant. He was getting ready to wire the dog tunnels, so since I could put off my clothing inventory a few more days without any serious effects I thought it would be a good thing to help him. Also, he asked me if I would about a week ago. We decided to put three lights in each tunnel and one light at the head of each crossing of tunnels. So we were busy all afternoon measuring out wire splicing on bulb connections and also trying to each complete wiring a switch so that each dog driver can turn on or off the lights only during the day.

We thought that we would be able to put the wire up today, but we barely got the things rigged up before dinner.

Tonight I washed my hair, which was a major undertaking especially since I have so much. Three or four of us have decided not to cut our hair, well right now mine is growing way down my neck and getting curly.

Paul has propounded another theory as to why Antarctica, which appears to be the real McCoy as far as geology is concerned. He has lateral forces working around a resistant mass, folding, etc., then a terrific pressure or force hits upon the resistant mass causing sinking and the Horst fault, which is known to exist. I think he has something there, the whole thing sounds reasonable, not a mere coincidence.

Tuesday, April 16

I guess I am a full fledged electrician. Pappy R. in jumping down from a ladder last night hurt his arch, crippled him up so that he can hardly walk. So I did the wiring of the dog tunnels today. I feel pretty proud, I spliced into hot wires, the main line, without even one shock. It's fairly easy, all you have to do is remember not to bare both lines at once and also to not let both ends of the wire touch. In other words, just don't grab on to both ends of the wire at once. Oh, yes, I had one casualty today—a burnt out fuse, which was not entirely my fault. The switch for Doug's tunnel evidently was bad. After completing the wiring, I turned the lights on. Not much happened but a dim flicker in his tunnel, a short which blew out the fuse. That is, I thought it was the switch, but after trying a couple more with the same thing happening I gave up and decided to try again tomorrow. My hands were getting a little cold as all of the work had to be done without gloves. After talking to Pappy he thinks that possibly it might be one of the light sockets, so I will try them tomorrow. The first one we did was Warner's tunnel. We made one mistake in that we uncoiled the wire along the floor and before we knew what it was all about, nine nice little dogs pounced upon the wire and proceeded to chew the hell out of it. We had to rewrap most of it because nice little teeth marks bared the wire here and there. Well, we learned a lesson—you can bet that we didn't give the next bunch a chance.

After lunch our side filled the snow melter which I guess is getting to be a habit I would like to get out of, but I am afraid that I am doomed. At least for a year.

Wednesday, April 17

Wind picked up a little last night and this morning—a nice friendly blizzard which proceeded to tear off the tarp which covered the Beechcraft, fill in the excavation dug for the blubber house and chop house which only yesterday Dick had taken off the temporary roof to build the structure for the building, etc. Who would have thought that it would blizzard. Dick didn't. But after a full day of digging, redoing work, I think that Dick and Jack B. will never trust old Antarctica again. Oh, yes, several other minor things such as snow drifting in through cracks in several tunnels, and F. Alton not being able to find his snow measuring sticks which every late afternoon he religiously makes the rounds to each one. These same snow gauges we so industrially painted on the *North Star*. Also, Fitz almost got lost coming back from his shack. The only thing that saved him was a light. Where it came from, whose it was he doesn't know, but such is the life in Antarctic in a blizzard.

I finished wiring the dog tunnels this morning and found the trouble in Doug's. It happened to be a punk socket. This afternoon I did a little inside work, helped Pappy finish wiring the science lab building. His foot isn't any better, but he is hobbling around on one crutch. Just came in from talking to Paul, I am still convinced that he has really found something. In fact, I am so interested that I am going to try to name the various poles, I think it can be done. Show night, so I helped Nib with the dishes, also breaking Toney's record time of thirty-eight minutes. The picture was "Paradise For Three," very funny. Ralph Morgan and Robert Young with supporting cast, quite capable of adding to the fun.

124

Thursday, April 18

A perfect day—I just received a message from Alda. If she only knew how much I count on hearing from her. It's a funny thing, whenever there is nothing really pressing—no planes to dig in, no dog tunnels to dig and we could, say, sleep an hour longer in the morning, wouldn't you know that that &!;#%!¢ cook would have to get up on time and have breakfast at 8:00 on the dot. When we really want to get up, have a big all hands job ahead of us, he will over sleep and we will get breakfast around 9:00 or so. I have never seen it to fail. I did a little wiring job this morning, putting in a switch on the line leading to the clothing and meat cache. Since that tunnel is not a main thoroughfare, it is not necessary to have the lights on all the time. Then during the afternoon I put up a few boards, supports to reinforce the roof over the clothing cache. Also started to finish my inventory, which I am afraid promises to be a job. "I guess a fellow can't even have peace eleven or so thousand miles from home," says Nib, because here he was sound asleep and one of the fellows woke him telling him that he was wanted on the phone—an amateur from his home town. He will be able to talk to his family tomorrow night. I would like to contact Alda but will wait till things quiet down a bit—too many fellows hang around the radio shack to really have a halfway private, decent conversation. Of course only about ten thousand or so amateurs will be likely to listen in and half of the population of the world, at least those who have short wave sets.

Friday, April 19

I'm staying up later every night. In fact, haven't been to bed before 11:00 for so long it isn't even funny. And now that the work has let up some, it has been midnight, 1:00 o'clock—and it's getting harder to get up at 8:00 every morning. I hope they make it 9:00, or else just let us get up when we want. I worked on clothing all day, opening boxes, checking and re-counting everything and getting things in order. It's rather cold work even though it is in the tunnel, but I guess there's nothing I can do about it.

Saturday, April 20

Had a rough day today, breakfast at 9:00 and talked to Paul till about noon, working on his theory. It so happened that I didn't dress for breakfast so when I finally got around to it just before lunch I certainly took a beating—sleeping all morning, lazy, etc.

During the afternoon I worked on clothing and have just about completed my inventory. It was still more of a job than I figured and it is still a darn cold one. Helped Nib with the dishes tonight, along with Tony, Klondike and Pappy G. We broke our record of last Wednesday and completed the job in about twenty-five minutes. Show tonight was "Mad Miss Mouton." I had seen it before but enjoyed it thoroughly. I don't know what it is, but the pictures play such an important part down here—we all look forward to them like a bunch of kids. Coach goes on mess duty for next week and the boys have already started a pool as to the number of dishes he is apt to break. The number ranges from all of them down to five. I am sorry, but no one seems to have any too much faith in the Coach as a dishwasher and waiter.

Sunday, April 21

What a wonderful sleep—up at 11:30, breakfast then a bath. I have sort of a system worked out—a bath once a week (whether I need it or not) and wash clothes once every two weeks, works out very well. Today was official setting of the sun and we all turned out about 12:30 for "flag lowering." A very interesting and impressive act. The two Marines, Walt and Pete, did the lowering, Paul gave commands, Shirley had his camera on hand. It's too bad we didn't have a trumpet so we could have had "Call to Colors," but the whole ceremony went off all right. Everyone took their caps and hats off when they were supposed to and the Marines lowered the flag at just the right speed. Worked with Paul all afternoon plotting important stress centers of the U.S.—very interesting. If Paul's theory is accepted and correct, it will put the "think" side of geology upon a more or less "know" basis. Poor Al doesn't know what to think, he does not want to believe a word of it, but darn it, he's got to a little because Paul's really found something.

Special holiday dinner today, turkey and all the trimmings. Why, we even had a punch. Doc Frazier very reluctantly broke out two quarts of our best stock (Old Log Cabin). He's a teetotaler and "Nibble" did honors by mixing grape punch and very strong, too. I happened to have charge of the whiskey, Doc turned it over to me and some of the fellows were on hand during unwrapping. And in fact, Klondike did it all, saying "A pleasure task," but also he took a little nip from each bottle while Toney begged to have a little left out of each one for him to sample. It's a wonder any of the stuff actually got in the punch. Just to prove that the holiday spirit prevailed, we even had a show, "Mysterious Avenger," a cowboy thriller. The boys really whooped and hollered. It so happened that the villain's name was Lockhart. Earl certainly took a beating. I have been passing cigars out every Sunday. I still think that Toney gets more good out of them than anyone in camp. First he smokes them, chews the butt, and saving the ashes he cleans his teeth with them.

Monday, April 22

I guess I am downright lazy or else it's spring fever, which couldn't be because it has been better than fifty degrees below the past few days. I guess maybe I am keeping too late hours—but there's nothing better to do at night than read, and for some reason I don't get sleepy till 1:00 or so. Today I worked with "Nibble" getting "Dolly" started. That's some tractor, she started right up. We did, though, have some trouble getting her out of the garage, practically had to stand her on end, the drift was so steep. Finished the clothing, also in the morning, and after lunch helped Nib shovel snow out of the garage—quite a job as we had to relay a couple of times. Toney and Klondike came to our rescue.

For the past week or so we have been digging various odds and ends out of drifts but Doug and H.H. bit off a little more than they could chew. They tackled a lumber pile under about seven feet of drift. They would have had to do a powerful lot of digging, but "Dolly" to the rescue. We got the majority of them out with the tractor, jarring the others loose which were easy to get out. Oh, yes, Nib and I collected the two tractor sleds and the caboose, but we have not been able to find the snow scoop. Pappy G. broke out the metal detector. Either he didn't know how to work it or else it's no good. Anyway he held it over the tractor which is certainly made of metal—it didn't even phase the darn instrument.

Tuesday, April 23

Woke up this morning—hating to get out of my bunk as usual. However, I have it timed fairly well. I manage to get to the table just before things are cleared away—at least I get there in time for seconds. Worked for Pappy R. today putting a line out through the science tunnel and rewiring the tunnel to the "head." It so happened that when Pappy originally wired the tunnel he wrapped the

127

wire around the bamboo poles. But since then the roof has sagged some, causing a tremendous strain on the wire, which would, eventually, probably break. And at the time, Clay thought that we were getting some leakage there.

When I did the job, I hung the line loosely from the bamboo, fastening it by copper wire, hence in case any more of it sags, the wire is loose enough. In fact, the other wire had so much weight on it that in some places I couldn't pull it out.

Wednesday, April 24

First blizzard for quite a few days. We were going to take the tractor out and drag in seals but it would be impossible when one can't even see the nose on one's face. And how would it be possible to drive, steer the tractor safely around the maze of wires, gye wires, antenna poles, etc., which exist around camp, besides missing the many tunnels?

I worked all day in the science building getting Larry's and my section fixed up. I built shelves and helped Al open the lead boxes for the cosmic ray outfit. Our picture tonight was "Return of Cisco Kid." Zeke took a beating because of Colonel Bixby—gentlemen from the old school. It sounds like the wind is picking up a bit. I can hear it flapping the canvas tarp over my head—a section of the food tunnel.

Thursday, April 25

Wind acted up all day and at present (midnight) appears to be going strong. It is drifting pretty bad as it is possible to hear it on the roof of the head, which for some reason does not drift over. Didn't do much this morning as I haven't been feeling very well. Kind of off my feed. Maybe I am too particular or something, but I just can't go some of the chow we have around here. Some meals everything is perfect and others, the food stinks (pardon). The best meal we have is the evening meal, while others are thrown together in a hurry, in a careless sort of way.

During the afternoon I finished wiring out in the dog tunnel and the blubber and chop house. Dick and Jack B. did a wonderful job on the construction of the building. It would make a good bunk house. Seems a shame that they will have to smell the place up. Perk is going to use half of the blubber house to cut open seals, work on anatomy. I always did think that wiring was a cold job and today was no exception. The trouble is, in the first place it is necessary to wear leather faced gloves, which are darn cold, then too, having to work with tape with bare hands doesn't help matters any.

Friday, April 26

Worked all day getting in seals—total number was twenty-eight and some of the fellows talked about getting them in all in one day. I drove the tractor and it took all morning to uncover them, by means of the scoop. Just like riding over a corduroy road, rather hard on one as the seals are naturally frozen stiff. The tractor bumps, plunges and dives along. Several times I almost bumped my head on the windshield. Oh well, only one hundred and fifty more to go. By afternoon we had them uncovered enough so that we could put glorified ice tongs through the eye holes (which, incidentally, were long ago deprived of their eyes by the skua gulls, large flocks of them would feast merrily on such tidbits), and by means of the winch and I will admit that I did get a little cold and was glad when Nib came to relieve me for a cup of coffee.

It gets dark around here at 3:00 o'clock, but we worked till 4:00 o'clock since today was mail bag. I really did very well. Folks, Alda, Bob, Lois, Mary Beth and Dr. Jenson. After they finished reading the letters, WGEO played records while they were waiting for us to acknowledge the broadcast. All during the program they would ask us to come in on channel three or four, please. Clay was in his bunk and Paul couldn't do a thing simply because we did not have permission from the commission to have contact with WGEO. It kind of burned us up a little. Here we have $60,000 worth of radio equipment, those fellows at WGEO stay up till 1:00- to 2:30 reading our letters and we can't even answer to let them know we have heard the broadcast. If I were them I would tell us to take our Antarctic Expedition ———. Anyway, Paul I guess decided to take things into his own hands, so after a talk with Clay, the latter went over to the radio shack and started to call WGEO. After some effort and time he broke through and had a two-way conversation, Paul explaining that this contact was not official, asking whether or not they had received anything which would make such a contact authentic. Well, much to everyone's surprise they had received permission that very afternoon from the radio commission permitting a two-way conversation from the time completion of reading letters till 2:00 o'clock. That was why they were so insistent about our answering them. Also they had a stenographer on hand to take our reply messages. By the time all of this was hashed over it was too late to take any of our messages. Besides, we were not prepared, so the whole thing was postponed till next mail bag, and arrangements were made which seemed to satisfy all members concerned. I have just been checking over the number of messages I have received from Alda—nine all told.

Saturday, April 27

Up at usual time, hit breakfast just right and was even dressed by 9:00 o'clock. Nib and I started the tractor and while it was warming up we went into the machinist building and warmed up. I was to take the tractor the first part of the morning. Last night Nib fixed the generator so we at least would have lights. I don't think I could possibly have picked a colder job than running the winch, unless it's working with wire. Anyway, it was pretty cold and just enough wind to make it that much worse. I stood facing the wind a couple of times just to see how long it would take my face to start to freeze up, to burn. I didn't have a watch, but I don't imagine it took more than five minutes at the most before my right cheek started to burn, pain, then numb. But even with my back to the wind I was continually nursing this or that part of my countenance back to a painful realization of life.

My hands caused me the most trouble, though, since I had to handle rope in working the winch. In keeping tension on the rope the circulation in my hands was a little thwarted and they would more or less freeze in a grasping position. Need I say that I was extremely glad to see Nib relieve me every hour or so. We quit at 4:00 o'clock because it was too dark, and since it was probable we would get a little blow over Sunday it was decided to cover the seal tunnel. That consisted merely of putting plywood over the end. The seal tunnel, by the way, extends out from the chop house and is approximately fifty feet long. At present it contains seventy-three seals, which is its capacity. The rest we will have to pile up at the end of the tunnel to be pulled in when needed. I guess we have over seventy more to pull.

Sunday, April 28

I don't know what makes me so tired but I slept until 11:00 this morning. After breakfast I took my usual Sunday bath and washed a few clothes, then I spent the rest of the day in my bunk reading. We always have a late dinner on Sunday, today being around 6:00

o'clock. Afterwards Fitz, Earl and myself played a few records—kind of music appreciation gathering. We would pick at random from Paul's numerous classical selections a group of twelve records, play them, and try to name each tune and the composer. A very pleasant way to pass the time, also very instructive. Nib made some ice cream (strawberry) which we had about 9:00 o'clock. Naturally, I ate two dishes (soup bowls) and some of the fellows had nerve enough to comment. I forgot to mention the picture last night, which was "The Big Broadcast of 1938," which most of the fellows thought was bunk. I had seen it before and my opinion still stands —I didn't and don't like it. I thought that W. C. Fields, who is naturally funny, overplayed his part. Oh, well, what's the difference—I'm no movie critic.

Monday, April 29
Griffith is mess cook through this week and darn it, since Murry is on night watch now, it will be impossible for Grif to sleep late. I had high hopes of him sleeping through so that we could all get an extra hour or so, but I guess it's no go. We've had it pretty tough the last two weeks. Nib and the Coach were both on time every morning and I guess Grif is going to follow suit. Such is life. Got a big shock this morning. Just as I was going out to help Nib start the tractor our cubicle was reminded that we were to sweep, clean and swab down. What a way to start out the day. Since Fitz had to go out to his shack, Larry and I did the job. I went out to relieve Nib at 10:30, so worked the winch till lunch. Nib then took it till 2:00, and I relieved him and we finished getting all of the seals in by about 3:30—a total of about one hundred twenty-five seals, which will last very nicely through the winter night.

It's really taking one's life in his own hands when driving the tractor into the garage, and every time I go down the ramp I feel like we will go straight out the other end. It's quite a grade, and "Dolly" stands practically on her head when going down. Incidentally, the brake does not work so hot when in motion, and when I do try to slow down a little the brakes throw the tractor into the left snowbank or else into the door, whichever happens to be in the way. And it does not do any good to try to go down in low or second gear because "Dolly" rambles along just the same. Well anyway, we have had no accidents up to now and since we finished our last job with the tractor and Nib has boarded up the garage it looks like my record is safe, at least until next spring.

Had a pretty hard time getting up again this morning. I meant well, I tried, but I just couldn't move. Don't worry though, I made breakfast all right. Worked on the tents today. What a job. The tent pegs are at least four or five feet down under drifts; besides, the inside is completely drifted over. We had a heck of a time finding all of the stuff, but after some effort I managed to get together all of the fur sleeping bags, matts, skis, etc., things which are to go in my cache. These things were all stored in the old sleeping tents which were fairly tight till Jack Richardson put two of his bitches in there. They proceeded to rip and tear the hell out of the side, hence a perfect setup for old man blizzard. Not only did they ruin one of the tents but also chewed up one of the sleeping matts beyond repair. I can't for the life of me figure Dinah and Gray out because they seemed like such nice dogs. And to deliberately destroy Uncle Sam's property, tsk! tsk!

Ike, Malcolm, Joe, Larry, Perk and myself worked all day and only got one tent, the pyramid, dug out and down. But we have plenty of time and only six more to go. Dick used his team today to haul in some dog equipment which he had cached over by the tents. He had quite a bit of digging to do himself, as you just can't leave things around without expecting, the inevitable. There are still a couple of good days to be spent out there. We didn't get a chance to bring in all of the gear as it got too dark and the temperature dropped (minus forty degrees), so Dick thought it best to put the dogs up. Beautiful—just as we were coming in and the Southern Cross was very plain. That's at least one consolation, the nights are very beautiful down here.

May Day without a "May Pole Dance." Whoever heard of such a thing? After breakfast Paul and I went out to the science lab and ran a temperature freezing test. Worked fairly fast, taking approximately three hours. Every minute or so we take readings on rate of freezing of the water and about every five minutes get air temperature. There is a certain point when she starts to go fast and we were both caught off guard. Once it started it was about two and one-half degrees per thirty seconds, and it's a job to keep up with it— we use a U.S. bridge. Also about every half hour we go out and take an anemometer reading; along with this we stand facing the wind and clock ourselves to see how long it takes before our face takes on that first sting or ping of freezing. In exactly three and one-half minutes my right cheek started to burn. It's a very interesting experiment.

After lunch I went out and helped Ike, Larry and Jack B. haul in some of the gear from the tents. Was too cold (minus forty degrees) to have the dogs out, so we had to man haul them. All of the tents are down now except the two used for cook tents. Show tonight was "The Great Man Vetor," John Barrymore. Thought he was very good in it. Afterwards I went out to the lab and worked, building shelves and cleaning up in general. Shirley moved his film drying rack which was on half of Larry's and my work bench. I put up a Miami U. geology sock on the wall, just so we will feel at home. So I guess we can really get to work now.

Tuesday, May 2

Everyone had a growl for Grif when he woke us this morning and the consequence was a nice argument with all hands putting in a few cents worth here and there. Of course, I didn't say a word. The whole thing so happens that Sig (cook) just won't get up, and Murry has to wake him about eight or nine times, then it takes him about half an hour or so to even move. Well, he's up late, and then has to hurry breakfast (which is usually late). And when he does finally have it ready, he then tells Grif to call us, expecting us to hop right out of bed and be at the table in five minutes. Then the trouble begins, the cook walks up and down yelling at everyone to get up, making imbecilic remarks, trying hard to be funny and talking to Grif in such a voice loud enough for all of us to hear, saying that they have had such a hard time—to go work at 9:00 o'clock and quit at four, or if we don't hurry he will throw the chow out, etc. Well, this one morning he really got told in no uncertain terms —a big growl. He was kind of taken back because he has been rather quiet all day. It does, though, get a fellow to have such goings on when there is a poop sheet on the bulletin board telling him when meals are to be and where and what time we are to be awakened, twenty minutes before the event. Oh well, the great winter night has really started with a bang. Paul and I ran the experiment test in the morning and in the afternoon. I went out and helped finish with the tents.

Friday, May 3

It was actually nice getting up this morning—really quite. And

Grif, incidentally, woke us twenty minutes before, which was according to Hoyle. I still can't believe it. I expected any minute to hear Sig's insulting voice yelling at us, calling us lazy, etc. Murray went to Paul after yesterday morning's episode and told Paul that he wouldn't stand to have all of the fellows yelled at, blamed by the cook for being lazy, when he himself had to be called about a dozen times then practically dragged out. Murray had a plan to call Sig only once then go back to bed. If he didn't get up then, well that would be too bad. The whole camp would sleep and the cook would get the blame. Paul said he would let him try it if something he had in mind didn't work. Well, evidently it did, because this morning was according to the book. Paul and I were fifteen minutes late for lunch because of our experiment, it worked rather slow because of no wind, which would average approximately one-fourth mile per hour throughout the experiment.

After lunch I worked on graphs, plotting some wind chill, temperature and wind velocity recordings for Paul. The science lab is fast getting inhabited. Of course, the radio and weather station have been in for some time. And the photo lab has been completed also. The above, so it seems, are the main stays of the expedition. In other words, as many say in a sarcastic sort of way, "Oh, didn't you know, we came down here just for the weather observation," etc. Nonetheless, we lesser departments are striving forward trying to get our allotted places fixed up in working order, even if it did mean shoveling snow all day then doing our own work at night. So Murray and Perk are pretty settled, as is Fitz. Earl has started work in that he has been making blood sugar tests for analysis later on. Of course, Larry and I are fairly well fixed—shelves, etc., while Al, who is right across from us, has been busy with his cosmic ray and various other sounding and temperature recordings. Even Gil is all fixed up with a desk and shelves which run clear to the ceiling, which are piled with office supplies from a mere paperclip up to notebooks, pencils, etc. In a far corner beyond the door, Zeke has finally finished his desk which is more or less of his own design—a drawing desk, drawer and bookshelves combined. Across from Paul and Lon is a long low table for map making. So just one big happy family, hoping to do some darn hard, serious work. Shirley finished all of the flight pictures and has almost all of his stills, camp shots, complete. He works mostly at night so that when the negatives are drying there will be less dust.

134

I got the most wonderful message from Alda last night. Wasn't much to look forward to today except the show tonight, which was "St. Louis Blues." It was a very good picture, incidentally, the music especially, with Maxine Sullivan. Made the run this morning, taking three hours. During the experiment Doc Frazier is taking out various fellows to see how long it takes them to freeze their face. This work is in connection with a part of our temperature run. It's very interesting. While some of the fellows stand out facing the wind for as long as ten minutes with no effects at all, others are not out for more than fifteen or twenty seconds till they get their first ping. My record is twenty seconds which I clocked while getting the wind velocity which Paul or I have to get at least four to five times during the run. The heck of it is after the first pain starts I have to stand till two minutes is up so as to get the wind reading.

Today my nose really took a beating—first time out fifty-five seconds, and second time thirty-five seconds. Now it is as sore as a boil and about as tender.

During the afternoon I worked on graphs and figured out the mean temperature for our runs. So far Doc Frazier is running some blood pressure tests and I happened to be in at just the wrong time because he nabbed me. First he took about a dozen or so tries so as to get my average, then I stripped to the waist and we went outside in the tunnel and took about eight or ten more. I practically turned purple and had goose pimples all over me, shivered and shook, but the hardhearted Doc couldn't or wouldn't be touched. Well, my count or pulse seemed alright, although high at one fifty-four/ninety-nine or thereabouts. Toney had the highest with one sixty/one hundred. So the cold has a definite effect on one's pulse, etc.

Sunday, May 5

Up about 10:00 o'clock. I don't guess I would have slept much longer, but why do people always have to carry on such loud confidential conversations on Sunday, the day of rest? And it always seems to be those fellows with voices like the well-known foghorn. I can't mention names because that wouldn't be nice. Cooked my own breakfast which consisted of two slices of fried bread. I was going to eat more but the cook informed me that breakfast would not be till 11:00. He as usual was growling about something. I don't know why it is, but all cooks, especially Navy cooks so I'm told, always think that they are being picked on and abused. Well, ours is certainly no exception. He is living up to the Navy tradition or something. Well, this morning he was blowing off about everyone coming in and getting their own breakfast and that he had to clean up this and that or had to work till 1:30. He mumbled around, I didn't quite get all that he was talking about. Anyway, we are all getting so we just ignore him anyway and let him rave on. Fitz, who happened to be a culprit, also told cook that according to the poop sheet on the bulletin board breakfast was to be at 10:00 o'clock. Then Sig really blew up, said he didn't give a damn about that, he didn't pay attention to it anyway. Well, I guess Paul will have to iron him out or something. He is the only one who has the authority to tell him what's what.

After a very pleasant breakfast I went out and took my bath, which is now getting to be a regular ritual with me—bath and wash clothes. I hit it rather lucky today. Toney was doing a small wash so I stuck mine in with his. I really did a good job on myself today, used almost two buckets of water. Washed my hair and scrubbed so hard that I was red as a beet. Boy, I certainly miss a shower. The first port we hit on return I am going to spend all day just sitting in a tub, or at least take four or five showers. Took the temperature run this afternoon, but only took about one hour to complete it. Very cold, about fifty degrees below zero but very little wind, plus eight near where our thermo-bulb cylinder is located, which happens to be on a pole from the roof of the service building.

Had a wonderful meal tonight. I'll say one thing, Sig can really cook if and when he wants to. But gosh, can't a guy cook and be pleasant at the same time? I don't know how it happened but we had a show tonight, rather a re-show of "Rose of Washington Square." Still was a good picture—at least I liked it. Afterwards I worked out in the science building (lab) a while, studying up on a little historical geology, which brings me up to now, 1:00 o'clock.

Monday, May 6

Everyone seemed to get up without much trouble this morning, even yours truly. In fact, I was up before I knew it—it really surprised me. I usually eat breakfast in my P.J.'s and a jacket, then hang around the stove till everyone leaves and I begin to look conspicuous. Then I hustle around very important-like, getting dressed, ready for the big day ahead, but really wishing all the time that I could get back in my bunk.

It is now 1:00 o'clock and I just finished repairing our cylinder. It seems that while heating it this morning prior to our run, I heated it a little too much and the pryolin melted—just a bit, but enough so that the thermo-bulb was allowed to touch the side of the cylinder. Well, neither Paul nor I noticed it at the time but continued to make the run. Everything went normally till we reached minus thirty-one hundreths C where the temperature of the water is supposed to remain constant for some time, but today it was only a matter of ten minutes or so before she started to go down again. This was odd, entirely unlike all of our other experiments. Well, then it dawned on us what had happened. You see, where the thermo-bulb was allowed to touch the side of the cylinder, it being copper, acted as a conductor, hence ruining the whole experiment. However, we went right on through with it just to show or get the curve that such a set-up would give. I had quite a job getting it back in line. Now that I wanted it to melt just a little, you think it would?

After lunch I started to work on assembling the anemometer which Court is letting Paul and me use. It is to be put on the roof of the science annex, alongside of the pole used to hang our containers. It will have a blinker system so that we can get a wind reading anytime during the experiment without having to go outdoors. The instrument will be right next to the cylinder or close to the cylinder. It will be a big help. It was pretty cold last night and today the temperature was around minus sixty degrees and at present is minus fifty-four degrees. Well, it just goes to show that even way down here at Little America one can't escape from the inevitable—school. Yes, we had the opening class in navigation this afternoon, taught by none other than Coach Ike Schlossbach. The University of Antarctic will meet every Monday, Wednesday and Friday to study navigation from the hours of 3:00 to 5:00. All of the fellows who will be on the trail are supposed to attend because everyone has to know how to navigate.

This evening at 8:00 o'clock we had a short meeting of the scientific staff, purpose being to just get a line on things and to let us know that every Monday we would meet and, as assigned, various members will talk. Poor Nib has even turned scientific on us. Paul has him working on the resistance of different types of snow surface obtained by pulling loaded sleds of given weight, using a spring scale. I think they hope to try several kinds of runners—metal, wood, etc. Grif is going to work with him on the project. Nib has been busy the past week or so tearing the tank down. He feels that with a little less weight he might be able to do something with it next spring. So he is taking off as much of the plating as he can. Yes, this proves to be a really busy winter night, and I can't see how it can be so very long till we will be on the trail.

They say a man's home is his castle. Well, here it's a man's bunk. I always feel so good when I am up here, kind of secluded and private like. It's really kind of nice because this is one place I can really have a few minutes of peace, a few minutes to myself. I just like to lie here and dream. It's my own little world.

Tuesday, May 7

Still pretty cold today but no wind, so Paul and I decided to make a still air run. This means that we placed the cylinder and the thermo-bulb in Al's ice crystal pit which is located at the end of the science cache. Al, Larry and I will use this pit to study ice crystal structure. The temperature in the pit was around minus thirty-six degrees and the complete run took from 9:30 A.M. till 5:30 P.M. An all day run—was very tiresome and my eyes ache. In order to take the reading and read the instrument, especially when a degree passes every thirty seconds or so. And it is the most helpless feeling to be caught alone when there is a rapid drop—just can't keep up with it. Several times both Paul and I have been caught where one or the other of us steps out for a few minutes. The funny part about it is that you lose two or three degrees before you actually catch on. They just sort of slip by. Or else if you are trying to get on to a degree, you find that you missed it, taking also a loss of degrees before you catch up with the thing. Worked on navigation till about 2:00 A.M. getting ready for the next class. We had to construct a mercater chart and get a few definitions, etc.

Wednesday, May 8

Couldn't move this morning, I was so tired and sleepy. Breakfast as usual, 8:00 o'clock or thereabouts. I guess someone told the cook off because he has been keeping fairly close to the galley instead of trying to be funny. Excellent day for our experiment, blizzard conditions with approximately a thirty mile wind. I went out on the science roof to take the first wind reading, and when I faced the wind I couldn't breathe. It almost knocked me over. But after two minutes I did not notice any frost pain, except my face stung a little from the drift. It was nice and red all over and very wet. We used a cube container today larger than our cylinder, holding eight hundred grams of water. The run was beautiful, reached zero degrees C in about thirteen minutes. On taking another wind reading I was received a little differently in that in thirty seconds my nose started to pain, in forty-five my neck pinged, and after about one and twenty-one hundreds minutes I noticed a dull ache, a pain across my forehead just above my eyes. And oh yes, after fifteen seconds my wrist (exposed, holding the anemometer above my head) burned like mad, more like a cold metal burn than anything else. By the time the two minutes was up I was more than glad to make a dash for the stove. I felt pretty miserable. Paul got the first ping to his nose after about five seconds. During the afternoon we ran both containers at once and the same good results.

At 3:00 o'clock this afternoon we had navigation class which consisted of working problems. Ike gave us a problem to work, charting on a mercater chart. If we can, it more or less completes the course, or should. If we could do it, we're able to navigate so well I don't see why any of us are taking a navigation class. We are supposed to go ninety degrees to beacon, around crevasses, tell the distance, variations, etc., and a lot of things I have never heard of. I am afraid that Coach is a little ahead of himself. Navigation in two easy lessons. I haven't tried to solve it yet but I imagine I will have quite a bit of trouble. He should have spent more time on fundamentals. After all, we've got all winter.

Pete called me into the radio shack just before dinner. They had contacted Dorothy Hall in N.Y. and a schedule is all arranged for May 23, 11:00 o'clock EDT. Alda had written here and she read the letter. Show tonight was "Three Loves Has Nancy." Very funny. All of the fellows enjoyed it. A show helps a lot around here—it is a wonderful means to relax.

Thursday, May 9

What a day—it is now 3:00 o'clock Friday morning and I just got to my bunk. I worked all evening on the navigation problem that the Coach gave us and it was a doozy. What made it so tough was the mere fact that the whole thing was not clear. But to say the least, it was not at all boring because all the time while working it, I found out more about the original problem—data which had been left out—so I had to continually change my work, or after pondering over some part of it I would find that a particular part had been changed or else stricken from the problem altogether. In the case of the crevasse the bearing given was impossible (209° N., 103° S.) because to take such a bearing one would have to be in two places at once. Also, after having the crevasse all nice and situated it was decided that it should be at 89° 10′ instead of 88° 10′. Oh well, such is the way it goes. Anyway, I finished and think I did all right.

The day was perfect for our run. We used both the cube and the cylinder. The method is to take the small two hundred and fifty gram cylinder out first. It reaches freezing in thirteen minutes first, and remains constant for fifteen minutes to a half hour. Then we take the cube out, which is supposed to reach freezing before the cylinder starts down to air temperature. We hit it lucky today and everything went off perfectly and the whole run was over by noon. It was quite cold, about minus fifty degrees, and a wind of about twenty-seven to thirty miles per hour which made the experiment go fast. Unless we make two runs a day, or if one happens to take all day, my afternoons are usually spent plotting the results or else in figuring the average wind temperature and loss of calories per minute. That is probably the toughest part of the whole job, trying to keep up the paper work. It's rather slow work, this plotting.

Friday, May 10

Another day—I am enjoying my work here and am having a good time. Well, today was one of the coldest we have had, minus sixty-five degrees. I had to go out to put up the cylinder but I can assure you that I didn't tarry long. The wind was not very bad, about five miles per hour, but that was cold enough. My nose froze in the time it took me to walk to the roof (only a few seconds because I don't exactly mope along on such days). It took just about two hours to complete the run, and for once Paul and I got to lunch on time. I don't know what is wrong with me lately, but I haven't had much of an appetite. And I might add that the lunch we had today didn't improve matters any. Now, I usually like rice, but I swear that what we had today would bounce.

Saturday, May 11

I don't know what's the matter with me but all I want to do is sleep. I can't seem to get enough. If I were the only one I would worry, but most all of the fellows sleep and sleep. Al says that there must be something about Antarctic which is conducive to sleep because on the last expedition he says that all he wanted to do was sleep. Nothing exciting happened today, just the same old routine. The run this morning took the usual three hours. During the afternoon I worked on graphs trying to get some sort of temperature degree curve out of our work. The hardest part was getting a scale. However, after a few failures I think I will be able to get a fairly comprehensible scale and curve merely by omitting the period at which the water remains at zero, hence enabling me to get all of the curve on the paper.

I forgot to mention yesterday's mail bag. As you might know, just as my letters were read, static became quite apparent, hence I missed both the folks' and Alda's, but heard Aunt Nellie's and Bob's very plainly. Very fortunate though, because being a two-way contact Paul asked if the first group of letters could be read over again, so my disappointment was quickly rectified and was happy to hear that all is well at home and that Alda quit her job and is getting ready to take her exams.

Saw "Stage Coach" tonight, very good picture. I had seen it before but I was sitting on the edge of my chair along with the rest. It really holds one in suspense.

Sunday, May 12

What a sleep—which proves that there is something around here which makes one want to sleep. I clipped exactly twelve hours and still feel tired and sleepy. Well, you might say, shucks, you slept too long. And to that I would reply that I have tried the other too, getting some nights five to six hours, and I am still tired. So I guess the answer is to try to gain a happy medium—say eight hours. Either that or else it's the climate. But I might mention that Toney, who goes to sleep every night around 9:00 o'clock (except movie night) sleeps right through to 7:00 o'clock, and he's still sleepy. Had a very delightful bath this morning, two buckets of water. Very extravagant, but it was worth it. I also washed out a few things. I find that it is easier to do a small washing once a week rather than let things collect for a week or so. Some of the fellows are just now taking their first baths since Wellington, as well as attending to their clothes. It took Douglas a whole day to do his—looked like a washing for a family of four or five.

Paul and I worked on graphs all afternoon and averaged the

winds and plotted them. We are trying to get some sort of picture in relation to temperature, wind and loss of heat. Very good dinner (I would never tell the cook). Fried chicken, sweet potatoes, corn, etc., and I was really hungry because in my seeking of cleanliness I more or less missed the breakfast hotcakes. I did, however, have a bowl of cold cereal. Quite a surprise tonight, had another show. A re-show, really, "Arkansas Traveler," plus "Gunga Din" (the last three reels—of all the pictures to be incomplete!). We planned just to show it but Paul thought it would be better to show a complete picture, then kind of sorta throw in the misfit. Made three temperature runs after the show, got to bed around 2:00.

Monday, May 13

All today would have to be is Friday and it would have been complete. To make a long story short, the weather did us a mean trick. That is, the temperature raised a little, was minus fifty degrees, hence making it possible for us to go out and work, wasn't that nice. For the past two weeks we had all been hoping that the weather would remain minus fifty-five degrees to minus sixty-three degrees, because in such temperature we do not go out and do any strenuous work because of getting lung frost. It is very necessary to take it nice and easy when the thermometer gets down around minus sixty degrees, because any vigorous exercise will naturally cause a heavy breathing. And if you have ever done any heavy breathing in such temperature, you will understand what I mean. First, I guess you just kind of forget and possibly work a little too fast. Well, that first deep breath, one lung full, will soon break you of that habit. It's hellishly painful, and the coughing makes "whooping cough" look like a piker.

The only thing to do when such happens is to tear for the inside and stay there. Mac has sensitive lungs now because he just had to take too many deep breaths. The whole trouble is the thing might develop into T.B. later or unless you get over it before you leave here. Klondike knows of several fellows up north who contracted T.B. through frosted lungs.

Well, getting back to everything, we still have Fitz' tunnel to dig come the first nice day, and today seemed to be it at minus fifty degrees. Well, all hands turned (almost all, a few always manage to hide out) and by dinner time the thing was almost finished. I worked on the wall near the "absolute house" which is the furthest from camp. For a couple of hours in the morning it was light enough so that we could work without light, but later on Vernon had to get the put-puts on and the flood lights. I didn't particularly notice that I was cold, but when I got in for lunch my old standbys were well taken care of, meaning my nose, chin, cheek and forehead. The only part I noticed was my head, my forehead, just above my eyes. I could hardly stand the pain. And if sinus trouble is anything like that, well I don't think I'll have any. It's the second time I have experienced such a headache. It's really hard to explain exactly, except that it just ached and pained. Al and Larry got the same thing, and Al said that he has never had such a headache. Well, we got half of the tunnel covered. It's surprising how much work can be done when all hands are around. I had to go in about 4:00 o'clock. I thought maybe it was just me, I couldn't take it, but when I noticed quite a few of the others doing the same it rather salved my conscience.

But I guess there's no rest for the wicked. Nib was there and needed help with his sled runner testing, so Al and I went out and helped him. Al and he pulled, and I read the scale. We had three types of runners, being enamel, icy and wood. The wood seemed to be the best, taking only about a one hundred pound pull to start a two hundred pound loaded sled, while the enamel took about two hundred and ten and the icy one hundred and thirty or so. And in a steady pull the wood pulled through with a seventy pound pull while the enamel runners were much more. This was all on hard surface. On soft there is some difference, they were all harder to pull. No navigation this afternoon because we had to take advantage of the wonderful weather. Also, we did not have the scientific meeting, the boys were just too tired—of course, I wasn't.

Tuesday, May 14

The boys thought that the world had come to an end because I was the first one at the breakfast table. Of course they didn't know till later that I had to get up at 6:00 to let Earl give me the works. That is, I was his subject this morning. He tested my heart and pulse, sampled for sugar, etc. It was all pretty nice. The worst part is getting out of bed, and then the mad dash over to the science lab. But once there I hop into an improvised bed that Earl has acquired for his subjects. It happens to be the basic wire structure. However, it was fairly comfortable and I was able to practically sleep through the whole thing. The object is to take all of the various tests, etc., while the patient is relaxed, my heart being forty-eight and my respiration being eight breaths per minute. Earl was through about 7:30 so I went back to the bunk house and dressed, then read till breakfast. It was funny to see the expression on Nibs' face when he saw me sitting by the stove. I am usually one of the last to get up.

It was beastly cold today, minus sixty-three degrees. Paul could not order or force anyone to go out and work but the tunnel had to be finished, so he more or less asked for volunteers. About everyone turned out and the job was finished by noon. All that had to be done was cover about one hundred feet of tunnel, the whole tunnel being about three hundred feet long. Of all the days for me to get ambitious and want to finish wiring up the wind anemometer! I was almost afraid that I bit off more than I could chew. If you have never worked with bare wire at sixty degrees below, there is really something in store for you. Paul finally came to my rescue and helped with the wrapping. It was necessary to heat the tape then make a mad dash outside. But no matter how fast we moved, our only reward was a piece of tape stiff as a board. Well anyway, I am glad that little chore is done. It is really nice now because we do not have to go outside to take a wind reading, but merely watch the gauge which is fastened to the wall in front of my desk. Incidentally, my desk, such as it is, has turned into a "climatologist's" station or something. Anyway we have our wheatstone bridge, plus the instrument for recording wind velocity and directions, etc. Larry said he tried his best to save Al and me but to no avail—Al is taking all kinds of temperature readings as well as taking care of the seismic outfit. What a disgrace for a geologist, but our day will come when we take to the field. Tonight after dinner Paul and I made a run due to the fact that we didn't have time to get it in any earlier. Even then we could not let the thing get to be constant because of the scientific meeting which was to be at 8:00. However, we got in our critical points plus two and plus/minus seven. The talks tonight were very interesting. Court gave a very good progress report, as well as did Weiner and Al.

Wednesday, May 15

Well, I kept my word. Yes, I didn't budge this morning till I was sure that everyone else was up or at least getting up. After all, I have my reputation to uphold. I can't understand it. At home I never had trouble arising, but down here it's different. Maybe I am getting old. We finished the run by 11:00 o'clock this morning using the two hundred and eighty cylinder, temperature being about minus fifty-eight degrees and wind three miles per hour. Then, I don't know how it happened, but I took apart the wind instrument and rewired it so that we could run it off without unhooking the battery, also putting switches in so that we could turn off the direction lights and the velocity light, hence enabling the use of a buzzer.

It is rather hard to watch a light, the time, as well as record. However, I don't think we will be able to use the buzzer as it plays hell with the radio which makes Clay very unhappy. Larry strung up the wire for lighting our ice house, so this afternoon I went out and spliced into the main line. We have been getting some pretty good radio programs, yesterday Bob Hope and this afternoon Fred Allen and Kay Keyser. It certainly helps a lot.

Navigation classes this afternoon and the Coach gave us another one of his problems. I will give him credit though, it isn't as mixed up as the other. We also worked a few compass problems in class. The whole thing is gradually dawning on me that I might be able to navigate some yet. Before dinner, Al, Larry and I had a little gab fest over the glaciology program. It seems that I am to take over the layer and structural work as well as compression. I think it will prove to be very interesting work. The fellows who have been here before talk about the long winter nights. Well, from the amount of work that is in store for us I don't think they will be long enough.

The picture tonight was J. E. Brown in "Wide Open Faces." Incidentally we had a double feature, "Torchy of China Town." I hope that we don't have many more like these two.

Thursday, May 16

The usual task of getting out of my sleeping bag. I suppose that you will get tired of hearing me harp about this sleep business, but I assure you that the whole thing is very, very real. Especially having to unzip a nice warm bag and get out into the ice cold. Every morning this bunk house seems cold as outside. My teeth chatter and I know my knees would gladly knock, but since they are already quite that way, I have to be satisfied and express my dislike by just plain growling. Here we go to all the work of bringing down nice warm quarters, only to be frozen out by a few fresh air fiends who open the doors. Oh, yes, also because they did it on previous expeditions —I mean slept with the doors wide open. Another example of such stuff is in getting in the seals—Buck wanted to have four men carry one seal with grappling hooks, just because they did it on Byrd Expedition Number 2. Of course it wouldn't be right to use the tractor because, after all, shouldn't we do it the hard way. Well anyway, back to the present. I will admit that it's wonderful sleeping in the cold, but the darn place is so cold all day. I guess it's just a question of having your cake and eating it too. Under Fitz' bunk on the floor in the corners are nice little puddles of ice, and if we leave our shoes on the floor over night they either freeze to the floor or are so stiff in the morning that it takes some time to thaw them out. The main trouble we have is keeping our feet warm. In the science hall we have to wear fur mukluks because on the floor it's about forty-two degrees plus, it's pretty cold. Of course the bunk house goes down to the tunnel temperature which varies from minus thirty-eight degrees plus, and everything in the place freezes —even my cod liver oil, which I am very earnestly taking three times a day (I even like it). I am still very fortunate to have an upper bunk because they are much warmer. The fellows in the lower bunks are having trouble with their mattresses getting mouldy. I don't see how I get off the subject, go on such a tangent, but anyway I did get up this morning and I am ashamed to admit it, but Perk got up after I did. I can't understand how I slipped up.

Kind of windy today so we hurried and got in a run this morning. Nineteen miles per hour. Since the wind light was flicking so fast and since it would have been impossible for Paul to watch that and record too, (I read the bridge), we hooked in, or rather we added Malcolm to our number figuring that he had a little more time than some others and would be more reliable. As a result, today's run went haywire. While getting Malcolm squared around so that he could record we didn't notice that our stop watch was losing minutes, hence throwing all of the readings off. The way we work it is, take a re-set watch, correct it with a chronometer, then start the stop watch on even seconds. Also, the watch time is noted at the same time. Usually we try to start on half hours. Well, today after the experiment got started we all had our own jobs, had our hands full, so to speak, and we simply failed to notice that the minute hand on the stop watch did not coincide with that on the watch until at least twenty-eight minutes had passed and the damage had already been done. We finished the run and I have been trying to figure out the time by plotting the curve we got, then comparing with a similar case. It worked fine, our first twenty-eight minutes were off three. I spent all afternoon plotting runs, so far I have about half done. We are getting some beautiful curves, and a strange thing is that all of them seem to have a hump between plus five and forty-four degrees. We haven't quite decided what it means, but have given it up as a mere happenstance. Took a nice nap before dinner. Doc put some stuff in my eyes and they feel much better. I guess I will have to start wearing my glasses.

The wind has picked up quite a bit this evening, thirty-one miles per hour. I went out to see if the anemometer was alright. It is supposed to have three braces to hold it up, and so far I have only two on it. I hope that the wind doesn't get too strong. Boy, it really isn't fittin' for man or beast tonight. A flashlight didn't do me any good, drift too thick. It's heck when you have to light a match to see if the flashlight really is on. However, I am glad to report that everything is intact. Gosh! the wind is really howling. I am certainly thankful that we are all safe.

Friday, May 17

Boy! What a night. The wind howled and carried on all night, reaching about forty-five miles per hour in the early morning. It makes a terrific noise. This afternoon Phil called me into the radio shack to show me the static electricity, a flash fully two inches long, cracks like a rifle.

Would probably knock one plenty flat. Everything we touched in the radio shack gave us a shock. After all, fifteen hundred feet or so of wire are bound to cause some sort of an electrical center or something. It burns me up, I stayed up last night to take a run (that is, if the wind picked up) and no sooner do I get to bed than it goes up to forty miles or so. However, this morning we had a thirty mile wind which gave us a nice wind. The temperature was minus twenty-five degrees, and tonight it is minus eight degrees (and the wind is about the same). This afternoon I again did graph work. I hope to be caught up with our runs one of these days. It's fairly easy to take the run, it's the work afterwards that takes time— plotting curves, wind curve, time and degree curve, figuring out averages, etc. It keeps me busy. And to think they say that the winter night drags on—why, I haven't had two minutes to myself since it started.

At 3:00 o'clock we had navigation class and Klondike gave us the dope on a transit, and at 4:00 we had our first radio class. Pappy Reese drilled us on the code. I didn't do so well. For some reason I don't seem to be able to hear so well, can't distinguish between dots and dashes. However, I suppose I will get onto it later on. Had my usual before-dinner nap. Very refreshing. When we don't make a run in the evening and there isn't a show, I spend my time studying geology, historical and Paleo. I'm going to get it cold so that then I will be all ready to go. Also I plan to take a large map of the U.S. and plot in different horizons, different fossils found, etc. It will help me to study.

Got a nice telegram from Alda today.

Saturday, May 18

Up bright and early (8:00 o'clock) had a miserable breakfast (oatmeal) and was hard at work by 9:00 o'clock. Had a nice run today, Doug is becoming very expert as a recorder. At first he was a little confused and Paul had to help, but this morning Paul worked on maps. Doug got along alright. It was a long run lasting from 9:00 till 2:00. Wind was fourteen miles per, but the temperature was minus nine and seven tenths degrees which is fifteen degrees above zero F—practically hot. We had to eat lunch one at a time with Paul relieving us. Today was the first day I had both temperature and water on the high scale. It was easy to get both readings. On the other hand, when the water is on high and temperature on the low scale, I always miss one water reading in taking a temperature. Paul and I really are perfecting this experiment, we have been kind of polishing it up so now it is fairly accurate, except for the instrument error which varies with the temperature. Something went haywire with our wind instrument, none of the lights would go on, so I worked on it in the afternoon—that is, the vane part, not the anemometer. When I got it all back together, oiled and everything, the east light burned continually, regardless of direction. There is a short somewhere and the joining wire is under about four feet of drift. Looks as though I have a job on my hands.

The war is quite a topic of conversation around here, and work stops at 3:00 for the NBC news. The radio gang is kept busy copying news flashes at all hours of the night and day. First thing that's heard in the morning is "What's the news? Any news last night?" Why, the fellows don't even growl in the morning any more. We have been getting some pretty good programs—dance music, Sammy Kay, Hal Kemp, etc. The programs are in the afternoon from four to five. It makes it fine because I am working on my graphs, which does not take too much concentration, so I can divide my attention. And I might say that the division is uneven—need I mention that more goes to the music. The picture tonight was "Joy In Living," Fairbanks Jr. and Irene Dunn. It was received very enthusiastically, will probably be a re-show.

Sunday, May 19

What a wonderful sleep—in fact, 11:00 o'clock came around too soon. Toney woke me to tell me that there was hot water, so I hurried out to the machine shop, had my bath and did quite a washing. I know that once a week is not often for taking a bath, but I really make up for it. I simply shine when I get through, sometimes I wonder how my hide stays on. Well, anyway, I make attempts at keeping clean while I know some who have not had any baths at all. (Incidentally, their underwear is a very dirty gray.) Court was one of them. I say "was," because he finally broke down a week or so ago—not only took a bath but washed all of his clothing. It was actully funny when he brought in his clothes. The underwear had been so dirty that one washing did not make much of an impression on it. Did not make a run today as conditions were too similar to the other day. However, did spend the afternoons reading historical geology and doing a few more temperature curves.

Had chicken for dinner, sweet potatoes, spinach and pie—very good. Larry started mess duty today. Fitz and I gave him a hand because of a re-show tonight. Had a cartoon comedy, "Angels With Dirty Faces."

Monday, May 20

I still can't believe it—I got right out of my bunk this morning. The only explanation I have to offer is that I wanted to impress Larry or something, uphold the dignity of our cubicle. It would look bad if the mess cook's bunk mates were not on hand at meal time. (On time!) Oh yes, Dick and Jack B. left for Little America, to stay till Friday. They are just getting a little trail experience together, and also to look around the old building for various necessities which we could use here. So far I don't think Clay has heard from them. I know he tried all last night and also most of the morning. He can hear Jack's carriage, but not his key. Evidently he had the polarity mixed—shortened. Doug and I had a nice run this morning, finishing just in time for lunch. Temperature was two degrees below zero F and wind was about eleven miles. Just can't seem to get caught up on this graph work. I have been trying to do the day's run as we do it (that is, the same day), but I still have about ten back experiments to chart.

Had a scientific meeting tonight with E. A. presiding. Fitz was first speaker, giving us the dope on magnetic observance. He thinks there is a definite effect on aurora by magnetic change, also he hopes to find how variations affect radio. Earl gave a very interesting talk on his work. He finds that our basal metabolism here is lower than in temperate climates. My percentage is plus/minus two here, which is about thirty-seven or thirty-eight out of normal hours. The others range from plus thirteen, minus seventeen, up to plus three/ten, which is Doc Frazier, who has sugar diabetes. He takes shots almost every day. It's a shame—he had the whole thing licked at home, not a shot for over two years. But either the diet here is not right, or something, so he is taking shots again. Also, Earl hopes to take water samples and try to grow culture, if anything is present. He has a bug catcher which he will put to use as soon as he can get around to it. After all, his day starts at 6:00 and he often works till 12:00 or so at night, getting ready for the next day's experiments. Doc Frazier then concluded the meeting by giving some results on his blood pressure work.

Tuesday, May 21

Got to sleep last night about 2:00 or so. Just can't seem to get to bed any sooner, there is so much to do. If I do any reading it has to be done late at night. Up to now I have read thirty-two books of various natures. Hope to read around one hundred or so. We have some very good books here, both fiction and non-fiction.

Arguments start around here at the slightest provocation. For instance last night about midnight a terrific discussion issued forth from the galley, something about frozen oysters. Cook, Mack and Boyd evidently started the whole thing and before long the whole camp had entered in and the discussion touched not only oysters but also fish. Sig claimed that they never freeze fish (evidently he has never visited Boston Fish Pier). Everyone else claimed they did just to be contrary and to get the cook. He finally broke out a Navy cook book which didn't prove a thing. He certainly took a beating. Pappy Grey was in the thick of it. He is the darndest guy, everything will be nice and quiet and all of a sudden an argument will break out started by the one and only (Pappy Grey). Then when it gets going strong he kind of slips out then stands aside seemingly enjoying the whole thing. Our table got into a big discussion the other day on the color of cream cheese and American cheese. Pappy was in the center of things. It doesn't make any difference what the subject is, if there are at all any possibilities we argue on it. They are not really arguments where anyone gets mad, just friendly ones. They seem to stop just before the blows take place.

The run was fairly fast this morning, started at 9:30 and was over at 11:30. Temperature was about minus ten degrees Fahrenheit and wind was around six miles per. Doug is getting along a little better, still do not think he is careful enough in reading the time, because when I plot in the curve I find it is not true as it should be. However, after a little finagle I can even them up. But maybe that isn't according to Hoyle. The whole trouble is Doug can't keep his mind on two or three things at once, and today was a madhouse. For a science building, well, this building is nice and quiet like a playground. The radio blares forth at all times, and I might as well mention it, I can't quite understand radio men. They don't seem to be able to tune in music. They don't seem to understand that it should be at least soft music to be audible. Instead they blare it out with as much volume as possible so we not only have music good and loud, but also a little code and static. When they do get a good program and by some act of God get it turned down to a halfway decent volume then some one of them changes it or at least plays up and down the dial, ruining the once good program and increasing the noise to squawks and screeches of uncertain origin. Besides all of this quiet, the fellows working carry on a continual crossfire of conversation which consists mostly of ribbing. Then to complicate the picture a news flash will come over the air and all work stops, all hands gather around the speaker. All but Malc and I, our experiment requires that we stay by the instrument till the run is over. I am used to all the noise, etc., and can carry on regardless. But poor Doug—it all seems to confuse him.

Wednesday, May 22

The strays returned back to the corral early this morning. In fact, they sneaked in about 3:00 o'clock—hoping, I think, that no one would be up, but they certainly were fooled. Old Murray was up and he proceeded to take a picture of their arrival. I haven't seen it but I guess it's a doozey, since they certainly were a sight according to reports. Jack Richardson was up also. Clay contacted them last night for the first time and it seems that they had just arrived at

Little America that afternoon, late. It was really funny, about three or four of us were sitting around in the radio shack, plus Clay, Walt and Phil. They were all trying to figure out what Jack was sending. I guess he and Dick were having trouble with their set. Anyway the whole thing messed up. Probably it would have been more clear if they had cranked the generator a little more—that is, if Dick had worked a little harder. First when we heard them Jack ran his code all together. That plus the weak generator made it pretty bad. Clay talked to them by phone and told Jack that they heard him and were trying to outguess him. That must have had some effect on Jack, because his next transmission was much better, except for the fluctuation of sound due to the weak generator. Anyway they said that they were coming in "The Still of the Night." We didn't get the real low down until navigation class this afternoon when Dick got up and told us of their trip.

No sooner had they departed from here Sunday than it started to snow, and after going seven miles they had not hit Little America, so they decided to stop and camp. Since it was bad Monday also, they decided to try out their sleeping equipment. They had put up their trail tent, mixed up some pemmican and I suppose were fairly comfortable. That is, till they tried to sleep. Jack said he had never been so cold in his life, he says that the sleeping bags were too large. They at first tried sleeping with just the underwear on, but soon gave up, put on all their clothes (even their fur parkas) and even then I don't think they spent an enjoyable night of sleep. If, in fact, they slept at all.

Anyway, Jack woke up early Tuesday morning and found that it had cleared up and the moon was shining. So he woke Dick about 4:00 o'clock so that they could eat, break camp and get started in time to take advantage of the lightest part of the day, which is from about 10:00 A.M. to 1:00 P.M. They didn't have any trouble getting to Little America from their camp, simply followed the pressure ice. From their camp they could see the light of West Base—our beacon on top the machinery building. They didn't, however, have to travel during the light time of the day because they recognized where they were. They got to L. A. about 6:00 o'clock, spent the day rummaging around getting the few odds and ends needed here. They then contacted us on Tuesday. They had quite an experience. They used the compass on their sled but it did not do them much good because it was not calibrated for down here.

Navigation class consisted of the Coach talking on the celestial sphere and astronomical navigation. Walt took a radio class, and I even surprised myself and was able to copy about four words a minute and made very few mistakes. Shirley developed all of my film for me and it turned out very well. I spent the time prior to navigation class making a booklet to keep them in. The only ones that didn't turn out real well were those taken on Pitcairn, I had some trouble with my camera there. The film got jammed and those that I have seem to have dust specks on them. However, I think they will print all right.

The run today was very successful, exp. number twenty-eight, the temperature was about minus thirty-nine degrees centigrade and wind was one and eight tenths miles per hour. Paul and I have to give our results up to date at the next scientific meeting. I have been working like mad trying to get all of the graphs caught up. They are going to be quite complete, they will have the temperature curve, water freezing curve and wind bars on them, plus the figures, calibrations of heat loss, average wind and temperature. I think Paul is quite pleased with them. He has left the whole thing up to me now, as he has turned his attention to maps and several of his proposed theories. It has been beautiful out nights, wonderful full moon and beautiful displays or aurora.

Tuesday, May 23

Woke up this morning with a start—I knew I forgot something last night. Didn't bring in the cylinder. As a result I had to try to thaw it out before breakfast. Well, I didn't succeed because I was a victim of circumstances, today being snow melter day, besides being my turn to sweep up in the bunk house, also I promised to get Shirley some water. Hence, Doug and I did not get started till after lunch. Temperature was still minus thirty degrees centigrade but there was hardly any wind at all. For about twenty minutes, the anemometer didn't turn at all.

Today is the day I was to talk to Alda. I say was, because the band was just dead. I have never been so disappointed in my life. Boy! It would have been wonderful to talk to her now, to hear her voice. I hope we can hear the mail bag alright tomorrow, maybe I will hear from her then. Helped Charlie tonight file some of his pictures—he has taken about seven hundred still shots and is indexing them so that we can look them over. He has a good one of what he calls a "jam session," although I think it is a little falsely titled because I hardly "jam" anything. It is a picture of me sitting in my bunk playing my clarinet, with Al, Weiner and several others as an audience.

I don't know what, but Larry being mess cook must have a good influence on me or something. Anyway, I hopped right out of my bunk this morning at the first sound of the gong (frying pan and spoon)—well, maybe the second. Since we can't shave any during the day because of the radio, I have been shaving right after breakfast. There are not many schedules that early. Chuck has a mirror and light fixed up out in the carpenter's shop, which makes it very nice. I kept my beard for a while but it bothers me quite a bit and when I gave the electric razors out, I started to shave. Of course I kept my mustache (if one could call it that)—I might say, I kept the fuzz which happens to be on my upper lip. Some of the fellows have been getting haircuts but I think I am going to keep mine long. What convinced me was the haircut Nib and Toney gave Pappy G. Boy, it's a doozy, he looks like a jail bird. They took the clippers and cut his hair high all around his head, almost skinned him alive. Now with him as a living example of their work they are trying to drum up a little business. "The Antarctic Barber Shop Corp." Malc, Toney, and Pappy Gray. They had to take him in to keep him quiet after butchering him up—they want to work on me next but I am afraid I don't like the idea.

Had a nice run today, took only two hours—wind about five or so and temperature minus thirty-seven and fifty hundreds degrees centigrade. Since I had a little time before lunch I worked on negatives. They all turned out pretty well. All of them are a little dark, but they will print all right. Plotted the day's run right after lunch, very nice curve. Navigation class was at 2:15, since mail bag program now comes on at 3:30. I am pretty far behind in class, don't seem to find the time or something.

However, I will take a day off soon and really get on the ball. Mail bag program came through very well. Got letters from the folks, none from Alda. I don't understand unless she counted too much on our contact last night. The first part of the program was from Detroit, and was not very clear. Today's program was also a two-way contact and Paul talked to WGEO.

Saturday, May 25

Gosh! This month has passed quickly, or should I say is passing quickly. Anyway, Vernon strikes off time by the weeks so I guess I can hedge by a few days. Personally I wish it was next spring so that we could start on the trail. Have been having quite a blizzard, last night and all day today. Temperature is rather low but the wind is about thirty miles per. A few days ago it got so warm that it actually snowed, hence there was quite a bit of loose snow around so it will probably drift badly. The run today was pretty fast, about an hour and a half. Uneventful, except for the fact the counter jammed and we had to count the wind by putting marks on paper. It kind of confused things a bit, but I am pretty sure that we did not miss any. While Doug was watching or marking time, I would have to watch the light and count the number of flickers. I have rigged up a new light system for Doug this morning, he claimed that he couldn't watch the other. So I disconnected it, lengthened the wire, and the light now sits right under his nose—in fact, right between the watches. I know that if there are any errors in wind recording, it shouldn't be the fault of the position of the light.

Spent the afternoon working on graphs, getting a few of them completely finished so that they can be used for Paul's talk Monday night. The picture tonight was "Of Human Hearts," a very good story. We also had a news reel which consisted of a few of last fall's football games—really a treat. Oh, yes, and the invasion of Poland. I guess we can't get away from that stinking war no matter what. All during the day, the least hint of war news, the boys would hover around the radio shack. Got a message from Alda. I certainly wish I could hear from her more often but I do suppose she is pretty busy. Besides, the band is so indefinite, I have had a message in the radio shack for her for about a week and it has not been sent yet. Conditions are so bad that Phil, if he can get through at all, is only able to send a few. However, mine should be coming up soon.

Sunday, May 26

This is the one day I look forward to (I mean the mornings) because that means one thing—sleep! I got up about noon and Toney told me there was plenty of hot water so I proceeded to take my weekly bath and do my wash. Jack R. comes out just as I finished washing my underwear and towels (white things) so I threw in some of his stuff before I washed my dungarees. It seemed quite a shame to throw away the water, because after all it was clean—besides, it's some job to get it. I carried snow till I was blue in the face before I finally got the tank filled again. Decided to take a run today since the wind was still up and we wanted to get a check on yesterday's, which we were not too sure of because of the broken counter.

I had a heck of a time getting out of the tunnel to take the cylinder up to put in place. Snow had drifted over the trap door, or hatch, and when I put my head to it (I usually start it with my head since my hands are full, then ease it with my shoulder) well, that didn't work. Reward, sore head. However with some persistence I did manage to crawl out. Incidentally, the entrance was full of drift and I had to crawl out on my hands and knees. What a guy won't go through for science. Boy, it was really nasty out. I couldn't even see the light on the cruiser and there was a nice high drift on the roof, which you can be sure I didn't see. Results, I fell flat on my face. It's the darndest thing in walking along to hit a drift or else fall in a hole left when one of the fellows dug out his skiis, or else just a valley. I guess I will have to get Douglas on the ball. I think he needs a little exercise anyway.

Well, I got back in and to my amazement the water temperature had already started to fall, it was at plus ten degrees already. I couldn't understand that as it had never before done that, besides, I heated it enough so that it should have taken at least ten minutes before it started down. Well, it turned out that the needle on the galvanometer had gone haywire, was stuck, so there was nothing to do but go out, set the cylinder, warm it and start over again. The trouble is, fellows take temperature readings during the day anytime and forget to clamp the needle, hence the slightest jar such as the door slamming, walking, or even sitting on the desk causes the needle to quiver, getting it off kilter. Well, our second attempt was a success and I am anxious to plot the curve. I think it will be a perfect one. I didn't help with the dishes tonight, simply because I helped Larry all last week. Besides, I wanted to give some of the other fellows a chance. You see, on show nights everyone pitches in and helps clean up the dishes. Since Sunday was a re-show night, the mess man gets help three nights a week which isn't so bad. Incidentally, I go on mess again in sixteen weeks—worry, worry. The show tonight was "St. Louis Blues." Some of the fellows wanted "The Awful Truth," but after taking a vote Dorothy

Lamour won out. Some of the fellows still think the voting was crooked. Imagine thinking that I would use cigars (expedition cigars) to further my own cause. I also voted "St. Louis Blues" and I did pass out cigars, but I can assure you that I did not pad the ballot box in any way. Some of the fellows suggested that for, say, two cigars, they could forget their honor and vote for the Blues, but I was above that. Oh, I might have used a couple of extras for that, but nothing to be alarmed about.

Monday, May 27

Stayed up last night till about 2:00 o'clock working on graphs, getting ready for the meeting tonight. These darn things certainly take a lot of time to complete. The actual plotting isn't so bad, but the figuring of the average temperature, wind, changing the wind from miles to miles per hour, and then plotting them also on the graphs makes the job rather tedious. I am certainly thankful that I brought my glasses, because if I hadn't, my eyes would certainly have gone bad on me, the work is so close.

Clay has shown me the ropes on working the receiver and last night I got WIWO, Ciney, some "hillbilly" program, one of their early morning specialties. It is possible to tune WIWO at almost any time, they have a fine news broadcast. News of the war kept coming in and the fellows got a big kick out of kidding Murray about Hitler. He's scared to death, thinks the Americans better pitch in right now and finish things. They always retaliate with "If you are so worried why don't you go over and join the allies?"

Didn't put out the cylinders today as I worked on the paper for tonight, completing those graphs which I intended to use, also making a master summary of all the experiment runs to date. The meeting was quite long tonight, lasting till about 10:30. On the program was Paul and Perk, I should say Paul and two of his many enterprises—mainly cartography and climatology, my branch being climatology. Our paper came first and Paul started off by giving them the history of the wind chill index and the background for his interest in the subject as a geographer. His talk was very interesting. I followed by giving the working technique of the equipment, explaining our early methods, some of the pitfalls, and our improvements. Well, I was going strong and everything was fine till I got to the graphs. I had been sitting up till then, thinking everyone could see the charts a little better, I stood up. Then things began to happen. I started to move around, my knees started to sag, I couldn't talk, everything went blank and I just made the chair in time. I would have dropped myself all over the place. It's the first time that's ever happened to me. Why, to even think about fainting, absurd. But nevertheless it almost happened. Doc brought me a glass of water with some kind of medicine in it and I felt a little better. Mac, who was sitting in his bunk to one side of me, said my face got as white as a sheet. Paul carried on and gave his summary. It's a shame such a thing would have to happen when it did, but it couldn't be helped. Anyway, I am glad that I didn't pass out sooner.

Berlin was the next speaker after an introduction by Paul to the subject of map making—cartography. Klondike told of his transit angle shots on West Cape, Floyd Bennett, East Haycock, East Cape, and it seems that the whole thing is moving out to sea, toward Bay of Whales, moving approximately seven feet per day. Len figured that in five years the Bay of Whales would be closed in. Well, that doesn't worry me because I won't be anywhere near here in five years. Then Berlin told of the method of plotting Mt. Peaks, getting their angle from photographs, and Zeke told us they are then projected onto a finished map. The whole meeting was very interesting. I turned in right after that.

Tuesday, May 28
Felt a little better after a good night's sleep. After breakfast Doug and I put out the cylinder. The run today took about three hours, remaining about an hour or so in freezing stage. The temperature was minus twenty degrees centigrade and wind was eighteen miles blowing quite a bit, yet there was not much drift. Most of the loose snow had been taken care of Saturday and Sunday. Charlie S. developed the rest of my film last night, so I spent most of the afternoon making containers for the negatives and filling them. I have had wonderful luck with my pictures, they all turned out fine, I think they will print. The trouble is I am missing one roll, the one I took of the crossing of the equator. I hope that I can find it because they were some good shots. I finally had to get Ike a couple pairs of stockings. I guess he can't darn or something, anyway he has been using adhesive tape over the holes in the heels till they finally gave out. He claims that he lost or had stolen all of the socks I gave him but two pair, and although that can be possible, since I know Ike and can see his bunk I am more inclined to think that they are probably under his mattress, his pillows, or even in his

sleeping bag. I asked him if he was sure they weren't around. He says he's looked, so I can't let him go barefooted. I know that he will find them, though. It will probably take a little time because his bunk is a perfect picture of chaos. Poor Gil has a heck of a time. Ike will dress in the morning and have all of Gil's clothing on, or else he will have on one of his stockings and one of Gil's, or he has been known to have on one of Gil's shoes, say a left, then just to make it complicated he will put on a left of his own.

Wednesday, May 29

Just another day. There is really no difference in the days now. The same thing day in and day out, our activities are so limited. The only time I get out is when I take the cylinder. I have been wanting to go skiing but for some reason I haven't gotten around to it. Today it was beautiful out, aurora, and it was almost light. The snow is as hard as a rock, and every step we take is accompanied with a familiar crunch, crunch. It's really sort of a weird sound. Lying in the bunk at night it is possible to follow the night watchman by his steps as he makes his way through the tunnels as his routine takes him from building to building, checking fires, seeing that everything is fixed for the night. It's impossible to realize the desolation one feels when going out into the night darkness, in leaving the warmth and friendliness of our camp tunnels and our buildings.

I noticed it even in making my short trip to the roof of the science building with the cylinder—the quiet stillness of the Antarctic night literally engulfs one. There is not even the angry cry of the skua gull or the impetuous squawk of the penguin, only the hum of the antenna wires or the muffled sound of the put-puts. However, on really windy days the wind mill generator functions. I will never forget the sensation I felt when I first heard the uncanny voice of the blades cutting the air. I immediately ducked. At first I couldn't place the noise, a thousand thoughts passed through my mind. I could have sworn that a lost plane was floundering over camp.

Doug and I started the run about 9:30. Malcolm took up the cylinder and I began to record the wind velocity. Zeke had asked me a couple of days before for a couple of mirrors. Chuck was making him some sort of a tracing device. And since I thought I had plenty of time, he checked the wind for me while I went to get the mirrors. Well, when I got back things had happened, the water temperature had dropped to plus five, meaning that I had missed plus ten, which didn't make me any too happy. There was nothing to do but get the cylinder, warm it up and start over. We did much better the second time and everything clicked off nicely. Temperature minus forty degrees centigrade and wind was nine and five tenths miles per. We were through by lunch. Pappy Gray was cook today. Gosh, he's a funny little fellow. Our table has a new name for him, "Feather Merchant." He looks just like one too. He's quite a cook, he makes Sig so mad because he really dishes out the food. For instance, today he gave us toast for breakfast and toasted cheese sandwiches for lunch. Boy, did that burn Sig up. He told Pappy he should have given us crackers—using too much bread. Says it takes five hours to bake. Pappy got mad and told him to go to hell and told him he was through. I can't understand what Sig wants to do with the bread. Keep it to look at or something. It is for eating (I think), anyway, we have plenty of flour. I think he is just too lazy to bake. I guess they got it smoothed over some way. I suppose Pappy told Sig that when he was cook, he'd put out what he wanted to. Anyway, he cooked dinner—steaks, and the best we've had.

Pappy and Nibble are still trying to get me to let them cut my hair. Boyd cut Paul's last night and they said that they could put the job to shame and want me to be the victim. However, I'm not too anxious. I still look at Pappy and get kind of scared. Worked time problems in navigation class. Shirley was all set up and took movies of the class, also the radio class. I am doing a little better at copying, but it's kind of discouraging. The show tonight was "There's That Woman Again," Virgina Bruce and Melvin Douglass, rather humorous. Yes sir!, the best part of the day is from the time I hit my bunk till I am literally forced out in the morning. I usually get to bed by midnight, but often read till the wee hours.

Thursday, May 30

Decoration day, and by rights should be a holiday. Some of the fellows took half days—of course I didn't (well, maybe I did take it a little easier than usual). Coach is giving us a navigation exam for Friday and he said we could all have today off to study. He said after all, it is a holiday. Well for some reason it didn't work out that way. I did, however, get in a good honest studying during the afternoon. Doug and I ran the experiment in the morning. The temperature was minus thirty-three degrees centigrade and wind sixteen miles per, run lasted for one hour and fifty minutes. It's such a relief not to have the experiment drag out and go through lunch.

Typed a poem for Toney this afternoon—"Lure of Little Voices." Very beautiful verse, very appropriate. Well, it so happened that since today was a holiday, for some anyway, the fellows put up a big howl for a show. So everyone pitched in with the dishes and we had a re-showing of "The Awful Truth." I think everyone enjoyed it more this time. There are so many good cracks that it is hard to get them all the first time.

Friday, May 31

I studied some last night but soon got tired and read "So Free We Soar," by Dorothy Hood. Of course I can read a novel, but am too tired to study. Oh well, that's the way things go. I don't know, but for some reason I can't get very interested in navigation. I guess it's all right for those who like it. I think the main reason is that I don't have time to get the work done. It burns me up, some of the fellows take expedition time to study, do nothing but that all day, while I have to run the equipment in the morning and try to work up the graphs and such. I really don't feel like tackling a navigation book. I did want to read a couple of geology texts, but from the looks of things I guess I won't make it. Today's run was rather interrupted due to the fact that Charlie S. started to take pictures of the science building. And as usual, he had a hard time getting anyone to be in the pictures, simply because all (or most) of the fellows were busy taking pictures with their own cameras, taking advantage of Shirley's flood lights. He just finished the machinery building and pictures in the food cache. He got movie shots of Boyd, Chuck, Pappy Reese working at their respective benches, also of Toney opening food boxes, carrying in food, and of Malc carrying in a bag of coal. Incidentally, the bag was filled with straw. Here in the science building Charles took movies and still shots of every department at work. I had Dick take some for me with my camera, because the water temperature would be on a rampage. This place was really a mad house, some of the fellows were taking pictures with three or four cameras at once, standing on tables, chairs, getting in some of the most awkward positions. Anyway, everyone had a good time and everyone had his picture taken.

After lunch I took a nap before class, but Gil woke me up and wanted me to act for them. He and Shirley were taking movie shots in front of the bunk building, he wanted someone to come out of the door and walk down to the tunnel. My first acting, public appearance and I wasn't scared a bit. One time I walked to the clothing cache and next, I came down the tunnel from the head. Coach started putting the questions up at 2:00 o'clock, so Fitz and I started taking it. It certainly covered everything. I think I did all right. Some of the fellows worked on their papers after dinner, as the questions were probably a little longer than they should have been considering the fact that we had radio class at 4:00 o'clock. Pappy Reece sent about seven words a minute, which I copied without much trouble. But when Pappy hit the numbers I kind of fell down a little, simply a case of neglect. I didn't learn it, and I am ashamed.

Saturday, June 1

I am so used to writing May that I almost slipped here. Yes, it's June the first and I still have to say "who would have ever thought that I would have been way down here, Little America, on June 1st, 1940?" I didn't sleep very well last night. Don't know why, but I tossed and turned till about 4:00 in the morning. And of all the nights not to get some sleep, I would have to pick last night, especially since it was my turn to be Earl's patient again, meaning that he woke me at 6:00 A.M. However, I didn't have much trouble in getting up, but I didn't waste any time in getting over to the science building. It's not exactly warm running through the tunnel, sixty degrees below, with only pajamas and slippers on. Boy, I was certainly glad to hop in Earl's basket stretcher bed. I rested for about fifteen minutes or so, then he put the rubber mouthpiece in my mouth and I breathed for a while in the bag in order to clear it and get some of my gas in it before actually starting. Then the mouthpiece was removed for about five minutes to begin the ten minutes of observation, Earl watching the number of respiration and also taking my blood pressure, pulse, etc. After the ten minute period, during which I was not to move, Earl took my temperature. My respiration was fourteen breaths per minute, blood pressure one hundred and six/seventy and pulse was forty-seven and fifty. As usual, the fellows were shocked to see me up. I did go back to bed and tried to sleep but it didn't work.

Didn't run the experiment today as the conditions were similar to yesterday. However, the temperature is rising so Sunday is apt to be a good day as it will probably blizzard. We had quite a shock tonight. The show was going to be "Going Places," so Gil, myself and several others decided that it was the "Going Places" with Dick Powell, Louis Armstrong, Maxine Sullivan, etc. But you can imagine our surprise when what should appear but a series of short subjects narrated by Lowell Thomas. The one that Shirley picked for reel number one of "Going Places" was one on Pitcairn Island, Easter Island. We all got quite a kick at the thought of seeing the Pitcairn one and it was easy to pick out Fred Christian and others. Larry and I tried to find Warren, the fellow we stayed with, but no luck. Several of the fellows during the picture would point out the ones they stayed with. I still think that if nothing else, our trip was a success in getting to stop there. I really enjoyed it. Shirley hurried out and got another film and it was "Wuthering Heights," one show I had not seen. I thought "Hound of the Baskervilles" was gloomy and morbid, but I think "Wuthering Heights" had it beat. The only laughter in the whole picture was during one of the dances and even then one would feel that something mysterious was trying to stifle it. It certainly had an effect on the gang and I noticed several of them with rather red eyes. Of course, it didn't phase me, well, I might say that mine were a little watery.

Sunday, June 2

Toney woke me at 10:00 this morning, I asked him to do so after he had finished his washing. Jack Bursey is this week's mess cook and had already started to set the table for breakfast. The water was nice and hot and plenty of it, so it didn't take me long to finish my wash. I washed everything I wore during the week and it's rather funny because I have nothing to wear during the process. That is, I don't like to put on clean clothes while I am washing, hence I kind of drape a towel around my waist. And unfortunately I happened to touch my leg against the hot water pipe. As a result, I have a nice burn and either I will have to be more careful or else devise some other means of dress, because it is kind of cold running out into the tunnel for snow. That's the bad part about doing a washing down here—the effort and inconvenience of getting clean snow. That probably sounds funny, but actually clean snow comes at a premium. It's either full of soot or else an oil barrel sprung a leak, or better still, there seems to always be a cigarette butt in evidence. However, recently we took a piece of pipe and stuck through the tunnel, so on blizzard days we get some clean snow. I suppose we will have to start a tunnel or something. I can't understand it though, because a certain area south of camp was designated for snow—that is, we were not to drive dogs, tractor or anything in that region. I always feel so clean after a good bath, which always follows the huge washing, five pieces. It's kind of hard to get used to one bath a week when at school I took at least two showers a day. Doug wasn't around when I was ready to start the experiment so Toney helped me. I read the watches and worked the bridge while he counted the wind. We got along very well. It seems that Doug had been skiing. Ordinarily I would have waited for him but Perk told me that Doug said that he'd be darned if he was going to wait around while I took a bath, etc. He was kind of burned up because I started without him. I think it also griped him to think that Toney could do it as well as he. He came in and said "Oh! I see you have started." I told him that Toney just helped me get it started while we were waiting for him.

He mumbled something in his beard, stalked out of the building almost tearing the door off its hinges. He's such a baby—after all, Toney is helping him out. He hasn't spoken to me all day.

We had a good old Virginia baked ham for dinner—raisins, pineapple and everything. It was very good. I'm a little late, but Pappy Gray had a big surprise yesterday. He got a wire from Washington, the Navy, informing him that he made "Chief." Yes sir, that old "hillbilly" hung around the Navy long enough to make "C.P.O." At least, that's how he said he got it. (He's the aviation mechanic.) Murray's term as night watchman finally expired, much to his relief. He said he will be glad to eat regular and get a little sleep, although he sleeps all day. At least he is in his bunk all day, it is impossible to keep the fellows quiet. They mean well, they start out in a quiet, subdued voice, but soon a small argument will start, probably over who will win the war or possibly who will be the next president, reaching a crest, shortly accompanied by an increase in voice volume. Actually, one would think that murder was about to be committed. But yet they always seem to end friendly. At least they all have so far, and when they start ending the other way I hope I will be miles away from here.

During the later afternoon I read a chapter of historical geology, then helped Shirley file a few prints. Then one of those petty arguments I just spoke of happened to start. First Zeke and Shirley were discussing the question of the government having a right to our film. Then one thing led to another till the Civil War was brought up and then immediately Zeke and Shirley sided up, the rebels of the place against some of the others. They went around and around. Finally Mac came in and wanted to know what was the show for tonight. Well, that started it. What could be a better way to spend the half hour before dinner than trying to decide about the evening

164

performance. Well, there seemed to be differences of opinion. Some wanted "Dodge City," others wanted "Three Lives of Nancy." I wanted "Dodge City" so I started to campaign, saying that I would be glad to give anyone who would vote for that picture an extra cigar. (Just kidding.) The discussion got a little heated since we won out last week by getting "St. Louis Blues," and the other fellows still thought we cheated. So Mac got a poop sheet and went around to get the votes. Everyone voted but Pappy Reece, and since Nancy's were one ahead of us, we shook Murry out of a dead sleep to talk him into voting our way. He is in a stupor, a fog, and said he wanted "Torchy of China Town." Well, that just about finished things. After dinner I went around starting to agitate, saying that we got swindled, and asking how many really wanted "Nancy." Well, I could only find eight fellows, and fourteen were supposed to have voted. Mac got on his high horse and wanted to know if we were doubting his integrity. After all, he said he also wanted "Dodge," and he even took the paper around, even had the pencil, and still lost, you can't blame him for any crooked work. I told him the only thing we had against him was that we didn't win. Well, things turned out all right, we had "Nancy," and everyone had fun during the voting. They even had the nerve to call me a crooked politician, just because I offered cigars.

Earl hasn't been feeling very well all day. I didn't know it till I missed him at the show. He always sits by me. Incidentally, I have a box seat. It's the only way to see over all of these guys around here with bushy hair. My sea chest makes a very good platform. After the show I went to the science lab to write a little. Larry and Paul came in and before we knew it we had a nice bull session started. Paul told me how he met Ruth, his courtship, etc. He also told of several experiences on lecture tours. We talked of various universities and I found out quite a bit about Allegheny College, both Paul and Ruth went there. Ruth was working in the registrar's office at the time. One thing led to another till at 1:30 I finally gave up and went to bed. I had my sleeping bag out to air all day and I would forget to bring it in till then. So I had to stay up an hour or more so as to warm it up, and when I finally got to bed there was still some snow at the foot of the bag. Read for a while, then to sleep.

Monday, June 3

Jack B. is much more gentle at waking us up than any one man we have had so far. He has a bell, something like a cow bell, it actually has a pleasant sound, much more refined than a skillet. Got a sweet message from Alda yesterday. I sent her a message today—saying whatever she does will be alright with me. Clay is certainly nice about sending messages for me. He says that if I wanted to send one every day it would be okay with him. I guess he just likes me, he has told others to cut down a bit. I forgot to bring in the cylinder last night but didn't notice it till after Doug had started the wind count. Naturally it was impossible for us to go on unless we used the cube, but it would have taken too long because the wind velocity was too slight. So I told Doug I would go out, get the cylinder, and that we would start at once. I think he was a little mad because he had everything ready, etc. Besides, he hasn't gotten over Sunday. I spent the morning by starting to type up the experiments, one original and two carbons. I am afraid that's going to be quite a job, at least it's going to take some time. The hell of it is, the days are too short now, or at least they seem that way. It seems that no sooner do I get up in the morning than it's 1:00 or 2:00 the next morning, and after being busy all day, I seem to get nothing done. Oh, I do, but it piles up and if I want to do any studying I have to sacrifice my other work or else stay up late—it defeats me. They all talk about half over and we haven't even finished radio or navigation, let alone make any preparation for this spring.

After lunch I noticed that Malcolm was in working with Paul, so I guess he either forgot about the run or else he was giving me the air. So since the wind was so slack I decided to run it myself, which I did. It wasn't bad, all I had to do was watch two watches, record time, watch the light, count the wind and work the bridge. Outside of that nothing was doing. The wind was two and six tenths miles per hour and temperature was forty-eight and fifty-five one hundreds degrees. Everything went fine even though I didn't get to finish it because of Court wanting to make a balloon run. In opening the balloon hatch my temperature is affected, so it was useless to go further. Besides, I had gone beyond the critical point. In navigation class we reviewed the exam papers. Didn't do badly, got everything all right but rating a chronometer. Pappy Reece really gave us the works in radio class—twelve words a minute. I even surprised myself. I got at times two or even three words in a row. Maybe there is some hope. Boy, there's not a minute's peace around here. Scientific meeting tonight. Nibble with Paul as his "mouthpiece" gave a report on his "sled runner" experiment. Coach and Joe gave a report on their work and Court told us about the "heat of radiation" and Al finished up with cosmic rays.

Tuesday, June 4

I guess I will never learn—up last night till 2:00 or so, reading. Consequently I had a tough time getting up this morning. Of course, that is nothing new. I will swear that some of these fine mornings I am going to just say "the hell with things" and sleep all day—I'm desperate. There was a big bull session last night in our cubicle, which helped keep me up. Larry, Gil, Fitz and Perk were settling world problems from the war to the slums of Boston, including all of the larger cities which had been visited by any of these learned four. Temperature run today ran off very smoothly, temperature being minus twenty-five and sixty-five hundreds degrees centigrade and wind about eighteen miles per hour. Doug finally swallowed his pride or else thought he had punished me enough. Anyway, he was on hand by 9:00 o'clock ready to go. Lasted one hour and forty-five minutes. Shirley wanted to take some pictures of the clothing cache, so since I'm head man I went out and posed for him, took some shots with my camera. After lunch I worked on temperature and wind calculations, which I don't enjoy any too much. Right now my eyes burn like mad, even though Doc treated them for me. Poor Doc F. is having a heck of a time. He says someone took his ski boots—he looked high and low for them, but no luck. I suppose they are under his bunk. At least that's where one eventually finds things around here, or maybe in the bunk. About a week ago I couldn't find one of my deck shoes, three or four days later I found it in my sleeping bag. Now I know that I haven't been sleeping with my shoes. Still I'm not sure, my bunk is pretty crowded. Washed my hair today before dinner. I was going to just let my hair grow, but I am afraid I will have to weaken one of these days and get it cut. Grif does a nice job—crew cut, all the cruiser bunch has one.

Wednesday, June 5

I don't see how I can keep finding things to write about. No fooling, the same thing day after day. But I shoot the bull on and on. It is now 12:30 A.M., Thursday morning. I am sitting at my desk in the science lab, writing and listening to some music coming from

Australia—very beautiful, but sad. Some girl is singing war songs, sweetheart, lover songs. They'd tear the heart out of a chap leaving home for the trenches. I still can't believe that such a war is going on. We're supposed to be a civilized world. I hope and pray that the U.S. will stay out. Pretty cold out today, forty-seven and forty-one hundreds degrees centigrade with about a five mile wind—took Doug and me about two hours to finish our run. Earl is some better, Doc is giving him injections. I suppose he will be up in a few days, kind of miss him at the theater. He seems to have amoeba dysentery or something, got it when he was studying in Sweden last year. Paul has put trail information on the bulletin board. Berlin is leader of our party which is the "Pacific Coast Party." I'm geologist, biologist and meteorologist, Moulton is assistant observer and dog driver, while Bursey is radio man. Larry has been put in charge of the group that will work in the Edsel Fords, he will spend all of his time working out that region.

Jack Perkins has charge of a small party working from the Fords locally in search of plant life. Nibble has Grif as his relief driver. Fitz will have a station out in the Rockefeller mountains. Only a few of the fellows have been named permanently such as Berlin, myself, Larry, Perk, Fitz. The rest of the parties will be picked later on, etc. I am glad Lon is going to lead. He is navigator of our party, he has had so much field experience up north. He was the logical man, also he is the oldest. I think in our group, though, we will all have something to say, and I hope I do, especially as to the length of time to visit a peak, depending on the "geology." Show tonight was "It Could Happen To You," Stewart Erwin. Just a picture. Navigation class was a flop as far as I was concerned. Coach got all screwed up, and got everybody else the same way. However, I think I am getting it all right. Pappy R. sent us from six to eight words a minute, which I got very well.

Thursday, June 6 (134th day)

I almost slept in this morning, but the weather was such that I thought it better to make the run. We got started at 9:30 as usual, temperature was minus forty-nine degrees centigrade and wind seven miles per, which is cold and windy in any man's language. We were through about 11:00 A.M. and five hundred and ten calories of heat per minute was given off. I almost forgot to bring in the cylinder last night which would have been tragic. I was in bed, and for some reason I didn't feel right, knowing I hadn't done something I should. Well, it was the cylinder and did I ever hate to get up, dress and go out. My nose got nipped in the short time it took me to walk on the roof.

I haven't been feeling very well lately, seem to continually have a headache, and my head is always hot. I guess I am going to have to get more sleep, but it is so hard, especially when there is so much to do. Right after lunch we filled the snow melter. I didn't stay out long because I only had on a pair of dungaree pants, deck shoes, one pair of light socks, a beach jacket and helmet. Hardly the outfit to be caught out in. The wind numbed my legs before I even got to the place where we were to get the snow blocks. As for my face, I got a nice "bite" on both checks and nose. I can take it all right but believe me it was really foolish to stay out and literally "freeze to death." However, I did stay about fifteen minutes. My thin deck shoes immediately started to freeze and my ankles felt like I had a dry ice poultice wrapped around them. I guess I will learn. It's impossible to realize how necessary our windproof outfits are, today being the first time I had so much as ventured out without mine.

The same thing this afternoon as any other—I am still trying to get caught up with my graph plotting and temperature, wind, calorie units. I don't suppose that I will ever get done, but I keep at it. The 3:00 o'clock news of the "American Hour" certainly is a drawing card. At five till about half of camp is standing around the loudspeaker in the science lab and it is sacrilege for anyone to even so much as take a deep breath. All work stops because, after all, we do need food for thought. But I admit I am a little tired of hearing "war" discussed so much. I got so sleepy around 4:00 o'clock that I just quit and turned in. Had a nice nap till dinner. I swear that if we have any more meetings in the evening we are going to have to make the week longer or something. Since preparations are being made for the trail it has been decided that those fellows apt to go on the trail will meet two nights a week to discuss problems and hear Paul and Al talk on various ethics of the trail, etc. So Monday night a science meeting, Tuesday trail meeting, Wednesday show, Thursday trail, Friday, well, don't worry, they will find some way to take it up, Saturday show, and Sunday re-show. So out of seven nights there is only one not taken.

At the meeting tonight Paul talked. Most of the operations will be east along the coast as far as possible. To the southeast along the horst known as Queen Maud Mountains. Very important that the tractor can work all right. Will add fifty to seventy-five percent to trail operations. Difficulties for the tractor are soft surface and ramp at Mt. Grace McKinley and Mt. Haines area. Hope we can reach Mt. Rea where we will establish a sub-station for seismic work. Will also be depot and take off place for planes. Tractor will leave as soon as possible in the spring around September.

Berlin, Passel, Fitzsimmons and Warner will go with the tractor. If the tractor will not work, it will throw a heavy burden on the aviation unit. There will be three major flights. D to south and join flight made in fall at Thorne Glacier to trace Mts. to east and southeast to come back without retracing steps. Probably early in November E and R to start from sub-base and support Pacific coast party. F to start out and continue along coast to flight A. A landing near Mts. will be made if possible. Should pass or reach one hundred twenty degrees meridian, return inland approximately half way between coast and Ellsworth flight, to be made after dog teams have departed from sub-base. G to be made from sub-base south, pick up flight D at Herlich Mts. Continue S.E., return between Ellsworth's track. Hope to land for ten days or so for geological work. Beechcraft to act as reconnaissance plane to reach outlying peaks that dog teams cannot work. Flight H, stop at Mt. Sidley and Mt. Hall Flood for specimens. Possible to have Beechcraft and Condor fly down to edge of Polar Plateau taking seismic soundings. Would like to find out what is under Polar Plateau, do not know as yet. Flight C—Beechcraft flight across section of Ross shelf ice to determine if high point east of here sighted on Fall flight is really an island. Also along edge of Ross Shelf ice to map edge and study breaks.

Dog team parties—Pacific Coast Party to travel fast through Edsel Ford Mts. and to N.E. and E. as far as possible. Perk's teams and one of Larry's will act as supporting party for Pacific Coast Party. Ford geological party will do detailed geological study in Edsel Fords. Biological party will join Pacific Coast Party and support them. After reaching one hundred miles beyond sub base two of the supporting teams will return to sub base while others will travel back more slowly working Mts., etc. Biological party will probably return two or three weeks earlier than other parties as Perk has work to do around here—skin seals, etc. Also while in Mts., Perk hopes to visit rookeries. Al then told us a little of the geology, explaining that all mountains would have to be observed; hence would have to know a little geology, at least the difference between pink granite and sandstone.

Friday, June 7 (135th day)

I almost stayed in my bunk today. However, the weather tricked me up again. Wind was about nineteen miles from east and temperature was thirty-six degrees centigrade, a perfect five hundred day, taking one hour and twenty minutes to get from plus ten to minus thirty-six degrees centigrade. Shirley took some portraits of me the other day, posed with a fur parka on. Larry took some shots with my camera which Pete developed last night. They all turned out okay, all but one. Larry evidently didn't focus the thing. Also on the roll were shots taken in the tunnels, my cache, etc. They all turned out fine. This last bunch of negatives brings my total up to number five hundred and fifty-two, which is pretty good for a beginning. I ought to have quite a collection by the time I come back from the field and go to East Base, Valparaiso, etc.

I only hope that the hypo has been washed off sufficiently so they do not turn yellow at least till I have a chance to re-wash them when I get home. I am pretty proud of my work so far. I don't even claim to be an amateur photographer. In fact, I know nothing about it except that the camera has to be pointed in at least the general direction and snapped. Most of my outside pictures, shots were taken f8 or 9 at 50th, 100th. Some of the negatives are pretty dark but Shirley says that they will print okay. On the whole, though, I have fairly good negatives. I can't get over Alda giving me the camera, it was so sweet of her.

After lunch I started to work on my clothing issue, trying to bring my books up to date. I don't know how they are going to work it, how far I will be held responsible for the issue. But to be sure I'm not caught "holding the bag," so to speak, I am going over individual issues with the fellows so that we more or less agree on what was received, etc. Also to get signatures for clothing up to date. All I hope is that when I am all through with my books, issues correspond to the original received. I won't feel so badly if I am out, say, maybe a pair of mitts or a pair of socks, but no more than that. After dinner the wind had increased so that we thought it would be wise to take a temperature run. We were not able to get started till about 9:30 as our light blinking affected the radio. Phil was trying to contact WIWC and was having quite a time—signals very weak, band has been gradually fading out since about the middle of mail bag program. I had just finished working on my books and it was getting near mail bag time when Grif and Sarg came up and said that they were going to listen from the cruiser and wanted me to go along. So I put on a jacket (Beach), helmet and leather faced gloves, already had on deck shoes and dungaree pants. That's the same fatal snow melter filling outfit of the day before, but I thought it would be easy to make the two hundred yard dash to the cruiser without much trouble. Well, I guess I don't know the Antarctic yet because in that short distance I almost literally "froze to death." The wind had increased to about thirty-five miles per and it was barely possible to see the cruiser light. We had to follow the light wire which had blown down and as yet had not drifted over, it was silhouetted against a blowing background of white. It was hard to breathe, almost impossible to breathe through my nose. Tried to hold my breath only to give in, gasping mouthfuls of that precious element vital to life.

It was certainly wonderful when we did finally reach the trap door which let us into the privacy of the tunnels. Wiener was already there, as were Al and Phil. It was pretty cold inside, they had to quit burning the oil stove because of fumes. One lone electric heater was trying bravely to heat up the living quarters. Phil already had the station tuned in and we all settled down to listen to the pre-mail bag program from Cincinnati. It had no sooner started than Jack R. came in saying that Clay hadn't gotten the program yet, that Walt was outside checking all of the antennas, etc. Clay was still trying to contact WGEO. Nib pipes up and says, "I'll be damned—about $100,000 worth of radio equipment and we can't even get one program every two weeks." Well that does seem true, but still it just happens that conditions always get lousy around mail bag time. We got very good reception though, and I heard one from Alda. I didn't get all of it as luck would have it. I got a letter at the very first, but did not understand it. For about a day after the program all of the fellows asked one another if they heard such a message for them, or if they got a certain part, or who it was from? Right after I heard from Alda the band started to die out and I did get one from the folks, which I was sorry to miss. The trip back to camp was even worse than going over. Nib and I came back together and a couple of times we got a little off our course. But by yelling at each other and following the power line we made it all right, but not without freezing my face, meaning my nose. I never thought that I had an overly large "proboscis," but I guess I have. Anyway, it is certainly vulnerable.

After dinner, when Phil got through with WIMC, Doug and I started our temperature run. Being 9:30 and fairly late we were thankful that it moved so swiftly. The wind was thirty-three miles per and temperature thirty and forty hundreds degrees centigrade. The water reached zero in about thirteen minutes and we kind of took it easy waiting for the water to complete its freezing process. This waiting merely consists of counting the wind and every five minutes recording it along with the air temperature, and also keeping an eye on the water temperature just to catch it when it starts down. In other words, we were half asleep when Grif ran into the building all full of snow, no hat or jacket, and said "Fire in the blubber house."

He didn't seem very excited or sure that there was really a fire, he merely made the statement. Doug said that since he belonged to the dog department he'd better go see what it's all about. The rest of us and about all of the fellows in the science building were at work or at least "shooting the bull." Gil was typing, Larry and Jack R. were sending and receiving, Fitz was working up some reports. After Doug left, Larry and Jack got ready to leave and I didn't know whether to go or not. I hate to leave the experiment, but when Shirley came in with a box of recently born pups, indicating the fire was pretty bad, I also tore out, but immediately returned, dressed and started to collect shovels and anything that might be helpful to fight fire. Pappy Gray was running all over the place collecting fire bombs and extinguishers.

I tried to reach the blubber house by the long tunnel, running past the head along the dog tunnels, but the fire had burned through the wire cutting out the lights. And the smoke was so dense my flashlight wouldn't cut through it.

I couldn't breathe and my eyes burned. I did manage to crawl back to the science building, climbed through the balloon tower, stood up on the roof and was immediately blown off, landing in a none too soft drift. It took me a few minutes to pick myself up and get oriented, starting in the general direction of the blubber house. My flashlight didn't do much good. After falling over several large drifts, stumbling in a couple of sastruga holes, I got to the blubber house. Quite a few of the fellows were already there, shoveling snow down the ventilator.

Flames were shooting out of both the ventilator and the smokestack. I grabbed a shovel and with Nib holding a light I tried to put snow down the smokestack. It was a hopeless task. The wind would tip my shovel and empty it before I could even get it up to the stack. In the meantime some of the fellows were chopping holes in the main tunnel roof in order to clear it of smoke. Dick opened the end of his tunnel, as did Jack B. The dogs were in great danger, especially Perk's team and the larger puppies, Perk's tunnel being the last on the starboard side before getting to the blubber house and the pups had short tunnels perpendicular to the side of the house.

As soon as some of the smoke cleared, Toney, Pappy Gray and myself jumped down through the hole in the main tunnel. It was terrible, the smoke now heavy with chemicals as the crew topside had steadily been pouring and throwing everything available, fire bombs, etc., into the house and through the door, down the ventilator and the smokestack. It burned our eyes, got in our lungs, it was impossible to breathe. However, by using our flashlights we managed to crawl to Perk's tunnel. Dick's tunnel, which was right across the way was free of smoke and we were able to get a few needed breaths of none too fresh air before we continued on into Perk's tunnel.

Tosk, lead dog and closest to the main tunnel, seemed alright. But as we continued deeper into the tunnel we found the dogs in pretty bad shape, most of them seemingly out. We carried them out one by one and shoved them out the hole in the roof to some of the fellows outside. I had particular trouble with one dog. When I knelt down to take his chain off I thought he was down and out, but suddenly he jumped up and pulled away from me, tightening the chain around his neck. And before I knew it he and I were having quite a tussle, which ended up in my coughing and more or less "tossing my cookies." Finally, however, he gave up, I got the chain off and carried him out. He was limp as an old rag. Thank goodness he was the last one to take out because I don't think I could have made another trip. In spite of it all, it was kind of funny to see a little puppy dragging out a dog about twice his size. We made a hurried survey of the rest of the dogs and found them okay.

The fellows by then had opened holes in the other tunnels and they were clear. Jack R. dropped down in the tunnel and said he was going to try to get to the puppy tunnel. So he and I worked our way along the side of the blubber house, which by then was a mass of flames and the timbers right over our heads had started to burn. The tunnel floor was covered with about an inch or two of hot fat and we had to step pretty lightly because our feet started to get a little hot. We didn't have much trouble getting the tunnel gate open. We jumped, greatly relieved because some of the snow blocks

174

had melted, and that little pool of water was certainly a god-send. Just as we got in the tunnel Dick completed chopping a hole through the roof, so we did not have much trouble getting the pups out. They had not been affected as yet, but they were a little scared. One of the larger ones, a black and brown malamute, had dug himself into the back end of the tunnel and all that showed was his tail. We almost missed him.

After work was done in the tunnels we climbed out to offer our help in fighting the fire. Well, that was hopeless. The whole building was ablaze by then—a beautiful but horrid sight. We all just stood around fascinated. A small group of men witnessing destruction by the Antarctic's dreadest enemy. There was nothing we could do.

All of the dogs were saved. Dinah, who at the time was having puppies in a small pen in the blubber house, had been turned loose in the magnetic tunnel. Dick picked her up and the puppies had already been taken in by Shirley. The wind being from the east probably would not shift and the fire could not spread. We could not stop it, so there was nothing to do but return to the bunk house and let her burn.

When our bunch got to the house, Paul had a "poop sheet" and was counting noses as the fellows came in. We were all thankful that all were accounted for, but such a bunch as I had never seen— dirty beards and faces all iced, clothing torn. There was quite a commotion while the fellows were returning borrowed clothing, flashlights, everything from mitts to shirts. We all made such a mad dash once we realized that there was really a fire, grabbing anything we could get our hands on. The closest piece of clothing was ours for the asking. While we were out Doc Frazier made some coffee and set one of the tables with cookies, cold meats, etc., so between mouthfuls the evening's experiences were told and re-told. It seems that the fire was caused from hot blubber boiling over or exploding. Dick had just stepped out to the bunk house to get something. The only reason he was working in the place at all was to have it warm for Dinah while having her puppies. So when he got back (I guess he was gone about ten minutes) the section of the wall near the blubber stove was a blaze of fire. He immediately threw all of the fire bombs he had on the blaze and for a minute he thought he had it put out, and he would have if he had had more bombs. However, it got the better of him so he turned Dinah loose in the tunnel, grabbed the pups and ran to the bunk house for help where most of the fellows were playing a game of "Dictation." Shirley took the pups to the science lab and all hands ran.

All of Perk's dogs and the larger puppies were turned loose in the science lab and after a short period of recuperation they soon were all over the place, each trying to contribute a part of his personality to the general aspects of the place. We had no sooner finished our lunch than Jack B. came in to announce that the tunnels were altogether clear and that we had better cover up the holes or else we would also have a tunnel shoveling job as well as our other troubles. So Jack, Larry, Lon, Zeke, Dick and myself dressed again and went out. At that time the excitement had kind of worn off and I realized how tired I was, how much my face hurt, how it was to try to fight a fire at minus thirty degrees centigrade temperature with a thirty-four mile wind. We had all produced, worked in a mad frenzy to defeat a possible death.

All during the work I was not aware of my face, which in its ice covered condition seemed warm enough. The first time I went in, Doc Frazier said it was pretty bad and massaged it back to a tiny tingle, and I guess my second time out really did the job. It did not take us long to cover the holes and we were certainly glad to get back to the warm friendliness of our respected companion, the stove. Doc again came to my rescue, revived my face, and after putting on some dry clothing I almost felt good except that my face hurt like hell and had started to swell a bit. I guess I was a pretty sight all right. I will never forget tonight as long as I live—stumbling blindly through the night, eyes blinded by the snow and ice, my face an impassive mask of ice. Moving forward against destruction by Antarctica's bitter enemy, fire.

Saturday, June 8 (136th day)

Boy, was I ever glad to hit the bunk last night—I think I fell asleep immediately. But this morning was a different thing. My face was swollen and sore, and with my cauliflower ear, plus a headache and one or two sore muscles, well, I not only was in a bad humor but looked like something the cat drug in. Oh yes, I forgot to mention, I was also a little sick at my stomach. Didn't even feel like eating my breakfast, but did manage a bowl of fruit. After breakfast Doc fixed my face up but there is not much he could do except put on tannic acid, which only acts to keep the wind off. Boy, how it burned. I couldn't smile, and to open my mouth at all would only add to my discomforts. I spent all morning in

176

my bunk trying to sleep, trying to forget those little pricks of pain that seemed to have possession of my face. Doug woke me out of one of my beautiful, wonderful trances, dreams, and wanted to know if I wanted to try a run after lunch. Well, I had another bowl of fruit and after lunch with the temperature minus twenty-six degrees centigrade and the wind twenty-two miles per, made a brave attempt at sitting through the experiment. But I couldn't sit still and after fifteen minutes of it I sent for Paul, who relieved me. I remember freezing my ear once, but it couldn't possibly have been as bad as this or I would have gone mad long ago. I went back to my bunk, half asleep, half dressed, till almost dinner time. I did manage a bowl of soup but I couldn't keep anything else on my stomach. Now it would take quite a bit to keep me away from a show, especially a free one, so I did manage to sit through "Holiday," Kathryn Hepburn and Cary Grant. What a picture to show, especially when it hurt to laugh. However, I did get along fairly well with just chuckles.

Earl was feeling a little better so Doc permitted him to lie in Larry's bunk, which with the aid of about six pillows got along very nicely. Gosh, I almost forgot. My face was not my only worry but also both wrists, which Doc bandaged up. However, I do not notice them particularly, so I guess they are not too bad. The thing that makes me feel so badly about the other night is the fact that Dick practically built the blubber house single handed. It is true we all helped with the hole, with the digging, but the plans, construction and initiative was all Dick's. It was his baby and he did a fine job on it and he had a right to be proud. We didn't lose much except alpine rope, which was a very important trail necessity, plus a few odds and ends, some extra sled parts, harness webbing, etc. Dick, only an hour before the fire, had brought in his duffle bag with personal clothing, some shirts, a suit, etc. Well needless to say, they were lost as well as Dick's fur parka and mukluks. Dick certainly is a dejected looking sight, I feel sorry for him.

He thinks it is all his fault but that's absurd. It just happened, and it was a good thing it did because now we will be more careful.

Sunday, June 9 (137th day)
Went to bed last night around 12:30 but did not sleep very well. In fact, did not get to sleep at all till about 4:00 or so. Everyone slept late this morning, waking up around noon. We had a rather

177

late breakfast. Petras is now mess man. Missed my bath today, for some reason. Mainly that there was no water due to the fact it has been too nasty out to get any snow. Besides, my face still burned and was plenty sore even though the swelling has gone down considerably. Didn't do much all Sunday afternoon but lay around, reading to try to take my mind off my own miseries. I had little success, but by dinner time I felt much better and was plenty hungry as I had eaten very little the last couple of days. Just before dinner Paul called me into his office and showed us a message from Ruth—a seven pound eight ounce baby girl. He was so happy and excited he could hardly stand still and was having quite a time writing her a message. Not many in camp knew it, Al was to announce it during dinner, so I got a couple boxes of cigars and Paul passed them out. Boy, the fellows really kidded him. By that time most of the fellows were seated, and when Al announced it I thought the house would come down. Talk about noise. Oh yes, I forgot, Nib, Al and I mixed a little punch for the occasion, using three quarts of Schenley's. It was kind of strong, but the fellows really went for it. Paul even drank a couple of glasses. We really had a fine time. A good meal—chicken, frozen fresh peas, frozen fresh beans, a meal fit for a king, and Paul was certainly the king. I have never seen him so happy. I hurried to know that our promise still holds. Even the re-show of "Dodge City" was a big success. In all of the excitement I even forgot about my face. It had stopped paining and burning and started to itch, which was a relief in itself.

Monday, June 10 (138th day)

Boy, what a relief to get a good night's sleep. I only woke up a couple of times and that was when I turned my head, putting some weight on my ear. Doc F. changed the bandage on my right wrist and found a nice large blister which he proceeded to cut off, applied tannic acid again and bandaged it. My other wrist did not blister so he did not bother to bandage it. We didn't take a temperature run today because conditions were too similar to another run. Besides, I thought that it would be a good chance to get caught up on a little graph work, on which I am sadly behind. Worked practically all day on them so by tonight I have a good headache and in a lousy mood. The wind had died down some so the fellows, Dick, Larry, Burney, Perk, etc., worked out in the ruins of the blubber house trying to salvage a few items such as dog chains, clamp on's, etc.

178

They worked all day and I guess it was plenty dirty work as they came in looking a sight. However, they accomplished quite a bit in that they had chopped and dug out all of the snow drift, which had so nicely filled in the pit after the building crashed in. Tomorrow they plan to put a new roof on, probably a canvas one. The new blubber house will not be a nice wood building, but merely a snow pit with a roof. The chop and blubber house will be one. A funny thing, the wood floor of the house was hardly damaged at all except for a few of the boards. That's some help, I think. There were several seals in the chop house. They'd been dragged from the seal tunnel into the chop house, ready to be chopped for dog food. They were fried, boiled and cooked, all in one. In fact, I guess there wasn't too much of them left. That type of work is certainly hard on the clothing, half of the fellows came in with their windproofs torn. So that means another issue as soon as they finish the work.

Right after dinner Nib wanted to know if I could run the tractor for him, help him jar the tank loose. He and Grif have been hard at work the past few weeks taking off some armor plating. In fact, they have taken off anything they could to lighten the weight of the tank and still leave enough of it so that it could run. They took off the front plates, side plates and the armored trap doors. Chuck replaced all of these with plywood. I wonder what the army would say if they could see a plywood tank. Just about the only metal left is the frame and necessary wheels and gears of locomotion. Grif took the metal plates, etc., and made elongated groussors to fit on the track, hence giving the tank a wider tread. Should give it more bearing surface, and with the decrease in weight and the increase in surface hardness the tank should work and not bog down as it did in the spring. Nib and Grif spent all day digging a ramp from the garage, and since blizzards spring up at the least expected time they thought it would be best to take their test run regardless of how late it was. Well, I backed the tractor out, and after it warmed up, I ran up and down the ramp several times so as to smooth it out, kind of tramp it down. Well, everything would have gone alright except they couldn't get the tank motor started. It almost started a couple of times. The trouble was it could not be primed enough. So after about an hour or more work, it was decided to try again tomorrow and in the meantime Nib would work on the motor and they would try heating it. So I brought "Dolly" back down the ramp and put her in the garage. The scientific meeting tonight consisted of talks by Jack R. on "Pilot Balloon Runs" and Court on "Radio Sound Balloon Runs," also Al Wade gave us a summary of his work up to date.

Tuesday, June 11 (139th day)

Well, you might know that since the fellows had the blubber house all cleaned out it would blizzard today—yes, a forty-four to fifty mile wind, recorded by Court's high elevation anemometer, and plenty of drift. So today was more or less a holiday for most of the fellows.

Nib, Mac, Pappy Gray, Grif and a few others had a hot game of "Dictation" which lasted most of the day. Of course, the garage ramp would have to fill up, but such is life and luck in the Antarctic.

Our anemometer recorded the wind as twenty-nine and eight tenths miles per hour and the temperature was minus twenty-one and ninety hundreds degrees centigrade. The run lasted an hour and a half.

Dinah and her pups are doing nicely. One, however, died the other day, it was the first born. Jack R. tried to nurse it along, had it in a box by the stove, fed it with a medicine dropper. But the poor little fellow just couldn't make it. But the rest are fine, five in all, one male and four bitches. Dinah, I am afraid, is not a very good mother. They are her first litter and she doesn't stay with them very much—the modern young mother, bridge at two in the afternoon and she stays out late at night too. She's quite a problem but I imagine that after she gets over her nervousness she will be a model mother.

Doc F. has been tending to my wrist, changing the bandage, etc. It's coming along alright. Still sore but it is starting to scale over. A funny thing happened last Sunday. Doug has been coming in to see Earl quite often, asking if there was anything he could do, you know how it is. Well, I guess Doc F. got kind of fed up on hearing Malc blow off saying he would be glad to do this or that, so about the latter part of last week Doc told him that if he really wanted to help Earl he would do his laundry for him. I guess that was quite a blow to Doug because Doc said he didn't come around for a few days. Guess he got scared out and I don't blame him because Earl hasn't done a bit of washing since he left Dunedin, and probably since Boston. Well anyway, Doug stopped in the clinic Sunday morning to pass the time of day, etc. Doc happened to be there and mentioned that Sunday might be a good day, since he had the whole day to himself, to do Earl's laundry. I guess Doug was kind of stuck and to save his face he had to do it. He worked all day Sunday, had to carry snow to fill the "machine shop melter" because it hadn't been filled at all because of blizzards. Doug got his snow from various places along the tunnels where it had drifted in. Well, in fact, he didn't even get to the show on time, I think it was rather mean, but Doug ought to know better than to stick his neck out, especially around Doc F., because, well, he doesn't think too much of Doug anyway. At least Earl profited by the ordeal. He, however, didn't want Doug to do it, just didn't like the idea of someone doing his work. Earl's condition seems improved. He's getting shots every day, last couple of days he has had a temperature of one hundred and one.

Wednesday, June 12 (140th day)

Woke up this morning with a nice headache. Evidently Vernon forgot to open the door and with the door closed it gets pretty stuffy and hot in the bunk house. Vernon caused quite a commotion last night about midnight. It seemed that there was something wrong with the snow melter, so Vernon proceeded to fix it. I thought the house was coming down and he seemed to delight in his hammer because it took him just a little longer than usual to drive each nail. Of course, the howls of protest did not have anything to do with it, and Doug, who is very childish about some things, threw a couple of big shoes against the galley door, which added to the din. Everyone seemed to add his two cents worth. However, it didn't seem to phase Boyd who calmly finished the job. Believe it or not today was actually a still day, no wind to amount to much and the temperature was about twenty and a perfect day to work. So Paul called all hands available to go to work on the blubber house ruins. I didn't go out because of my face which was starting to peel, and Doc F. advised against it. Malc reports that at noon the hole was filled clear to the top with drift and only the day before yesterday they had it all clear. That's what makes work down here so hard, so discouraging—things have to be done over and over again before they are actually completed. I spent the morning working on graphs. We did not make a run as Doug went outside and worked. After lunch Nib said he planned to warm up the tank and take a trial spin. He and Grif had worked on the priming pump and pronounced it okay. In the meantime, Nib wanted me to drive the tractor, go over to the outside gas cache and shake out ten drums of gas for the tank and to be used as the load for the trial run. Mac and I went over. In going along with the tractor I had to change my course a couple of times because of "grounds" which were half exposed and there is nothing that makes Clay more angry than to cut his "grounds," which the tractor does very nicely. Most places, however, are well drifted over. Also, the antenna poles are a constant worry when driving a tractor during the winter night around camp, especially since Nib took off one of his headlights for the tank and the other one does not work. But the rear one works so it's merely a question of going in reverse, which is nothing new. We found the drums all right, they were about a foot under surface. It didn't take us long to get them out.

By the time we got back to the garage Nib had backed the tank out and he and Grif were finishing putting on the rest of the groussors. Nib then got in the tank to go over and pick up a sled, but instead opened his trap door and asked for a flashlight. Then he disappeared for a while only to appear again with the information that he had broken his "oil purifier" which meant the trial run was out. But Nib said he would just try her out around camp, just to see how it worked, so he again disappeared. The trap door closed, the motor roared and he was off. She worked, the tank didn't sink in or bog down at all and today the snow was probably as soft as he would ever see it. In fact, Joe Wells, after coming back from reading his thermometer, said that several times he waded through snow up to his waist, which would mean at least to his ankles or over his knees.

Nib took the tank around by the Condor hanger, to the Cruiser and back without even stopping and drove down the ramp to the garage. Boy, was he happy, and he well had a right to be because he'd worked like hell. When everyone else gave the tank up, Nib stuck it out, figured, and worked it out. Result, she works. There is quite a bit of drift around camp and the tank bucked like a veteran. All Nib has to do is fix the oil purifier. The show tonight was "Romance of the Redwoods," and pardon me, but it stank. It no doubt will not be among our re-runs.

Thursday, June 13 (141st day)
I still can't believe it—we all slept till 11:30 and believe it or not, another blizzard, and a honey at that. Wind about forty-five miles

with temperature minus twenty degrees centigrade. Boy, the month of June would put March to shame. We have had blizzards continually since the first of June and it looks like they are going to remain with us. I guess everyone was tired out. The fellows finished digging out the blubber house and put the roof on yesterday, and that was a day's work. Paul probably told the cook to let us sleep, not to have breakfast till late, and there wasn't a peep out of the fellows all morning—not even Joe Wells, who usually gets up at 6:00 or so starved. Had hot cakes for breakfast with cane syrup (molasses), was very good for a change. Doug and I started our run at noon, finishing up at 1:30. Our anemometer reading was twenty-five miles, which is obvious, since ours is at a lower elevation than Court's and is probably sheltered by the balloon tower.

Friday, June 14 (142nd day)
Dragged myself out of my bunk with much effort this morning. I still swear that I am going to sleep in one of these fine mornings and I am getting closer and closer to it every morning. The only person who sleeps later than I do is Zeke. (I'm not proud of the fact.) Our bunk has regular routine each morning. First Larry gets up, then Fitz, and last but not least, me. Some mornings, however, I manage to get up before Fitz, but not often. Our temperature run lasted for over two hours today. Temperature was minus fifteen degrees centigrade and about a fifteen mile wind. Heat calibration was two hundred sixteen and fifty-four hundreds, meaning that wind chill would be low. Have started "Gone With The Wind." Have been going to tackle it all winter but couldn't get up enough nerve. Imagine one thousand and thirty-seven pages. Had a long talk with Paul today about this and that. I found out that he hadn't seen Alda's picture so I got it for him. He was very favorably impressed. We talked about whether the Senate was going to appropriate us any money to get out of here. Charlie (Boston) read a piece out of the paper to Clay over twenty meter, saying that someone in the Senate said to appropriate $117,000 to bring us home and then quit the U.S. Antarctic service once and for all. Well, it will take probably at least $100,000 for the ship, $17,000 for food and incidentals, so I guess there will be no increase in salaries as was hoped if the appropriation would be $250,000 as originally asked. So I guess I will have my twenty-two and one-third cent per day cut.

Well, the only thing to look forward to today is the show. Same old thing day after day. If it wasn't for such things as shows, mail bags, messages, etc., I'm sure that I would go stir crazy. The temperature run today was uneventful except that we are having trouble getting the cylinder out. We have had so much bad weather, blizzards, that our hatch opening has drifted over, which has to be dug out every morning. That's Malc's job since the Doc still advised against my going out, especially since the wind is so bad. We keep a length of pipe where the hatch should be, then Doug digs down till he hits the pipe. Then he fastens the connector end to the pipe and I pull it through while he goes back on the roof and fastens the cylinder. This has to be done fairly rapidly so as to get the cylinder up before it starts or gets to plus ten degrees centigrade, so we heat it before we take it out and Doug keeps it wrapped in a scarf and in his parka pocket. After I have connected the contact end to the bridge contact, which is just outside the door, I make a mad dash to get back in to take the plus ten reading. Often times I have gotten there just as the needle passes plus ten, so have to be contented to start the experiment with plus nine, and often times we have missed down to plus seven. The temperature today was minus twenty-nine and sixty hundreds degrees, wind was fourteen miles per. As soon as we get a fairly nice day without wind I guess we will have to clear out the hatch and fix up some kind of a stovepipe arrangement end through the pipe. Show tonight was "My Darling Daughter"—third time for me.

Sunday, June 16 (144th day)

Gosh, I forgot about the great change in my schedule in that I did my washing yesterday afternoon. I was afraid I would get in a rut. Besides, I like to sleep and rest on Sunday, have a little time to myself. Chuck, Toney and I spent about three hours yesterday afternoon cleaning up the tank. Boy, it was a mess. Some of the lunkheads around here can't seem to realize that it takes clean snow to produce clean water. Well, the last person or persons got their snow from the tunnel somewhere and it was full of oil and corruption. As a result, the sides of the tank had a layer of oil about an inch thick. We had to use lye, alcohol and everything else before we could even phase it. After finally getting it halfway presentable we rebuilt the fire which we had to let die down so that we could empty the filthy water. We started to fill the tank again from snow blocks which Chuck, Joe and Toney cut while they were out filling the snow melter. It was really wonderful to take a bath. You see, I missed last week due to the blubber fire, blizzards, etc., and I was beginning to feel uncomfortable. I also did my washing and a couple of things for Joe. I think I will stick to Saturday from now on because this morning it was so nice to sleep late.

Got up for breakfast knowing that I was clean, my clothes were all clean and that I didn't have to rush out to the machine shop and spend half of Sunday carrying snow to fill up the tank.

Today was quite a day because Jack R. became a man. Yes sir, and for a gift he got the mess job for the week (which in my way of thinking isn't such a hot gift). And evidently Dick, Ray, Arnold and Doug didn't think so either because they relieved him of the duty for today saying that it was beneath a newly made man's dignity to start out on the threshhold of manhood by being a mess cook. Toney helped me with the run today, as Doug has to wash dishes. Temperature was minus thirty-five degrees centigrade and wind about twelve miles per hour, but no drift. I guess that all of the loose snow has been drifted up long ago, because this month we have really had our share of blizzards. Dinner tonight was a treat, as are all of our Sunday meals—fried chicken, fresh peas and lima beans, with sweet potatoes. The fellows all sang Happy Birthday for Jack, and Sig presented him with a nice cake (I might mention in passing that I had three good sized pieces). Paul received a message from East Base. They are all fine. They lost five dogs from dampness and fighting. Dustin went back, probably because he and Ronnie could not agree on Rickie. Also Hawthorn returned. We had a re-show of "Love Affair," which gets better every time I see it. I think Irene Dunn is wonderful in it, as is Charles Boyer. One day last week Wagoner of the General Electric Co., who handles the mail bag, sent Paul a message asking who we thought were the most popular actor and actress of the pictures that we have down here. Although we have not taken a ballot on popularity of players, we did take one on popularity of re-shows, etc., and from voting Irene Dunn and Cary Grant were the best liked since the pictures they are in are among the leading ones.

Monday, June 17 (145th day)

Boy, since I have started reading "Gone With The Wind" I have practically lived with the book. Stayed up last night or this morning till 3:30, but I finally won the Civil War. It was a tough battle, but it was worth it. I did, however, think a little differently this morning, especially around 7:00 o'clock when the breakfast gong (a spoon and a pan encouraged and aided by H.H.) announced that breakfast would be on the table in half an hour. Well, I swear that I almost said "to hell with it," and turned over to continue my peaceful dreams. But my conscience got the better of me. I guess I felt a little guilty, and after about a half hour or so of arguing within myself I did manage to get to the table just as it was being cleared. After a breakfast of hot cakes, I went out and worked on the hatch through which we take our cylinder. Didn't take a temperature run today because similar to another day. Besides, there wasn't much wind so thought it would be a good idea to work outside. Larry and Al were working in the ice house, digging their pit deeper. I put a stove pipe through the roof so that we will be able to drop the contact end into the tunnel. This method will eliminate the every day shoveling which has taken place the last few days.

Had navigation class this afternoon, started on latitude. Radio class was a big success as far as I was concerned, got about ninety percent or so of all the words and Walt sent about twelve a minute. Not much happened tonight at scientific meeting. The fellows are starting to growl a bit—don't like the idea of having so many meetings. I should think that the fellows could have evenings to themselves, still things have to be done and time is so limited. Fitz explained the function of his magnetic equipment and Doc Frazier read a "poop sheet" in which he just rambled on. But he did state that down here would be an ideal place for tuberculosis patients because of the dry air. Of course, some of the bunch wanted to know if there would be nurses.

Tuesday, June 18 (146th day)

Tore myself away from Scarlett last night about midnight and did manage to get some sleep, so feel much refreshed this morning. Got the temperature run started off bright and early this morning at 9:00 o'clock. Temperature was minus fifty and forty-five hundreds centigrade, and wind velocity five miles per hour. Total time was about an hour and a half. After lunch Nib wanted to try another trial run with the tank so I drove the tractor for him. Mac and I went out with the tractor, got a sled and went out to the gas drums we pulled out the other day. We loaded them on the sled and waited for Nib to come with the tank. Gosh, it was cold today.

The minute I got outside my face started to burn and after about a half hour or so my hands were practically useless and I had to work the hand levers on the tractor with my wrists. There is not a colder job than driving that little red tractor. The doors can't be closed because the windows ice up. And even with the doors open it is necessary to open the rear window and windshield—in other words, a kind of open air job. I was certainly glad to see the tank approaching the gas cache, looking very grotesque bouncing and plunging along at the amazing speed of five miles per hour with the one lone headlight trying bravely to light the way. With the added reinforcement of Toney and Paul, Grif and Nib, it didn't take us long to finish loading the barrels. Then Nib backed the tank and we hitched on the sled—the trial run started and it was a success, so I heard. After the sled was loaded I made a beeline for the garage, it was just too cold for me to linger. After about fifteen minutes Nib brought the tank back to the garage. Boy, I have never seen him so happy—his beloved tank was a huge success. The only difficulty was that it kicked up so much snow that it was impossible to see out the windshield, so Nib immediately started to work to devise some sort of a fender guard. Tonight Paul called a trail meeting and we talked over plans (now for certain including the tank).

Ike was made head of trail activities, having complete authority during preparations. Of course Dick and Jack B. will be in charge of making blubber, Jack B. will make and repair sleds, Perk on the tents and I will work on food and clothing. A very fine meeting while it lasted, but toward the end turned into a general bull session.

Wednesday, June 19 (147th day)

It's a funny thing, but I can't think of a darn thing that happened today. That's the trouble when I miss a day, I forget so easily. Well, after all, not much happens anyway. It's just another day. Temperature today was minus thirty-seven and 70 hundreds degrees centigrade and wind six miles per hour. Doug and I had a very successful run taking two hours. Got a nice curve. Oh yes, as usual I am still having trouble getting up mornings. This afternoon I worked out in the clothing cache moving the fur sleeping bags out to the housing cache away from the building. Will probably move all of the extra clothing out there just in case. Ever since the blubber house fire we are taking extra precautions because if this building or any of the others would go it would be just too bad. Because if one goes they all will go. We would probably move to Little

America. It's a good feeling to have such a place. Of course, some of us could live over at the cruiser, and if worse comes to worse we could all live there. Well, not exactly a pleasant thought, but one can't afford to be literally "caught with our pants down." Spent the time during navigation class working some time problems. Walt took a radio and sent us about twelve words a minute. I did fairly well. I know I can copy ten all right and thirteen is just a little too fast for now. Show tonight was "Big Town Czar," which, incidentally, will not be re-shown.

Thursday, June 20 (148th day)

Today is just a repetition of yesterday. I hate to say that I am becoming a little tired of this life, but I am here and there is no getting around it. Quite a bit of excitement around here today. Since Paul sent Wagoner the "poop sheet" saying that we thought Irene Dunn and Cary Grant were our choices for popular actress and actor, it was decided that we would actually take a poll. So Gil typed a list of the stars, made a few carbon copies and passed them around. So the conversation for the next couple of days will be centered around our favorite Hollywood folk. Due to the fact that we had seen more pictures with Cary Grant, I picked him as my first, then came Clark Gable as second, followed by Gary Cooper, Spencer Tracy, Errol Flynn. It's hard for me to say because I like them all, each has his good points. I would have really picked Lionel Barrymore first, then Charles Laughton, because they are still the best. Of course I picked Irene Dunn, because she has contributed much to our entertainment down here as she has been in about four pictures, and every one a good one. Next comes Betty Davis, and for third I would say Katharine Hepburn. You know, there is a difference whether the actress is being chosen for her ability to act or for her umph!—half of the poor misguided souls down here picked Dorothy Lamour, but personally I can't see how. I guess she is beautiful and appealing and all that, but isn't beauty really skin deep? Well, tomorrow is to be a legal holiday down here, June 21st—midpoint of our winter night. Yes sir, from then on it's all downhill. We're over the hump, so to speak. It will all be over but the shouting. So tonight during dinner some of the fellows started agitating for a show since it would be possible to sleep in. So Charlie said it was alright with him and Paul agreed. Of course Jack R. was in favor of it since he was on mess duty and that would mean help. So since I was among those who started the movement I helped with the dishes. Not very smart to be caught like that, but I couldn't make a graceful exit. Fitz, Dick, Doug and I helped Jack. We had a re-show of "Love Affair." I don't know why, but some pictures are better when they are seen a couple or three times. "Love Affair" is that type of picture.

Friday, June 21 (149th day)

After the show last night I finished "Gone With The Wind." I was up till the wee hours, but I was determined to finish it. I don't think I could have lasted much longer—that darn book has kept me up now for the last couple of nights. So I made one desperate attempt to finish it and succeeded. How could any one person put so much in one book—one thousand and thirty-seven pages. And they aren't ordinary pages, but fairly small print and oh, so many words per page. Joe said that was the only book that ever made him stand up and read it. He practically lived it. He'd sit in a chair till he couldn't stand it any longer, then climb in his bunk and read till his back was sore from lying down, and would finally end up by reading standing up. I guess I was almost that bad. It did give me some satisfaction to fight the Civil War and see Scarlett through three marriages, though. But I still didn't particularly like the ending. It seemed like Miss or Mrs. Mitchell just got tired of writing and stopped. I would have had the book end much differently—endings should always be happy. It was wonderful to sleep this morning. A regular holiday and today is one day I really rested, didn't even take a temperature run. Got up about 1:00 in the afternoon and by the time I finished breakfast and cleaned up a bit it was time to go over to the cruiser to listen to the mail bag program. What could be better—sleep late, rest, and the mail bag program all in one day. It was wonderful. The program came in very well. We're still having two way test contact with WGEO. I received messages or letters from mother and dad and Aunt Nellie. Also they re-read the message from the last mail bag program, that is, the last half of the program, and sure enough, the folks' letter was read. I didn't hear it last time because the program died out. You know, the only thing I don't like about these holidays is the meal arrangement. I got so darn hungry by dinner, which is usually around 7:00 o'clock. Joe says the critters take a delight in seeing how long we can go without food.

Well, the meal we had tonight was worth waiting for. Turkey dinner and trimmings. Sig was at his best. And just to prove that it was a great holiday, I passed out cigars. But darn the luck, it wasn't great enough to have punch. But then, it won't be long till the fourth. We hadn't gotten half way through our dessert when the fellows started to talk show. So we had a show—a re-show of "Joy Of Living," and of course it was Irene Dunn. This bunch around here have gone show crazy and I guess I'm just as bad as the rest.

Saturday, June 22 (150th day)

Holidays always tire me out and I had a plenty tough time crawling out of my bunk. But rest assured I still make it to the breakfast table in time. But I will admit that I had several close calls—got there just as the mess cook was clearing the table, or just in time to save my fruit. Fruit is a premium around here and if a fellow isn't careful one of these crooks will grab it off. Doug and I were back in the harness this morning the same as ever. Right after lunch I worked with Paul going over some of the data we have gotten up to date. We worked out several graph arrangements to help show the advantages of our temperature runs, such as temperature against wind, temperature against calories, and wind against calories. After we finished we didn't quite know what we had and still don't. It will take some time to study the graphs in order to understand them. Shirley was busy all afternoon taking pictures in the bunk house of the various cubicles, so there was a mad dash as fellows tried in vain to make them look half way presentable. Paul's office is always a sight and now especially, since he has been working on the flight pictures. But he made a brave attempt to clean and straighten up and not ten minutes after he had finished I asked him for his scissors, and darn if he could find them. And they had been in plain sight before he started straightening up. It's really funny, he gets a streak of tidiness every once in a while and spends all afternoon cleaning his office and putting things in shape. Then for a couple or three days after that he can't find a thing. Then in about a week things will be all scattered around again and he feels much better. All you have to do is ask him for something and he'll say, "Oh, yes, it's under these papers," lift them up and sure enough there it is. Al Wade is the same way.

In the late afternoon I excused myself, telling Paul it was Saturday and time for my weekly bath. Since Chuck, Toney and I have decided not to clean the snow tank fixed for wash water, I wish you could see it. It kind of burned us up. We'd spent all day Saturday cleaning it and filling it with nice clean water. Well, if we were lucky we could take baths, wash and use the water once before the rest of the vultures got to it. Chuck usually washes after the show Saturday night, and he used to say that at least a dozen fellows would come out to use the tank—yet none of them will clean it or fill it. After we clean it, it usually stays clean till Monday night, then someone starts using tunnel snow and the sides of the tank become filthy and greasy. So this Saturday we decided to clean it but to fix up a container for our own use since we seemed to be the only ones who cared whether the water was clean or not. Chuck didn't have time to rig the thing up so I took a tub and a Von Prague and melted enough snow to take a bath and wash a few clothes. Then by leaving enough hot water in the tub it was simple for Chuck and Toney to melt enough for them.

The show tonight was "For Love or Money." I wasn't too much impressed, in fact, can't even remember who played in it. We had a short technical color subject about Canadian Mounties, which was a joke. A singing Mountie for a hero, who even sang at his wedding. I don't guess it will be re-shown. Got a very sweet message from Alda tonight, saying she was sorry she missed the mail bag.

Sunday, June 23 (151st day)

I can't get over all of these holidays. I'll be getting downright lazy if things don't change, and that would be terrible. Got up at noon as per usual on Sundays and we had a breakfast of hot cakes and fruit, plus toast and coffee. Didn't make a run today as conditions were similar to yesterday. Spent most of the morning working on graphs and in general messing around. Someone found out that we had a Chinese checkerboard so Shirley, Murry, Earl and myself played a couple snappy games. They almost succeeded in starving us out today. I was actually weak by dinner time, and we would have my favorite—baked ham, June peas, corn, mashed potatoes, tea and fruit jello—a feast fit for a king. I finally had to give up after a couple of helpings. Passed out cigars again today, these double holidays are hard on cigars, to say the least. We only have enough for a couple months more. But we will be on the trail anyway, so that will be that. Dick Moulton is on mess duty for this week and he is carrying on Jack R's habit of turning on music to wake us up. It's surprising the nice effect it has on one in comparison to beating on a pan with a spoon. Yes, it's really wonderful to wake up to Guy Lombardo playing "I Love You Truly." I helped Dick with the dishes tonight, Grif and myself. I don't mind washing the dishes but I certainly hate to handle the pans. The cook is very careless about pans. Not only does he seem to use quite a few but he also lets stuff harden in them, which no good Navy cook does, I am told. They at least put water in the pan and set it on the stove, but not our little Sig. I guess he doesn't know any better or something. The show tonight was a re-show of "Dark Victory."

Monday, June 24 (152nd day)

I can't get over how fast the days slip by. Here it is almost the end of the month. Well, personally they can't go by fast enough for me. The sooner we leave for the trail the better I will like it. These all have been wonderful experiences, and I am glad I came on the expedition. Read last night till about 2:00 or so, "Adventures With a Lamp," by Ruth Partridge, a story about a student nurse. It seems to be very good so far. It was highly recommended by Malcolm and Joe liked it. Doug and I got started on time today but the run was very slow, lasting till noon. And rather than miss lunch we stopped a few degrees before the thing reached stability. The wind was ten miles per hour and temperature was minus twenty-one degrees centigrade. After lunch I worked on graphs again trying to make something out of the work we did Saturday, but for some reason could not get very good curves. The wind didn't seem to be accurate in most cases and I think possibly the error might be due to the critical points we picked to take the average. Our critical points are plus two and minus seven and we take the average wind between these two points. But often times our wind reading, which is taken every five minutes, does not fall at the same time the water temperature reaches plus two and minus seven. In some cases it has been necessary to go four or five degrees above or below the critical points in order to get the wind average. Well, that means a lot more work but it doesn't make any difference anyway because I am so far behind now that nothing seems to matter. I have finally given up ever trying to keep up with the graph work. Maybe I will have some time on the ship enroute home—that is, between sunbaths.

Our side had been filling the snow melter this week. It's a fairly simple job now that there are drifts clear to the roof of the buildings and all we have to do is walk up and dump our block of snow

31. The author with two other members of the Antarctic team—Dr. F. Alton Wade (middle) and Larry Warner (right). All three men were associated with Miami University in Ohio.

32. The buildings all covered with snow.

33. Entrance to buildings. Paul Siple standing in entrance way. After a blizzard, we shovel out again.

34. Digging a tunnel for the dogs. This protects them from the high winds and extreme temperatures during the winter night. Example: if it's 50 degrees below zero outside, it could be about 30 degrees below zero inside the tunnel.

35. The dog crates are inside the walls of the tunnel so each dog has its own house. Since they fight they are always on a tethering line unless let loose to exercise. When they are exercised in the tunnel the driver always has to be present to stop fights.

36. Paul Siple hitching up dog team.

37. There is usually no horizon.

38. An Army tank sent with the expedition for testing in cold climate. From left, the author, Sgt. Asman (Army) and Clyde Griffith.

39. The tractor trailer with a wheel cyclometer shown, which measures nautical miles. From left, Sgt. Asman, author, and Paul Siple.

40. The T-20 International tractor clearing a path. The tractor could only be used in reverse because of traction.

41. Pumping gas. The drums are under the snow.

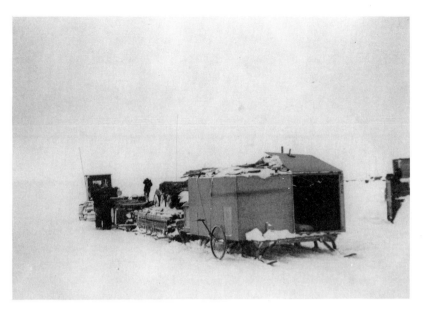

42. The tractor taking a load out to the 60-mile cache. Load consists of dog food, airplane fuel and man food.

43. We hitched our trailer sleds behind the tractor. The dogs tired easily when we first started on the trail. The normal load for two sleds was 900 pounds.

44. We traveled in single file with one man skiing ahead to break the trail.

45. A forced rest stop because of a blizzard.

down the snow chute. It only takes about fifteen minutes a day which gives me just enough exercise to get by on.

As usual, navigation class was in a turmoil. I don't know who is the more mixed up, the Coach or some of us. His pet stooge is the inevitable Malcolm who keeps the Coach on a rampage most of the time by getting things "bassackwards." He gets things all screwed up, a definition wrong, or some theory of his own, and winds up by trying to defend himself by giving navigation experiences while a Boy Scout or when he sailed about five years back, or something as absurd. The trouble with Doug is that he learns a thing once, and one way—well, he just can't change or won't change. He's right and there is no getting around it. That is, he's right till the Coach takes him down a notch, which he does every Monday, Wednesday and Friday from 4:00 to 5:00 in the afternoon. We had a little quiz in radio class, Pappy R. was kind enough to give it to us. Wasn't it nice of him? He sent us about seven or eight words a minute. That is, he sent five lettered codes, mixed numbers, and code. I missed seven letters. It seems that I am missing my B's and six's, am interchanging them. B is —••• and six is —••••. I haven't quite got the distinctive sound between the two. Scientific meeting was a success tonight. I gave a little summary of the progress of our temperature work and I didn't faint this time—I remained seated. I presented a few curves for comparison purposes and told of our trouble in plotting on our final graphs. Berlin gave a short summary of his work, saying that the map would probably be finished in another month. Also that he took a shot of West Cape on June nineteenth and found that it had been moving fifty-two inches a day, an increase since his last shot which I think was sometime in February or March. The West Cape seems to be moving a little north and east. One of the fellows asked if maybe we were possibly moving, and naturally there is no way of telling at present, but Berlin hopes to make a survey at Little America. They have longitude and latitude shots, etc., taken from previous expeditions, and if Little America is moving then we probably are because of the short distance, a little over five miles. The main paper or talk of the evening was Paul's "poop sheet" on his Polar theory which I think rather astounded the boys, although most of us know a little something about it. I feel quite sure that his circles are not just a coincidence, but I can't understand why someone hadn't thought of it before, why someone hadn't put a mercator grid around other than the two present poles. However, Paul has a lot of work to do yet and I know he will be only too happy to get home. He will be able to get hold of some good maps and some good geology reference books whereby he can determine the age of his so called "Footprints of Imprints of the Poles."

Tuesday, June 25 (153rd day)

I had a tough time getting out of bed this morning. I didn't stir till 9:00 o'clock, almost missed breakfast. We got the temperature run started by 9:30, lasting until noon. The wind was twenty miles per hour and temperature was minus twenty-two degrees. It is now 1:00 o'clock Wednesday morning and as I write it is blowing quite hard. What a weird, terrifying sound, the wind howling, whistling down the ventilators. On a good windy day the radio wires fairly sing, accompanied by the "putt-putt" of the exhaust of the generator engines and the roar of our windmill. Spent all afternoon working over a list of clothing which would be desirable for trail use, typing out enough copies to give to the various members of the parties. Most of the data I got from Paul's thesis. The main object of the list is to tell the fellows what they are to take on the trail, then to have them check the list against the clothing they have, testing the quality and the condition of the clothing. Just before dinner (which, incidentally, was chicken—which I can't understand, so don't ask me) I went out in the clothing cache and did a little straightening around. Also got Earl some extra blankets for his stretcher bed. He has been up for the last couple of days, although he is fairly weak he seems much like himself. Tonight I was all settled to do a little reading and studying when a trail meeting was called so that Paul could read and comment from the log of his sledding trip last expedition. Very interesting and will give us some good pointers.

Wednesday, June 26 (154th day)

Paul took us up to the one hundred and fifty mile beacon last night, and even though "the trail" sounds pretty tough I am still anxious to get started. They got started last time about the thirteenth of October and the temperature was plus four but after a couple of days the temperature dropped to minus thirty-five degrees and minus forty degrees. That's what worries me. It's not particularly the cold but the wind which makes it so uncomfortable. After the first day out they had a dog fight and a dog by the name of Will Rogers got bit on the leg. He was on Al's team and a very good

194

puller. He never recovered but kept getting worse every day till finally Al had to shoot him. It seems that the most difficult thing on the trail is keeping footwear dry. After skiing all day, naturally your feet sweat and your boots become hot. Then they freeze overnight and from what Paul says it really is no fun trying to put on frozen shoes. And there is hardly enough kerosene to thaw them out completely every morning. Well, it's something to look forward to, anyway. The temperature today is similar to the other day and wind about fifteen miles per hour. The water was almost an hour and a half in freezing, however, we did manage to get through by lunch.

After lunch I read a little historical geology and finally got out of the Devonian, also Walt sent me a "poop sheet" by code. I thought I had better do a little practicing because Pappy might give us another quiz. There are getting to be fewer and fewer of the fellows showing up at navigation these days, and we are getting started later, too. I don't know what's wrong, but it's pretty bad—it must be the professor. Dick seems to have given up and Bursey thinks he is too good to show up. In fact, not a good half of the trail members come to class any more, only now the old stand bys, myself, Larry, Perk, Doug, Jack R., and Earl. As for radio, things are about the same. Only a few are getting it and according to Paul no one goes on the trail unless he passes radio as well as navigation. Well, if that's the case we're going to have a small trail party. But even when things look the darkest there is always hope, so I just know that everything will turn out all right. Boy, we really had a thriller tonight. "Gorilla," with the Ritz brothers, what a screwy picture. After the show there were little groups of fellows centered all around the place trying to figure out who was the "Gorilla," what was what, who was who and which was which.

Thursday, June 27 (155th day)

Started out the day wrong this morning by getting up fifteen minutes early at 8:45 and I knew I would pay for it, that something would go haywire during the day. Well, I was rewarded. Doug and I got all set to take our temperature run. In fact, Malc had already taken out the cylinder and things were all ready to start. But nothing happened—the bridge, the galvanometer needle wouldn't work. Messed around for about ten minutes trying to find the trouble with no luck, but by that time the water had probably already started to cool. We would have to start all over anyway, so Malc very reluctantly put on his wind proofs (snow suit, as he calls it) and went out to get the cylinder. Well, Al, who was nearby, took a look at the bridge and before we knew it he had taken the whole thing apart. I guess we spent at least an hour or so, pulling here, wiggling wires there, testing. Pappy R. even came with the radio department voltmeter and still we couldn't find anything wrong with the thing. In fact, we had given the whole thing up when Al, in putting the galvanometer back in place, was screwing down one of the screws which secures it to the bridge and noticed the needle jumping. It seems that this screw has to be just right or the whole thing is shorted out. We had it too tight before. Doug has certainly had a tough day. Yesterday I told him that we wouldn't take a run today, that I was going to work with Larry and Al in the snow pit. But when I awoke to a thirty-five mile wind and a minus twenty degrees centigrade temperature, I decided it would be best to make the run. Doug in the meantime had planned to wash his clothes, along with Paul. So the two of them worked last night till the wee hours carrying snow blocks to fill the wash tank. So he was rather put out when I said we were going to take a run. Of course, I didn't know of his plans. So he went to see Paul who told him that the washing could wait and that he had better stick to me. Then after getting all set to go, having taken the cylinder out, to have the instrument not work—well, I am afraid it was too much for Malc. He didn't know what to do. Then when I hunted him up and told him everything was all set, that Al had fixed the galvo—well, I'd rather not say, but he said something about my making up my mind. He's such a fiend for routine that a day like today would naturally upset him. We finally got under way at 11:00 o'clock, which meant we missed lunch, but did finally reach minus eighteen degrees centigrade by 1:00 o'clock. Dick had saved us some food but when I found out it was bologna omelet I had a nice dish of cold cereal and a cup of cocoa and called it a meal.

After lunch, spent time on historical geology, almost finishing the Mississippian. Later I went out in the clothing cache and straightened up a bit. I seem to spend most of my time trying to keep that place clean and in order. I can readily see how much work there would be in handling stock in a large men's clothing store. I am gradually getting all emergency clothing moved away from the building to the housing cache. Had quite a time checking up on the ground mattresses. I had only fourteen in the cache, but after snooping around found the remaining eight in various fellows' bunks being used as pillows, mattress covers and mattresses. I should have known where they were because when we were in the tents most everyone had a ground mattress under his sleeping bag. When we moved into the building they just sort of hung onto them, and some even thought it was general issue although Paul made it clear at the time they were given out that they were to be used on the trail.

Oh well, such is the life of a supposedly supply man. As usual, at night there are little cliques of fellows playing this game or that. Chinese checkers has taken the camp by storm, but "Dictation" is still going strong, and Earl and Arnold even play a couple games of chess every once in a while. As for cribbage, I think Gilmore is champ. He spends quite a bit of time playing Doc F. and F. Alton. Of course, Pappy Gray is the A'cey Deus'y champ, defeating Grif about every time they play.

Friday, June 28 (156th day)

Woke up this morning to the tune of "St. Louis Blues." What a song to wake up to, especially when one has a headache. I guess I'll have to stop reading, but darn it, that's the only real relaxation there is around here. It's really wonderful to crawl up in my bunk nights, get all ready for bed, then read, write in my "poop sheet" or just to think pleasant thoughts. This morning I worked with Al and Larry, hauling snow out of their ice house. They have reached a depth of twenty feet and the old hoist would creak and groan as box after box of porous ice was cranked to the surface. Either Larry or myself would turn the crank and we had Al down in the pit. It was a fairly simple process. After Al would fill the box we'd crank it up, then dump it. We reached the twenty foot level about noon. They didn't need any help in the afternoon as Al was going to drill holes for more dynamite, so I worked out in the clothing cache till time for navigation class. Radio class was a success, I seem to be getting a little better every class.

Saturday, June 29 (157th day)

Boy, I like to see these days fly by! More power to them, the faster they go by the better I'll like it because that just means we will get out on the trail sooner. Made the run today and finished by noon.

After lunch I went out to the machine shop to take my bath. Chuck was making a stand out of pipe to hold our GI can water tank, our personal tank exclusively for myself, Chuck, Toney and Joe. He hadn't quite finished making the thing so Toney and I went out and cut snow blocks. It was very nice out, not too cold and just enough wind to keep one moving. We cut about twenty-five blocks, enough for all of us. Chuck was still working on the stand so I made a temporary stand out of two horses, started the Von Prague and spent the next two hours melting snow. Had some trouble with the Von Prague as Chuck and Joe (the dopes) last time they used it put kerosene in it and for some reason, since it's supposed to burn gasoline, well, kerosene doesn't work very well. I finally ended up dumping the stuff out and filling it up with good old gasoline. By 4:00 o'clock I had about two-thirds of a tank full of hot water so started my washing. I have quit using the washing machine as it's too dirty. For some reason the fellows just won't clean it up, so rather than struggle with trying to keep it clean I wash my few clothes out in a bucket. I have changed my bathing techniques somewhat. I still wash out of a bucket but instead of trying to rinse as I go along, I get all soaped up then stand in a tub and pour a fresh bucket of water over me. It's much more satisfactory. By dinner time I was cleaned up and shining, glowing like a spanked baby. We had shrimp for dinner, quite a treat—fried shrimp, the first I had ever eaten. I'll give the cook credit, he can put out when he wants to. Helped Dick with the dishes tonight, as well as last Sunday and Wednesday, Larry and myself. The show tonight was "Judge Hardy's Children." Either it was good or else the fellows were in a good humor. Anyway, everyone laughed. Mickey Rooney is good.

Sunday, June 30 (158th day)

The last day of June, and another month gone by—Boy!! The mess cooks for this coming week have been posted as two "dark horses," but when Al asked us for an alarm clock I knew that Wade and Siple were our men. Four hundred and forty pounds of mess cook. The boys will really have to hop out of bed now. Pancakes this morning, our regular Sunday breakfast. After breakfast at 1:30, Doug and I took the temperature run. The wind was six miles per hour and temperature was minus thirty-six degrees centigrade. We finished up by 3:00 o'clock, spent the rest of the afternoon sending and receiving with Earl and Doc Frazier. Doc is still having trouble with his S's, H's and I's. I swear, you send him "I" and he will put down an "S," send the "I" again and he will put an "H." I guess he just hasn't tuned his ear to the sounds of these letters.

We had fried chicken tonight, good old country fried chicken, and it certainly pleases me to know that we have plenty of chicken. Why, gosh, I've eaten more chicken since I've been here than ever before in my whole life. Helped Paul and Al with the dishes tonight —not that I am trying to "kiss in," but since I enjoy the movies as well as the next fellow, I think that by helping with the dishes on show nights I am at least doing my part. The show tonight was a re-show, "Paradise For Two," which still got plenty of laughs. Also showed "The Sun Never Sets." That is, we showed the first three reels—the rest is missing.

Monday, July 1 (159th day)

We are still trying to find out how "The Sun Never Sets" ended. Murry was the only fellow down here who had seen it, and that numbskull forgot. Well, when I get back I will haunt every theater till I find that show. I probably won't, but it's something to think about. Woke up this morning to the New World Symphony, a very delightful way to awaken, if I may say so, no beating of pans and the cook was actually quiet—of course, it couldn't be due to our messmen Wade and Siple. Of course, after getting the cylinder out this morning and all ready to start the temperature run, the damn instrument went haywire so poor Doug had to march out and bring it back. Luckily it hadn't started to form ice and while Malc was warming it I worked on the bridge. Fortunately I got it to work again by turning a few screws which I know nothing about, so by 10:00 we were all ready to start again. Temperature was minus thirty-four degrees centigrade and wind twelve miles per hour.

After lunch I took a little walk around camp just to look things over. Boy, things have certainly changed since we have been holed up here—huge drifts forming deep valleys run north and west at an angle to the main dog tunnel, and about all that shows of the buildings are the roofs and, of course, smoke stacks, radio equipment, etc. The snow cruiser light is friendly looking, a ray of hope in isolated darkness. And our own finder atop our highest radio pole on the machinery building throws a welcome light over the whole camp. I was in a fog all during navigation class as I hadn't done much studying on our new work. However, I will get to it so I do not feel particularly bad. But in radio class I was in my element.

I made few mistakes at nine to ten words a minute of five letter code, and eight words a minute of letter and number codes. There wasn't much doing at science meeting tonight. Arnold gave a short talk on heat radiation, but none of the other fellows had anything to report so the whole thing ended in a huge bull session.

Tuesday, July 2 (160th day)

It's almost a pleasure to get up this morning, especially in such a gentle way. Music and soft voices and no cook yelling like a mad man, insulting. Doug and I got started on the temperature run by 9:00 o'clock and we finished at 11:30, the wind velocity being about fifteen miles per hour and the temperature minus twenty-one degrees centigrade. After lunch I studied historical geology till time for the "Barr"-Gelanto fight. You know, "I'll moider dat bum, Gelanto." There were quite a few bets made but since very few of us have any money, we bet our cigars or candy issue. We usually watch the way the Coach bets because when he makes a bet he usually picks the winner, especially when there is a cigar at stake. I think he would almost rather lose an arm than a cigar. He is one fellow that truly enjoys smoking them. Of course Barr won. Personally, they ought to ditch Gelanto. All he can do is drink beer. Have been busy the last few days getting extra clothing, fur parkas, etc., for Weiner and his party, which includes Felix and Fitz. They are going out from camp about twenty miles, the purpose being to take aurora shots simultaneous with Al and Shirley at camp. That way they will be able to determine an aurora altitude. The tank will take them out, Nib and Grif. They will take one tractor sled of dog food plus the caboose.

Wednesday, July 3 (170th day)

Boy! I got the shock of my life last night when Gil asked me if I would like to cook Wednesdays, that being the cook's day off. At our table the boys have been talking of my cooking ability, kind of kidding me along, and Gil must have believed them. I tried to talk Gil out of it, I thought up a hundred different excuses—the temperature run, class, etc.—but I was stuck, so there I was at 11:00 o'clock Tuesday night with a cooking job on my hands. I thought and thought what to get for breakfast and finally fell asleep with a vague idea of giving them "fried bread." Vernon woke me this morning at 6:45, and it took me a couple of minutes to come to and realize what the score was. It was still kind of cold as Vernon had only built the fire about half an hour before, so once it dawned on me who I was, where I was, and what I was doing up so early, it didn't take me long to dress. By the time I got to the galley Joe was out there drinking a cup of coffee. I looked at the fire in the galley range, then put on the coffee pots. Then I mixed up my batter, which was done more or less by hit and miss. I'd dump a little of this in, then a little of that, then taste it. Finally I got a concoction which tasted rather pleasant. The grid iron of course was not in its usual place, and after looking all over the damn galley I found it under the snow melter. It was frozen fast to the floor, incidentally, meaning that I had to spend more precious time chopping it free. Al came in about seven-thirty and started to set the table. Then Paul dropped in, looking somewhat in a fog, as if he wasn't quite sure which end was up. By 7:45 we were all set for the mob and Paul started the music. Joe and Nib were already seated at our table so I started my bread. What smoke. Before I had finished frying a half dozen, everyone was up and squawking—I literally smoked them out. On the whole, the breakfast was a huge success (except for the smoke, which couldn't have been helped), and several fellows came back for seconds, and one even for thirds. As for Toney who never eats breakfast, well, he ate four and Ike even tried one.

After the breakfast mess was all cleaned up I went to my bunk to read till time to fix the noon meal, which I hadn't given a thought to till then. It was too late to bring in anything from the outside so I looked over the contents of the galley shelves and spied some canned chili. That was my lunch. Of course, canned chili all taste the same, but by doping it up a bit I did manage to get it to taste fairly well. Anyway, the fellows seemed to like it. I slept for an hour or so after lunch till navigation class, then I went out to the galley to start my evening meal. I had decided on fried ham, German style fried potatoes, succotash and hot applesauce with peaches for dessert. And oh, yes, tea. Toney gave me a hand with opening the cans. It takes three men and a boy just to handle that job alone. And Joe cut the ham. In fact, about everyone at our table came out to give advice or taste this or that. Well, my meal was a success. The fellows really liked the spuds—I guess they were getting so tired of mashed potatoes, besides, the onions added somewhat. Of course there was some smoke connected with frying the ham, but no one seemed to mind. I guess they were used to me by now. And oh yes, I had mushroom soup which went over big. So I made my

201

debut as a cook and believe it or not I feel quite proud. The show tonight was "Yellow Jack" with Robert Montgomery.

Thursday, July 4 (171st day)

Yep, the fourth of July and our time to go on the trail is about here. Today is a legal holiday. Got up this morning at 12:30—to music, of course. Larry mumbled something under his breath, "Do we even have to wake up on holidays to music?" After breakfast I went out to the science building with the idea of studying, but Weiner had a list of a few items he forgot so I went out with him. After that I think I did manage to study a paragraph or two. Earl, Larry and myself practiced a little radio, then I happened to think that I wanted to send Alda a message, which Clay was able to get off. Gil decorated the place all up today, hung flags all around and put favors at the places at the tables. I got our best brand of cigars and helped Al mix the punch—extra special punch, lemon flavor with about four fifths of white label scotch, which made it very tasty indeed. The meal was the best Sig ever put out. Everything from shrimp cocktail, soup to nuts. The turkey was very good with sweet potatoes, June peas, cranberry sauce, asparagus, and for dessert, plum pudding. I thought I'd eaten so much I couldn't get up from the table, but I managed somehow and immediately went out to the galley to start washing dishes. Since today was a holiday, naturally we had a show, so I helped. Jack B. and I had them all done before Paul and Al had even finished their dinner. Coach did the pans and believe me, every pan in the place was dirty. Dick did the silverware. We have quite a system and it doesn't take any time at all to clean up. We were to show "Dawn Patrol" tonight, but as Charlie got ready to re-wind the film he found that it was split and that the salt water had stuck it together some way. You see, our shows came down on the *Bear* and I guess they were almost certainly under water. Ended up by showing Shirley Temple in "Sue of the Mounties."

Friday, July 5 (172nd day)

I didn't get to sleep last night till the wee hours. I tried a couple of times and finally gave up and read. Then for some reason I was hungry so made a trip to the galley and had a cold turkey sandwich. I suppose the turkey was for today's lunch or soup or something, but I didn't see any hands off signs on it so I ate the critter. Got up this morning at 8:30 and I would have sworn it was Monday. It's hard enough telling the days down here without having holidays to throw one off. Doug and I had a two day rest, so we started our temperature run right on time this morning. The wind was six miles per hour and the temperature was minus twenty degrees centigrade, and the total time was three hours. It gets kind of tiresome just sitting and waiting for the water to freeze, so lately Doug and I have been talking a little geology. Today I gave him a lesson in elementary structural geology—a good review for me. Our anemometer has been giving us some trouble lately so since there was not much wind this afternoon I went out after lunch, took it down and brought it in to thaw out. I then cleaned and oiled it—now it works perfectly. The whole trouble was the contact was all iced up.

Went over to the cruiser to hear the mail bag program. The first part of the program from Los Angeles did not come in too clearly and we missed most of what Olivia De Havilland had to say, but Bing Crosby came in wonderfully well. I got a sweet letter from Alda, and was glad to hear from the folks that everything is fine at home and at the farm. Doc Frazier, Al, Toney, (Tony), Grif, Phil and myself were at the cruiser. The rest of the fellows at camp made trail flags while listening to the programs. Weiner will need about four hundred for his proposed trip. Paul carried on quite a conversation with Wagoner of General Electric in informing him that June was the windiest so far recorded on three expeditions. The average for the month was sixteen miles per hour. They talked for quite a while, just shooting the bull in general.

Saturday, July 6 (173rd day)

Just another day. The whole thing is, there isn't enough outside activity around here to keep our interest. It's true I'm taking the temperature runs, studying quite a bit and reading, but for some reason I still don't feel very active. But I suppose things will be different in about a month when we start work outside—good hard work to build a little appetite, get a little exercise. I laughed at first when I heard fellows talk about the dreaded winter night. Well, my laugh has changed to a grin, almost a chuckle, and I'm wondering. The temperature was minus twenty degrees centigrade today and the wind was practically still, so our run took a long time. We didn't get started till 10:00 o'clock and finished at 1:00, missing lunch which didn't particularly worry me because it was hash. I was very contented with jelly sandwiches and cocoa. After lunch I went out to start heating my water for a bath, etc., but I have never seen the machine shop such a scene of activity, getting ready for the aurora party. Chuck was finishing a running tower for the tank, Joe was busy at his sewing machine working on trail flags, and about five others were doing this or that, so my bath was out of the question. I spent most of the afternoon getting furs for the party as well as Nib and Grif. Dick, myself, Larry and Doug did the dishes and had them done before the Dark Horses even finished their meal. The show tonight was "Dawn Patrol," just a reminder about war—personally I don't want any of it.

Sunday, July 7 (174th day)

Read till late last night, "Rocks and Rock Minerals," till I finally fell asleep. Woke up this morning around 11:30 and had a delightful breakfast of corn fritters. Toney (Tony) is the new mess cook. Since we missed two days last week Doug and I decided to take our temperature run today starting at 1:00 and reaching minus thirty-six degrees centigrade by 3:00 o'clock. The wind was about five to eight miles per hour. I spent the rest of the afternoon cataloging negatives till time for dinner. Big surprise and shock, we actually had a Sunday dinner on time and it's a good thing we did because I was beginning to feel a little faint. Had Virginia baked ham which really touched the spot. The re-show tonight was "Only Angels Have Wings." I hate to admit it, but my eyes got a little watery toward the end. It's beginning to get a little lighter day by day, or should I say a little less dark. Anyway, we are beginning to get a little lighter to the north and today there was actually a sunset—that is, a little coloring on the horizon.

Monday, July 8 (175th day)

Quite a busy day. Weather was bad, blizzard conditions, so postponed digging out the garage. Nib has been having trouble with his tooth, it's abscessed, so Doc yanked it out today. Poor Nib had a tough time of it and Doc had to give him ether. As usual, the tooth was a wisdom tooth and the roots had curved under the tooth next to it. Nib feels a little better now, but the effects of the ether are beginning to tell on him. He has been taking a beating all day. The fellows have been kidding him about calling for "Marge" while he was under ether and Nib just as seriously as you please replies, "That's funny, I don't know any girl by that name." However, his little operation changes all plans for the aurora party. So Paul, Al

204

and the party got together and the outcome was me and the little red tractor doing the honors, so I have been busy getting her ready to go. Grif will still go along so he and I changed the oil, fastened a large search light to the roof, and various odds and ends of little jobs. I stuffed all of the most conspicuous cracks and bolt holes with rags, as well as the floor board, also made a canvas covering for the hood to help keep the motor warm. We then rigged up a blinker system in the cab so that the fellows in the caboose can keep me on a straight course. Final touches were putting in a couple of fur skins for kind of seat covers and the tractor is all set to go. We plan to leave late tomorrow providing the weather is okay. At the meeting tonight Arnold gave summaries on his radio sound work and Al furthered his talk on glaciology. After the meeting I packed my duffle bag with a few extra socks, this and that, and I'm all ready for tomorrow.

Tuesday, July 9 (176th day)

For a while today it didn't look like we were going anywhere, but after talking to Arnold and taking several looks outside Paul decided that it was alright with him if we got underway, but that we would have to decide. I will admit that the weather could have been more desirable, but after all, it could have been much worse. So Grif, Nib and myself hurriedly put oil in the tractor, got her started and made several adjustments on it. By that time the fellows outside had finished clearing out the driveway and had the garage doors open. So I backed "Dolly" out, going over to the gas cache to pull out the three barrels of gas which we were to take along. Malc was out there and with Grif and Nib had the drums pretty well dug out by the time I got there. After gasing up, the next job was to pull out the caboose which has been parked along side the food cache most of the winter night. It wasn't much of a job pulling her loose, as well as one of the tractor sleds, and after some maneuvering got them both lined up and all set to go. We have been missing the snow scoop for some time and since the tractor was out Nib thought we had better locate it and drag it out to the surface. Pappy Gray came to our rescue having seen it last between the caboose and a bamboo pole, so they prodded around in that vicinity and there it was. It didn't take long to pull it loose. In the meantime, Murray, Fitz and Phil were busy loading their gear into the caboose. As for Grif and me, ours was pretty well taken care of consisting merely of gas, oil, funnels, gas pumps, and a box of tools and personal gear such as sleeping bags, tents, primus stoves, etc., which we took along just in case. Dick packed it all on a dog sled for us to be hitched to the back of the caboose. It didn't take long for Grif and myself to carry our gear out and load it on the sled, and we were to pick up the gas on the way out, so we had a little time to rest. By then, however, it was 5:00 o'clock so we decided to leave after dinner, which was a good idea because it was steak (and I for one appreciated one last good meal, because one never knows).

After dinner I finished dressing, putting on my seal pants, fur mukluks, a couple of shirts and my beach jacket. It certainly weighs one down to have on so much clothing, but it's a necessity. We finally got underway about 7:00 o'clock with half the camp out to see us off. And believe me, it was bitter cold, somewhere in the minus fifty degrees. Shirley took several pictures and Paul, Al and several others followed us out to help load on the gas barrels. I tried going forward, which seemed to work very well till we got a half mile out where we bogged down. At the half mile mark we met Larry and Dick who had skied out with a primus lantern so that Fitz could set our course due east by lining up with the "findus" light and the light which Larry and Dick had with them. Dick later told me that he certainly didn't envy us leaving in such cold weather because on the way back to camp he froze his fingers on both his hands. Well, I admit that I wasn't too elated over the thought of leaving nice comfortable, warm quarters for the unknown blackness of an Antarctic winter night.

Wednesday, Thursday, Friday, July 10, 11, 12

First I would like to say how glad I am to be back in my own bunk after what surely must have been a bad dream, a nightmare. After leaving Larry and Dick we plodded on in reverse for four miles, stopping every eighth or quarter of a mile to put up a candle arrangement trail marker devised of a coffee can on a six or seven foot pole with a candle in it with a glass cover and a large red trail flag. This was our method of navigation by sighting along the row of markers which were lined up with the "findus" light. Between these lighted markers small trail flags were put along the trail about every one hundred feet or so. At four miles Phil had a radio schedule so we all thought coffee would touch the spot. Fitz made it, and I don't know where I have tasted more bitter stuff. It was fairly comfortable in the caboose with a primus heater going. The only trouble was that the rime, frost on the ceiling, melted and the drops of water were very consistent in dropping down our necks. The fellows had the caboose fixed up quite home like with furs on the floors, and electricity supplied by a twelve cell battery furnished us with light. In one corner Phil had his radio set up. In all, things were very crowded but we all could manage to squeeze in at once. I had on three pairs of socks plus my fur socks and one would think that would be enough, but while we stopped I got another pair out of my duffle bag and put them on. My feet had been cold ever since we left camp. However, the extra socks fixed things up for the time being.

After gassing up we got underway only stopping long enough to put up the candle marker until we reached nine miles, at which point I was told we would eat a bite. Of course I didn't argue against it because I had been driving steady for approximately twelve hours, and there is one experience in store for you if you have never driven a tractor in reverse over the barren wastes of the Antarctic with no lights. The search light on top of the roof of the tractor went out shortly after we had gotten underway. Not that I am particularly afraid of the dark, but just before we left Paul had told me to watch out for crevasses after about seven or eight miles. Well, there I was, bouncing along, bumping over sastruga at least two to four feet high. The tractor would climb up, then drop down the other side. And personally I was a bit worried because I never knew what drop might be permanent, into a nice deep crevasse. Of course I have never seen much of this grand, wonderful continent, but I never realized that it was so rough and rolling. However, after some talking I finally convinced Grif that the light ought to be fixed. At the time the only light was on the front of the tractor, which didn't do me much good except to let me know that the load was still with us.

So while Fitz was preparing our feast Grif fixed the light and I gassed up, and together we checked the oil. I never realized that such a simple thing as checking the oil could be such a distasteful task. In the first place, the new oil was frozen. We hated to shut the motor off because of the possibility of it not starting again. Besides, every bit of metal that we touched burned our hands like dry ice. But it had to be done, so while Grif was heating the oil we had to have a pint for the valves anyway. I turned off the motor with a prayer, crawled under the tractor and worked on the frozen oil jet. Either the wrench would slip and I would skin my knuckles or else I would bump my head on the pan. Why do they always

207

put such things in the damndest places. But I finally won out after uttering forth a stream of profanity that even surprised me. Well, it so happened that no oil issued forth when I had the cockpit open. So closing it again I hurriedly started the motor, striving to at least keep it warm while waiting for Grif. After putting in two quarts more I stopped the motor and checked it again. Still no sign of oil. By that time the oil in the can was so stiff it wouldn't pour and Grif had to heat it again. We put in two more quarts, checked it again, still no oil. Then it dawned on us that probably the oil jet was frozen, so decided not to add any more oil as the tractor only takes six quarts to begin with.

Well, I don't know when a meal ever tasted so good; that is, if you want to call pemmican, coffee and crackers a meal. However, it was the best we had. We wasted about two hours at the nine mile stop. When we did get underway Grif noticed that we were a little off our course due to the fact that at camp they had turned on the "findus" lamp again, and in lining up our markers Murry took the light at camp as the third candle marker back, as it was the last bright light seen. Hence we were making a circle instead of a straight line, and Grif noticed that the angle was increasing instead of decreasing. At that time, however, they did not know it was the camp light. We, however, turned around and started back to the trail trying to line things up. In the meantime Phil had contacted base and did find out that it was the "findus" light. And after they turned it out it was a simple matter to line up three, four lights, hence getting on our course.

Before we left our nine mile stop I turned the tractor around and gave it a try at going forward, which worked fine except for a couple of times I bogged down. The last time which I thought was a bog down happened to be a wreck, if you can imagine such a thing in the Antarctic. When the tractor treads just spun around without moving I backed a little and gave her another try. Nothing happened, then Grif yelled at me, I looked around and there was a real wreck. Somehow the sled rope slipped off the tractor connection and the caboose pulled up on it, turning the sled clear around with its rope caught underneath it. What a mess. But after a little engineering we managed to get things straightened out and got underway again. The wreck, however, literally wrecked our blinker system of navigation, which I am more or less glad of.

It seems that the tractor cut the wire in a couple of places. The whole thing was a lot of trouble anyway. It did work all right, though, when it was used alone. One light for right turn and two for left, but when the man standing on the sled, the man putting out the small trail flags, tried to steer me also, I must say that things got quite confusing. That is, from the inside of the caboose they would flash me a right turn, which was fine, but when at the same time the man on the sled would flag me to the left, well, I don't know. Anyway, I met them both halfway by going straight ahead.

Our next stop was at fifteen and eight-tenths miles where we gassed up and had a radio schedule and coffee. Just as we were getting ready to leave to start again it started to blow, for no apparent reason, blowing a driving snow from the east. This didn't make things so hot, besides, it blew out our third candle and the rest were hardly visible. It was impossible to go to the aurora camp of west base. The cyclometer read fifteen and eight-tenths, but one and six-tenths was considered as distance covered (or lost) during forming of circle and retrack.

Grif and I turned back hoping to get back to base before the blizzard completely covered our tracks. We left the caboose and a half drum of gas, taking with us one sled and the dog sled with trail equipment for us. Fitz wanted us to stay for a cup of coffee but we were too impatient to get started. Besides, a delay might be costly as the blizzard was becoming more active. So after very cheerful fare-wells and goodbys, under the circumstances, we departed with both of us sitting in the tractor cab, going forward for a change, and in second. I will admit that the odds were against us. The tracks ahead were filling in rapidly and in some places it was impossible to see them at all. But luckily in such cases a trail flag would come to our rescue. We went along fine till about 9:30. The reason I know the time is because we were supposed to send up flares at 9:00 o'clock to let Murray and the rest know of our progress. We had been on the trail for four hours then and I imagine we must have been averaging at least two miles an hour. But it was all too good to be true. We stopped to gas up, got underway again, but it was impossible to see the trail. So Grif got out and walked ahead of the tractor with a flashlight trying to pick out our tracks. A seemingly hopeless task, but Grif was uncanny. I thought we were lost several times and just when I would give up we would pass a trail flag. I guess Grif must have walked for about three miles that way, and I mean the going was really tough for him—plodding, dragging himself along through heavy soft drift after having been on the go for at least forty hours. I guess it was beginning to tell on both of us.

He finally came back and said he would have to ride a while. He again squeezed in our two by four cab and we went on again. I thought I could go a little further, besides, I saw the camp light. Grif, I guess, thought I was crazy because he said he didn't see one. But crazy or not, I was determined it was our "findus" light, so I departed for it. Then after some time I didn't see any more trail flags. I didn't exactly panic, but started to turn around to try to get on the trail again. Well, in turning around the tractor bogged down and it didn't take us long to decide that we had better call it quits, stop and camp. We were completely washed out. Grif later told me that he was so tired that he was afraid that while walking in front of the tractor he might fall and I would run over him. Funny, but I thought of that also, and although it was impossible to see out of any of the windows, I did manage to keep pretty close tabs on him by leaning out the door. I know the last time we gassed up I felt a little dizzy, my head was reeling, going around and around. It would have been impossible for us to go on even if we could find the trail. We were licked physically as well as mentally.

So I shut off the tractor (which was a mistake) and we went about the business of unpacking our emergency equipment which, thank God, was all intact. Now neither of us had put up a trail tent, but it's surprising what one can do in case of necessity and we were no exception. In ten minutes we had ours up (ordinarily it takes two or three minutes) and in no time had our fur sleeping bags inside and in less time than that we were in them. I will never get over how wonderful those little trail tents are. Outside it was blowing, the drift was driven hard against our faces stinging like a thousand little needles, but when we got in our tent it was like another world. None of that mad forceful blizzard, just we two, at home in our temporary shelter.

We both slept with most of our clothes on and I was comfortably warm except for my feet. I guess there must be an art to sleeping in a fur sleeping bag, especially the ones we have. I got into mine alright, but couldn't zip it up over my right shoulder as it should be. Hence I had a nice draft of cold air blowing in all night. I tried several times to plug up the hole but I guess I failed, because my feet were cold all night. I slept with my head out of the bag in the hood, but my head was right against the side of the tent and the wind kept flapping it against me all night, dropping snow from the ceiling (where it came from I still don't know) on my face. And the collection of rime around the hood eventually ended up on my face. Grif, however, had a little different idea of sleeping in his bag. He crawled all the way in, his head and all, stuffing up the hole for his head with a blanket. His method though didn't prove any more satisfactory than mine because he was cold also.

We woke up to a nice calm day (at least the tent wasn't flapping), and how long we had been asleep we couldn't tell. I looked at my watch which read 9:15, which didn't mean much except that it probably stopped at that time in the morning or evening of the previous day.

Maybe you didn't think it was cold. If it hadn't been for Grif getting enough move to lean out of his bag long enough to start the Von Prague I guess we would still be there. It's really a dangerous thing to light a Von Prague in a tent, but we had to have some heat in order to thaw out our kerosene so that we could use the primus stove. How I finally managed to get out of my bag and get my mukluks on (the only thing I'd taken off, and my fur parka), I can't say. Incidentally, I put on a pair of blanket socks which brought up the sock total to four pairs of heavy wool, one pair fur socks and one pair of blanket cloth. Grif slept with his helmet on, but I didn't. It was more like a football helmet than anything I can think of. I did, though, manage to thaw mine out enough so that I could put it on.

We were very much undecided as to what we should do. We didn't like to admit we were lost, although we were rather worried. I hope I never again experience such a hopeless feeling as I did the night before. I am convinced of one thing and that is the Antarctic doesn't give a damn who you are. And I have never seen anyone or anything so relentlessly put one on the defensive for one's life. Anyway, we were certain of one thing and that was we needed something hot, but neither of us were hungry. I suggested a broth made from a cube, so Grif said he would take a look around, trying to find the trail, while I got our so-called breakfast. After about fifteen minutes he returned saying he couldn't find a thing. By that time I had snow melted and the water boiling. Grif went out to get some more snow and I heard a yell from him, "The light, there it is!"

All I can say is the saints were good to us. Grif still couldn't believe it and after our broth breakfast we both went out and sure enough, the light was there—just a speck on the horizon. I got our very pistol and fired a couple of shots just to attract attention, so we would be sure it was really the light. We didn't get any response but that was natural, because we didn't know whether it was 6:00

o'clock, the hour for us to communicate with base. Well, seeing the light at least settled a few things. We had thought of back tracking to find the trail, leaving the tractor and skiing in, and even sending up a red light denoting we needed help. But these were all out now —just follow the light.

Our next big problem was starting the tractor. We used every stove we had to heat her up—the small primus cooker, the heater and the Von Prague and several times we caught the wind proof heating tent afire. But in about an hour priming her a bit I started to crank, with Grif sitting inside with his foot on the clutch. The very first turn of the crank and she sputtered and coughed. I primed her again and she started. What a wonderful, heavenly sound—anything to break the dreary stillness of the Antarctic. I still marvel at how it was easy to start, and even Grif couldn't get over it. What more could we ask for? Our light was still there, our tractor was running again and the moon was even beginning to peer through the haze above. What difference did it make if we did forget our shovels and had to dig the tractor out with a ski and a cooking pan? It took some time to break the tractor loose because she sure was stiff. When she did finally crawl out of her hole I don't think you could have found anywhere two more happy lads. I needn't say that it didn't take us long to break camp, pack up and get underway. Oh yes! Our lights went out completely only five minutes after we got the tractor started again. Grif walked on ahead with a flashlight still looking for a trail of some kind, but still following the light. I don't think we had been going more than an hour when Grif ran back to the cab asking for the very pistol, saying he saw some activity near the light. We both looked and sure enough, there was a white flare, so we sent up a white one and then a green one meaning that we were all right and that we were coming in okay, under our own power. They answered with the same, meaning that they had seen us.

I can't explain the feeling of joy, of thanks, the relief that swept over me after seeing their flares. There was no more guess work. Now we were sure that was a light and that was camp, our home in the Antarctic. So we got underway again, going in reverse because the drifts were so heavy and soft that the tractor wouldn't go through them going forward. But in reverse she plowed right along. Grif rode on the sled awhile, then when we stopped to gas up he had piled in the tractor with me. I was so impatient to get back, and the tractor goes so slow, but the light did seem to get larger. Of course we would have to almost run out of gas. We had hoped that we had gassed up the last time enough to carry us in, but evidently not because "Dolly" started to miss out. So I switched on the emergency tank and just caught her in time. And this time we were confident that we would get into camp on two of those extra gallons. But "Dolly" thought different because we ran out of gas about one-fourth mile from camp. Well, need I say more. That was the last time we gassed up and in a half hour we steamed into camp, at all of a mile an hour, stopped the tractor by the machine cache hatch. Leaving her idle we went inside to the galley where we were met by Al and soon the whole camp was around. None of them had expected us although it only took us six hours from our camp. We answered a thousand questions and we had a truly wonderful homecoming. Everyone seemed relieved to see us and both Grif and I were plenty glad to be back. Sig fixed us something to eat.

Pappy Gray pinned a large medal on Grif. Shirley and Court had rigged up a big "Welcome Heroes" sign with a picture of Grif and myself standing by the tractor prior to our departure. Arnold had written a "poop sheet" on our trip. We were both tired and the shot that Doc gave me just made me that much more sleepy and tired. Although we got in about 10:30 P.M. it was midnight before I got to bed. Woke up this morning around noon, just got out of my bunk long enough to fix a sandwich and some hot chocolate, and crawled back in again and slept till dinner.

Now I feel just a little better, still stiff even though Doc gave me a nice rub down just before dinner. I guess I will live through and probably recuperate fully after a good night's sleep.

Saturday, July 13 (180th day)

What a hectic day—you might know it was the thirteenth. Gosh, I wish I had stayed in bed. Oh well, I guess everyone has to have their off days. Today has certainly been ours. After breakfast Vernon and I went out to start the tractor. We put a primus torch to her and in no time had the motor running, but the clutch was another story. In order to crank the beast it is necessary to hold the clutch in since the transmission grease is so stiff, so we used a stick to hold the clutch in. Then the problem was to let the clutch out. I kept working it in and out trying to get it to take hold. Every morning we ever started it, we had to do that very thing. But Vernon said that would ruin the clutch and to let it out half way. Well, after all, this is my first expedition so I am supposed to take the advice of the older fellows, so I did it his way. Then he got in and relieved me, for, after all, it was in the minus fifty degree range and that was pretty cold, anyway you take it. Well, finally the clutch started to smoke, but by that time it was time for lunch. So Vernon put the stick to the clutch again and we went in to eat. That's just about as hard on the clutch as anything.

After lunch Grif and I went out. We both took turns working the clutch, and after applying heat, Grif, who was in the cab, told me that it was all set. So I took his place, preparing to start her and put her in the garage. I put the clutch in. Well, it didn't feel or sound right to me. The motor didn't change a bit. Then I tried to get her in gear but with no luck, and things were really happening down around the clutch, a kind of scraping, grinding noise which means only one thing, shot. Yes, what a day—only a burned and worn out clutch. I wasn't at all surprised because she slipped with me a couple of times out on the trail. The only thing that really concerns me is putting in a new one. Of course that's Vernon's job, but we've got to think of some way to get her into the garage because it would be bad trying to work on her outside even though we could throw a tent around her. Well, there wasn't much to do after that but shut down the engine and cover her up till Monday to decide as to who, what and where it's to be done.

Grif and I then carried in all of our gear, etc., which we used on the trail. I did manage to have a little time out of the day to take a much needed bath. The picture tonight was a double feature, so to speak, "Colorado Trail," cowboy stuff, plus "News Boys Home." In case you have forgotten, it is still the thirteenth, and even if it isn't Friday things can still happen. As if the clutch wasn't bad enough, oh, no! The movie picture projector had to go on the blink. The speed regulator or something went haywire. We saw at least half the picture anyway, so it really wasn't too bad.

Sunday, July 14 (181st day)

Good old Sunday—the day of rest. And I mean I really rested. Got up this morning around noon. I swear no matter how hard I try, I can't eat any more than two pancakes. I'm almost ashamed of myself—must be losing my appetite. If I could only eat four or five, then I could at least last throughout the long afternoon. Doug and I made a temperature run right after breakfast, lasting till 3:00 o'clock. The temperature was minus forty degrees centigrade and wind about thirteen miles per hour. After that I intended to study a bit but instead messed around in general, getting in a bull session here and in an argument there. On the whole spending a very enjoyable day. Mac is the new mess man, Toney finished up last night. Gosh, I'm afraid I'll be coming up again soon. Oh well, this time it will be simple compared to the last time I was on mess duty. Passed out cigars to go with dinner. The fellows certainly enjoy their cigars, it's a shame that we don't have enough for two or three times a week. Dinner this evening was wonderful and I really made a pig of myself. Fried chicken, sweet potatoes, June peas, etc. I ate about everything on the table. I still say that I believe I have had more turkey and chicken since I have been down here than in my whole life. I helped Mac with the dishes tonight just to keep in shape. The same bunch helps every time—Dick, Toney, Larry, Jack B., Pappy G., and myself. The picture tonight was a re-show of "Brother Rat." For some reason I like it better this time than before, it being the fourth time I have seen it. Got a sweet message from Alda tonight. I was getting kind of worried, hadn't heard from her since the twenty-seventh of June. Conditions here have been pretty bad the last couple of days. The bands have been dead and WIMC had been closed down due to his moving his station down to Gainesville, Georgia.

Monday, July 15 (182nd day)

Blue Monday—I guess they are all the same, the world over. I have been in a fog all day and so sleepy I practically fell asleep standing up a couple of times. Boy, we've really been getting the cold weather. While Malc and I were taking the temperature run, the temperature was minus sixty-five degrees Fahrenheit and now at midnight it is minus seventy-three degrees Fahrenheit. Boy, I bet the fellows out at the Aurora Base really have every stove they have going full blast and I don't blame them. Al and Murray have been very successful in their Aurora shots, and ever since they have been out Clay has been up all night receiving them, as well as Larry who has been recording for Al. They must have at least a couple of dozen shots by now. Spent all afternoon working with Shirley who is making a series of photographs of our clothing and equipment. This afternoon we took the trail clothing which will be used by one man this summer. Paul wanted a record, a picture record showing the various things and the quantity. Well, it made a lot of extra work for me, and you should see the clothing cache now.

215

After all my pains and time spent out there straightening things up and taking inventory. Well, it looks like a cyclone had struck it or something. About everything I wanted was in a different box. Got another wonderful message from Alda, also one from mother and dad. This has got to be my red-letter day.

The science meeting tonight started without our senior scientist, F. A. Wade, who happened to be at the cruiser asleep, and he certainly needed it. Not only has he been carrying his own work plus the extra Aurora work, but has been looking after Fitz magnetic work as well. Paul opened the meeting and started it by giving a brief talk on geography and its importance to us this summer, then Lon gave us a few points on field surveying. And lastly but not leastly Larry gave a "poop sheet" on geology, what to look for, how to map, etc.

Tuesday, July 16 (183rd day)
Wednesday, July 17 (184th day)

Well, the unexpected happened. Here I was feeling so secure, so safe here at camp, feeling sorry for the fellows at Aurora Base, of course not realizing that late last night Al had a contact with them making arrangements for them to come back. Meaning that Nib, Grif and myself have to leave our happy house, traipse all over the Antarctic continent after them. Al told us this morning at the breakfast table. We are to leave as soon as possible, but at the moment the temperature was about minus sixty degrees and the wind was a good fifteen miles or so—just a little too cold and windy. However, we had to be ready and after the temperature run which was the highest calculated loss yet (six hundred and seventy-five plus), I went out in the garage and helped Nib. He and Grif were gassing up the tank and I got all of our emergency equipment together, tent, sleeping bags, food, etc. Also got ten gallons of kerosene, and five of white gas for the large primus heater used to heat the tank motor, just in case. Also cleaned up and tested the primus stove and heater which we had with us last time. By dinner time we were all ready to go, depending on the weather. So after our meal Nib and I went out to take a last look at things and found that the wind had practically died down, and except for a little haze around the moon it was a clear night. So we decided to leave right away, as soon as possible. Paul came out and after looking around a bit said he thought it was okay to go as we would have the moon with us all night. He immediately got the bunch together to dig out the ramp to the garage and Nib, with Petras helping him, started to heat the tank. I finished packing gear, with Jack B. giving me a hand. Dick, Larry and Ike spent all afternoon carrying dog food out from the blubber house as we were to take one sled along with us and make a cache at the twenty mile beacon.

Grif started to put the groussors on the tank and by 9:30 or so all the work prior to our little trip was done. The tank was out of the garage, the sleds all loaded, hitched and lined up. Nib pulled the load a few feet just to take some of the slack off the line. The dog sled with our personal gear and emergency equipment was tied to the back sled. Our train consisted of two sleds, the first being eight barrels of gas, the second with dog food, gas hose, funnels and a box of gear to be used enroute. We left the tank running while we came back to the bunk house to dress in our furs and drink a cup of coffee. We finally got underway amid the cheers from the fellows who braved the cold to see us off. Shirley took a picture of us three, then some more shots of our departure. Dick Moulton skiied out to the trail and set up a lantern in line with the "findus" light so that we would have something to go by. For the first mile or so I rode in the tank, standing up in the conning tower relaying Nib's signals which were given to me by Grif who was riding outside working the light, trying to find the trail flags. The tank worked fine, its powerful motor breaking the Antarctic stillness with a steady drone. After about two miles we lost the flags so we decided to use the "findus" light, keeping it directly at our rear—that is, as long as we could see it.

I changed places with Grif who was getting rather cold. This is all easy to write about, but to perch atop a slick plywood roof, trying to keep from falling off a plunging, leaping tank and still watch out for flags, keep the "findus" light lined up and work the search light—well, it's no fun and I really don't care to attempt it again. We hadn't been going again long before Grif decided to ride back on the load. I forgot to mention that it was rather drafty in the tank, in fact it was colder than outside. I thought we had gotten started again and were really on our way for good when Grif, who had walked back inspecting our load, yelled that we had lost half of our gas load. So we pushed the four remaining ones in the center of the load and secured them after a fashion. The tank is all right, but it's a little too fast, a little too powerful, and barrels of fuel or anything fall off at the least provocation. And our speed of five miles per didn't help matters at all. It wasn't long before I lost sight of the camp light and we steered by a compass, which Nib had in the tank.

About 1:00 o'clock we had gone ten or twelve miles and had not seen a single flare or signal from the Aurora camp. They were supposed to send up a flare every half hour after midnight. We got kind of worried, thinking possibly that we were off the course or something, so I got out the Brunton and according to it we were going due north. So when we started again we turned what we supposed was east and after going a half hour or so still did not see any signs of a signal. We still were not sure of our course. Besides, the moon and wind were not just right, so we decided to turn back to our original course before reading the Burnton, travel till 2:00 o'clock, at which hour we were supposed to gas up. And if we didn't see any signs of a signal, then turn back and start over again.

Well, luck was with us, or shall I say luck was with the boys at Aurora camp, because at 2:00 o'clock we saw a red flare to the left of us. So I immediately answered with a white one, then sent up another one so they would answer and we would get a check on our position. We were off about fifteen degrees, in other words, we were to the south of them. So we got in line with their signal and Nib followed his compass till we were able to see their light. Once we saw their flare the trip was uneventful except for stopping every so often to put a gas barrel back on. Boy, that was work. By the time I could signal Nib to stop we would be some distance past the barrel, hence Grif and I would have to roll the *%¢&$* barrel up to the sled and I suppose we spent a half-hour trying to get one drum back on the sled.

The tank traveled along nice, taking the sastruga like a veteran. And if it wasn't for the cold and the trouble I had sticking on, I might have enjoyed the trip. Well here I thought I was going to be nice and comfortable riding inside the tank, but instead there I was perched on top, outside in the cold and the temperature was in the minus fifty degree's then. I had on a complete fur outfit and with the exception of my face and hands I was fairly warm. My hands suffered due to the fact I had to handle the searchlight and couldn't work it with my fur mitts on. As for my face, it seems to always be stuck right out there taking it. I hadn't shaved for a couple of weeks or so because of these trips and what happened, and I got large icicles on my fuzz (beard), which for some reason insisted on freezing tight to the fur on my parka hood. I would stick my chin down inside my parka collar with just my nose out, then when I would come out of it I would almost leave half of my upper lip

218

behind or at least pull some of the hair out of my magnificent mustache. As soon as we got about a mile or so from their camp, I sent them a "poop sheet" by code, using the search light and strange as it may seem, Phil got most of it, especially the part where I said "Boy that coffee smells good" and as a reward they had hot cocoa ready for us.

We arrived there at 5:45 A.M. and I guess they were pretty glad to see us. They had quite a nice little camp, which consisted of a tent and the caboose. They also built a nice high beacon. While we were eating a tasty meal of pemmican and cocoa, they took down their tent and packed their gear. Then we unloaded the dog food and stacked it next to the beacon, along with a couple barrels of gas. Then after gassing up and hitching the caboose on, we got underway. We took the dog sled and pulled it up and lashed it on one of the tractor sleds. We left there at 7:40 A.M. following our old trail back till we came in sight of the base light. Nib had the tank in second gear for a while after leaving the Aurora camp and we must have traveled along at least twenty-five miles an hour and over high sastrugas, well that was really something. It was all I could do to stick on. Of course I rode on top again and worked the light and several times I almost slid off, if I hadn't grabbed that light in time I would be a goner now. I am certainly thankful that it was at least bolted securely in the tower roof. Incidentally the wind was so strong that it broke out and cracked all of the pyrolin out of the tower windows. I didn't have much trouble guiding Nib home, as he could see the trail fairly well and when he missed it some, all I would have to do was swing the light in the direction I wanted him to take. We went along fine till we came to an intersection in the trail, a place where we turned around to pick up a drum of gas—well, I stopped Nib while we checked up on the trail, and the tank motor died. Nib tried to start it but the battery was dead, so Nib and Grif changed batteries with the rest of us offering encouragement and doing anything to help as much as we could. I got down in the tank and by some miracle tugged and lifted the other battery in such a position so that Wiener and Fitz could pull it out. I don't see how Nib can stand working with his bare hands, but there he was working with cold stinging wrenches and pliers, changing connections on the battery while Grif undid the plates that held it in place. Luckily one of the fellows spied the light just before we got ready to start. Nib had finished changing batteries, and with a breath of prayer on our lips we all stood around waiting to hear that welcome voice of our tank motor. Nib worked with frenzied haste, hoping to get the new battery connected before the engine got too cold, which would mean we would be hours heating it up again. His work was amply rewarded, because with only a few tries the motor bounced to life and we were on our way again.

We made a beeline for camp. I steered Nib for a little while till finally he was able to see the light. We got to camp around 1:15 P.M. and the fellows gave us a big welcome. We just missed lunch but after a few sandwiches and cocoa we all felt better. Upon arriving we immediately put the tank in the garage and Vernon took care of it. We left the place where we had battery trouble at ten minutes to twelve and I imagine we were at least three to four miles from camp, so we made fairly good time. I turned in at 2:30 and slept till dinner time. Then I crawled up in my bunk and dozed off till Larry woke me for the show, which was a re-show of "Wings of the Navy." Shows are getting pretty scarce now and we have to show two re-shows a week with only one first showing. I didn't dally long after the show but went right to bed and really did some serious sleeping.

Thursday, July 18 (185th day)

Boy did I oversleep—didn't wake up till almost noon today. You know, all it takes is a little trip out in the cold, cruel winter night to make one really appreciate the comforts of home here. Just to get up to a nice warm bunkhouse is enough, not to mention the good food, radio, movies, books and electric lights! After lunch I went out and started to unpack the sleds but decided it was too cold, minus sixty degrees below, for me to be running around. So I settled by washing my hair and shaving, cleaning up in general, then took a little nap before dinner. I didn't get in again on the dozen jobs around camp that await me.

Friday, July 19 (186th day)

After a good night's sleep I'm beginning to snap out of it a bit, not in such a fog. In fact, I got up this morning bright and early at 9:00 o'clock and ate a huge breakfast. We had prunes and it seems that about half the fellows at my table don't like them and my bowl was full to the top. I ate about half of them and managed to sneak the rest in Pappy G.'s dish before he came to the table. Doug and I ran our temperature equipment, the wind being about eight miles per and the temperature in the minus forty degree centigrade range. The heat loss per calories was four hundred and two grams. Today being mail bag day I didn't start anything after lunch, but read a little geology till 3:00 o'clock. Then I went over to the snow cruiser to listen to the program. Al was already there so we played a game of Chinese checkers (he won) till time to hear the part of the program to come from San Francisco. Murray and Grif came in a little later, also Petras who woke up Phil who had been asleep since 8:00 or so the night before. San Francisco's contribution to the occasion was a trip around the fair grounds, which was nothing more than a big publicity stunt. None of us paid much attention to it. Just our luck it came in fine today, but last time when we wanted to hear the stars, etc., it was lousy. Oh well, such is life.

Ed Day (ham radio operator) should be back on the job the next couple of days or so. Boy, I'll be glad, then I can start getting and sending regular messages again. All of ours here at camp have been accumulating for the past two weeks or so, and I have about three in the bunch that have not gotten to Alda yet. I hope that she will not worry or think I have forgotten. Also I hope mother will not worry. Their letter today was nice. It is certainly a relief to know that they are well and that everything at home is okay. They finally got through—a two-way contact with KRTC East Base, and we heard one side of the conversation. Wagoner of course talked, asking Dick Black of East Base all kinds of questions concerning the camp. I was surprised to find that their temperature today was eighteen above and at the time of the broadcast was only twelve below, their lowest temperature being minus thirty-eight degrees below, while our lowest temperature was minus seventy-three degrees below zero. Quite a difference.

Toney was proud to hear that his friend Joe Healey had the finest, longest beard in camp, and there are only four fellows there without them, while almost all of the fellows here are clean-shaven or at least with only a week's growth or so. Carl Ecklund and Paul Knowles' wives were able to talk to them, which made it very nice. Of course, I guess they were plenty excited and I'll admit that the conversation didn't make much sense, mostly "what's." Still, just the sound of their voices were enough. Shirley, Court and Petras last night went down to the pressure ice to photograph it. They left here about 8:00 o'clock, getting back at 1:00 in the morning. The outcome of the thing was oh, they got their pictures all right, but Court's face is swollen up like a balloon. And I guess they all spent pretty sleepless nights. Pete says it takes a marine to stand anything.

Saturday, July 20 (187th day)

Here I am two days behind in my writing. It certainly is hard to keep this thing up, especially when nothing exciting happens. We do the same thing day in and day out. Our temperature run this morning was a success, calorie loss four hundred nine and three tenths. After lunch I went out to the machine shop and started heating my water for a bath. It usually takes about two hours or so to melt enough snow for a tub full of water. Jack B. was out there and is making his little girl a sled, a miniature dog sled, and he said he would be glad to make me one.

While I was waiting for my water to heat I went out and brought in my skis and gear which were packed on the dog sled. Had a big shock and a bit of bad news last night—Murray didn't get any Aurora pictures. It seems that his shutter was frozen or something, anyway, all of his negatives were blank and Al had at least twenty-five or so. It's a darn shame, all that work for nothing. From the way they talk we will try it again as soon as the moon is less obvious. At present it is very full and very beautiful.

I had quite a time darning a couple of stockings. The holes were so large that the electric light bulb which I was using would jump right out when I tried to pull the sock tight around it. I always feel so clean after a good bath, well, as good and clean as can be expected. I certainly miss taking showers. Boy, when I get back to civilization I am going to spend the first week in a shower. Well, a tub, anyway. After dinner I helped Mac with the dishes. The show tonight was Arson Lup in a real thriller. Boy, I can't get over it— why, in about two-and-a-half months we start on the trail.

Sunday, July 21 (188th day)

Sunday and slept till noon. I cheated a little today and slept till 1:00 o'clock. I just couldn't budge till then. I'll be glad to get back to the states so I can get ambitious and work again, get out of this lazy spell that I seem to be in. I don't want it to become a habit. Larry is worried also, he spends quite a bit of time on the flat of his back, too. I don't know what it is but I feel good and tired most of the time. I ate quite a bit for breakfast this morning, which is most unusual. I actually ate two whole pancakes and chiseled a glass of tomato juice from Sig. Was going to take a temperature run right after breakfast but found that Doug forgot to bring in the cylinder last night. Hence that was out because naturally the thing was frozen solid. That's about the fourth time he's done that. I guess I'll have to take it out and bring it in from now on. At least if I forget it I can't bawl out anyone but myself. You see, we have seventy done, and I do so want to get one hundred.

Had some good programs coming in this afternoon. The Hour of Charm, a couple good bands and part of an opera at the Cincy Zoo. Boy, that brings back pleasant memories. Just before dinner I crawled up in my bunk for a nap, something different. Of course we had chicken for dinner of which I ate my share and maybe a little more. Larry, Dick, the Coach and myself did the dishes. The re-show was "Mad Miss Mouton," which was very good. Afterwards Larry, Earl and myself went to the science lab and practiced a little radio. I am pleased to find that I haven't forgotten it as I haven't done much practicing for a couple of weeks. Just came from the galley where I polished off a nice toasted peanut butter sandwich, which is getting to be a nightly affair.

Monday, July 22 (184th day)

Getting up this morning was a bad dream. The trouble with our bunks is that we can only get out of one side, and that usually is the wrong one. Didn't finish breakfast till 9:30 so Malc and I didn't get started till late. The temperature was minus thirty-two degrees centigrade when we started at 10:00, then dropped to minus thirty-seven degrees centigrade by noon, the wind was around seven miles per hour. After lunch I went out to the machine shop and started to sand down the runner on the small sled that Bursey is making for me. It's really going to be a nice one. After that I went in and studied a little historical geology till time for dinner.

Oh, yes, just before dinner Grif and I got in a little discussion trying to settle the state's military problem: should we have compulsory military training? Naturally I am not keen on it, but if we have to have it I should think that it would be less harmful to our youth to have one year, ages from eighteen to twenty-five. This would follow right out of high school and would take a year during which most fellows are more or less undecided anyway. Either that or compulsory training in high schools, which I don't think would be so hot.

After dinner I crawled up in my bunk to take a nap, but before I knew it I was in a heated argument with Shirley, Chuck and Giles on the merits of higher education, etc. I was kind of outnumbered but held my own till time for the science meeting. The whole thing started when half asleep I heard "college boys" mentioned. Well, I was out of my bunk like a flash. The service fellows are always talking down college boys and I did my best to defend us. At the meeting Shirley gave a clear talk on problems which we would be apt to encounter in our trail photography. Then Perk gave us the dope on lichen moss and birds, which we are to pay particular notice to. A long meeting, did not adjourn till 11:00 o'clock.

Tuesday, July 23 (190th day)

Got a big surprise this morning, Malc gave me coffee in bed. His ruling had always been anyone over forty was entitled to java in bed. I can't understand it, surely he doesn't think that I am that old, does he? I can't understand it, because I have been so consistent in my morning arising, almost the last one up every morning, quite a record to be ashamed of. After breakfast I spent a little time philosophising, spreading a little good common sense to the morning group which after breakfast always gathers around the stove. Doug and I did our temperature work, the wind being seven miles per hour and the temperature minus twenty-eight degrees centigrade, quite warmish out. Spent most of the afternoon in the science building studying historical geology and a little radio practice. Jack R. sent some pretty fast code to me. Boy, that science lab is beginning to smell rather like a zoo since they have the pups in there. Dick, Earl and Jack R. between them have managed to keep them alive, although the poor little devils were pretty full of worms. However, now they are coming along all right and are getting full of the old Nick. In fact, it's almost impossible to keep them in their box.

Last night after the science meeting Paul, Al, Murray, Fitz and myself had a long talk about the possibilities of another Aurora trip and it was finally planned that we leave this coming Friday morning. At present it doesn't look like we will make it as it is starting to blow. Of course Nib and Grif and I will take the party out in the tank, but there is a slight change in the personnel. Perk will go in Fitz' place. Fitz would like to go but feels that he shouldn't neglect his work too much. We will not take a payload so should make pretty good time.

Wednesday, July 24 (191st day)

Just before I fell asleep last night Paul asked me if I would cook the next day and I vaguely remember my answer as being yes. Anyway, I was rudely awakened at 7:00 this morning by Zeke who was relieving Vernon as night man. It took some few minutes before I realized what the score was, but by the time I got to the galley I was pretty wide awake. Fitz and Vernon were out there making some coffee and toast. Fitz got up to go out and take some dip reading or something and Buck, well, you just can't tell when to expect him. He seems to be up and around at the most odd hours. To start the day off right the eggs were frozen so I had to work with them longer than usual. I decided to have French toast. Well, the batter was so good that I ate half of it testing it while I mixed it. The cinnamon did the trick. Besides that we had apricots and coffee, plus cold cereal if the fellows wanted it. The fried bread went well and some of our more hearty breakfasters had three and four pieces. I thought it was very good. I had three and Ike, who never eats breakfast, had three also. So I guess it was a success.

After I cleaned up in the galley a bit I crawled up in my bunk to nap till 10:30 when Pappy G. woke me. For lunch we had spaghetti and sliced fried corned beef and apple sauce. Everyone seemed to get filled up so what more can I ask?

Boy, this cooking is tough work. I slept till 3:00 then started getting dinner. I decided to have hamburger and Pappy G. cut the meat up while Toney and Nib put it through the grinder and mixed it. That's one thing about our table, the whole gang chips in and helps. Joe sliced the corn beef for lunch. Besides hamburger I had mashed potatoes, sugar corn, tomatoes and fruit salad. I tried to use some dehydrated cauliflower but it didn't turn out right. The stuff didn't come out in the three hours that I soaked it, so the next time I will put anything like that to soak the night before. Also I tried some powdered rhubarb and what a mess. When I finally got through with it, it tasted more like apple and looked something like apple butter. Oh yes, I also had mushroom soup. I started frying hamburgers about 5:00 o'clock, everything else was on the stove cooking. Nib came out and helped wash the spuds and watched and tasted the vegetables. Al came in and worked over the soup and added more sugar to the rhubarb, and with Pappy G. and Toney in the galley it looked like a big hotel kitchen. Four of us were working over the range. Of course I would forget about thawing out the tea bag, but good old Nib got there just in time.

The meal was served on time and all in all it was darn good, even if I did dirty up about everything in the galley and had to throw out the cauliflower. But you know what they say about good chefs —they dirty every pan in the kitchen. So I must at least get a good one from that score.

I guess the hamburger and onions were a treat, at that. Fitz ate eight and most of the fellows averaged four. In fact, while I was frying them, Grif had two, Malc had two, Toney about three, Nib two, and Al must have had at least four. They were just tasting to see if they were being fried right. Oh well, such is the life of a cook. I must have felt rather guilty about all the dirty pans because I helped with the dishes—Fitz, Coach and I. We started to have a show tonight, a re-show of "Big Broadcast of 1938," but the machine went haywire and the combined forces of Pappy G. and Walt could not fix it offhand. So the thing was postponed till tomorrow night. They are going to tear it down tomorrow and I warrant that between them they will either ruin it for good or it will be humming like new.

Thursday, July 25 (192nd day)

Boy, I feel wonderful, got a nice sweet message from Alda. I wish that Ed Day would hurry and get back so that our messages would go out. Got up this morning and not with a will. In fact, if it hadn't been for the temperature run I would have stayed in my bunk and really slept. The temperature today was minus fourteen degrees centigrade and wind was twenty-five miles per hour. Just before we started the experiment I went out to see if the still air pit that Doug had dug a couple days before had started to fill up. It was, so I got a piece of plywood to cover it. Well, it was nip and tuck there for a couple of minutes whether I was going to get it out through the hatch or not. The wind was coming from the southeast and blowing right against the hatch cover. I could get it about halfway open, brace it with my head and shoulders trying to lift out the plywood, but about that time the wind would seem to center its activities in my vicinity, knocking me down, closing the hatch cover again and messing things up in general. When I did finally get it out, the wind about got it away from me. Well, I finally got the pit covered, holding the plywood down by shoveling snow over it. Boy that was cold work. My face started to burn and my wrists, which

226

for some reason or other were sticking out big as hell where my coat and mitt meet, got kind of frostbitten. Wind burned or something. The worst difficulty in being out in a blizzard is breathing. I was panting like I had just finished a one hundred yard dash. The wind literally takes your breath away. After getting thawed out a little I went back out to put the cylinder up, and doing so, I took the can cover off our stovepipe connection to the tunnel, laid it down, turned my back a minute during which I untangled the wire of the cylinder, then reached for the can to put it back and it was gone. Disappeared into thin air. And I mean it must have sailed. I should have known better. Well, if nothing else, today I learned one thing and that is never try to cover a pit during a blizzard. Always have them covered before the blizzard.

The run lasted till 11:30, then I went out to the machine shop and cut another can to cover the stovepipe. Just before lunch I took it out and brought the cylinder back in. Spent all afternoon typing up some field rock definitions, a "poop sheet" which Larry made up. I added some things and Al thought the finished product was okay. Oh yes, I forgot, but today was a big holiday. We worked today the same as any other weekday, but in spirit we were supposed to be celebrating. "Utah Day" for Doc Frazier, he even had his Utah flag up and Sig gave us turkey tonight for dinner. We even had punch which happened to be one of Nib's concoctions made out of alcohol. We must be out of whiskey or something. Anyway, Nib came in the science hall late this afternoon with a little pint bottle to bum some alky off Perk. I took one sip of the stuff but couldn't go it, a little too strong for me. Why, I would have been drunk on the one drink, so I gave it to Joe Wells who, to show his appreciation, gave me a bar of candy. Ike did pretty well at his table. All of the fellows gave him their drink, so he got an old medicine tonic bottle and filled it up. Washed dishes for Mac tonight. Jack rinsed, Pappy G. did the pans, and Grif cleaned up. The boys, Giles and Pete, worked almost all day on the projector so we had "The Big Broadcast of 1938." Shirley's feet do not pain him so much and he is walking around a little. Doc thinks he will be all right, just lose a couple of toenails or so.

Friday, July 26 (192nd day)

We got a real scare today. Malcolm didn't show up for dinner and he is usually very prompt. So Dick and Jack B. looked all around camp, in Dog Town, at the medicine shop and everywhere they could think he might or could be. But they didn't find him. And when everyone thought about it no one had seen him since after the snow melter fill party, and the last I saw him was when he brought in the cylinder about 2:00 o'clock. We took our temperature run as usual, the wind chill being four hundred twenty-nine and five tenths plus, the temperature in the minus thirty's and the wind about fifteen or so miles per hour. During the run Doug had a run-in with Doc Frazier. I suppose they were both to blame, but for some time Doc has been heckling Doug about taking the news "poop sheets." Well, I can see no reason why Malc shouldn't take them after we are through with them. He likes to save them and I know that he does wait till they have been laying around a couple of days or so. Well anyway, they discussed the matter in no uncertain terms. In fact, they almost came to blows. I guess that upset Doug quite a bit because he didn't say much after that. Then he didn't show up for the evening meal.

Well, Al, Jack B., Jack R., Dick and myself immediately got dressed and started to make a complete circle of the camp following Al's thermometer line. When we came to Ike's trap line, Dick and I followed around it while others completed their circle of camp. I guess it took us about an hour or so to walk the mile and a half. The going was pretty bad as the wind had picked up and the sastruga was fairly rough, making it hard to walk. Dick's flashlight went out, the batteries froze up. Once we thought that we saw fresh tracks but decided that they were made by mukluks and were probably made by Joe Wells, and probably any tracks made that afternoon would be drifted over anyway. And these tracks were in the hard snow beneath the drift and sastruga.

I have never experienced such a feeling and I can't explain it, but as soon as Dick and Jack couldn't find Doug around camp in the tunnels or in some of the buildings, or feeding his dogs, we all knew that it meant one thing, that he was lost. That he had probably gone outside for some reason and wandered off or had gone for a walk and got lost in the blizzard. While Dick and I were walking we didn't say much, we were too dumbfounded. We couldn't believe it that one of us was actually wandering around or stumbling along blindly, maybe so close to us that we could touch him if we only knew which way he might have gone. I flashed my light all around as we walked and had near failure several times. Sastruga casts the most grotesque shadows and some could even be mistaken for a man lying down exhausted. My light started to weaken just

228

as we got to camp. Before we reported in, though, we took a look around the airplane hangars and in the near vicinity of the buildings, but no Malcolm. Al and the rest were already in the bunkhouse when we got there and they had the same luck we had, couldn't even find any tracks.

We didn't stay in long before the complete camp personnel was turned out and divided into searching parties. Mine consisted of Dick, the two Jacks, and myself. We were to go east as far as we could and still keep the "findus" light in view. Other groups covered north, south and west. We spread out and must have gone a good mile and a half before we had to stop, the "findus" light being barely visible. Besides, two of our flashlights were frozen. After going east as far as we could we turned north and continued in that direction till we could see the other parties' lights, then we headed back for camp covering a new territory as we went. The cursed darkness—Doug might have been lying behind any sastruga, we might have skied right by him. It was such a hopeless, helpless feeling and everything seemed against us. All of the parties were to be back by 11:00 o'clock. Ike, Joe, Earl and Klondike were the last fellows in. All had the same report—failure. While we were getting warm Paul and Al debated what to do. And after arguments from all sides, pro and con, it was decided to wait till morning, till we could take advantage of the few hours of light (twilight) which we would get providing it didn't blizzard. We did all we could, covered the ground thoroughly as possible for at least a good mile all around camp. It could have been suicide for us to go beyond the vision of the "findus" light. Well, we were a pretty miserable bunch who went to bed that night, but all looked forward to the next day, hoping for a good clear day. I talked to Paul before I turned in and he said that if Doug kept his head and dug in he would be all right, because it wasn't so bad out. The wind was pretty high but the temperature was also high, being about minus ten degrees, so there was no immediate danger of his freezing to death.

Saturday, July 27 (193rd day)

I didn't sleep worth a damn last night, tossed and turned all night. I couldn't get my mind off Doug out there all alone, because I've experienced what it is to be lost. But we'd had light, a tent, food, in fact, everything, while Doug didn't even have a flashlight. Oh, if we could only have clues or something. We were powerless. The blizzard was still going strong today and the highest wind velocity recorded during the night was thirty-five miles per hour. We more or less just stood by today hoping and praying that the storm lets up so that we could get out and make one last desperate effort to find him. A kind of quiet came over the whole camp and there wasn't much camp work done. Fellows spent most of the day in little groups, talking in hushed tones. At lunch Paul asked Jack and myself to pack up Doug's things and clean up his bunk. I guess Paul had lost all hopes, but Dick and I still couldn't believe it and I felt that Paul was a bit hasty in checking Doug out, but later found out that he had gone through Doug's papers, etc., to see if there was any reason or motive for the disappearance and merely thought it best to have things put in his lock box to keep them intact and in order. Well, I certainly hated that job and it got worse as the afternoon went along. I kept getting lower and lower in spirits. After all Doug was (and is) my very good friend. If it hadn't been for him in Boston I would have been lost. Such a quiet had descended over camp that it was still decided to have the movies, the picture being "Risky Business," which did a fair job of boosting up our spirits. After the show Gil pointed to the screen. You see, Doug always took it down. I did it tonight.

Sunday, July 28 (194th day)

Sunday morning Dick woke me at 8:30 to carry out our plans made last night to take Dick's team and head toward Little America, then swing up through the pressure ice, along the barrier, then back to camp. The trouble is, there's no telling where a fellow might wander to. The blizzard had let up and it was fairly light. Boy, talk about excitement, I just turned around and Doug was there.

Doc Frazier, Paul and Dick were cutting his clothing off him. Paul, Ferranto and Boyd took a look out the hatch right after breakfast to get another line on the weather and they saw someone walking in the vicinity of the snow cruiser. At first they thought it was Pete, but they'd just seen Pete. It walked, shuffled like Al, but not quite as tall. They all made a dash at once, it was Doug. Boy, what a happy Sunday. He was completely exhausted, and pretty badly swollen, his aviator's license bracelet cutting into his wrists, also breaking the strap on his watch. His left foot, three toes were badly frozen as was his right foot. I had his sleeping bag out to air so hurriedly brought it in to warm. They got all of his clothing off and wrapped him in a blanket. And after his drinking about four cups of coffee and about as many cups of broth, Doc bandaged his burns and put him to bed. During all of this he told by bits, in jerked sentences, his story.

It seemed that last Friday after he brought in the cylinder he decided to go for a walk. He was still a little worked up over his run in with Doc and thought that a walk would do him good, give him a chance to think. So he walked west following along the trail flags that head to Little America. He had no flashlight and had no intention of getting out of sight of the camp light. He went west till he was afraid to go further for fear of losing sight of the light, then he turned south planning to circle the camp, just keeping the "findus" light in view. For a while the light was in plain sight, then it disappeared. He kept on walking thinking eventually that he would find it or see it soon. Well, he walked till 9:30 then turned in. He dug a shallow banana shaped ditch and lay down to rest. He must have fallen asleep because when he woke up there was about four inches of snow over him and the air was beginning to get stale. So he got up and walked again, then dug in again. How many times he did that he doesn't know. He thought he would never make it because in the dark he wrote a note and pinned it to his shirt. Then, too, he said he was afraid that it would drift over and that we wouldn't find him, so when he dug in he would leave one leg or an arm out of the ditch. How he ever dug these ditches with his knees, I don't know. His hands were too sore and swollen and the snow was too hard. Then he says the last time he dug in, he woke up and it was clear and he saw the camp light. It would be impossible to imagine the joy, the relief that possessed him when he saw the light, and he walked into where Paul and the others found him. Afterwards Vernon, Ferranto and Perk followed his trail back and found where he had stayed last and they estimated that it was about two miles or so, and north of camp. I talked to Doug. Just now he is still quite shaken up as might be expected because he went through hell. He said he never expected to see camp, his home, again and thanked God that he was still alive.

Monday, July 29 (195th day)

Didn't sleep very well last night, again. I guess I'm still worked up about the weekend. Spent all morning digging out the garage ramp prior to our leaving tomorrow morning. Dick and Jack B. left this morning about 8:00 o'clock with Dick's dog team to lay our trail more carefully, to put in more flags and closer together. After lunch I packed our large tool box with odds and ends of gear, gasoline, kerosene, funnels, primus stoves, etc. Then lashed it onto the sleds, as well as Nib's tool box. We had never unpacked our emergency sled, so it didn't take long for us to get ready. Grif and Nib did odd jobs on the tank and dug out a couple barrels of gas. Murray, Perk and Phil have been busy all afternoon getting their things together. Clay heard from Dick and Jack about 5:00 o'clock, they had gone eleven miles and were camping for the night.

Tuesday, July 30 (196th day)

Boy, what a jolt to be awakened at 7:00 o'clock. Yes, Nib wanted to get up early, heat up the tank and be ready to go by 9:00 o'clock, so he woke me. I was a little bleary eyed for a while and it took me some time to get oriented, but I finally thought of what I had to do. And after a cup of coffee I went out and tied our tent on top of our emergency sled load. Perk had fixed us up a tent the night before. Then I did a few last minute odds and ends, and by breakfast time was hungry enough to completely devour four hot cakes, literally swimming in hot butter and honey. Grif actually got over here in time for breakfast then went out to relieve Nib with heating the tank. After breakfast I put on my fur outfit, replenished my supplies of flares, got three chocolate bars and some cigarettes, and I was ready. We did actually get started by 9:45. Murray, Perk and Ferranto delayed us some in lashing up their sled, but on the whole we left camp fairly on schedule. Most of the fellows were up and out to see us off. There is something fascinating about the tank, it's like some fiery monster, snorting, roaring, impatient to be off. We stopped out at the gas cache and picked up two barrels of gas, then we were really off. A very pleasant day, about minus eighteen degrees, and a wonderful wind being about ten to fifteen miles per hour. And the best part being that we had some daylight. That is, if one stared real hard one could make out one's nose on one's face. Anyway, it was such a relief to be able to see anything at all.

I rode on top of the tank and worked the light. Dick and Jack B. did a fine job of laying a trail. I had no trouble at all in picking up the flags with the light. The rest of the fellows rode back on the sleds. It wasn't very comfortable riding, though, because the tank threw up a steady cloud of drift. And from any position I couldn't even see the sleds, let alone the fellows on them. I was getting my share, too. The wind was just strong enough to be uncomfortable, blowing the drift snow from the tank groussors back over the front of the tank and right into my face. The little particles of snow would hit my eyes, get in my nose, long icicles hung from my mustache and would stick to my fur parka hood. The snow hitting my face would immediately melt, then freeze, and by the time we got there my face was a mass of ice. I finally had to sit up on my knees to escape the blast of snow. That was some help except that it was harder to stick on, and at present I fear I have house maid's knees. But I guess one has to take the bitter with sweet. Well anyway, getting back to things, we made darn good time, stopping only once and that was when, for no apparent reason at all, the trail just stopped. No more flags. But just as I saw the last flag, I saw a light ahead which evidently was Dick and Jack camped at the sixteen mile beacon.

So we started again after Nib saw the light and had something to go by. I turned out the search light and he went on into camp by their light. We arrived there at 12:30—Dick and Jack B. met us with cheery "hello's" and immediately invited us to come into their tent and get warm. Well, I'll admit I did. Dick spent the next five minutes or so rubbing my face, kind of thawing it out. The first thing Jack B. said when he saw Murray was "What the hell kind of a trail did you set out—we had a damn hard time following it." I guess poor Murray will never hear the end of it, but he will admit that he did set the flags too far apart. Dick said that he got up at 5:00 this morning and it took them till 10:00 o'clock to find the next flag from their camp. Also they saw our light when we left camp. Another thing they kidded Murray about was his beacon there at the Aurora camp. He said he built one twenty foot high. Well, it turned out to be about seven foot, so Jack had to rib him about that.

It didn't take us long to get the tank turned around and gassed up. Dick made some cocoa which touched the spot and we were ready to take off again. Dick's team was all harnessed and ready. They were going to leave immediately after us, following our trail till they got to the good flag trail. They intended to drive right on through that night if they could, because a blizzard was starting to stick its ugly head up from the east. The sky was getting quite dark. Grif drove the tank and I rode back on top. The return trip was tougher than our coming out, as the wind had increased some and our trail was beginning to blow over making it hard for Grif to see. It was his first try at tank driving so we did not make such good time. But even at that we got into camp in four hours.

We stopped a couple of times, once to pick up a fur which I had under my knees—it had blown off and luckily Nib saw it. Also, I heard Nib yell once, looked, and he was waving his arms for us to stop. He walked up and picked off the muffler which had come loose and was about ready to fall off. Then we had to stop again because the pipe where the muffler had been was taking in snow and causing the motor to miss out. And our last stop before camp was when Nib relieved me. I had to go back on the sled, turn my back to the wind and go about the business of thawing my face out. I don't know why but my puss always seems to take a beating to every trip we've been on so far. In fact, it is always getting burned. We kept watching for the camp "findus" light and when we did find it, it was a sort of a glow on the horizon. And by gosh, the next minute it was right there and we saw the roofs of the buildings and even the antenna poles. I guess we weren't more than a quarter of a half a mile away. It was funny because usually we can see the light about nine miles away, it being just a speck. And on a real clear night the fellows at the Aurora camp say they can see it. So I guess it had really started to close in after we left on our return trip.

We pulled up by the garage and I ran down to pull down the plywood doors and got it ready to drive the tank in. As I was going back up the ramp to tell Nib all was okay, Grif came walking, kind of staggering, down. Nib said he was sick, that when he got out of the tank he took a step then fell. He got a little gas from the tank and not being used to it like Nib, it made him sick and he felt faint. I guided Nib into the garage. We had a little trouble because of some new drift, but Paul, Toney and Coach came to our rescue and did a little shoveling. I don't know why, but I am always glad to get back. My old bunk always looks good, especially when I thought that we were going to have to spend another night out in the Antarctic winter night blizzard.

Wednesday, July 31 (197th day)

Boy, we really traveled yesterday—thirty-three miles in six and one-fourth hours. Fastest ground travel ever seen in Antarctic. That tank really tears along. I was certainly hungry at dinner last night. We didn't bother with our lunch, so by the time we got back to camp I was weak from hunger. My three or four morning hot cakes wore off long ago. After dinner I got up in my bunk and kind of took it easy, I was plenty stiff and sore and my face started to hurt a bit. Boy, it is certainly a sight, all scarred up and dead skin starting to peel off. I must have dozed off some, because suddenly I jumped up with a start and for some reason I was thinking about wooden spoons. Then I happened to remember that I didn't give Murray any spoons for the trip. When he returned from his last time out I gave them to Dick and Jack B., thinking that they would be back before we even got started. Well, they weren't, and while we were out there I didn't think to give them ours. So I went to Al and Paul about it and they both said not to worry, that they could cut some out of their food box or from a sled slat, or anything they had, for that matter. I couldn't help but feel a little uneasy about it, but when Murray asked me I told him that they were all gone. Anyway, Doc F. came to my rescue by telling me that he saw Murray take three spoons from the galley—what a relief. Just before I went to bed Paul asked if I would mind cooking on Wednesday or whether I would need a day to rest after our trip. I told him I would, so went down and asked Nib if he wanted to cook too. He said yes, so 7:00 o'clock this morning found both of us standing sleepily in front of the galley range wondering what it was all about. We had cereal, fruit, coffee, and I made some toast. Nib tricked me, because after I left him last night he went out to the galley and put the cracked wheat to soak. It's a good thing he did, otherwise it would have been as hard as nails. And strange as it may seem, it was very good and tender.

After breakfast I turned in asking Nib to wake me in time to help with lunch. Well, I finally woke myself up and it was 11:30—boy, I jumped into my clothes and made a mad dash for the galley, only to find Nib and Toney there. And apparently everything was under control. At least it looked that way, no one was excited. Toney was making spaghetti for lunch and he was busy stirring the tomato sauce, Nib was waiting for the water to boil before throwing in the spaghetti. Well, the lunch was good. The only thing is they forgot to put any salt in the water and I remember distinctly asking them if they did. So I asked Walt to make an announcement telling all of the fellows to use plenty of salt. It was a little late though, because the bums were already beginning to squawk about how awful it tasted. But the salt did make it fairly palatable. I promised to bake a cake for dinner, so after Walt had the galley cleaned up I started in.

It was really very simple. That is to say, all I had to do was add water to a ready made cake mix. At least I thought it was that easy. Well, it called for a moderate oven so I threw a couple shovels of coal, greased a pan with butter, put my batter in and put her in the oven. The Boston cook book said that a devil's food cake (layer cake) would take twenty-five to thirty minutes to bake. Of course, what it should and what it did are two different things. Anyway, when I took it out I thought it was done. I stuck a broom straw in it and it came out clean. But here's the part I can't understand. When I dumped it out on a board it fell all to pieces and ran all over the place. In other words, it wasn't done. I hurriedly cleaned it up before anyone could find out, then I started all over again. The second time, I left the thing in for an hour almost, just to be sure, then tested it with a straw and pronounced it done. What luck! When I dumped it out of the pan it turned out to be a cake and really stayed together. By that time Nib had come into the galley and started to cut steaks. I then made a fudge icing, and when the thing was done I was even surprised at myself. It even looked good to eat. I then opened some cans of spinach, put the potatoes on, made some broth and turned my attention to some cauliflower which I had been soaking all morning. I give up on that stuff. It still didn't look right but I boiled it for a half hour or so and called it done after pouring a little butter over it. Nib started the steaks about 5:00 o'clock, so by 6:15 we were ready to serve. All in all, the meal was a success. The cake was even good. All except the cauliflower which was just plain tough. If I ever try to serve dehydrated food again, I'm going to soak it a week or so. Had a re-show of "Great Man Votes."

Thursday, August 1 (198th day)

Paul made an announcement last night that we would have to be a little more strict and careful in regards to quiet hours. What brought it all on was a "Dictation" game the night before which was going strong at midnight or so. Also that the breakfast dishes would be cleared away by 9:00 o'clock. That kind of hurts me. I had to get up at 8:45 this morning so that I could make breakfast in time. Ruined my beauty sleep and I really needed it. Spent most of the morning with Paul talking over plans for spring operations. After lunch I got out some things for Shirley to photograph. He wanted to retake the glove and mitten group, the picture didn't turn out very well. The mittens blended in too well with the background and he wanted more contrast. Also took various views of our sleeping bag and the fur one.

We had chicken tonight for dinner. There evidently wasn't any

236

real occasion so I said it was Indiana Day. Why not, didn't Utah have a day a while back? I can't let Doc and Malc get ahead of me on that score. I still don't know how it happened but Al said something about wanting to see a movie, "Holiday," in particular. So I started campaigning and Dick and I helped Walt with the dishes. Then news came from the radio shack that a show was out because they had scheduled something. So I went and talked with Clay and he said he would be through about 8:40 and that he would not mind seeing the picture himself. I went to Shirley, he and Petras didn't know anything about it and wouldn't show one unless Paul gave his okay. So I went to Paul. Guess I'm just the fall guy around here. Anyway, Paul said it would be all right with him, then I went back to Pete and he ran the machine. Boy, they really had me on the merry-go-round there for a while. I probably got a couple of fellows mad at me, in fact might have lost a friend or two. But when Al said he would shoulder the blame, I didn't worry any more. I used to have nice square broad shoulders, but since I have been on this expedition they have become rather beveled. So need I say, we had a re-show of "Holiday" with Kathryn Hepburn and Cary Grant. Oh yes! Coach suddenly became very much enthused about seeing the movie, and for once he really wanted one.

Friday, August 2 (199th day)

This early rising is going to be the death of me. I remember the good old days when I could sleep till 9:30 and still make breakfast. Since Malc has been laid up I haven't been making any temperature runs, but today I talked Larry into helping me. Incidentally, Doug is coming along fine. He has recovered nicely from his experience and he told me today that there is a chance of saving the toes on his left foot. For a while Doc thought that he would have to amputate, but when we looked at them today there seemed to be a slight red tinge, a sign of blood and life in them. It will mean all the difference in the world to all of us and to Doug especially, because they depend on whether or not he goes on the trail. The temperature today was minus thirty-six degrees and the wind ranged from five to three miles per hour. After lunch I got some clothing together for Dick who modeled for Shirley. Took pictures of Dick in long handled underwear, union suits, P & S suits, our gray outfits, red outfit and a ski outfit. Dick's beard made him look like a real explorer.

Boy, am I taking a beating around here ever since that compulsory military training question has come up. All of the service men kid me about being in the army, navy and marine corps. Nib says I ought to get in the tank division and that there is nothing that would please him more than to drill me. In fact, there is even talk of leveling off a place near the Condor hangar for drill purposes for the benefit of us civilians. Grif thinks I would make a good gob, so he is talking up the navy. I really hate to disillusion them all, but I don't think I would like any of it.

Went to the cruiser to listen to the mail bag. Doc, Al, Pete, Grif and myself. Of course everyone would have to hear Alda's message about an apartment. I guess I will never stop being kidded about that. Pappy Gray especially. Then Grif says he swears that he heard the name Bob somewhere in the message. It wouldn't do any good to get mad so I guess I just have to take it. Clay has been clearing our messages right along and cleared something like fifty tonight. Boy, Alda will really be surprised when she gets four or five messages all at once. Clay just told me that on one of mine to her he signed "Charles and Clay"!!

Friday, August 3 (200th day)
Didn't do much of anything today, just one of those days. Spent most of the morning sending and receiving with Doc F. I haven't practiced for some time but still can receive about fifteen words a minute and that's good enough for anyone. After lunch I went about the serious business of taking a bath and washing my clothes. Len was using the machine so I washed by hand. All I had anyway were a pair of socks, dungaree pants, PJ's and my underwear, but even at that it took me all afternoon by the time I heated my water and all. I missed taking a bath last week and really needed one. Helped Walt with the dinner dishes. The show didn't get started till 9:00 o'clock as Clay wanted to take advantage of the good weather and try to clear our messages. The show was quite a thriller tonight, "Drooganmen's Courage." After seeing the show Larry decided to change over to soft rock geology. It was a mining picture with several mine cave ins.

Sunday, August 4 (201st day)
Slept this morning till noon—clicking off twelve hours like it was nothing. After polishing off four hot cakes I found out from Court's weather report that the temperature was minus sixty degrees Fahr-

238

enheit with a five mile per hour wind so I asked Paul if he would help me take a temperature run as Larry was busy. We finished up around 4:00 o'clock. Got my clarinet out today to fix it and was surprised to find it okay. The new pads I put on had set themselves.

Turkey for dinner with all the trimmings—very good. Afterwards I helped Len, new mess cook, with the dishes. Show did not get started till 10:00 o'clock. Clay cleared seventy-one messages tonight, expects to finish up tomorrow night. Pappy G. and Grif have taken on Chinese checkers now instead of acey deucey, but they still can't get along without spats. Poor Pappy really takes a beating. He swears that everyone gangs up on him and that when four are playing, two of them block him while the third one wins. I have been learning cribbage, a very delightful two handed game. Al has been teaching me. If I get nothing else done down here I will know a little more about bridge, know how to play cribbage, have read some geology and a few novels besides getting plenty of sleep. Not bad!

Saturday, August 5 (202nd day)

Vernon played a mean trick on the cook this morning. He only called him once, which meant that we had a very late breakfast. More power to Vernon. Temperature was minus sixty degrees Fahrenheit with about a five to seven mile per hour wind, so I decided to take a temperature run. Both Larry and Paul being busy I made the run myself. Everything went smoothly except I was busier than the proverbial one-armed paper hanger. Calorie loss was in the five hundreds. After lunch I worked in the clothing cache getting ready to issue trail clothing. I at least got started on the job by getting Dick fixed up. I hope in the next few days to get all the fellows who are going on the trail all clothed. I only hope that I have enough to go around.

Boy, is it ever getting light days now. From about 10:00 A.M. to 2:00 or so it is very light. Yesterday visibility was about ten miles and that color in the west certainly looks good. I'm all for it, and ready for it. Yep, the sooner the sun gets here the better I'll like it. Filled the snow melter today and afterwards had our first practice of the West Base football team. Used an old can as the football and had a right nice fast workout till we all about dropped, puffing like steam engines. Toney, Nib, Gil, Ike and myself had a science meeting tonight with Court holding the fort. Gave us a darn fine "poop sheet" on what to look for and why in the meterological world. I guess I'll have to discover Passel's halo. I am to be weather observer of our party.

Tuesday, August 6 (202nd day)

Got up early this morning. I was rudely awakened by Earl to go sleep in his basket to be the specimen for his metabolism tests. My pulse was fifty-one and respiration was three and four per minute. He and Doc Frazier then took a blood sugar test (sugar in your blood should be about one hundred and eighty, mine was two hundred and thirty). If it were more I would have diabetes. I found out later that I had a one hundred percent increase of sugar in my blood, although a urine sample showed no sugar. I asked Earl what a one hundred percent increase means, but he doesn't know yet till he takes a few more tests. Spent practically all day issuing clothing, taking care of Berlin, Larry, Nib, Toney, Earl and H. H. I am kind of worried about our hose supply. Most of the fellows today wanted five pair. If it keeps up I am afraid that we will run out. That means that those getting five more pair will have had a total of twelve pair instead of the original plan of ten pair. It did my heart good when Earl only needed two pair.

I hope I have more like him tomorrow. Al sent morse code before dinner to Doc, Earl, Larry and myself. It was good practice. After dinner Doc, Joe, Earl and myself played four handed cribbage with, of course, Pappy Gray and Al as hecklers.

Wednesday, August 7 (203rd day)

Boy, I take a beating all the way around. Nib was going to help me cook today but something turned up which altered plans somewhat. It seems that the boys at the Aurora camp want to come "home" and I don't blame them. For four days the weather has not permitted any aurora picture shots and there isn't really much to do out there to take one's mind off things and after all one can't sleep always, and besides they ran out of books. Ferranto read "Gone With The Wind" in a day and a half and Perk half waded through an American Literature book. And I guess things weren't going well all around. From reports by Phil, Murray was kind of bossing things and such—well, anyway, they were ready and wanted to come home. In fact, Phil and Perk wanted to ski back leaving poor Murray there alone. Poor Murray. Since we were to leave on

240

Thursday, Nib had to do a few odd jobs on the tank while I would have to squeeze my work in between meals. Buck woke me at 7:00 this morning and the same thing happened this morning as last Wednesday. I got up in a daze and before I knew it I was out in the galley stirring the hot cereal. Luckily Nib had put it to soak the night before (cracked wheat). I woke Len up about 7:30, and it didn't take him long to set the tables. Besides the cereal we had toast, coffee and fruit.

After breakfast I turned in and slept till 11:00 o'clock. Pappy Gray happened to see me in my bunk or I would have slept right through lunch, I mean at the time when there was supposed to be a lunch. I fixed spaghetti, good old Italian spaghetti with tomato sauce. That is, I dumped a few cans of tomatoes in a pan, added a little of this and that plus some flour, and lo and behold, a fairly good sauce. The worst thing about being a cook is that I have to taste my awful concoctions first, but actually it was good. I had quite a time with the spaghetti in that I got hold of the wrong pan, too small, and I couldn't put it all in at once. Hence the outcome was each section was a little different. But on the whole, none of it was too sticky or too uncooked. Nib came in just before I was ready to serve and helped pour the water off the spaghetti and in doing so got burned by hot steam. He almost dropped the whole business on the floor. I didn't get very many compliments on my lunch, but still, the Doc didn't have a rush of business so I guess everything was all right.

After lunch I went outside and repacked our tool kit and all of the gear we have to take for safety's sake, for emergency, and just plain usable items such as gas pumps, funnels, etc. At 3:00 o'clock, Nib and Toney stormed the galley and started to make hamburgers. They started out to make just a couple but before they knew it everyone in camp was crowded around, all hungry—in fact, Grif said he was starved. The meat course for dinner started out to be fried ham but ended up baked ham with brown sugar (an inch or two) topped with pineapple. Nib helped me and we had peas, spinach, mashed potatoes and asparagus soup. Everyone seemed to enjoy the meal. Oh yes, Nib made some chocolate nut ice cream for dessert. Helped Len with the dishes—that is, I did the pans while he and Dick did the dishes, and Coach washed the silverware. Big surprise tonight. We were all set to see a re-show, and what pops up but "Blondie." I can't quite decide whether or not I had seen it, but I can't get over the part where Dagwood leaves for the office, next it shows letters fluttering aimlessly around and the mail-man flattened out, also the sandwich episode. We all got a big kick out of it.

Thursday, August 8 (204th day)

Boy I was tired last night. Meant to get to bed early, prior to the possibility of our leaving for the Aurora Base, but at the last minute the weather turned for the worse, the wind picked up to fifteen miles per hour, so I read late. But much to my surprise I was awakened at 7:00 and informed that the wind had let up and the temperature was only minus twenty degrees Fahrenheit and that we would leave as soon as possible. Nib had already gone to start thawing the tank. I had brought in my furs the night before so it didn't take me long to dress and eat breakfast. By that time Grif had arrived and after we finished eating, relieved Nib. I went outside to finish tying on our load, and it was a perfect day (with the exception of the sun, of course). I would say a beautiful August day, very light, and no wind at all. I had no sooner finished lashing up when Nib backed the tank out of the garage and we hitched the sleds on.

There wasn't much of a ceremony this time. In fact, no one came out. Why, after all, it was old stuff now. Hadn't we already made three runs, dashing out to the Aurora Base? Fitz decided at the last minute to go with us since it was so clear out and it would be possible to take star sights, or at least shoot the moon. However, there wasn't a star in the sky. But the moon was shining brightly and the sky was a clear blue with a red orange to the west and north. So we silently, unobserved, sneaked away from camp at about 10:15 A.M. with a roar as the powerful tank sprang to life under Nib's expert guidance. I rode on top of the tank, with Grif and Fitz riding back on the sled.

Did I say it wasn't cold. Well, before we had gone a mile my face started to burn and the tip of my nose showed signs of freezing. One good thing, I didn't have to do much in the way of helping Nib because he was able to see the flags very well, so I kept my parka hood well pulled around my face with only enough space to peek out every once in a while. Of course this had its disadvantages because my breath would freeze my face and any hint of a beard to the fur on the parka, which really didn't bother me a whole lot till I would try to push the hood back.

Then, well, one can imagine. Then, too, the fur around the hood

242

would get all iced up and any place it would touch my face would cause it to burn. However, I was thankful that I didn't have drift blowing in my face as was the case the last trip, and also was double thankful that it was daylight. I never realized how much difference light could make and oh, boy, when that old sun returns, won't I be happy.

We stopped a little over a mile out to pick up two gas drums that we had lost on our second trip out. Dick and Jack had found them and had them marked with trail flags. Didn't take long to load them on and with Nib being able to see the trail okay, we didn't have a bit of trouble. We didn't make another stop till we got to the Aurora Camp, arriving there at 12:15 A.M., making just fourteen plus nautical miles in two hours. That's really traveling, Antarctic speaking. After we got to the end of the good flag trail (Dick and Jack ran out of trail flags), Nib was able to follow our previous tracks of a week ago and the fellows had a red flare set out which I saw about ten minutes before we got there. Oh yes, in pulling into camp we happened by mistake to tear down Phil's antenna. But they were so glad to see us that I think we are forgiven.

We didn't waste any time. Phil, Perk and Murray had already started to break camp, Fitz immediately started to shoot the moon and also was able to get one star, the only one in the heavens— Sinus. Nib, Grif and I gassed up and turned the tank around getting ready to line up the sleds. Perk had some cocoa in the cook tent so one by one we would get one last cup full before the tents came down. Grif was to drive back and we left there about 1:30. We were detained some by Fitz and the final lashing of the Aurora equipment which Nib insisted had to be extra secure, because when you travel seven miles per hour over sastruga—well, nothing stays intact.

The trip back was uneventful except that it was cold, the temperature being down to minus forty degrees, and as luck would have it, the five mile wind had shifted and was right in my face. I can't understand why it has to play such tricks but it was in my face on the outgoing trip, then, as nicely as you please, it switches around so that it is in my face on the return trip. Now a five mile wind never meant much to me back home. In fact, I just never thought about it. But a five mile wind minus forty degrees Fahrenheit, well, you really got something and my face really took a beating. Then, too, I had to use a scraper on the windshield to free it from ice, and even through my mitts the metal of the putty knife which I was using burned my hands. We got to camp around 4:00 o'clock and as usual

243

I was happy to get back. Gosh, it was wonderful to actually be warm.

Friday, August 9 (205th day)

Was busy all day issuing clothing to the men going on the trail. I don't know what it is that makes me so darn tired, but after that little jaunt yesterday I was completely bushed. I didn't even have enough ambition to get in a good bull session, which is really something. When we got in yesterday afternoon Doc and Earl took blood sugar samples of us. Earl later told me mine was two hundred and forty, which is pretty high from a normal of one hundred and twenty to one hundred and thirty. I slept like a log last night and almost slept through breakfast, which would be a calamity. Afterwards Paul asked if I was going to take a temperature run. He said it might be a high one since the wind was about twenty-one miles per hour, and the temperature was minus forty-eight degrees Fahrenheit. So I went over to get ready and much to my surprise and chagrin had forgotten to bring in the cylinder from the last run. In the meantime, I had the stop watch synchronized with the chronometer and Larry helped me by checking time and counting the wind. We finished up at 12:15 and the calories of heat loss per minute were six hundred and fifty, which is one of my highs. After lunch I worked out in the cache trying to straighten it out a bit.

I guess Murray's name of Old S.B. has stuck. Malc started calling him that after seeking W. C. Fields in "The Big Broadcast of 1938." S.B. were W. C. Fields' initials in the picture and he was supposed to have been connected with every major disaster since the sinking of the Titanic. So since Murray's failure in his first attempt at getting aurora pictures he has been known as Commander S.B. Wiener. The funny part of it was that he thought S.B. meant something else and when we went out after them he asked Grif about it. Well, he's been taking a beating ever since. Poor Murray.

Boy, all hell has popped loose here the last few days, and of course I would have to be more or less the cause of it. Al, Larry and I think that it is not necessary to send a geologist on the Pacific Coast Party since in the first place there will not be enough time to do any accurate or detailed, careful work. Al and I figured it up the other night and found that at the most, there would only be fifteen days in the field from Hal Flood, which means that when it is all boiled down, a geologist would be lucky to have five or six days to work.

244

Al maintains that it is a waste to send a geologist on such a party, that any of the other members could do what routine collecting has to be done. Besides, there is no definite proof that there are sediments present there, let alone fossils. So in a "poop sheet" to Paul, Al tells of his plan which is to have Larry and me work together in the Edsel Fords, which will give us at least thirty-five to forty days of actual work. Naturally I came down here to geologize, which means making a detailed map. And I would also very much like to find fossils, for age determination. To travel such a long distance without possibly having any time to work, we geologists think that it would be to our better advantage as well as the expedition's to stay in a known region. It would be best to work on the map with Larry and take a chance on finding fossils in a region, although none have been found. Al sincerely believes that there are fossil bearing strata present.

He says that no particular effort has previously been made to find fossils. Whereas if I make the Pacific trip, I will of course go in a virgin region, but what good will that be if time does not allow the making of a map of some sort or other? Al made only a brief geologic map when he was in the Fords in 1934 and he was in the field for at least twenty-five to thirty days. So what work could be accomplished in five or ten? We'll see what Paul has to say.

Saturday, August 10 (205th day)

Spent practically all day issuing clothing. Got the plane crew fixed up with the exception of Shirley. He is the darndest guy to get along with of any of the fellows down here. I have never known a fellow to argue like he does. Half joking, half in earnest. And he's always so dead sure he is right. Anyway, he asked me if I had any large ski boots, to which I replied no but that possibly we could arrange a swap. To which his answer was that any guy who would trade his large boots for smaller ones was a sap, or words to that effect. Then Shirley maintained that he had been asking me about different boots for a month or so and that I knew that his were too small. I know very well that he has never said anything to me before today about his ski boots and I told him so, to which he flared up and said, "So you are calling me a liar." I was plenty burned up by then, so I told him he was if he wanted to take it that way. I don't know what it is about him but it is impossible to even start a friendly discussion with him but what it will end in a heated argument. And he can never be convinced he is wrong. Anyway, he raved on about this and that, and that there were favors being paid certain men in camp in regards to clothing. He was wrong there, because as far as I am concerned I issue everything alike unless Paul tells me different. Well, the thing ended by his saying that he wouldn't ask the *'% ¢/* Expedition for another thing. Several fellows heard the argument and later came to me to tell me what they thought. Everyone seems to think I am fair and square in my issue with Shirley.

The strange part about it, from the second week on ice till the time he froze his feet he had said nothing to me about ski boots being too small. Then he froze his feet due to his own stupidity and carelessness, and now says his boots are too small. In the first place he bundled his feet up, wearing socks and sheep lined slippers in his boots—couldn't move his toes. He probably wears an eight or nine shoe, his ski boots are elevens. That's at least two sizes large. Mine are only one size larger and my feet are always warm as toast—I only wear one pair of socks. The thing that gets me is when I gave out the boots, and all the clothes for that matter, everyone sang about how everything was so darn large and wanted better fits. Then when I tried to give them smaller sizes, thinking that would satisfy them, they ran back saying I gave them this or that too small. If I ever have anything to do with issuing clothing again I hope someone shoots me. If I had only known!

Went over to the cruiser this afternoon to check up on some clothing I packed for them on the ship. I was very much surprised and relieved to find that they needed very little, only one pair of socks per man. Doc was there as well as Al, and Larry came over, so we talked about the coming trail operations. Al still can't see what good a geologist will do in the Pacific Party. He is sincere about wanting Larry and me to work together, so I guess we will. After all, Al is still senior scientist of this shooting match, and what he says, goes. Helped Len with the dishes tonight. The show was "Ex Champ," and before the show Gil and Fitz swore up and down that Wallace Beery and Jackie Cooper played in it. Well, you can imagine the ribbing they took when it turned out to be Victor Melegan and Tom Brown. Didn't get to bed till the wee hours as Larry, Earl and myself practiced radio and shot the bull in general.

Sunday, August 11 (206th day)
I think I got caught up on a little sleep, just clipped off twelve hours of good sound slumber. Chuck, who is the new mess cook,

woke me up at 12:00 o'clock. Didn't do much all afternoon but type copies of Gil's press notices. He has given his permission so I have almost completed duplicates of his press or progress reports to the committee. Most of the "Mama" boys, as Pappy R. calls them, talked to their wives and gals today. The same bunch—Mac, Pete, Shirley and Giles. They are the only ones who ever get contacts. Pete practically monopolizes the radio shack and the amateur band. He talks to his wife at least three times a week, at least, he takes all the time when the band is open. I heard him last Sunday talking to a fellow, a station where Lockhart could make a contact, and the band was open fine. But Pete said that sure they would be glad to make a schedule sometime when conditions were better, then he turned right around and talked to his folks for an hour or so. When I had the schedule, I mean when I was supposed to have a schedule with Alda, these guys didn't pay any attention to it. In fact, Pete didn't once enter it into the schedule book. Conditions were bad that night or I would have raised plenty of hell around here. Another time I had a successful contact with my folks. I was supposed to have another one two weeks later, nothing was done about it. I guess you have to be the privileged to make use of the radio twenty meter phone, but I still don't think things are run quite right. Even Paul hasn't had contacts. Pete says he tries but still the same stations monopolize the thing and the same few fellows talk. Oh well, such is life.

Didn't feel very well tonight and took a nap just before dinner. Helped Chuck with the dishes, Joe Wells, Ike and myself. The show tonight was a re-show of "She Married Her Boss."

Monday, August 12 (207th day)

I came so close to sleeping in this morning that it wasn't funny. I just got to the table as Chuck was clearing away my plate. Spent all day issuing ski pants and ski shirts. Boy, this issue job is a pain in the neck. I had about six pairs of size forty-four pants and only three fellows who can wear such a size. Well, the pleasant part of the job is trying to make a fellow with a size thirty waist or so appreciate a size forty-four pants. I usually have to end up taking the forty-four myself. Doc and Earl took a blood sugar test on me today, which was two hundred. I have been doing a twenty-four hour urine test for Earl, and no sugar present. I'm glad of that because I'd hate to have to give up my weekly candy ration.

Tuesday, August 13 (208th day)

Stayed up pretty late last night reading about the Scotts and Shackelford Expeditions. Paul wanted us to read of certain expeditions. I guess it's not a bad idea—learn through the experience of others. Got up this morning around 9:00 o'clock, almost missed breakfast again. Well, I wouldn't have minded it this morning, though, because we had eggs but no fruit, hence I had nothing but toast and coffee. Didn't do much this morning but issue towels and clean pillow cases. Used all of our supply of towels but half a dozen, so need to keep them in reserve. Paul asked me to cook the next day so got to bed fairly early. Got a sweet, wonderful message from Alda last night.

Wednesday, August 14 (209th day)

Buck woke me at 7:20 this morning, and as usual I staggered into the galley half asleep and before I knew it was stirring the cereal (the cracked wheat which Nib had put to soak the night before). Got Chuck up at 7:45 and we had breakfast ready promptly at 8:00. It didn't take him long to set the table as all we used were bowls, cups and spoons. Breakfast consisted of hot cereal, fruit, toast and coffee. I then took to my bunk and slept till 11:30. It was lucky I woke up, I thought, but Nib had started things. He had put on the hot dogs to boil and thaw out an hour before and had started to fry them. I opened up a few cans of beans and hurriedly heated them, and with a little applesauce (also from a can) we had lunch. Oh, yes, we had coffee and bread. I got compliments on the beans—that is, the flavor of the beans. Of course, Phillips Canning Company put the beans up, but Chef Passel flavored them with one can of tomatoes. Even I had to admit that it was fair. Had hamburgers at 3:00 this afternoon. Toney and Nib served. Had roast for dinner, was surprised that it was so good and that it was so juicy. I put it on at 12:30 and it cooked all afternoon, but about every half hour I would baste it. About 4:00 o'clock I cut the excess fat off and turned it over. Then after about an hour I cut into it, cutting with the run of the fat, and by 6:00 o'clock it was perfect. I flavored it with garlic salt, etc. Also had canned whole potatoes with asparagus soup, coffee, and peaches for dessert. Al came in about 5:30 and tasted the soup. And, as usual, I didn't have enough salt in it. That is one of his jobs on Wednesday, testing the soup. He also cut the meat for me. Nib came in and helped put things out. Well, the meal was really a success, especially the meat. The only kick was from Al, Paul and Fitz, who like their meat rare. But you can't satisfy them because they are practically cannibals at that table and like their meat raw. If it isn't dripping blood they don't like it.

We had a trail meeting last night and Paul told us of the work of the various divisions. It seems that the number of plane flights will have to be cut down because of a gas shortage since the tank and plane use the same gas, which is eighty-seven octane. We have plenty of white tractor gas, so there is some hope of working it into the plan somehow. Also Paul told of the change in trail personnel to begin the Pacific Coast Party—Berlin, Moulton, Bursey and Richardson; and in the Edsel Ford Biological Party, Warner, Passel, Gilmore and Wells. So overnight I became a dog driver. It hasn't been decided as to what team I will take, but Dick and Jack B. are going to get together soon and rearrange the whole thing. I am glad that Gil and Joe will be in our party. I think they will be fine. Our party is to have two dog teams and I guess Gil will drive the other. Boy, that will be something. We'll all have a lot of fun. The picture tonight was a re-show of "I Am The Law."

Thursday, August 15 (210th day)

Woke up this morning about like a wet rag or something and thought I might sleep in since I had so long promised myself such a treat. But Nib came by and said that he would like to try to get the tractor in. So reluctantly I got out of bed, dressed, and by the time I had eaten breakfast I didn't feel so badly about being cheated out of a morning in bed. Just before we were ready to go out the Doc called Nib in and told him that he had better not go out—that is, after looking at his throat. Nib had been having trouble with his tonsils again and his neck is still swollen quite badly. So I asked Dick if he would give me a hand and we could heat her up and see if there would be any chance of getting it in gear.

It wasn't so cold out, about minus twenty to minus thirty degrees Fahrenheit, but it was quite windy. Dick and I spent practically all morning digging out from underneath the tractor so as to be able to get our heaters under the pan and transmission. We then put canvas tents over the front radiator and one to cover the back extending from the winch. The sides are pretty well drifted up, so it didn't take much to fill in any open place. When we got through, the whole thing was pretty air tight. Then began the business of starting the "pot," or Von Prague heater, and the primus torch.

Dick took the torch meaning to heat the transmission, while I was going to use the "pot" for the pan. Well, neither of us seemed to be able to get the darn things to burn.

The main thing was that we weren't able to get them hot enough. We must have worked for an hour or more to no avail. In the Von Prague there is a cup around the coils in which gasoline is poured. Then by lighting that, it is supposed to heat the coils, and when it gets hot enough and the right pressure, it takes off. Well, I did everything I could think of. My hands were getting cold and my legs were cramped because I wasn't built to sit half way under a tractor. Besides, I caught the canvas cover afire a couple of times.

Well, I finally gave up, took the "pot" in, and Pappy G. looked it over and found that the air jet was frozen (plus a couple of other things). So I started another one inside and was lucky enough to make the tractor before it took a notion to stop on me. So anyway, we had a "pot" going under the pan. In the meantime I guess Dick was having his troubles. He couldn't get that darn torch to burn to save himself, and his feet were getting cold and he thought his heel was beginning to freeze up. He went in to get warm, taking the burner and line part with him to see if the line was frozen or if something was haywire with the burner. You see, the primus torch is comprised of a tank with an air pump connected to it, then a line runs from it to the burner proper. Dick thought that possibly condensation had taken place in the line. I got back under the tent over the front to watch the "pot" and change it around.

Dick came back soon carrying a small hand torch, and it wasn't long before we had the primus torch going full blast. It was quite a simple process by merely heating the large with the small, but it meant that one of us had two heaters going full blast—and was it ever hot and wet. Naturally, the whole underneath part of the tractor was caked with ice, as well as every nook and corner in the body, so we literally had our first Antarctic rain. At noon Nib came out telling us it was time for lunch, but we told him to save us chow as we were going to at least get the motor started before we came in. It didn't take long to heat up the oil, and in the meantime I had cleaned out the cab which was full of snow and had taken the hand torch to the engine, which was caked with ice. I primed it a couple of times and the engine started right off, and after a few minutes Dick and I thought we might at least try it in gear before we went to lunch. So Dick crawled out from underneath and I climbed in, hitting the roof with my head. I had my doubts because

I pushed the clutch in a couple of times and it just didn't feel right. Well, I managed to get it in low gear. I let out the clutch and nothing happened. Then I tried reverse and every other gear on the darn thing. No luck.

Well, by that time I'll admit it was time to quit, at least for lunch, so I left the motor running and we went in. Just as we started to climb down the hatch, the fellows were coming out to fill the snow melter. Chuck had saved us some food and I am afraid that we more or less wolfed it down. We talked over the situation while eating and I thought that there might be some possibility of getting the winch in gear, and if it worked we could use the winch and a dead man to get her in the garage. So Dick and I went right out again after lunch and after about ten minutes of persuasion and clashing of gears I managed to get the thing in gear and a shout from Dick informed me that she was working. Good old winch! Well, the next thing to do was to get a dead man sunk. So we picked a place over a drift directly in line with the winch and it was only a matter of a few minutes till we were ready to see what the winch had to offer. Dick watched to see that the dead man didn't pull out while I gave the motor the gas and started to wind the rope around the winch head. Well, the winch seemed to take quite a bit of strain and it even seemed by jerking the rope to jar the tractor a bit. When it got to a certain point it would stop dead but the motor would not change tone. I knew then that something was definitely wrong about the clutch, because before if the winch had too big a load it would stop the motor. We tried a few more times but couldn't budge "Dolly" so we decided to get the primus torch going again and heat the length of track which was in the snow and which was obviously frozen in. Boy, it didn't take long to turn all of the snow under them and around them into slush.

Then we tried again and it moved so easy it was like a dream. Even the tracks moved. But like a dream, it was short lived. As soon as it started to climb the drift, the winch would stop. It worked fine on the ten feet of level ground, but the winch wouldn't take the grade. I decided to try the gears again, so I got in and after a little difficulty clashed her in low and she jumped forward for about twenty feet then ran into a soft drift, a grade, and stopped. So I backed up and tried it again. Even reverse worked, which was a surprise to me when before none of the gears seemed to take hold. Well, we were in rather a depression, so we thought that if we dug a path through the soft drift and got her out on level ground she would run all right. So we dug like mad for the next half hour or so. Then the question was whether it would be possible to turn enough to get out through the path we had dug. I went back and forth, each time turning just a hair, and each time taking a little longer to shift the thing in gear. Then finally couldn't get it in gear at all. I guess I worked for twenty or thirty minutes trying every gear in the place. So I got the winch in gear, and even though it was off at an angle we thought we could straighten it up again and possibly figure up some way to use the winch, if it meant digging away the whole damn barrier. Well, it was getting a little dark and either we just didn't think or completely forgot, anyway the tractor ended up in our heating ditch and the winch line got tangled up and was pulled tight so we had to take out the dead man in order to get the line free.

We figured we were just about finished but decided to try the gears once more. So I hopped in the cab and after a few minutes of crashing (and cursing) I got her in low, immediately jumped out of the ditch and went right along our path out onto a flat surface, just as nicely as you please. It all happened so fast that I still can't believe it, but Dick says it's the truth and I know Dick to be an honest man. Well, now all we had to do then was get it up the drift and into the garage. So I followed Dick who walked ahead because it was getting fairly dark, and besides, the windshield had an inch or so of ice and snow. We tried several times to climb the drift which stood between us and the garage and finally had to change our course, gradually working our way out, so that we could follow the trend of the drift.

Boy, was I ever relieved when we were finally on top of the drift and all set to go in the garage. You could never hope to see a couple more happier lads than Dick and me. We ran into the bunk house to tell Nib the good news. He couldn't believe it. We were sure proud. The next thing we had to do was open the garage doors and dig away enough snow so that the tractor could enter. Nib came out and gave us a hand. Well, it was merely a matter of a few minutes to get the tractor put away. I just got it in gear enough to start it down the ramp and she coasted in. I mean, she would have coasted in, but some chunks of snow stopped her and I couldn't get it in gear again. So I turned off the motor then put it in gear, and with the switch off Dick then cranked her down the rest of the way. Anyway, "Dolly" is safe in the garage and now all that has

252

to be done is for Boyd to fix her. Paul was very pleased at our accomplishment and congratulated us both. He thought it would take the whole camp—it took us eight hours. Everything is simple in the Antarctic.

Gosh, I was tired last night, and went to bed early. I was kind of stiff from so much shoveling, besides being on my feet all day. Woke up this morning a little late for breakfast, but Chuck had saved me some. It's nice to have friends. Since it had been decided that I was going to have a team, Dick and I spent the morning down in dog town and I helped him change all of the dogs around. I really have a nice team, in fact a damn good team. I think five out of the nine are registered dogs, which is something.

My team consists of Rusty, the lead dog, Keela, Josca, Kazon, Myrra, Kotik, Alaska, Jad, Wanda and Tongas; since there are only nine dogs to a team one of the dogs would go to another team. Tongas was one of the malamute pups which were born at Wanna-laucet. He's about a year old now and is going to make a real pet. I'd kind of like to keep him. After lunch I went back to my dog tunnel to dig out the two sleds which Zeke had stored there as Jack B. wanted to fix them up. Dick came down and we took out Rusty, whom we thought was blind. Dick wanted to see if he could see anything at all. If not, he would hardly make a good lead dog. It was still very light out, but Rusty didn't do so very well. He'd stumble over the smallest sastruga. I went back to finish digging out the sleds while Dick said he would dig open the end of the tunnel so that we could set the sleds out. It all didn't take long and soon we had the sleds outside.

I spent some time then trying to clean up the tunnel a bit. It was hard to walk in it as there were so many icicles hanging down and there is nothing more uncomfortable than getting a neckful of ice. So I took a broom and cleaned the roof off the length of the tunnel. I later found that Zeke had been saving them for weeks so that he could take pictures of them. In fact, he was coming down the very next day. It was kind of funny.

When Dick brought Rusty back he said he had been leading him around and said he thought the dog couldn't see a thing. Hence, no lead dog. Dick said I might change if I wanted so I took a Sib, a bitch pup which I named Toske, after her mother. I haven't yet decided who I will have for a lead dog, but I would like to make a lead dog out of Tongas. I don't know whether I will have time to teach him anything or not.

My first try at cutting seal meat. Dick showed me the best way to chop it. Boy, is that ever hard work. The meat is frozen actually so hard that it dulls and chips the ax blades. During the mail bag program this afternoon we made the trail flags. I got a message from Alda. I can't understand why Alda hasn't received messages from me. I've written, sent them to her regularly. Also got letters from mother and dad, and from Howard, talking of his wonderful vacation. Guess I'm jealous. Just before dinner I went out to feed my dogs. I was surprised to find them so well mannered. Not one made a grab for their meat but would take it only after I had given permission, then they would only take it very delicately.

Saturday, August 17 (212th day)

Up as usual at 9:00 o'clock. Was going down to help Dick work clearing up the blubber house, but I got started on making my whip a little shorter and before I knew it, it was noon. I had to rip the whip half way down and it was quite a job sewing it back. Made quite a respectable whip out of it, though. After lunch I went down to my dog tunnel and worked in it a while, trying to dig it deeper so that I don't have to crawl through it on my hands and knees. Then I went out to cut my meat—Dick was still working in the blubber house. After I finished chopping my meat I told Dick I thought I'd take my Saturday afternoon bath and he thought it was a good idea. So I told him that since I was heating a whole tub full he might as well use part of it. He thought that was a good idea, too. I then went to the machine shop, got a couple or three buckets of water from the snow melter, started the Von Prague and within a half hour I was taking my weekly bath. Toney put in a bucket full and took a bath also. Jack R., who was using the sewing machine to sew a zipper on his duffle bag, said that seeing us all taking baths made him almost ashamed. Besides, he thought that he had a definite "stank" about him, so he put in a bucket full.

It's a good thing that Dick got there when he did because a couple of other fellows were getting that Saturday bath look. Dick even went so far as to shave his beard. He certainly looks changed—he really got the bronx cheer when he came to dinner. The show tonight was Jane Withers in "Boy Friend." Oh, yes, a double feature! "Jones Family In Hollywood." Both were very over-entertaining.

254

Woke up this morning at noon. That is, almost noon—12:30. Had breakfast, then went down to the dog tunnel. I had planned to let my dogs out for a little run but it was blowing too badly, so I turned them all loose in the tunnel (I have a gate at the entrance to the main tunnel). What a mess, but at that, I guess I got off fairly lucky. Only had one dog fight, even if there were four dogs in it. Keela went into Myrra's kennel and I guess she didn't like it. Anyway, hell broke loose. Myrra went in after her and I still can't figure how the two males got in it. Just excited, I guess. Well, my whip was handy and it didn't take me long to settle things and peace soon ruled again. On the whole, everything went along fine. Poor Tongas thought all the dogs picked on him till he finally came and sat by me. Poor pup, he was scared to death. It seems a shame, a pup like that thrown in with older dogs. He wants to play and the rest don't appreciate him, even though they are mere pups themselves, a little over two years old. Dick came down and we talked about the dogs for a while. We then chained them again and went into the bunk house. I kind of decided to take it easy till dinner time by getting up in my bunk and reading "Dark River," quite a different picture than it seems. A very good dinner tonight, fried chicken—as usual, with all the trimmings. I helped Clay with the dishes. Poor Clay, mess duty finally caught up with him. I'll help him nights and all I can because he has various radio schedules which he has to keep also. The show tonight was a re-show of "Of Human Hearts," which really makes me stop to think. A very good picture.

Just another day and I about didn't get up for breakfast. In fact, I fell asleep again, but Dick woke me. After breakfast I talked to Gil and Joe to find out about clothing for them since they are definitely going on the trail. I got them taken care of, then went out to get Toney his fur parka. Toney tried it on and naturally it didn't fit, none of them do. They are all too large. Anyway, he took it off and threw it on the floor, said he'd be damned if he was going to wear it, it didn't fit him, besides it had been worn and I was always giving him worn clothing, which of course is not true. However, all of our furs have been worn by someone or another, because we only have so many and they are not personal property. Sure the one I gave him had been worn. In fact, it was used by the Aurora party. Well, anyway, he said he'd be &%!¢# if he'd wear it so I told him it was up to him, but I thought he was being a damn fool. It annoys me, every time one of these guys down here feel badly about something or have a gripe on they take it out on me by squawking about their clothing or by saying that I am playing favorites. I'm getting tired of the whole thing, trying to please such a bunch. Oh, well, such is the life of an expedition man. I just took the parka back and put it up.

After lunch I gave all of the fellows who are going to remain in camp a pair of socks, mitts and liners. When I went down to chop meat for my dogs, Dick and H.H. were in the blubber house making dog food. What a stench, besides being smoky. Had a heck of a time getting the meat chopped because it bothered me to breathe, and after about the first ten minutes my throat was dry. However, I did manage to get done. Earl came down after his meat but I had used the last of the seal, so we dragged in another and I helped take turns with Earl in cutting him in two. Decided I would feed my dogs at 5:00 o'clock daily. It seemed like a fairly good time and would give me plenty of time to wash for dinner.

Tuesday, August 20 (215th day)

Today has certainly been my off day—or was it. Anyway, I had a run in with Shirley again. I don't know exactly how it happened, but in talking to Pappy G. the other night I found out that he and Shirley and two fellows at East Base had blue ski shirts issued to them on the *Bear*. Well, I was glad to know that because I have been short two shirts. In order to give everyone in camp two apiece I would need sixty-six, well, I only had sixty-four. Two were missing and I knew that they were given out on the *Bear* but I didn't know two of our men got them. So I had to give the fellows going out on the trail two and the rest only one, keeping the rest as extras. Well, that isn't such a good arrangement because those not getting two were wondering why they didn't, and those getting the two, of course, had to make them very conspicuous. So I was really happy when Pappy G. gave me the information. So today I went over to Shirley's place to ask him if he got one, and to get it. Naturally he said yes, because Pappy was there, and I asked him for it back to give to someone else so that I could give everyone alike.

It was all right, but it brought about the old discussion of one guy having something another hasn't, and Shirley is like that. It burns him up to see someone with an item of clothing or something which he doesn't have. Well, it can't be helped, because some things

256

46. The teams get scattered out. In the foothills of the mountains.

47. Sometimes a team gets going too fast down a slope and the rear sled tips over.

48. Author skiing to inspect low outcrops.

49. Most travel days were all white (a whiteout), but some days we had clouds and shadows.

50. Stopped for sun shot and conference.

51. Camped at Mt. Rea.

52. Mt. Rea; light color is igneous rock, dark color sedimentary.

53. Unhitching a team.

54 & 55. The Beechcraft stopped by for a visit.

56 & 57. Geological party camp in the mountains.

58. A haircut on the trail. From left seated, Larry Warner, author, Gil Gilmore.

59. A stop to scrape ice off skis.

60. Charles F. Passel, 1939.

go to the dog drivers, we have some items of clothing for those going on the trail, and so it goes—but Shirley can't seem to understand that. Anyway, one thing led to another and he informed me that it all started back in Boston the day the Cruiser came in. It so happened that prior to its coming I told the watchman over at Army Base not to give the key to the warehouse to anyone but me, the reason being that different fellows were showing their friends, etc., around at all hours of the day and night. Twice I found the place wide open, hence my action.

Well, on this particular morning instead of going for the key, I went out to the gate and met the Cruiser and Phil asked me in, so I rode from the gate to the ship. In the meantime Shirley was looking for me so that he could get his camera out of the warehouse so that he could take pictures of its arrival. Boy, he was really mad, but after all, none of us were working because of the Cruiser coming in, hence no point in opening the warehouse. Besides, he didn't say anything to me about his camera being there. Anyway, I got it as soon as the Cruiser pulled along side the ship, but that was too late. He wasn't able to get pictures of the arrival. My fault. I started picking on him then. He said I was playing when I was supposed to be working. Well!!!!

Then, too, poor Shirley had arguments on the *Bear* with the officer. Then there were arguments whether he would stay here or at East Base. (I brought it all on, so he says. That is, I started it all at Boston.) Then, too, he has had to fight for any item of clothing that I have given him (he says). And besides, I didn't cooperate with him on some clothing pictures which Paul wanted taken. All I wanted him to do was to wait till I started issuing clothing, which meant delaying things a week, but that wouldn't work—instead I had to go out and open boxes specially for him. In other words, he doesn't think much of me. Besides being forgetful, he says that I'm not doing my clothing job right. Well, as long as Paul thinks it's being done well, the hell with Shirley.

However, after it was all over, he got the shirt. But he said that if he ever wanted anything else he would make a little "poop sheet" and give it to Paul, hence he would never have to have dealings with me. Suits me fine. I have never had the displeasure to meet such an unreasonable, stubborn, dogmatic person before, for which I am thankful. Besides everything else, he informed me that he didn't have to thank anyone for getting him on the expedition, which was just a dirty crack, because of Al. Well, it all ended very quietly. I

257

just walked out. Worked in the cache most of the afternoon taking inventory trying to get things all lined up for Murray, who will handle things when I am on the trail. The wind is still blowing fifteen to thirty, has been going strongly off and on since Saturday.

Wednesday, August 21 (216th day)

Murray woke me this morning at 7:00 o'clock. I certainly hated to get out of my bunk, but it had to be done. Last night Sig mixed me up some eggs for an omelet, so there wasn't much for me to do but put on the coffee and wait till time to serve. I decided to have short order service. Fitz, who is taking Clay's place as mess cook these last few days due to the fact that Clay accidentally (on purpose, so some say) cut his finger, and Doc thought it best not to get it in water. So poor Fitz, who was due the following week anyway, was pushed into service a little ahead of time. I woke Fitz about 7:30 and we were ready to serve at 8:00. Everything went along fine. I cooked the eggs while the fellows waited. The only trouble was that they turned out to be more or less scrambled, but they were good. We also had figs, coffee and toast. Oh, yes, I almost forgot to have toast, which would have been a crime of the first order. Fitz reminded me just in time.

After breakfast I went into the science building to type up Gil's latest press items, then Walt sent me a little code till time to prepare lunch. I gave them corned beef hash (canned), which I put in a flat pan along with catsup, using eight cans of hash. I also took canned beans and put them in a flat pan cutting strips of bacon on top, plus a nice layer of brown sugar. Well, to make a long story short, lunch was a success, especially with the Passel cocoa formula with a half bottle of malted milk for good measure. It was actually fun mixing the stuff. I'd add a little cocoa, then a little sugar, taste, then add more sugar and so on till I finally pronounced it good. Paul sampled it and put his okay on it. Just to make sure I put in just a bit more sugar and then the malt, which really topped it off. The fellows ate all the beans, they liked the flavor. Maybe it was the cinnamon I put in them.

After lunch I went down to the blubber house to chop my seal meat, but no seal was in from the tunnel so I had to drag one in. Luckily there was a fairly small one on top, but even then I had to do quite a bit of pulling and tugging before I could budge it. The seals, most of them, are too large for one man to handle and are frozen in solid. Several times this one had me whipped. However,

258

I did finally get it into the chop house, and after about a half hour of chopping I had my meat all cut. Damn, the seal meat is hard. It's pretty easy to chop through the blubber, but once one hits the meat, boy, it's like hitting steel with steel. How the dogs ever eat it is more than I know.

I got back to the bunk house about 3:00 o'clock and all the fellows going out on the trail were taking a navigation exam. Since I was cooking I couldn't take it, but will take it later. Decided to have liver for dinner and I really had a time slicing it. Having never sliced liver, I don't think I did so badly. Most of the cuts were about the same thickness. Dick came in after giving up the ship as far as the exam was concerned, so I put him to work. He cut up the potatoes for me, small potatoes, whole canned, into slices, which with onions and fried toast was pretty good. Along with the liver and potatoes I had tomato soup, peas, spinach, and coffee, plus fruit for dessert. Dick was certainly a big help, he fried the meat for me. Fitz didn't show up and I didn't notice it till 5:45. So I yelled up to our cubicle and sure enough, he was sound asleep. He really had to hustle to get the table all set up to serve by 6:15. Dick came to his rescue, too, by dishing up the dessert. Well, we served at 6:15 on the dot. Everyone seemed to enjoy the meal and even Sig complimented me on the dinner, and that's something.

After I had eaten I went down to feed my dogs. I always like to spend a half hour or so in the tunnel talking it over with my pups. They seem so glad to see me that it's really inspiring. The show tonight was a re-show of "Blondie," which came out in first place in our recent poll of movies to be re-shown. The fellows still got a kick out of it.

Thursday, August 22 (217th day)

I forgot that today was to be a holiday—yes, a big day—the return of the sun. I was awakened at 1:30 by Nib, who whenever he goes by our cubicle says "On the ball, Oscar." I was informed that we were to put the flags up at 11:00 o'clock, as at that time the sun would be at its maximum height. Al Wade came in to say that the sun was certainly up so after I dressed I went out to take my first peek at the sun. Well, I'll have to admit I was disappointed. I expected to see the sun, the sun I know. You know, big, red, and round. Well, all I saw was a red smear on the horizon. Of course it was a little cloudy, which might have been the cause of my not seeing it. But I was still disappointed anyway. The sun was back and it had its normal effects and everyone seemed happy, even though the temperature was minus forty-seven degrees Fahrenheit (which is cold in anybody's language). Well, at 11:00 o'clock we all congregated outside standing in a half circle around the flagpole. Nib and Chuck did the honors at hoisting the colors upon word from Paul, and we all doffed our hats, caps, helmets, or what have you. Quite an impressive sight, but damn it was cold. Shirley had his motion camera grinding away. Dick's nose started to freeze and no sooner had the flag reached the top than we all bolted for the hatchway. I beat Grif by a nose with Dick a hard third. We tried the science hall stove but moved on to the bunk house. We were for bigger and hotter stoves.

After we warmed up a bit we had breakfast. There had been talk of a baseball game, the service men versus the scientists, but one look at the thermometer discouraged that. Spent the afternoon working with Dick sewing my dog harnesses, which were a mess. It annoys me. If they hadn't been so carelessly mistreated, they wouldn't have been all chewed and broken up. Two have had the collars completely destroyed, while most of the others have at least two to five breaks in them. Zeke blames the dogs, saying they will chew anything. But we should have hung them so that the dogs couldn't get to them. Naturally dogs will tear up anything they can get hold of. So the thing to do is keep things away from them. Evidently Zeke didn't take a look at the harnesses.

The bunk house this afternoon looked like a Y.M.C.A. game room. I have never seen so many games going on here at once before. Earl and Arnold were playing chess, and of course the "Dictation" gang was strong at it. Gil and Al were playing a baseball game with Mac acting like an umpire, while some of the others were trying a new football game. Later on in the afternoon Paul, Nib, Shirley and Perk had some sort of a "pick up sticks" game, the object, I guess, being to see how high and what different designs one could stack little pegs. It was a close one between Nib and Al. At 5:00 o'clock Dick, Earl and I went down to feed our dogs. We had to drag in a seal as the little one I brought in yesterday didn't last long. Dinner was served tonight at 6:30, and what a dinner. It consisted of turkey, sweet potatoes, corn on the cob, fresh lima beans, spinach and peas with fresh strawberry shortcake as dessert. I ate so much I was actually miserable, but guess I was hungry and only had three helpings of turkey. Helped Fitz with the dishes, along with Gil and Dick. The show tonight was a re-show of "The Awful Truth," which I think is the best movie we have down here.

Friday, August 23 (218th day)

Boy! Won't this wind ever stop blowing? It reached a maximum velocity last night of forty-five miles per hour, and is going strong now at 12:30 P.M. Had a devil of a time getting up this morning, I wanted to sleep so badly. Fitz kept calling me, though, and I finally made it by 9:00 o'clock. After breakfast I started issuing fur sleeping bags, which is a tedious job since I only have twenty, and twenty-two men are going to be out on the trail. I went in and saw Paul and he said to issue to the men with the dog teams and to the plane crew, which is a total of seventeen men, and then to keep the other three in stock and possibly we will have to make a couple out of the fur skins. After lunch I wrote Alda, Mrs. Sibley and my folks. Then started sewing on my dog harnesses again. Boy, that is a job and my fingers are sore as boils. Well, I only have one more to repair, then I will be all set.

Saturday, August 24 (219th day)

Spent most of the day trying to round up and account for our ground mattresses which are to be used by the men on the trail. I found most of them under different fellows' sleeping bags—those fellows going on the trail! I merely issued the mattress they already had, the others I took back and re-issued. After lunch Fitz gave me a haircut, a kind of a short job, so to top it off I shaved and washed down to my waist. I did intend to take a bath but found that I had no clean clothing due to blizzard conditions last Saturday. I couldn't get in enough snow blocks to get water to do a washing. I didn't want to take too much out of the snow melter.

Yesterday Jack B. brought in Tim, one of his dogs, a huge fellow, part wolf, saying that he didn't think that he was well. He thought probably the dog was just chilled through and that getting him warm might fix him up. So he tied him in his cubicle and right after lunch the dog had kind of a fit, like he was strangling to death. Dick and Jack ran to him and got him quieted down. Dick said he had the funniest heart action he had ever seen—well, he had to believe it. Even at that he didn't like to, because normally a dog's temperature is one hundred and five degrees, old Tim was decidedly low.

I call him old Tim, but actually he was only four or possibly younger. He was a beauty of a dog, the largest in Bursey's team and the best puller.

About 9:00 o'clock last night Jack B. was in the science building typing, I was working on harnesses, when Dick came in and told us that Tim had passed on. Doc Frazier looked at him earlier in the afternoon and said that he looked like a dying dog. I went into the machine shop and got in on the autopsy which showed, according to Doc, that Tim had died of pneumonia. His lungs did certainly look sickly and congested. His heart looked strong and his stomach was normal. Dick thought at first that he might have died of some stomach disease. That is the third dog we have lost so far. Old Doc that was killed last summer, then Counvoa, who died about the middle of the winter night of a cause yet unknown. Earl, as soon as he can find the time, hopes to thaw him out and do an autopsy. Then lastly Old Tim. Well, frankly, we can't afford to lose any more. That puts the camp team down to seven dogs now as Jack took one of the Siberian Sib pups, which I think was named Chutcu.

Last night just as I was washing for dinner, Dick came in and wanted to know if I would help him for a few minutes. I said yes, and immediately put on my jacket and followed him, not having any idea what was to be done. But we went down to dog town going into the camp team tunnel. Dick stopped at one of the kennels, flashed his light inside, and there was Chutcu and six newborn puppies. Boy, was I surprised, but Dick said he had known it ever since the day we changed the dogs around. So we loaded the pups in a box and took the whole outfit to the machine shop and fixed them a bed. Dick took two of the pups and put with Snooks, the bitch with only two pups. She immediately cleaned them up and claimed them as her own. Poor Chutcu was so busy with the others that she didn't notice that transaction. Dick later told me that she had one more pup. The thing that puzzles Dick is who the father is likely to be. He hadn't planned any such affair.

The show tonight was "Charlie Chan in Reno," the last of our new shows. From now on we get nothing but re-shows. After the show Dick and I started to work making a breast plate harness, which we hope will be suitable to take the place of the collar harnesses. Got to bed at 2:00 A.M. Before we did hit the hay, somewhat earlier in the evening, Dick, Jack, H.H., Gil and myself went into the galley for a midnight snack, so to speak—cocoa and cold beef sandwiches, and later on Perk came in along with Fitz.

Sunday, August 25 (220th day)

Up bright and early today. Al was just sitting down to the table for breakfast. He wakes me up almost every morning. He informed me that the sun was really out, so I hurriedly dressed and ran to the hatch opening to see for myself. Sure enough, the sun was really there and it was a whole sun. Quite a wonderful sight to behold. Boy, I didn't know the sun could make so much difference. I'll never take it for granted. That's the trouble with all of us today, we take too many of the wonders of nature, etc., for granted, never really realizing what it would be like without them. For instance, not to see the sun for four months—well, I know. After breakfast Dick and I finished our special dog harnesses. I went down and got Mukluk, one of Dick's dogs, to try it on him. Took him into the science building and the harness fits perfectly, with a few minor adjustments. We then put on our jackets and took Mukluk outside and hitched him to the small airplane sled. Dick went, I rode on the sled. It was hard pulling because the surface was just like sand. However, Mukluk threw his whole weight into the collar and did manage to get to Dick all right. Our breast plate collar seemed to work fine, and our main objective seemed to have been fulfilled in that the collar didn't ride up on his throat causing him to wheeze. We couldn't stay out very long because it was too cold for the dog at minus fifty degrees Fahrenheit. At such a temperature not only is it bad for his lungs but the ice burns his feet. Of course not to mention what it would be apt to do to our lungs, but that's beside the point. We should know better.

Fed my dogs a little early, about 4:00 o'clock, then washed for dinner, finally ending up in my bunk till meal time. We had turkey for dinner along with the usual trimmings. The show tonight was a re-show of "Wuthering Heights," and it still affected me the same. Kind of gave me the creeps. After the show, Dick, Jack R., Larry and myself met in the galley for a little chow session and our main discussion was concerning Paul's announcement before the show started that all hands were to help dig out the Beechcraft Monday morning. Well, we all knew that the only reason they were getting it out was simply so that the service men could get their flight pay. An all hands job just so that three men or so could benefit by it. Well, it burned us all up. I know none of us would shirk from work, and would probably be the first ones out on an all hands job, but this was different. There is no earthly need to get that plane out for another month as far as the expedition is concerned. And yet we were all to put aside any jobs we happened to be doing to go out and dig. Well, the whole discussion ended up with none of us going out.

Monday, August 26 (221st day)

Nib woke me up this morning with his usual "On the ball, Oscar," then the next thing I remember was a conversation from somewhere concerning the weather, some saying the temperature to be minus fifteen degrees, others minus fifty degrees. I dressed and ate breakfast. Our talk at the table concerned the digging out of the plane. Some argued pro, some argued con, but most were under the impression that since only a few benefited, well, they should do the work. Besides, the whole thing was purely personal, so to speak, and not expedition. At the last minute Dick thought that he would go out just to see what was being done, so Jack and I said we would make dog food.

I went over and told Paul kiddingly that I didn't want to disobey orders, but that I didn't think I could go out as I would have to give a hand with the dog food since Dick was going out. And besides, I said, there are some of us who think that making our dog food is just as important as getting flight pay. I didn't mean to say that, but it got out some way. I felt kind of funny afterwards, but Paul didn't say anything. I guess he knows the set up all right. He could have said the plane stays in. Still, that could hardly be done and still keep peace in the family because then all of the service men would be down on him. I don't begrudge those fellows their pay, but I still think that they should have gone ahead and done the whole thing themselves. I knew I wouldn't have had the nerve to ask thirty men to drop everything they happened to be doing to help me get my flight pay. Oh, well, such is life.

Jack and I worked all morning making dog food. Gosh, what a job—a dirty, smoky, smelly job. Making dog food is a fairly simple job, but melting the seal blubber is where the smell comes in. The smoke from that simply burns your lungs, and before the morning was quite over I had a nice start on a headache, plus a good dry throat. Oh yes, and my eyes burned. Besides that I was in perfect condition, feeling fine.

We have a huge kettle and stove arrangement where we put the seal skin, which we slice from the meat when we feed our dogs. The skin will have anywhere from one to three inches of blubber on it, so the first step in the process is to melt the blubber. We then take a can of dry dog meal, put it in a tub and mix with the liquid blubber oil. Then by taking a mold we make individual pound blocks of dog pemmican, making approximately forty to the can. The blocks are then put out in the tunnel to harden, then the whole process starts over again.

Dick came down about 11:30, saying he was thoroughly disgusted. He said three men could have done the whole job, that all the fellows did was stand in each other's way. They used a chain to pull the plane out of the hangar and Dick said that they didn't even use that right. Then the thing that really annoyed him was the way Petras was running around with a camera when he should have been doing a little work. By lunch time we had made one hundred and ten blocks. After lunch I made another harness, a different type of breast plate collar, bringing up Jad to fit it on. Didn't have time to take him out and try it but plan to test it on our planned trip to Little America in the near future. After dinner Dick and I worked on harnesses till about 10:30. I sewed padding on the breast plate collars while Dick started to make another harness. Earl came in and said that he would like to "stick" Dick and me in the morning and that we shouldn't eat anything. But after a ten minute argument he finally consented to letting us eat if we would go in right away and eat. So we reluctantly quit work and retired to the galley where cocoa and sandwiches held the fort.

Tuesday, August 27 (222nd day)

Woke up at 8:00 o'clock this morning but stayed in bed enjoying the music Fitz has been playing when he wants us to get up. I stayed in bed expecting Earl to call me for my blood sugar test, but by 8:45 I got up anyway. Just as I finished dressing Dick came in and told me I was next. So for the cause of science, etc., I think I at least gave a quart or so of blood. The temperature today at 6:00 was minus fifty-nine degrees Fahrenheit, so after breakfast Paul suggested we run a still air temperature run. I hated to hear that because it would mean digging out our pit, which Doug had dug. Paul said he would give me a hand and together we had it cleaned out and ready for us by 11:00 o'clock. We came in and got warm, then tried to decide whether to start then or after lunch. We thought we might at least get it started so I went over and got the cylinder only to find it frozen, it had fallen to the floor. That kind of decided our little question, so it had to be after lunch. I spent the time till noon sending code to Earl.

After lunch we got started, the temperature had risen to minus forty degrees. I took the cylinder out to the pit, connected it up, then came back to record for Paul. After it had reached zero Paul left, saying he would come back later and relieve me. All I had to do was check the air temperature every five minutes and between times I sewed harnesses. Jack R. came in about 2:00 and wanted to know if I could relieve him from making dog food. He had hurt his wrist some time ago and the patting and molding the meal into blocks hurt him badly. I told him I would come down as soon as Paul relieved me. Paul finally showed up, he had forgotten all about the run. I told him the circumstances, telling him that I would send up Jack to record for him. It was 3:00 o'clock by the time I got down to the chop house. Dick and I worked till 5:00 o'clock completing five hundred blocks, we then brought in a seal and cut meat for our dogs. After dinner I brought in all of my harnesses, giving them a final checking. Bursey gave me an extra harness he had with his team, and out of those acquired plus the ones I already had, I managed to get a fairly good set of harnesses. Dick, H.H. and myself had our usual evening snack, consisting of cocoa and sandwiches.

Wednesday, August 28 (223rd day)

Up bright and early this morning as we planned to get an early start on making dog pemmican. But even though we got down to the chop house by 9:00 o'clock, we didn't get started till almost 10:30. There were the usual things which delayed us, such as bringing in a seal and taking the food that we prepared yesterday off the trays and stacking it in the old pup tunnel. Then, too, we had to wait while the blubber got hot. However, by noon we had three hundred and fifty blocks made. Nib took cooking today and he wanted me to show him how I fixed the spuds. So right after lunch Dick and I cut them up for him. Then we went out and filled the snow melter.

We were ten minutes late in getting back to the chop house—1:10. Tsk! Tsk! Boy, we really turned on the steam during the afternoon. At times the smoke and steam were so bad that we couldn't see each other. And need I mention the smell! By 5:00 o'clock I personally was glad to quit. My wrist was so sore I thought it would drop off. The way we have to get the block out of the mold is by jerking the wrist and it doesn't always drop out the first jerk. And there toward the last it seemed they would never drop out.

Anyway, by quitting time we had made eight hundred and twenty-three blocks. We decided to come back after the show and finish up since we needed only one thousand to complete the job.

Before we went into dinner we cut our dog meat. I helped Clay with the dishes, that is, I did the silverware and the pans. Fitz washed the dishes, Clay rinsed. The show was a re-show of Charles Boyer, Irene Dunn, in "Love Affair." My fifth time to see it and I still like it. I guess it grows on me.

Before we went back to the chop house we had a cup of chocolate and put on a tub of water for baths. We were getting to smell so bad that even we couldn't stand it. Personally I think that I smelled more like a seal than the seal itself. By 1:00 o'clock we had finished, making a total of one thousand and nine blocks. There was still some of the seal left that we had used to feed our dogs, so we decided to chip enough for tomorrow's feeding. Our baths consisted of quite a ceremony. We took the tubs over to the machinist building and each one found a secluded spot and in one half hour or so we all gathered around the galley stove—clean men. I have never seen my hair so filthy dirty as it was after my dog food making session—absolutely greasy. After partaking of a bit of food we all turned in, voicing that we would sleep till noon. We told Murray to tell Clay not to call us.

Thursday, August 29 (224th day)

I broke my vow of the night before and got up at 10:30. I really didn't mean to, but I had such a darn headache and was hot. I don't see how Murray and Chuck stand it sleeping days. Chuck has recently started to work nights, he says, so that he can get something done. I heard Clay come in our cubicle and wake Larry. Oh, yes, I also heard him set the table in his gentle way. He would hold the bowls a foot above the table and drop them. I spent the time before lunch receiving from Walt. Worked in my dog tunnel all afternoon cleaning it out and knocking down snow to lie on. Boy, it was back breaking work, but worth it because the pups seemed to enjoy it so much.

Friday, August 30 (225th day)

Had planned to have all hands help dig out the tractor ramp. But since the temperature was below minus fifty degrees Paul didn't ask all hands, but volunteers, so there were only a few of us out. I couldn't do much work as Doc thought I ought to rest my back.

It has been bothering me quite a bit lately and working in my dog tunnel the other day didn't help it any. Stooping over using a pick caused it to ache pretty bad. However, I at least lent my moral support, if that means anything. Nib, Dick, H.H., Vernon and myself were the first to brave the cold. Pappy Gray and Mac came out a little later. I have never seen so much snow drifted in one place. It had filled the ramp completely and was packed hard. After working all morning we had just about started to put a dent in it. It wasn't really cold, at least we all managed to work up a sweat. The high pile of snow on either side of the ramp of course protected us from the wind, and that's all that matters. So after lunch (that is, during lunch) Mac announced that it would be appreciated if all that could would come out after lunch and help finish the job. Incidentally, we had tripe for lunch, which I didn't eat. For some reason I just couldn't stomach the idea. Maybe it was because I watched the autopsy on old Tim and saw his stomach turned wrong side out. It didn't take long after lunch for the whole bunch to finish clearing out the ramp. In the meantime, Nib and I put oil in the transmission of the tractor. Vernon did a wonderful job, having to make a complete compression plate for the clutch. The old one was broken in three places.

Well, I had the honor to drive "Dolly" up the ramp, which was quite a job as they made the thing somewhat steeper than before. I had to try two or three times before I could make it. As soon as I got out I drove out a little way from the building so that we could dump off the cab. Since they have decided to use the red tractor for trail work, the cab would be a death trap in case of a crevasse, so off it came. Boy was it cold riding then—kind of a roadster effect in the minus fifties, and I will hurriedly assure anyone that it wasn't pleasant going. Nib and I then tried to move the old caboose which had been parked at the airplane cache, causing it to drift over, but we didn't have any luck. Besides, my face was starting to freeze up. We'll have to go out and dig it out one of these days. When we got back to the garage, Dick and Vernon had completed the assembling of their new sled, so I hauled it out for them and we gave it a test pull, ending up with leaving it out by the gas drums. Boy, it looks like it's going to work fine. Dick and Vernon sure looked happy. Just got inside in time for the mail bag program, received messages from Alda and the folks. I am so glad to hear that Alda is doing so fine.

268

Saturday, August 31 (226th day)

Here it is the last day of August, and am I ever glad. We'll be going on the trail soon. That's the reason we geologists are here. Dick helped me last night run a temperature run with the temperature at minus sixty-eight degrees below zero and a ten mile wind, which soon after we got started dwindled down to three miles, then it was still. Got to bed about 3:30 this morning. Paul thought it would be a good idea to run a still air, since the temperature had remained constant, or fairly so. I didn't bring in the cylinder last night, so while it was thawing out I went into the machine shop and used the sewing machine to finish a note book holder I am making.

I am becoming quite adept as a seamstress nowadays. We got the run started about 11:00 o'clock and by noon it was down to zero degrees centigrade, so I went to lunch while Paul held the fort. While the water is freezing, one man can easily handle it as all he has to do is record the air temperature every five minutes. I relieved Paul and about 1:45 the water was completely frozen. By 3:00 o'clock we had reached a water temperature of minus fifty-one degrees, and an air temperature of minus fifty-three degrees, so we decided to quit. Dick, H.H., Larry, Earl, Jack B. and Perk hauled in a few seals this morning. We had run out and these were brought into the tunnel from our supply of thirty, which are stacked outside at the foot of the seal tunnel. I was to help with the tractor but with a temperature close to minus seventy degrees Fahrenheit, it did not seem advisable to take it out and Doc forbids me to do any lifting. I had to be content with a temperature run. Helped Clay with the dishes tonight. A re-show of "Love of Money."

Sunday, September 1 (277th day)

Well, here it is the first day of September. Got a good night's sleep last night, getting up at 11:00 o'clock this morning. As usual on a Sunday, for breakfast we had hot cakes. Worked down in my dog tunnel most of the afternoon still trying to get it deep enough so that I can at least walk halfway upright. Zeke dug places out of the sides to store this or that, throwing the snow in the tunnel, hence filling up the passage way. That not only makes it impossible to walk, but also makes it uncomfortable for the dogs in that the snow would pack around their chain stakes, shortening their length of chain. They don't have any too much freedom to begin with.

Well, I have been spending my spare time with a hatchet and pick, chopping away that snow which due to circumstances, etc., had turned to ice, and what a job. Well anyway, I finished the job today by putting up side boards to keep the ice, snow and debris back in the walls. Incidentally, I can walk the length of the tunnel without too much danger of hitting the roof or the light cord, which always ended up with a shower of ice crystals right down my neck. Not only does the tunnel look better, but I bettered things for myself as well as for the dogs. Spent the time before dinner sewing on my note book holder.

We had chicken as per usual, and darn good too. Buck is the new mess man for this week. Clay finally made the grade. The show tonight was "Man To Remember," which I think was the best show of its kind that I have seen in a long time—wonderful acting. It was very true to life in that most of us do not really reach an ultimate aim or receive our just praise, the satisfaction of being a success, until too late, as in the case of old Dr. Abbott.

Well, we reached or got our coldest temperature last night, getting a station recording of minus seventy-four degrees (which happens to be too cold for me). Oh yes, I was out in it for a spell, but not too long. I had a little outside job to do in moving my two dog sleds over by my tunnel. But I can assure anyone that I didn't tarry. In fact, I hadn't even taken a step from the hatch opening when my face started to burn. Joe Wells went around the trap line and got a temperature of minus seventy-six degrees plus as a minimum.

Monday, September 2 (228th day)

Boy, was I surprised when I woke this morning to find it almost afternoon. Yep, 11:45 on the dot. Who would have ever thought it would be Labor Day here so soon? I guess everyone is getting home from the lakes today, I imagine the roads were crowded. It's really hard to imagine hurrying again, watching out for taxis, hurrying off to keep an appointment, rushing to a show, a dance—noise. Why, that will be unbearable. Our only disturbance down here is the howl of the wind, the steady drone of the generators, a few dogs howling and, oh, yes, the continual yapping of the Navy men about their beloved "Navy." I am so tired of hearing about the service that I am afraid it's becoming an obsession with me. Maybe it's the winter nights getting me. If it is, I'm not alone. Shirley, Boyd, McCoy, Schlossbach, Giles, Griffith, Gray and Petras daily get in at least one or two arguments (mostly friendly) concerning the

Navy. If it isn't how many ships it has, it's how many it's going to have. Or else whether one gun fires a three inch or a five inch shell, or at least about whether a BJ3 is better than a BS4. Darn it, it certainly gets tiresome. I asked Grif about it one day and he said we all love the Navy, we're just offering constructive criticism. Joe Wells is the only one who doesn't talk about the Navy unless to tell some funny story or something. He says hell, he'll have enough of the Navy when he gets back—let her rest.

Worked on a blanket liner for my fur sleeping bag, finishing it up just before dinner. Something new and different, turkey. Well, I'll give Sig credit, he certainly can cook when he wants to— especially dressing. Fitz, Larry and myself helped Boyd with the dishes. Had a re-show of "Yes, My Darling Daughter," the fifth time for me.

Tuesday, September 3 (229th day)

Well, I've finally decided Boyd is nuttier than a fruitcake the way he rants and raves around here mornings trying to get people up for breakfast. He really puts on a show for all of us. He kept blowing off at me till I finally got kind of peeved and told him rather crudely that he had done his duty, he woke me, and that was that. If I wanted to get up for breakfast, I would, and I assured him that the more he hollered around, the more apt the fellows would be to remain in their sleeping bags. I think I told him more, but I was pretty sleepy, kind of in a daze. Boyd's old story, and old cry, is "I wish I had an easy life. The trouble with you guys is you have never had to work. Just a bunch of college boys, there's work to be done and you're keeping me from it." Then he goes and sits by the fire for the rest of the morning. The whole trouble is that Vernon is still trying to carry the whole expedition on his shoulders, and he isn't strong enough.

Made a face mask for Nib this morning. I worked in the clothing cache most of the afternoon till time to feed my dogs. After dinner took a nap, but was rudely awakened at 8:00 to attend a trail meeting at which time Paul talked on safety first, common sense. Doc Frazier gave us a little information about first aid.

Wednesday, September 4 (230th day)

Well, I know one thing, I will never speak lightly of an Antarctic winter night again—I have been through one. It's something one just can't explain, but I know we all feel the same down here. Not that any of us are going screwy, batty, but still, it's beginning to tell on us. The monotonous life, same thing day in, day out, same faces, same arguments. It probably wouldn't be noticeable to an outsider but our whole existence now is built on tensions. The least little thing can easily blow up the whole works. We all make an effort to get along and respect the other fellow, his words and his privacy.

Woke up this morning, first Wednesday for some time that I haven't cooked. Nib took my place. Spent the time working in the clothing cache and I am happy to report that I am almost through taking inventory. Helped Nib prepare the evening meal. I baked the ham and fixed the potatoes. Ike made lemon pies, and what a mess. He started in right after lunch and when I went into the galley at 3:00 he was still going strong, covered from head to foot with flour, flour all over the floor, even on the door latch and snow melter water faucet. But that didn't phase the Coach, no, sir! He was making pies. (Incidentally, second attempt.) So there he stood cookbook in one hand, dough in the other. Well, the outcome even surprised me. His lemon pie was good. We sampled one right after he baked it—the first one, you know, just in case. But it did take Nib and me a half hour or so to clean up after him and Nib said he had been washing pots and pans after him all afternoon. My ham was a success, so they said. The show tonight was "Ex Champ" again. I have an idea it was voted in, just because of Nay Gray. Boy, what cold weather we have been having! The temperature dropped down to minus seventy degrees on the thirty-first of August and it has been minus seventy degrees or below ever since. In other words, it ain't been fittin' out!!

Thursday, September 5 (231st day)

I did a very foolish thing last night, I let Dick and H.H. talk me into trying out my fur sleeping bag outside in a trail tent. Well, we went out about midnight, but need I say we didn't stay long. In fact, 4:00 o'clock was our limit, but considering it was minus seventy-five degrees Fahrenheit—well, that wasn't bad. I was as warm as toast, my feet and upper part of my body, but my hip and thigh got rather uncomfortable. Poor Dick has had trouble with his feet, they have been cold every time he has been out. Whether it is minus ten degrees or minus seventy-five degrees, it doesn't matter. I think I could have stuck it out as I wasn't really cold, but since Dick decided he was going in, because it would be foolish to stay out and freeze, especially with camp warm and close by, well. . . .

Besides, our purpose was to try out our bags and if they didn't work, come in. I did have a little trouble with my hood which doesn't fit quite right. The temperature record of minus seventy-four and four tenths degrees was shattered today, reaching a new low of minus seventy-five degrees, which is the coldest temperature recorded for this part of the Antarctic in the last twelve years (some say thirty). Amundsen, I think, had a minus seventy-four degree temperature recorded and Paul says it beats all the Byrd expeditions, and that, at least, is something.

Well, as the result of last night's folly, I slept in this morning till 11:00 o'clock. Paul woke me then to help with a still air reading he and Doug had started. Doug is getting around a little better now. At least he only has two toes to worry about now as Doc took off the one bad one. But now, so Doc tells me, Malcolm is raising Cain and is mad because Doc won't take off the other two. Doc thinks they will regain life in a couple months or so, that is, they will slowly become normal, but that it will take that long. However, Doug wants them off so he can go on the trail. He says Doc is not cutting them off just to keep him from going. Well, either way he can't go and I certainly would think that he would like to have at least four toes instead of just two. Some of the fellows say that he just wants to be a hero, that he wants to complete a chapter in his book. I wonder. Anyway, since he is feeling a little better Paul thought it would be a good idea to give him something to do. Hence, the still air, and hence my getting up at 11:00 to relieve Doug for a while during the crucial part of the experiment and through lunch.

Earl and I have started to make small bags to hold our trail food in. I spent the afternoon running some of them off on the sewing machine. I am still not an accomplished seamstress, but I'm improving—did about two hundred. We are making them out of sheets, sheets from the U.S. Navy! It kind of tickles me the expedition wouldn't buy bags for such a purpose because they cost five cents, but Earl and I figured that the ones we are making are costing the government, just the way it does things. Went down to feed my dogs. I think I forgot to mention that Toska, my black bitch pup, had two pups of her own and very unexpectedly. However, since the arrival of Chutcu's pups I have been watching Toska, and Dick looked her over and said that he didn't think she was going to have any. So a couple of nights ago I noticed that she was in her kennel when I went by to the blubber house. I stopped and called her out, and there were her two puppies, dead. It was a darn shame, but we had no way of telling, as she was not bred. Dick thinks she was probably in heat at the time she was running loose in his tunnel after the blubber house fire. Her pups had probably been born in the morning and when I went down at 5:00, well, it was too late. I hate that.

Friday, September 6 (232nd day)
Woke up this morning bright and early at 9:00 and missed breakfast, not that I particularly cared, but Buck had thrown everything out. I don't think any of us down here are in a real big hurry. After all, we aren't going anywhere so I don't see why there is such a big fuss about breakfast being right on the dot. Paul and I ran a temperature run right after breakfast. We had what we thought was a good combination with a fifteen mile wind and minus sixty degrees to minus sixty-five degrees below zero, but when we got started the temperature raised to minus fifty-eight degrees, which ruined it as far as a record run was concerned. The sun caused both our thermobulb and cylinder to act strange. That is, the sun caused radiation of heat on the brass in the cylinder, hence the water started to freeze plus zero and eight tenths instead of zero to minus thirty and three tenths (thirty being the instrument error). After lunch I sewed some more food bags and started to work on my sled tanks, finishing them up. Had to put flaps on the bottom to secure them to the sled.

Oh, yes! I forgot Dick told me this morning that Toska had another pup. Found it at 2:30 this morning when he went down to look at the fire in the blubber house, and it was alive. He took it in and put it with Chutcu and her pups. He thought it would be best to let Toska dry up. Besides, he said she wasn't taking care of the pup. I haven't seen it but he says it is well-formed and well-marked, being black and white. A couple of days ago Dick and I moved all of the pups down to the blubber house, now that we are through making dog pemmican. Dick decided to keep a fire going down there at the time, just enough to take the chill off, then moved down Snooks and her two pups. Chutcu and her seven, Suzie Q, and Girt. We fixed up some pens and boxes for them and they seem quite comfortable. We take turns going down to check the fire. During the night Murray tends to it. After dinner tonight Dick and I worked on some more tanks, finishing two. I took some bedding down for my dogs tonight, some straw which our mirrors came packed in.

I put some in each kennel and each dog went in and very busily spread it all around to make a bed. Talked to Al tonight about getting a scholarship when I return. He said he had sent J.J. and Doc Shideler messages.

Saturday, September 7 (233rd day)

Boy, my busy day today. Got up in time for breakfast then worked in the machine shop making the sled tanks. When Joe got back from going around the trap line he helped me sew them, hence completing both Gil's and my tanks. I then brought in our trail tents, looked them over, hung them up to dry, then took them out to the clothing cache which for the time being is the collecting place for our trail gear. I spent most of the afternoon sewing food bags then went down to feed my dogs. Also cleared out the tunnel again, and the kennels, getting about a half-ton of seal fat and skin, which must have been fed when Zeke held fort because I always skin the seal before I feed. Dick gave me two stakes for my tethering line, stakes he made out of material gotten from Little America. Now all I need is a tethering line and I will be all set.

The show tonight was a re-show of "Dodge City"—sixth time for me. Gosh, it will be funny getting back home and seeing a show only once. Probably won't be able to get all of it because, after all, we do know these almost by heart.

Sunday, September 8 (234th day)

Slept till noon today, awakening to the tune of "Drifting Around And Dreaming," which I happened to be doing. Ferranto is now mess man, thank goodness Boyd's week is over. There was some talk of his taking another week. One thing is sure, if he had, I know he would have cracked. I shouldn't talk. I guess Buck's all right except he thinks the whole success of the expedition is on his own two broad shoulders and that he is absolutely indispensable. As in the case of refueling the diesel engines, he didn't say anything to Clay or Pappy, but he would show off to the group around the bunkhouse stove informing them that he wasn't going to refuel any engine as long as he had mess duty. All the rest of us carried on our regular duties when we worked in the galley. Clay carried on his radio schedules, as did Walt. The mess work is just extra! Well, as a result, we almost ran out of fuel, and if the engines had stopped it would have been too bad.

Vernon is on that old list, at least, with Clay, and McCoy is doing the refueling (and volunteered to do it). After breakfast of hot cakes I went into the machine shop and sewed more food bags. Then I went down and fed my dogs and called it a day by shaving, washing up and crawling into my bunk till dinner time. At meal time Paul announced that the *Bear* was to leave Philly on the fifteenth of October and the *Star* from Seattle on December first, and that all mail should go to the Department of Interior, Washington, D.C. Oh, yes, I almost forgot! Last night after the show I went out and did my washing, which consisted of two suits of very gray underwear, two P.J.'s, four pair of socks, four towels and one gray shirt. Since the washing machine is on the blink I did it by hand. What a job. Finished up about 1:30 A.M.

Wednesday, September 9 (235th day)

As usual, I hated to get up this morning. I don't know why, but it's so nice and cozy, warm in my bunk. I hate that initial plunge, so to speak, into the cold world outside. And let me tell you it does get cold in the bunkhouse. In fact, our drinking water freezes every night. Anyway, after breakfast I finished sewing up the food bags. Then Pappy Grey and myself got into a little discussion as to why he didn't have ski boots. Well, naturally, I had two strikes against me as I was acting under orders from Paul to save fur boots for spare emergency boots on the trail. Well it so happened that Pappy for some reason or other thinks he is going to be out on the trail—that is, if the plane operates out from Advance Base. But several times before I had asked Paul about it and he said he wasn't sure what the setup would be. Well anyway, I went in again to see Paul and it was finally decided to give Pappy boots because there would be a bare chance that he might be in the field a week or so. Also, Paul wanted these trail men who had Bass boots to have a chance to change to the Mc1 boot if they wanted to, the three men being Columbo, Richardson and Bursey. After seeing these fellows, found that Toney was perfectly satisfied but that Jack B. and H.H. would like to try the others. Well, it so happened that I had one eleven and one thirteen left, so the two drew straws for the eleven. Unfortunately for H.H. he was last, drawing the thirteen. Luckily H.H.'s Bass boots were size ten, which were just right for Pappy G.

Got the surprise of my life today at the breakfast table. Shirley came and actually spoke to me. That didn't particularly surprise me, but his subject matter sure did. His size thirteen boots were too large. I could hardly keep from laughing because he made such a fuss till he got the larger boots. So I gave him a pair of twelve Mc1 and I think probably he is satisfied, at least for the time being. Larry worked all day digging an extension to Gil's dog tunnel, a place to store gear. I worked most of this afternoon and should be able to finish it tomorrow. Went down to feed my dogs, and as usual, no seal was in. For the past two nights I have had to drag in seals, and luckily they have been small ones. But the one tonight almost had me stopped. I did manage to break him loose and had moved him a few feet when Murray came down—I put him to work. Cut up enough meat for both Dick and myself.

Tuesday, September 10 (236th day)

Up again this morning bright and early—9:00 o'clock. Had breakfast, then worked with Gil checking over sizes gotten in recent clothing canvas. We hope to get some sort of a semi-dress outfit for going home, going ashore possibly in khaki outfits, and thought it would be a good idea to come as close as possible to the regular sizes of the men. Doc Frazier x-rayed a tooth for me. It started to ache a few days before, but suddenly it stopped. Helped Earl sack sugar till lunch. H.H. had been helping him while I sewed the bags. We have eighty rations to fix up, which means eighty bags of the following: sugar, salt, cocoa, milk, fruit, bacon, etc. Most of the fellows were out today digging out the gas to be used in the planes, tractor, tank, etc. And from the reports I have heard it was cold work, the temperature being close to minus seventy degrees.

Went down to feed my dogs a little early this afternoon so that I could let them run loose awhile. I am happy to report that I had only one fight. The bitches in my team seem to be the trouble makers and they were at it this afternoon. Alaska got in Myrra's kennel and the latter didn't like it, hence went in and talked it over with Alaska. Well, the whip soon settled the dispute.

After dinner I was lounging comfortably in my bunk when Paul came to talk to Larry. I couldn't help overhearing that it was about the pending tractor trip. Paul was informing Larry that he was to be a member of the party and navigator, then he turned to me saying I was another member and was to act as radio operator and driver, with Dick and Buck completing the party. We are to leave Saturday morning, which doesn't leave much time and there is so much to do. This afternoon Paul and Al had a contact with Bob English and it seems that they are still working on our increase in salary, which looks very promising. Here's hoping!

Wednesday, September 11 (237th day)

Busy day today, getting ready for the tractor trip. Spent all morning sewing and making a tank for my trail radio which Pappy turned over to me the other day. Larry, Dick and the others worked outside on the gas again today—that is, till noon. But after lunch they decided not to work outside as it was blowing too badly (however, we did fill the melter—what a cold job). I think I was just as cold today as I have ever been. And it took me some time to thaw out before I went down to the blubber house. Larry and Dick were already down there working on dog food, that is, Dick was outside loading the bagged dog food into the sled as Larry pushed it up to him through an opening in the roof. As I couldn't do much to help them, I started to chop up a seal. Dick and I thought that we had better cut up a little more before we leave. Earl is going to feed my team as well as his own, while Jack B. is going to take care of Dick's, and H.H. will look after the pups. Didn't finish my seal before dinner, so after the show (which, incidentally, was a re-show of "Rose of Washington Square") I went back down to the chop house and worked till 2:00 o'clock in the morning. I don't want to brag, but I am becoming quite efficient with an axe. Personally, it will be a relief to get back and maybe just cut up some plain old wood instead of seal meat, which is hard as steel and very difficult and tiring to chop. After the show Larry and Dick went to the machine shop and worked on a sled which will haul our caboose.

Thursday, September 12 (238th day)

Boy, I just couldn't make it this morning, so I stayed in bed till 9:30. I did, however, manage to get some breakfast. I forgot to mention a few happenings of yesterday. First, to start the morning off right, Phil was late for mess duty and breakfast was not ready till 9:30. Incidentally, Ike was cook, and believe it or not we had fried bread. Well, what woke me up was Chuck and Phil having very tense words and the gist of the thing was that Phil thought Chuck should have walked over to the Cruiser after him, and Chuck in no uncertain terms told him that he was no different than the other fellows from the Cruiser and they all got there on time. And that if he couldn't make it, why didn't he sleep over here, after all, Grif and Pete did. That started the day off, as I said. Well, then too, the galley was a mess. Ike would put the bread in the batter then drip it on the floor, up the front of the range and all over the top. In fact, there was batter all over the place. Lunch was late as Phil had quite a job cleaning up. Ike had spaghetti, which was the best we have ever had, and that did burn Sig up. He ran around saying it was punk and even argued about it, although he was the only one who thought so. For dinner Coach had a good roast, plus apple pie—the first made down here so far, and it was damn good.

Our whole table helped with the dishes. Spent the morning re-sewing my radio cover and making a kind of reel on which to wind my antenna. After lunch I went down to the chop house and collected the meat that I cut the night before and stored it in my tunnel. Dick and Larry were packing dog food. I couldn't help, so I cut some more meat for Dick and myself. Our trail party, the great geological party, was to have a meeting tonight, but Gil was asleep so we postponed it.

Friday, September 13 (239th day)

Still getting ready for our little tractor jaunt. I guess we won't attempt to leave till Sunday or Monday. We are almost all ready, with the exception of putting the caboose on our newly made sled. The thing that will hold us up will be the work on the tractor. The hell of it is, the tractor has been outside every day since we were told about the trip so Buck hasn't been able to put a cab on it and do what work he has to do. This morning we brought in seals— Dick, Larry, H.H., Jack B., Perk, and myself, plus Buck and the tractor. H.H. and I worked in the tunnel, and as they were dumped in the end of the tunnel he and I pulled them up to the chop house. The fellows outside did the digging, they would use the winch to drag them to the tunnel. It was kind of funny, both H.H. and I working in such crowded quarters, especially since we both wear number thirteen and really do a good job of not handling them. I wear thirteen because of comfort, while poor Jack has to wear them of necessity. By lunch time we had twenty-five seals in the tunnel, which was about all it would hold. I suppose we could have squeezed in a few more, but gosh, we were all pretty hungry. After lunch some of the fellows worked to finish digging out the gas. Filled the snow melter also. Mail bag was from Honolulu today. I got letters from Alda, mother and dad.

Boy, I just made it to breakfast in time this morning. I really don't know why I bother, though, just for a cup of coffee and toast. We have been having eggs about every other day and personally I am sick of them. One day hot cakes and the next, eggs, and then sometimes a little cereal or fruit. Spent all morning working in the clothing cache getting a few odds and ends for different fellows, as well as getting Buck outfitted for the trail. Dick had to mop down alone this morning. Bursey and Klondike seemed to have deserted him.

After lunch I took all of my personal gear, duffle bags, a box and some trail equipment which I had in the clothing cache, down to my dog tunnel. Dick and Larry got the caboose secured on the sled. Went down early to feed my dogs and found a bunch of fellows down there sacking dog pemmican and carrying it out to the sled. There wasn't anything I could do so I cut Dick's and my meat. The show tonight was "St. Louis Blues." Had my first radio schedule test today and I didn't do badly. Earl located his set down in the blubber house and after he and I both checked in with Pappy R. we shot the bull back and forth for a while. Joe turned the generator for me. If I must say so, I was quite pleased with the outcome of things. My call for this trip will be NUWZ.

Sunday, September 15 (241st day)

Fitz and I helped Phil with the dishes last night. None of the other fellows offered to help because of the way Phil ran out last Wednesday. Oh well, what the heck! Woke up at 11:00 o'clock this morning to the beating of a pan by no one other than Toney who along with Earl and Perk are on mess duty for this coming week. For the next three weeks we are to do mess duty as a group—that is, the different trail parties—hence, the Biological Party. I got together our food today which was quite a job as I had to check over all of the trail food that I had put up last fall, and of course I would find the sugar sacks broken, and naturally the cocoa was spilled all over the place. I could never understand how they expected paper sacks to hold up and evidently they didn't but good old Navy sheets to the rescue. I finished up about 3:30 as Earl and I were going to have another little gab fest, but the CQ'ers were at it strong, as usual, so we didn't try. Shirley, Mac, Walt and Court had schedules. Went down to feed my dogs early again tonight. Dick had left me a piece of seal meat from that which we had cut for his dogs for the next two weeks, so all I had to do was cut it up in small pieces. Gil came down just as I was finishing so I gave him a hand, whereas he gave me what he had left over, and with that, when I got it chopped up, I think there will be enough to feed my dogs while I am gone. Helped the boys with the dishes tonight, I did the silverware and pans. The show tonight was one of our favorites. Irene Dunn in "Joy of Living" with Fairbanks. We have three Irene Dunn movies and we have seen two of them three times, and "Love Affair" four times. So I guess we must like Irene Dunn.

Monday, September 16 (242nd day)

I didn't think I'd make it this morning. I swear I don't know what's the matter, but I just don't seem to have any pep, and tired is no name for it. Why, I can chip off twelve hours of good sound sleeping without even batting an eye. Spent the morning doing little odd jobs such as getting the oil for the tractor, kerosene, primus stoves, funnels, fur robes, etc., and helped Larry take it all out through the hatch prior to packing it in the caboose. Dick had just finished securing the sledge meter. Buck worked on the tractor cab and made a drying pan to go under the hood so that we could dry mitts, liners, batteries, etc. After lunch, collected and washed up our trail cups and gave them out to the leaders of the various parties, then filled the snow melter. Had to wear glasses outside today as the sun is getting pretty bright. Earl and I then had a radio schedule, he in the blubber house and I in the bunk house.

September 17—October 3*
*September 17—October 3—Tractor Trip To Mountains

October 4

Returned last night from our little jaunt to the mountains. Tired, but glad to be back at base. Got in about 8:30. Sig fixed us some things to eat then Larry and I went over to see Al, who is in bed with tonsillitis. We shot the bull with him for a while, then came back and turned in. Gosh, it was nice to wake up to a nice warm bunk house. I really slept last night, a good nine hours. Had seven hot cakes for breakfast, which is not bad for a growing boy. Spent all day unloading our gear from the caboose and getting it cleaned up and stored away. Went down to see my dogs. They seemed glad to see me. Earl left me some meat cut so I didn't have to start out the first thing and chop seal meat.

Boy, what a sleep. I think I must have slept like a log. At least I know I didn't budge till Joe announced that breakfast was ready. He and Gil have been doing mess duty and they roped Fitz in some way because he was helping them. Larry and I were supposed to be on mess duty and Gil and Joe swear that we planned it so that we wouldn't get back in time. After breakfast I went down to my dog tunnel, dug open one end and put my dogs out on the tethering line. They were certainly glad to get out. I then started to dig out my kennels, and what a job. I worked all the rest of the day and managed to get eight of them out on the surface. They were sunk below the surface of the tunnel floor level, in some cases as much as a foot, and of course the tunnel had settled so that they were fairly well hemmed in. And I might mention that the dogs doing number one around didn't help matters any, and that helped freeze them in. Well anyway, I chopped and chopped, tugged and pulled, and as reward for my efforts, as I said before, I got eight out. Poor Keela had to do without for one night anyway. I hunted up a tea box for her but she wouldn't even consider it. I guess she couldn't understand why hers was so much smaller than the others. Anyway, I dug her a hole and she seemed contented enough.

I went over to cut my meat. Earl was there and it took us at least forty-five minutes to get our meat chopped. I guess I was just chopped out—my arms were like lead. I'd lift up the axe and it would hardly make a dent in a seal. I guess poor Earl was about as bad off. He and Jack R. had been down to the pressure ice the night before, took their teams and stayed overnight. I guess they had quite a time of it. Jack said his sleds were wrong side up most of the time. They came back this morning. H.H.'s team looks fine and old Prince and Blackie certainly add strength to his outfit. Jack is driving them at the wheel. Earl came in a little later than Jack. He apparently had trouble, for one of his dogs was tagging along a quarter of a mile back. Earl is now officially a dog driver. He said his team worked nicely, except for Dickie and Rex, two of Berlin's dogs who evidently are not trained. Earl said they always wanted to go when the rest of the team was stopped, which is not quite right. Show tonight was "Inspector Hornleigh," at last. Pappy G., Ike and four others had been yapping for a re-show for so long and finally when they had a vote I think they must have stuffed the ballot box.

A day of rest, but not for me. In fact, not for any of us. It almost reminds me of last fall. Well anyway, I woke up around noon, ate seven pancakes, which is a record for me (I used to be able to eat only two—I guess the trail kind of agrees with me, or maybe yesterday's little chopping session might have had something to do with it). I might mention I was a little stiff when I got up. Well, I dug out the remaining kennel, getting Keela situated and comfortable-like. I then cleaned out the far end of my tunnel, clearing it so that I could store my things when we hit the trail. By the time I finished cutting meat and feeding, it was time for dinner. Afterward I went over to the Cruiser to see Al who has been in bed the last few days prior to a tonsil operation. I guess they bother him pretty bad so Doc intends to yank them out.

Wednesday, October 7

Had a general meeting last night concerning trail operations. On our return trip we passed the tank at twenty-two miles out, camped with a broken sled, which Dick and Vernon fixed. Well, the next report from the tank put it at thirty-five miles, running into some soft snow. That was last Saturday night. Then Grif came through Sunday morning at 10:00 saying that they were having trouble with the tank mechanically, a knock in the transmission, but that they would take one sled and try to go on. So with that to go on we had a big meeting last night, sitting around for a couple of hours chewing the fat and getting nowhere.

Larry and Zeke got in a heated argument which was tending to get personal—something about weights. Larry told Zeke that he would probably have more gear than the rest of us put together. Well, it got around to the point where Zeke was saying that he knew more about the Antarctic than anyone here with the exception of Paul and Al, and yet he was not even going on the trail, so forth and so on. Just as things were nearing a crisis, someone butted in saying that that was all beside the point, then bringing up the tractor again. It was finally decided after hearing Buck's proposed plans to give him and the little red tractor a chance.

After breakfast this morning I went out to see if my dogs were all right since it had started to blow a bit earlier in the morning. All of them were in their kennels. I cleared away some snow that had collected around them, then shifted the kennels around so that the entrance was out of the wind. The darn wind shifts so swiftly

283

down here that before the day was over I had moved the kennels a couple of times more. Spent most of the day repairing my fur parka, trying to rescue it from a couple burned places received on the tractor trip. I had it hanging to dry on a line in the caboose while underway, and much to my own neglect the lantern swung against it. The result was two nice holes. It was kind of funny— when I finished my patching job I turned the parka back, fur side out, and there the patches stood out like a sore thumb. I evidently didn't match the fur lengths very carefully because the hair on the patches stood at least an inch longer than the rest of the fur. Oh, well, it will be warm, anyway.

Tuesday, October 8

We were supposed to start digging out the Condor today but there came reports that the temperature was minus forty degrees with a twelve mile wind, so we didn't have an early breakfast, but ate at the usual time. After breakfast I went out to take a peek at my dogs. They were all okay but a little cold, so I went in and got some excelsior from Pappy G. for bedding. They certainly knew what to do with it. Old Kusan immediately started to paw it around, getting it set. Well, the reports on the weather were rather false, for after lunch Paul and Mac took a peek outside and found it was fittin'. The reason for that was because after looking after my dogs I took a little walk around, and it wasn't bad at all. It wasn't exactly pleasant out, but after all, didn't we dig the &¢($%! Condor in in sub-zero temperature?

So after lunch all hands turned to, and started digging. Al sent word that he wanted to see Larry and me, so we went over right after lunch. He was still in bed but was feeling fine. He had received another message from the Committee wanting to know where he would suggest Larry and I do our work, what government department we would be connected with. Well, naturally the USGS would be the government department, and as for working up our material, Larry would work, if possible, at the John Hopkins, while I would do my work at Miami. Then in regard to salary it seems that the Committee could not see paying us money while going to graduate school as they would be contributing to our education—just a technicality, though, because after all we would be on scholarships. Or at least we hope so. Well, to get around that, Al suggested in his case as well as ours that we be paid a liberal salary for the months July,

284

August and September, hence getting around the little difficulty. It all remains to be seen, but here's hoping.

We shot the bull generally for a while, then left to contribute our bit toward getting out the Condor. Buck was warming up the tractor, and since he was busy with rebuilding a sled, I took over. It took about an hour or so to heat up and get started. Went over to the garage after the scoop and started in cleaning snow away from the front of the hangar. Buck just couldn't stay away (something novel, you know) so he worked the scoop. I took it for a couple of hours, then my feet got a little cold so I went in to change to my mushing boots. Oh yes, and also to have a cup of tea. We're all tea drinkers now. Anyway, when I got back Dick was driving, so I grabbed a shovel and did a little leaning on it. It had been decided that Phil would go with Buck on his trip to the mountains, so he relieved Dick. That is, Vernon showed him the dope. Phil did okay for never having been in a tractor before—he's from the Bronx. After dinner, Mac, Buck and Vernon went back out and ran the tractor a little longer, getting the front pretty well cleared away. In the meantime, some of the fellows were taking off the roof of the hangar as well as digging from around the tail.

Wednesday, October 9

Early breakfast this morning, up at 7:00. Worked all morning on the Condor. Richardson and I handled the scoop while Phil drove. By noon the roof was all off and we started on the front walls. And were they ever hard! And to think they were worried, afraid that snow walls wouldn't hold, so they made them several blocks in thickness. Well, they might have been snow when we put them all up, but they are ice now. A pickax wouldn't even put a dent in them. After lunch I relieved Phil for a while driving. My tooth finally caught up with me. Several times while on the trail, it ached, but I took a little "mist" and cleaned my teeth, and it stopped. But it got so that mist didn't do any good, neither did Doc's toothache drops of straight alky, so Doc said it would probably be better if I would have it out. He said it would be impossible to save it even if I were home and could get to a dentist. So when Phil came back out from his coffee, I went in and told Doc I was ready. I had been putting it off for the past month or so. He laid off during the afternoon so that he would not be nervous. I went out to feed my dogs, H.H. was kind enough to give me meat. I had started to chop some up when he came out and told me that he had plently for both of us. I certainly appreciated that because it was cold and my tooth ached. Then, too, the thought of having it pulled out didn't help matters any. So anyway, I got them fed and then got ready for Doc. It was about 5:00 o'clock then. Now that it's all over, it didn't hurt much—not much!! Doc said he put more novocaine in my gums than for Al's tonsil operation. It's a good thing Toney was there to hold me down because I was just getting ready to climb out of that chair when it came out. Doc couldn't pull it by a quick jerk, but had to keep working it back and forth, pulling at the same time. Well anyway, I'm glad it's out. The show tonight was "Gorilla," the Ritz Brothers.

Thursday, October 10
Friday, October 11

Breakfast at regular time this morning. They got along so well yesterday with work that Paul thought it not necessary to have an early reveille. But as soon as Mac took a peek outside, everyone got in a hurry. It was blowing, which put us in a rather embarrassing position as far as the Condor was concerned. It was all dug out and with an hour's work, such as splicing a bridle, etc., she would be all ready to pull out. Well, a blizzard, if it's a good one, can undo a lot of work, so the place suddenly broke into bedlam. By luck, Buck had started to heat the tractor an hour earlier so it wasn't long before it was running. The plans were to break the plane loose with the tractor, then take it and the tank and haul it out. They took a block and tackle, used the winch, and much to the surprise and joy of everyone, the tractor was able to pull her out alone. I know Nib was happy, as he was saved the job of heating up the tank, and that is a job.

Lunch was delayed till 1:30, but the Condor was out and that was all that mattered. Now the trail parties are free to get their own gear together and start out. I didn't go out for long this morning—just long enough to take a couple of pictures, my first in a blizzard. Charlie just finished developing them and they turned out fine. Pictures of the plane, buildings, etc. After lunch I gave out windproof P.J.'s to the trail men, then went outside to see if my dogs were all right. They were all in their kennels. I cleaned what little snow had drifted around the kennels, then went over and chopped my meat. I can't get over how well-mannered my dogs are. They never grab at their food or gulp it down like the Eskimos.

I'm rather fond of them. Always look forward to mail bag days. Heard from Alda.

Good old Columbus Day. Yesterday was a holiday, not only Columbus Day, which alone rates a large dinner, but also our last big dinner before we hit the trail. Sort of a get-together. Of course, it was supposed to be a holiday for the men, but all of us were hard at it all day. It's surprising, all of the little last minute things which turn up. I spent all day issuing various odds and ends of clothing to the fellows—things which they'd either lost, worn out, forgotten, or thought they would like to have. I'll be glad when it's all over.

Dinner was a huge success—tomato cocktail, turkey, and everything. After the meal, Paul gave a little farewell, an end-it-all, an after-dinner talk. And come to think of it, it does make one feel pretty sad when we think that the few days before going on the trail will be the last that we will all be together at West Base. Upon our return from the trail, the ships will be in and new men will come into camp. Things will never be the same. So we might never really be together again as there will be the others present. Besides, going home on different ships, and once we hit the states, boy, the fellows will really scatter. It's all very sad.

Fed my dogs late again tonight. I don't know how long they will put up with me. Show tonight, "There's That Woman," again, and a short on "The Colorado Trail," which, incidentally, we have seen for the sixth time. The fellows all like the Sons of the Pioneers. Dick and Jack B. made a little trip to Little America to hunt for rope, clothes, etc. They didn't have much time there, but did manage to pick up a few odds and ends.

Sunday, October 13
Gosh! It even surprises me—got up this morning at 8:30. Must be sick. Anyway, I went out to the galley and Fitz was making coffee, so I joined him. The bacon was good for a change—really fried. After shooting the bull for a little while I went out to the clothing cache and started to get some things that the Biological Party wanted. Several of the fellows gave me lists of gear that they wanted, so I did the whole job hoping to get it all over at once (but I don't imagine I'll have much luck).

I can't get over it. Roast beef on Sunday. I have gotten so used to chicken and turkey that I actually felt offended. That's what happens when we have a holiday on Saturday. After dinner I went out and fed my dogs. It had been blowing, drifting all day, and they were really snowed under. Dick helped me move the whole tethering line, then we dug out kennels. It was quite a job handling the dogs while we moved the line. Boy, Tongas is some pup. I'm going to have my hands full. The show tonight was a re-show of "Holiday." I like it better every time I see it.

Monday, October 14

Well, Perk was due to leave today, but the wind was blowing a bit, and I guess they are glad because they aren't quite ready. Kind of saved their faces. I spent all day taking inventory and am happy to announce that I am through. Yes, the whole thing is typed up and handed over to Paul. What a relief.

Tuesday, October 15

Didn't get to bed last night till the wee hours. After dinner I started to pack, wow, what a mess. I didn't know that I had so much junk. Helped the Biological Party get underway this morning. Earl, Bursey and I brought over the dogs from dog town to the vicinity of the tractor ramp where the fellows were loading their sleds. Gave them a hand with lashing their tents and various other items on the sleds, and the whole camp came out to see them on their way. The first field party to leave.

Wednesday, October 16
Thursday, October 17

Wednesday and Thursday were spent getting the sleds packed, re-checking the dog harnesses, going over the seemingly million and one things necessary for three months plus on the trail. I kept reminding myself that I couldn't run to the corner store for a needle or thread or whatever. We went over our various and sundry pieces of equipment such as sample map, geology tools, food, extra clothing, compass, radio, hand generator, and, of course, our primus stove and enough fuel to last for the trip.

It appeared after much checking and re-checking we were finally ready. So after lunch on Thursday the U.S. Antarctic Service Geological Party got underway with all the camp personnel wishing us luck and a safe trip.

288

Editor's Note: The following material is reproduced as nearly as possible to Passel's trail journal, which he kept in longhand in small volumes under trying conditions. Some niceties of punctuation and the like have been inserted for clarity and explanatory phrases inserted in brackets after the first use of an unfamiliar abbreviation.

Thursday, October 17
Camp No. 1

The first day out, at Meter reading 111.0, we left LA [Little America] West Base at 2:30 P.M., along with the Pacific Party, which had held over one day for us. Dick did not like for Gil & me to start out with our teams without either Jack B or him being along. Our party consists of myself and Larry Warner, Harold Gilmour and Loren Wells. Pacific Party consists of Leonard Berlin, Dick Moulton, Jack Richardson and Jack Bursey. Bursey and Richardson took the lead, Dick stayed back to help Gil and me. He expected that we would have trouble with our pups, but we both got along OK. All of the pups started to pull like veterans. All hands were out to see us off, and of course cameras were in full swing. Shirley was set up so that we had to go right by him. Joe & I almost ran over him; in fact if we had been any closer, we would have run him down. Gil said his team headed right for the camera. In fact, Shirley & Doc Frazier had to run for their lives. Joe & I sailed right along. I was using Keela as lead dog as "Gray," one of the bitches, was in heat; and "Grizzley," his lead dog, was constantly after her. But Gil, shortly after we left camp, had to change lead dogs as "Gray" one of the bitches, was in heat and Gil put Gray in the lead. Gil and I really had bastard outfits. Gil, I think, was a little worse off than I. My dogs were all good dogs, but they have never had a really good day's work. Butler had them before, and they would be tied up all day while he and Perk were sealing. As for Gil, Weiner had his, and they never made more than one or two trips a day from the cache, and when he did make trips, he would only have a few hundred lbs. on; then too, we had the pups which had never even seen a harness before, but we did pretty well. At start was a bright, sunshiny day, excellent for photographs, temperature about 25. But about an hour or so after we had started, the wind began to blow from SW. We made seven miles before we stopped, and by the time we had tents up, the wind was blowing about 25 miles per hour and could hardly see from one tent to the other. I tethered my dogs and dug holes for them. I hated to go back out and feed them, but it had to be done. I used seal meat, which I had cut back at base. I brought along enough for two days' feeding. Larry cooked tonight's supper or dinner or whatever it's to be called. Joe & Gil got their first taste of liver pemmican; of course Larry & I were veterans.

The second day out through the fifth day out was rather hectic as we were getting our system of travel worked out. We were also getting experience in setting up and breaking camp. We found that if each man did his part, it was rather simple unless the tent blew away. We had to try to catch it before it was several miles away. Also the dogs had not worked during the winter months, so they were pretty frisky, and we had many run-away teams. Also we were getting used to traveling long miles on skis.

Camp No. 2 – Second day out, Friday, October 18
Camp No. 3 – Third day out, Saturday, October 19
Fourth day out, Sunday, October 20   We held up for the day because of extremely bad weather. Did not leave Camp No. 3.
Camp No. 4 – Fifth day out, Monday, October 21

Sixth Day Out – Tuesday, October 22,
Camp No. 5

First halfway decent day we've had. The sun was actually out. Temperature: around −20. Made 11 miles starting at 11:30, camping at 5 P.M. The dogs were pretty tired, not to mention us. Have been having quite a bit of trouble with dog harnesses. Kusan's collar is small for him and chokes him. Will have to make breast harnesses for both teams. Stopped at 30 mile beacon for our noon lunch, which consisted of hot lemon drink, Army ration, semi-sweet chocolate, and eugenias biscuits. For me that noon stop is the worse part of the day—always get miserably cold. Had a delightful meal of pemmican-hooch, at night.

Radio sked [schedule] just completed.

Seventh Day Out – Wednesday, October 23,
Camp No. 6

Beautiful traveling day – made 11 miles; we seemingly can't do any better. When it got to the point that Larry had to help my team out with his man-hauling harness, we decided to call it quits, but, of course, not without putting in one more mile. Got underway this morning at 11:30, made 5 miles by 1:30 and had lunch. Passed 44.2 mile depot; at least that's the mileage we recorded on the tractor trip, but our meters read 5 miles at that point. Temperature this morning read −10 and probably reached +3 or 4 during the day. Joe just read the thermometer and temperature is now −25 at 9 o'clock. Radio sked ok. Listened in on some of the other parties and find Beechcraft intends to make flight tomorrow—Pete & Paul —flying to 250 miles east, stopping at 105 on return trip. Heard from Al himself that he was recuperating nicely from his tonsil operation—he had the other one out. Also that JJ is working on my scholarship for next year and that he thinks it will go through OK. However I will not know until March or so. Dogs seemed pretty tired tonight although I imagine we could have beaten, or hassled, a mile or so more out of them, but it takes more out of you than it's worth. I don't think anything tires one out any more than trying to make nine dogs pull, especially if they don't want to. I still can't figure out why they ever sent a dog (Bitch) like Wanda out on the trail. She hasn't pulled since we left LA. In fact, she is a drag on the team. I have never seen a dog stumble and fall as much as she does. Don't know whether she is just clumsy or what. At first I thought her feet were sore, but apparently they're ok. I guess she's just so light she can't keep her footing. Well, Gil's broken ski is becoming gradually shorter and shorter. He certainly looks comical kicking along on one long and one short ski. He's having quite a time with Mollie; he says she's a female sport, and that's really something. Today Gil actually ran out of cuss words and started drooling at the mouth, and of course Mollie was the cause of it all. Besides not pulling a thing, she has a bad habit of looking up, or looking back at Gil, and if a dog ever had sad eyes, she's it. I guess it kind of gives Gil the creeps. Well we got off to a good start this morning—Larry was just getting ready to get Gil's team under way when they broke loose, dragging him along, under the sled, for a few feet. He managed to get free, but they didn't stop till they had gone a hundred yards or so. It's a good thing they didn't start fighting because they would have been mincemeat before any of us could have gotten to them, and old Tip has a habit of starting fights. Well, whether the dogs are tired or not, I know I am, and there doesn't seem to be any chance of getting any rest. I haven't slept well since we left LA. In fact, I was up all night the night before we left. Either it's so cold I can't take it, or else my sleeping

291

bag isn't right. Any way I wake up about every hour or so, cold as a *&%#@.

Eighth Day Out – Thursday, October 24,
Camp No. 7

Woke up this morning about 7:30; heard Larry snoring away from some place in his bag and did manage to wake him. I slept fairly well last night; it surprised me. I have quite a system though by putting my fur parka at my feet inside the bag, then use fur mukluks underneath the bag, then use my blanket liner plus a couple of extra blankets and going to sleep fully clothed—I manage. It's funny though, but every time I wake up I am halfway down in the bag all curled up—I guess I have to come up for air. One of the blankets works nicely as a neck block. That's my biggest trouble— cold around the shoulders. Well we got underway as usual about 11 o'clock. Ran for 45 minutes, then rested the dogs; covered 2 miles in that time. At 5 miles we stopped for lunch. Boy if we weren't a pathetic sight, I imagine. There we were huddled on the lee side of a sled colder than hell trying to enjoy a very meager lunch of supposedly hot lemon and Army chocolate, which incidently has to be broken with an ax. Oh yes, I forgot to mention that the temperature was −25 and a young blizzard, just an 18 mile wind, which isn't exactly ideal for Antarctic travel. I don't know when I have been so cold and miserable. The wind was just hard enough to make it uncomfortable. Tonight my face is sore, frost welts all over it, yet the sun was out and except for that infernal wind and drifts it would have been a perfect day. While we were partaking of our lunch, the Beechcraft (2:15) flew over on her return trip to base. She circled a couple of times—what a sight, and to think that in a little less than 30 minutes, Pete and Paul would be back at camp hugging a stove—it took us eight days. Oh well, such is life.

We made 10.5 miles today, which I think is damn good considering. During radio sked, found out the Pacific Party and tractor are at 105 while Perk's party is continuing on to the mountains to break trail for tractor. Boy—Dick & those fellows really must have traveled—I knew they wanted to beat Perk to 105. After sked tonight, Gil & I were in our tent shooting the breeze when Larry yells in that the tank is in sight & sure enough, if Nib & Grif don't drop in for tea. They gave us all the latest news, etc. Gil was just saying that he bet the Pacific party traveled 24 hours a day. Nib said that they would travel so long, then rest the dogs for a couple of hours, then break camp and go again. And they did beat Perk to 105. He had camped at 98 while Dick and his bunch made 27 miles the last day, and it was quite a surprise, Nib said to wake up and see those fellow's tents. We fed Nib & Grif a little bacon and sent them on their way literally amid a swirl of snow.

Ninth Day Out – Friday, October 25
Camp No. 8

Bailed out this morning at 8 o'clock. Larry was up and had breakfast started, by 7. Temperature −16 and no wind—what a relief. I don't think I could have stood another day like yesterday. My face still burns and is rather tender. Well, after thinking it all over, I think that we'd better leave the racing and 27 mile days to the Pacific party; we'll be satisfied with our 10 to 12 miles per day. Besides I think our dogs would drop dead at the mere thought of a 27 mile day. However, they are coming along, and today we made 10 miles in a little under 3 1/2 hours, which isn't bad for a rummy outfit. At least I imagine that's what they are thinking back in camp. Well, all I have to say is that if any of them don't like our progress, let them try dragging nine dogs along plus a pair of 14 lb skis, not to mention none too light boots, especially after not having any sleep. I imagine that would slow them up. Saw the mountains this morning, so branched off the regular trail and headed in toward them. Surface today was wonderful for sledding, but not so hot for skiing, meaning, it was too slick. I had about all I could do to hold on to the "G" pole and keep on my feet. I did have several close calls. We got under way at 11 o'clock and in the first hour made 3 miles, rested the dogs, then had lunch at 2 o'clock after having totaled 7 miles. We made camp an hour early tonight so as to listen to the mail bag program. It came in fine. I got one from the folks, Bob & Lois. Boy, was I glad to hear from home.

It's getting a little colder. Joe took the temperature at 8 o'clock and it had dropped to −26, still no wind, but cloudy to the west. Radio sked was ok. Clay read me a message from Alda. Was glad to hear that the tank had arrived safely at camp, getting there at 9:30 this morning. Boy, Nib & Grif certainly looked like they had been through the mill. It really is a strange sight to see the tank traveling along—seems just like a roving snow bank, puffing & snorting along. After radio sked, I fed the dogs. I have been feeding both teams since I have to go out anyway and put the radio gear back on the sled. Gosh, the dogs are the ones down here that take a beating. They work hard all day pulling till they drop, being cussed at, then at night after it's all over, what do they have to look forward to—nothing but a bed of ice and a hunk, a block of darn hard dog pemmican. Well after it's all said and done, the only difference between them and us is that our pemmican is cooked and we can get warm, but we're still cold when we sleep. Still I don't think the score is evened. My ski bindings are starting to break. I can't understand why they brought such a binding for down here. A cable binding of all things—well, that's just one of the many things I can't understand—. The meter tonight read 179.2 and our camp tonight is a ground distance of 68.2 miles from camp.

Tenth Day Out – Saturday, October 26
Camp No. 9

Fairly nice all day. Temperature this morning was −9 with a min. about −7 and at 3 o'clock dropped again to −9 and now at 11 o'clock P.M. −20. I am in my sleeping bag, so to speak—my fur parka, 3 pair of socks, not to mention my extra blankets and, oh yes, I happen to have on my shirt, scarf and a pair of wool trousers. Sleeping in the Antarctic?? We made 13.8 miles today. My meter reading 198.5. We are exactly 82.5 miles from LA. The mountains are getting larger and larger, but they are still a good couple day's travel away. This is the darndest country for mirages. So far the mountains have been all over the horizon, and Joe swears he saw a light cruiser sailing by at full blast. Since yesterday, we have traveled just by sight of the mountains.

Joe has been skiing out ahead of the dogs, and he says he's not sure now whether there are even any mountains around here—he's seen so many strange things. We broke camp at 11:30 this morning and traveled 4 miles the first hour and a half. The surface is still smooth and hard, good sledding. The dogs fairly trot along. By 2 o'clock we had made seven miles and stopped for lunch. Of course we would have one thermos jug which keeps liquids hot and one that doesn't. It's just Joe's and my luck to get the cold one about every day. We traveled till 6 tonight and had the dogs tethered and camp all set up and were all in the cook tent by 6:45. We had a good meal tonight, something special, pemmican, and oh yes, we made Nib and Grif from a couple of cans of soup, so we had that plus apricots with all the leftover cracker crumbs to make sort of a pudding. It was very good, especially when you are hungry. Set all up for a radio sked, but no soap. Something is wrong with the transmitter. I seem to get plenty of power juice into the set but get no output. Something has gone haywire. I guess I'll have to wait till we come up with Phil and let him look at it. Boy I'm a whipped chicken tonight. Tired is no name for it, and sleepy, so here's trying.

Eleventh Day Out – Sunday, October 27
Camp No. 10

Perfect day for traveling. Made 15 miles in little under 6 hours. Surface still good except for occasional soft drift. The dogs would be trotting along nicely till they hit that soft snow; then they'd go head over heels. As far as using skis, personally I could have gotten along better with a pair of ice skates. We broke camp at 11 this morning and camped at 5:30. We stopped for lunch at 6 Mile Point and, as luck would have it, our only hot thermos bottle went the way of all flesh—it broke. We steered by boat compass today, course being 343. Larry had the compass lashed on one of our spare skis lashed on the top of the load of his front sled. Gil drove and Larry watched the compass while Joe skied along ahead setting a trail. Larry would wave him on the course. Tried a radio sked again tonight but no luck; could not transmit. In fact, I didn't hear Clay calling the other parties. I hope that we catch up with Phil so that he can take a peek at my set. Well, a week ago today we were holed in, but since then, with the exception of one day, we have had wonderful weather. Boy, the mountains certainly look good to me. I swear I have never seen a more sorry forlorn looking place than the Ross Barrier—nothing but nothing. Joe's comparison is the ocean. He says he could never figure out why people would want to take an ocean vacation trip—I can see his point.

Have been having some trouble with Grizzley—he just doesn't seem to understand the word gee; he always goes haw. I guess Murray must have spoken a foreign language to him or something. My meter read 207 tonight. Temperature at lunch was 0 and now at 11 o'clock P.M. it is −22. Larry just took a look around with the glasses and can't see hide nor hair of the other outfits—maybe we are at the wrong mountains or something.

Twelfth Day Out – Monday, October 28
Camp No. 11

Put in a pretty good night last night—the trouble is I want to sleep in in the mornings, and that just is not being done. It's a funny thing, but I get the sleepiest when I'm supposed to get up. We actually had a heat wave this morning, +10. It was almost comfortable outside. Got our usual 11:30 start and got to 105 camp at 3:15. Phil had skied out to meet us. Just as we pulled into camp, Dick, Earl, Perk and Jack H. were loading their sleds with the last of Fitz's stuff. I guess we hit it about right. I guess it's a devil of a trip up to the site for Fitz's base [camp]. He named the peak "Franklin Peak." It's a distance from here and at about 11 miles, the surface near there changes to blue ice—the dogs cannot get footing on the up grade.

Several of the dogs are laid up now. Mickey of Richardson team is about finished I'm afraid—a badly sprained back and fore quarters. Berlin says they might have to shoot him. Dick's Mukluk is all in with sore front feet. Several of his nails were torn off. There is some question on one of the Bursey's dogs—Moody. It seems that they have practically had to ride him on the sled and drag him for 30 miles—he's too fat and won't work it off. They might leave him here for Ike. Maybe Gil can make a swap, leaving Kodiac or Molly. I know we won't be traveling too fast. Phil fixed my radio today. The voltage plate or something on the hand generator had gone haywire. He used it on tonight's sked, and Pappy reported that it worked perfect. Well, it's good to have completed the first leg of our little summer trip, and we've covered 105 miles of our proposed 350 or so. If the weather is suitable, I think the Beechcraft intends to make a flight to Mt. Rea and on return will stop here for Al and Pete. This is quite a little settlement here, and I for one was glad to get here.

Thirteenth Day Out – Tuesday, October 29
Camped at 105 mile post

Boy, what a day. Just nothing but loaf around. Bursey got back about 2 this morning, but the rest stayed in the mountains to finish up today. Didn't get up till ten this morning. Took a bag of cerevim over to the Tractor to trade for some oatmeal, but Buck & Phil were not up yet. After breakfast, I was looking over my dog's harness when I heard confusion over at the Pacific Parties' tents. I went over just in time to get in a big discussion as to who had what right to take whose film. Jack, Len & Buck were in it. Stayed there a while and aired my views on the subject; then I returned to our camp. I started to work on a breast plate collar; one of my leather collars is starting to wrinkle up badly. I was afraid that it might start shoulder sores.

I sat in the cook fly with Gil and Larry and shot the bull. Larry was sewing on his knife case, & Gil was working on the trail journal. Jack B. came over, so we made a little lemon drink and continued our session. Phil had a 10 o'clock sked with Base giving them weather report. Our weather here was perfect, sun shining, clear sky, but at base 18 or 20 mile wind and a whiteout. We made up a list of food stuff etc. that we would like to have the Condor bring out, including such as tea, cerevim, coffee, dehydrated fruits, pepper etc., and Phil sent it in tonight. Paul immediately wanted to know what was wrong with the pemmican. Well, Phil told him it gave him heart burn, Richardson heaves it up, it does something to Jack B., and Berlin won't eat it unless he has to. I guess our outfit is the only one who really likes it. Joe has eaten as many as three bowls; oh yes, of course, Dick scoffs it up. I guess Paul was quite upset about the pemmican, and he wants to contact us again about loss of calories by not eating it before he sends other food. It's not that we want to eliminate pemmican; it's good, it's just that we'd like something else besides pemmican, especially since there is plenty at Base. Pemmican makes a nice meat course, but we like a little soup or fruit to go with it. Phil checked in for Jack and me. I listened in on my set.

Dogs are getting rested up fine. The dogs with sore feet are better. The wind started to blow a little tonight, so I went out and dug holes for my dogs. Little Wanda is the first one in hers. Well we are all standing by waiting for something to happen. If the Condor would only make its flight here, then we could be off. That is, as soon as the boys get back from Fitz's place & get rested up. I can't understand it, but we have had perfect flying weather for a week but no flight. Phil says Court won't give an inch if there is even a hint of a cloud—he's not sticking his neck out. Old Joe is getting to be quite a weather man. He will go out mornings, and if the sun is out and no wind & not a cloud in the sky, he predicts good weather. It's certainly good to have the sun back with us for 24 hours, even though it is hard to get to sleep. But since it's 1 in the morning, I think I'll try.

Fourteenth Day Out – Wednesday, October 30
Camped at 105 mile Depot
Boy what a great sleep. Didn't wake up till almost noon. I guess

putting two fur parkas under my body did the trick. Only time I woke up was when Dick & H.H. returned from the mountains. The dogs set up a hell of a commotion. They got in about 3:30 AM. I heard Dick speaking to Mukluk. I guess old Mukluk was glad to see the rest of the dogs. It has been a beautiful day, a little cloudy to the NW but warm, about +5. While we were having breakfast, H.H. dropped in on us and shot the bull for awhile. I spent the afternoon working over my sleds when I wasn't visiting around. I went over to the caboose a couple of times to say hello to Dick. I tried to get the 3 o'clock news. Berlin came in, and we talked things over pros and cons. He was telling us about his work in Alaska. Phil reported in for me again. I listened in on my set. I tried to get Larry a time tick, but no luck. The Base is still a haggling over H.H.'s ski shoes—today they wanted to know whether or not I gave them to Court. Well they have been on the subject for a week or more. They still have mix up about the food and where it will be dropped. I was just talking to H.H. It seems that he got up early this morning so as to make the morning sked. He had Phil send in a poop sheet to Paul requesting his removal from the Pacific Coast Party. I had expected as much in that he had two strikes against him before he left base in that Bursey does not like him. Bursey thinks that he is just a fresh young kid that knows it all. Of course, Bursey thinks that anyone who does not agree with him and waits on him due to his previous expedition is not worthy. Also, Len ordered Jack H. around and made life miserable for him. On the way to 105, one of Jack's dogs got a little lame and immediately Len wanted to kill it—well, to touch one of H.H.'s dogs just is not being done. It scared him plenty, had him worried. H.H. said that neither one of them spoke to him, and now Dick waits on them hand and foot. Good old easy going Dick; he can take any treatment just as long as he has his dogs. I guess all in all though he gets along pretty well with both of them; he just kids Jack B. along. H.H. says it's a crime though the way Dick does all the work. Not only does he help put up the tents and feed his dogs, but he also does all the cooking—Len and Jack B. sit in their tent—Dick hands their food in to them and lights the primus for them. In fact he just almost waits on them. Well I know Dick. Rather than cause a stink of any kind, he'll just play along, but some day I imagine Dick will get fed up and then look out. Well H.H. talked to Gil, and tonight Gil had Phil send in a poop sheet to the effect that they favored the recommendation. Well the answer came back, so H.H. is now

298

a member of the Biological Party. In his original message to Paul he said Dick advised that he keep his dogs. In his answer Paul said the division of dogs would be left up to leaders and that H.H. would be allowed at least to keep Kovac. I think that sounds like Al Wade. They know that H.H. wants to take Kovac back with him. Well, the outcome is that H.H. is going to take the little dog Chu Chu from Bursey's teams and give Bursey the two Blacks of Berlin's old team—Prince and Blackie. That's an even trade at that cause. Prince is a troublemaker if ever there was one. He'll fight at the drop of a hat.

Fifteenth Day Out – Thursday, October 31
Camped at 105 Mile Depot

Slept like a top last night, except I had to get up about 4:30 A.M. I heard a loud commotion outside, not the usual noises the dogs make while on the tethering line, but growls, etc. I guess I thought I must have been dreaming, because I didn't do a thing. Then suddenly I came to and shot out of the tent like a house afire. One of Perk's dogs was loose and near my bitch Alaska. Well I caught him and led him over and put his collar on again, and from then on peace and quiet reigned forth. That's one good thing—when a dog gets loose, the rest will tell on him—they are certainly jealous of one another.

Finally got word from the Base to move on because the plane would not and had not been able to fly because of punk weather. (We have had good flying weather for a week or so.) They said that they would try to contact us on the trail in the next 30 miles or so. Well with that we all spent all day getting our loads rearranged and dividing the dog food, etc. Perk and his party had come in from the Mountains the night before. Bursey yesterday hitched up and took Woody one of his dogs which was too fat to travel into the Mountains for Fitz. Perk says it was a funny sight seeing Fitz leaving their camp for his, skiing along, knapsack over back and with a 30 foot line tied around his waist and Woody at the other end. Boy, what a fix he would have been in if Woody suddenly decided to leave the countryside.

Radio sked tonite was OK. Pappy asked for a weather report, and there was a favorable report because when contacted, there was a slight wind from the NW, cloudy to the east but clear overhead; Phil said both planes would be ready to take off in an hour or so. At Phil's 10:15 PM sked they said that the Beechcraft had taken off three times but had to return—cold motor. Al & Pete intend to fly over Mt. Rea to try to find suitable site for a field.

Well Larry, Gil, Dick, Joe and Berlin were crowded into the cook fly, having a cup of tea when Larry said, "Here she comes." He tore out of the tent, and sure enough the old Condor was circling around for a landing. It was then midnight. Dick had previously put up a wind indicator. Mac, Pappy, Gray, Walt along with Ike & Zeke were in the plane. After "hello's" all around, we started to unload. Mac left the engines turning at a pretty good rate, and every time we would go in to get a can of gas, food etc. we'd freeze an ear, nose or at least a cheek. We finally got a system, as soon as a can would show up at the door, we'd make a mad dash for it, and I might mention, we didn't waste any time getting out of the wind. Pappy Gray had Lucky with him—Lucky was the only one of Toska's pups that lived. I gave it to the plane crew for a mascot. Pappy let him run around; I mean wobble around. Evidently he hadn't gotten his flying legs or something. Well we had no sooner got the Condor unloaded and Len & I were sorting out the food that was sent to the parties than someone yelled "There's the Beechcraft." She landed. Al & Pete stepped out of the cabin. They looked like they had just been in a coal mine instead of flying in the clean Antarctic—they were covered with lamp black. Paul dumped a sack of it in the cabin on their last flight. He started to make a trail with lamp black, and the wind caught it just wrong, and it all came back in the plane. What a mess. Well we had a little bull session with Al, & he gave me his pair of glasses since mine are all taped. I hated to start in on my spare pair. Phil sent in for a pair and Al was supposed to bring them. Well someone slipped up somewhere. Evidently Paul & Al didn't even get the message or something. After the Condor & Beechcraft took off, we finished dividing the food which consisted of extra milk, sugar, coffee, more concentrated broth, fruit etc. Pappy always brought Joe a gunny sack full of odds and ends, delicacies such as strawberries, chicken, canned peaches, tea etc. Sig sent each party some hamburgers—at lunch we fixed up some, quite a feast. Didn't get to bed till 3 A.M. Zeke and Ike pitched their tent and all quieted down, we thought; but Ike was still strolling around at 4 A.M.— crunch, crunch, crunch—and there is nothing more disturbing or annoying than to have someone walking around outside the tent— especially when one is trying to sleep.

Oh yes, a little earlier in the evening, I did a hair cut job on

300

Dick's noggin—a Marine crew cut. Well if you like short hair, the job is fine. Personally, I am right proud of it. In fact, Larry wants one like it.

Sixteenth Day Out – Friday, November 1
Camp No. 12

Well, starting today I am really a salaried man—50 bucks a month. I guess I really should have gotten up a little earlier this morning so as to get an early start and really earn it, but 10 o'clock was good enough for me. I guess most of the other fellows feasted last night because everyone was late in getting up. We were supposed to leave at ten. Well, we finally got underway about 1:30 or so. Zeke and Ike were up to see us off. The Coach looks like a changed man with his new wind proofs; he seemed mighty glad to be away from Base, and so did Zeke. In fact, Ike wanted to know who handled the real estate around here—he thought he might like to buy a lot.

It was a beautiful day, clear, temperature at 10:30 A.M. was +11. Dick and the Pacific Party took the lead with Len acting as navigator with a compass on Dick's sled. Next came the tractor. Then the rest of us got started. Boy were the dogs ever hopped up. Mine were really rearing to go, and I shot out from 105 like a house afire. But that didn't last long. After the first hour or so they started to settle down. I was surprised that they went as fast as they did. We were all pretty heavily loaded besides all of the dead weight, such as sleeping bags, duffel, etc. I had on my sled 2 man food rations (125 lbs.) and 5 dog food rations (about 300 lbs.) We had our lunch with the Biological Party. The tractor was a little ahead of us, and the Pacific Coast Party was a mere dot on the horizon. My sledge meter read tonight 227.6—we traveled 11.5 miles.

Seventeenth Day Out – Saturday, November 2
Camp No. 13

I swear to heck, I can never get to bed before midnight or so, even on the trail. Len dropped in to see Larry last night, and before we knew it, it was midnight. Len just shot the bull telling us about his work travel in Alaska—all very interesting. Well we did manage to get up around eight or so. Boy, what perfect weather. Temperature this morning was +1 with a max of +11. I skied along most of the day with my cap off and my shirt & underwear unbuttoned. We got under way about noon with the Pacific Coast Party ahead again. Our party followed the tractor.

Today was one of the worse days I have ever had. I'm dead tired tonight. We started climbing up on the Polar Plateau, and what a job—both on men and dogs! We climbed practically all day; some of the grades seemed as steep as 10%, although Len says the average was 6%. I know my dogs had a tough time of it, and I had to really drive them to get them into camp. As it was, I got in about 45 minutes after everyone else. I don't like to use a whip, but I had to today. It seems a shame to hit a dog when he is tired, but it's got to be done. If I didn't, I would still be about 4 miles from camp. The dogs try to bluff me every day and usually just a little slap will straighten them out. But late this afternoon they weren't bluffing, they were really tired! Oh yes, I forgot—yesterday the tractor fell in a crevasse, that is, just kind of dropped in, nothing serious, Phil just put her in second and pulled out. Phil was looking in the crack when I came along. I don't know how Buck missed that one. He has been walking along in front of the tractor taking soundings. He is dead afraid of crevasses. In fact, he will not drive through a crevassed region, and today was a bad day. In trying to pick our way up to the Plateau, we had to travel in some pretty tough country. The Pacific crowd wore their safety belts as they were laying the trail.

Sledge meter read 238.2. We made 10.6 miles & just between you and me and the gatepost, I couldn't make another mile, and I'll speak for my dogs also. My legs ache tonight for the first time since we left LA. Well it's from skiing up grade and pushing the load. I had to push on the Gee pole and the minute I let up, the dogs would stop. Oh well, such is life. Dick dropped in tonight for awhile. Larry & I looked over photographs and maps of the Edsel Fords. It was 1 A.M. before we got to bed. No radio sked as Phil is handling it.

Eighteenth Day Out – Sunday, November 3
Camp No. 14

Larry woke up at seven this morning. I bailed out at 7:45. Another beautiful day. Boy, we are certainly getting a break in the weather, clear with +1 temperatures this morning with a max of about +5. The only trouble is it cools down just when we stop to make camp, and I am always chilly then. Tonight at 8:30, temperature was −11. We got under way this morning at 11 A.M.

I lightened my load some by putting some sacks of dog food on the tractor and rearranged my load some by putting all of the heavy dog food, etc, on the front sled and leaving only gear on the trailer sled. Another hard day, up grade all the way. The surface was none too good today, rather soft, and the sleds really pulled hard. Up grade pulling really saps the dogs' energy. We had our lunch at 1:30 with the tractor and Biological party. Buck made us all some tea, which certainly touched the spot. We made a 30 mile cache consisting of dog food and gas. After leaving these, Buck took all of our trailer sleds and hitched them on behind the caboose. Boy, that certainly helped the dogs—they practically ran the last 3 miles into camp. Sledge meter read 249.7, making a total of 11.5 for the day. Gil corrected me saying we made 12 miles right on the dot. My meter, I remember now, was riding the rope once today, so that might account for the .5 difference. Went over to the Caboose for radio sked. Phil got a little news from camp. Condor made a flight 200 miles south to lay gas cache. Beechcraft went on flight around Okuma Bay. Phil also listened in on Fitz's sked. Ike & Zeke have not joined him as yet.

Nineteenth Day Out – Monday, November 4
Camp No. 15

Up bright and early this morning, at eight o'clock. I still can't quite understand why I am always so sleepy in the morning, but I am. I always get the sleepiest when I hear Larry starting the Primus Stove. Then too, there is no chance of oversleeping because Buck starts the tractor—no way we could sleep through that noise.

We got a fairly early start this morning. Pacific Coast party went first, and then the tractor and the rest of us kinda strung out. All of us but Gil had only one sled, so we would run a while and then stop and wait for the tractor to catch up to us. We seesawed like that all day. Gil with his heavier load came along steady. By 1:30 we had made 6.7 miles, so we stopped for lunch. Phil made us some tomato soup, which was really good. I am afraid that our one Thermos jug has finally given up. It kinda rattles inside and sounds like the glass is broken. Whoever heard of bringing breakable jugs down here in the first place.

Well, just one more thing that that Ronne messed up; need I mention the dog collars? My dogs really went fine today, didn't tire at all. I imagine I have at least 600 lbs. on my one sled. Part of the time I just hold on to the Gee pole and let the dogs pull me. We are still traveling over undulating country and still climbing, according to Len, about 20 feet to a mile. Well, as far as this Plateau is concerned, it's no different than the Ross Sea Barrier. They can give it all back to the Indians as far as I am concerned.

Earl took a nasty spill this morning. I was coming along behind him. I looked up, and noticed his dogs standing there, but no Earl. Well, there he was all the way under his sled. Apparently he was trying to ski sideways or something to avoid the wind, and he and the sled just tangled. Perk came along, and he and I lifted the sled off him. Earl had just twisted his ankle a little. The wind was cruel today coming SE right into our faces. My poor nose I am afraid will never be the same; it's one solid blister.

My sled meter read 264.1. We made 15 miles today before making camp about 5 o'clock. Larry & Gil did not get in for a half hour or so after we made camp. Joe and I put up one of our tents and waited there. Gil said his dogs pooped out on the last grade. Went to Caboose radio sked tonight. Paul wanted to know if we could get by without kerosene at Mt. Rea. Evidently they figure on carrying more safety gear, so Buck says. Anyway, we put them straight on the matter—we need the kerosene. We camped at Lat. 78.225′, Long. 152.05′ and our course was Mag 336, Var 93.

Twentieth Day Out – Tuesday, November 5
Camp No. 16

Course Mag 340, Var 92. True N 72 E. Made 11 miles today; sled meter read 274.6. Larry started for the Primus at 7:30 this morning. I got up about 8. We had our usual breakfast, Oatmeal plus cerevim as a second, tea or coffee and bacon. We got under way at 11 o'clock and made camp at 3 P.M. Len wanted to listen in on the election returns.

As long as we keep our 10 miles per day sked we're OK. We stopped for lunch, that is the tractor stopped to gas up, so we had a bite while we were waiting. Of course, we had our usual tasty lunch, hard Army chocolate, Euginas biscuits, a few peanuts and our drink, which was supposed to be hot, but isn't due to the fact that the thermos is broken. While we were stopped, we noticed that it was getting dark to the south of us and back east it looked like a huge bank of drift blowing toward us. Well, we had 5 more miles to get to the 60 mile cache. So we didn't even stop long enough to make use of the hot water Phil had. He was going to make tea, but when we saw that drift we just traveled. Well, it caught up with us, and since there was no wind, it couldn't have been a drift. H.H. thought it was a cloud; it was at least a fog. Nevertheless, we traveled close together. We fellows with the teams always kept the tractor in sight.

The Pacific Coast Party had already made camp when we arrived at 60 mile. Since they are not keeping up with the tractor, they travel faster. We have had a little wind all day, about 3 to 5 miles. There were a few clouds in the sky, cirrus. We are still climbing. Len estimated we must be 1800 feet above 105 mile cache. We had our evening meal early tonight. Quite a tasty dish of pemmican. Larry tried to make a custard out of eggs, powdered eggs sent from Base, but no luck. We have decided they are just the yolks. Anyway, he put apples with them, a little cocoa, sugar, and lemon, but still no go. We picked the apples and at least saved them. They will go in tomorrow's oatmeal. The tractor is certainly a traveling hospital. Snooks, one of the Perk's bitches, is riding in a box on the load, she had an abscessed shoulder; and Mickey, one of H.H.'s dogs that sprained his back in the Fitz Mountains pull, is also riding on the load. It used to be that when Perk would pass the tractor with his team, Snooks would whine, bark, and try to get out. Now she just sits there. In fact, Perk says she sticks her nose up at him. He says he'll have a heck of a time putting her in a harness again.

I noticed today a couple of sores on Tongas's forelegs. I can't imagine how they got there as his collar does not come down that far. I hope they are nothing serious. H.H. had a couple of dog fights today, and, of course, it was Pearl & Dina, mother and daughter. They always fight. I set up my radio to get Larry a time check, and then listened in on the radio sked. Nothing doing except the Beechcraft is going to fly here with ski bindings if weather permits. Well, by the looks outside, they won't be; it is still foggy. Temperature max today was +3, now −3.

Twenty-First Day Out – Wednesday, November 6
Camp No. 17

Last night we listened in to some of the election returns just getting an idea of how things are going. But so far we still don't know who was elected. I know I hope it was Wilkie. It's a funny feeling not knowing who the next President will be. Also, last night over WIWO we heard a few recordings played by Benny Goodman & Artie Shaw. Will it ever be wonderful to get back home and lead a more or less pleasant social life. Woke up this morning at 6 o'clock with the wind blowing a blizzard, so I turned over and went back to sleep. Next thing I knew it was 10 o'clock and Larry was starting the Primus Stove. He too had awakened early but went back to sleep and then heard someone stirring about outside. Well, the wind was still blowing some when we broke camp at noon. Temperature was +11, sun shining, and if it had not been for the NE wind, it would have been a perfect day to travel. I took several pictures of camp; everything was drifted over. We traveled till 1:30, and then had to stop as it had started to drift and visibility was zero. Len couldn't see to navigate. The Pacific Coast Party put up their tents. We put up one and nine of us crawled into it. We had quite a lively bull session. Let's see, there was Larry, Gil, H.H., Toney, Earl, Perk, Dick, Joe and myself, and Jack B. dropped in later. We had our lunch after starting a Primus and having a little hot lemon. The wind didn't let up till about 3:30 or so, and it did clear up in the East enough so that we got under way again.

The surface today is terrible. My legs are so tired tonight I can hardly move. It was just like skiing on sand; I had to drag the skis along. I am glad that the tractor still has my trailer sled, or I don't imagine I would have made it. Well along about six o'clock it started to snow a bit. The wind picked up again, and there was a surface drift. Oh yes, and it was quite hazy and foggy; in other words, it wasn't a fitting day to travel. Visibility was near zero to the East, and to the West the sun was shining, and we got a 22 1/2 percent halo. It was certainly a welcomed sight to see tents ahead because I know I could not have gone much farther. I was pooped. The Pacific Coast Party, having gone ahead, had already set up camp. Gil and Larry were just putting up one of our tents when I pulled in. We made camp tonight at 10.1 miles; my meter read 284.7.

We are just 173.7 miles from Little America; that is, we have traveled that far. We had to come a little out of our way in order to get up on the plateau. After leaving 105 we traveled SE for a day or so. Well, we climbed gradually today. The Rockefellow Mountains have been out of sight since day before yesterday. Temperature tonight is +9, and the wind has picked up. I imagine it's now blowing 25 miles per hour. Here's hoping our tents hold together. Larry just got in from putting snow around them. Nothing exciting happened today, except my team almost ran away. They got excited when the others started. If it hadn't been for my

306

old lead dog Grizzly, they would have been gone with the wind. But he held his ground so the whole team just piled up. Then came the sweet job of untangling them. I am lucky that my dogs do not tend to be fighters. Oh it's true they get in little scraps, but I have no real trouble makers. Well, I got them all straightened out except Wanda. She is such a small dog that she can get hung up in her harness with apparent ease. In fact, today I had to take her harness off her and start from scratch. She is a cute little dog though I imagine she weighs about 25 or 30 lbs. She is a good worker though. Phil held radio sked tonight but said Base faded out. It's 11 o'clock and still blowing. Time for bed.

Twenty-Second Day Out – Thursday, November 7
Camp No. 17

This is the third week we have been out. Yes sir, just three weeks ago today we were leaving Base amid cheers and clicks of cameras, curses, and shouts. In other words we left in a gale of snow and a shower of confetti. I can remember well myself hanging on to the sled for dear life while my dogs took off over the barrier, just missing the official photographer by a hair. Well we didn't travel today. It really blew last night. It has been estimated the wind velocity was from 35 miles to 50 miles, and I imagine we had gusts of at least 60 miles. I woke up this morning at 8 o'clock, and it was still going strong. Finally got out of my sack about 11. One of my dogs howled and woke me up. I dressed and went outside, still drifting. I had to dig some of my dogs out. Old Kotek and Kusan couldn't lie down because their chains were snowed under. Boy they were certainly glad to see me. After getting them all set, I went over to the tractor and dug out Snooks' box and got her situated OK. Meanwhile Larry had gotten up and fixed breakfast. Good old oatmeal with a few apples thrown in. I spent most of the day sewing on dog collars. I made two breast plate collars, one for Tongas and one for Myra. Gil, Larry, Joe and I sat in the cook fly; Larry was working on his man hauling harness, Gil on his journal, myself on the collars and Joe just working his mouth. Boy, he certainly can be a comical fellow. He has some stories about the Navy, different fellows he knew and knows. I went outside about 7 o'clock P.M. to feed my dogs. The wind had let up, but it was not clear. Everything was drifted over, including my trailer sled, as was Gil's. I went over to the Caboose for radio sked. Paul wanted to talk to Gil, Len, Perk and Earl. So I went after them and stopped in at

Dick's tent. They were eating, so I had a bowl of tomato soup and a cup of tea, kinda chatted awhile till Len came back. Larry called over that soup was on.

Gil gave us all the news after his talk with Paul. It seems that the Admiral had not resigned as was rumored. Crusan had been made second in command. Also the budget committee is working on the financial program that Al outlined, and Gil has been reassured that he will get to work on his own notes and will be retained a year after the expedition returns. I guess that cooks Hawthorne's goose. I can imagine coming down 11,000 miles just to have someone else take over your notes when we return. Gil swore that he would burn it or dump it overboard before he let someone else work it up, and he's right. Oh yes, the committee and the Admiral are going to try to work out or strike out Article 9 of the President's poop sheet concerning the keeping of personal film. That will certainly smooth things a little. After dinner we sat around and shot the bull till 1 o'clock, so it's time for bed.

Twenty-Third Day Out – Friday, November 8
Camp No. 18

Well we are now 82.4 miles out of 105, and I have up to date skied 221 statute miles, if I never ski another step. Here I am, a small town Hoosier, so to speak, who never even heard of skis, except see them in newsreels or something, let alone ever getting on a pair of the critters. Well I can handle them nicely now and only about 700 more miles to go, that is, from here back to Base. We made 11.9 miles today. We have kind of separate camps at this point. The tractor was not making such good time according to Buck, so we all took back our trailer sleds. Then he shifted into high and just walked away from us. Here I am getting a little ahead of myself.

In the first place I didn't sleep very well last night because the dogs raised cain all night. One day's rest made them kind of restless. Well that started things off wrong, at least for me. Larry got up this morning about 7 o'clock and I hauled out at 8. A perfect day, temperature being +14, sun shining, in fact a really nice day. We finished breakfast by 9, then spent a good hour or so digging out. We were really drifted under. By about 10:30 the temperature had risen to +24, and it really was hot. I worked around in my underwear without a cap or gloves. The Pacific Coast Party got under way about 10 o'clock, and the rest of us started about

11 o'clock. The tractor had to travel in second because of soft snow, so the dogs got a little ahead of it. We traveled ahead for about 3 miles, then we waited for the tractor. Phil wanted to tune in on the mail bag program, and they planned to make 15 miles, so they got in high and really traveled. Of course Dick and the Pacific Coast Party were well out of sight before we even got started, and naturally the minute we got back our trailer sleds, the going got tough.

We started up a grade, I don't imagine it was over a 6 or 7% grade slope, but it was at least 2 miles long. Boy, I thought the dogs would never make it, and the surface was the worse we have had so far. The sled dragged along like we were traveling in sand and as far as skiing was concerned, well I just walked along on them. Oh, incidentally, my legs tonight feel like a couple of dead logs. Perk and H.H. fell a little behind. Gil was up ahead almost out of sight. Doc, E.E. and I were traveling together. Our dogs stopped about every 100 feet or so. He finally decided to spell them a bit and wait for the others. They were not in sight yet, and Gil was getting out of sight, so I started again to catch up with them. Earl stood by to wait. Joe and Tony were skiing ahead of Gil. Well, I plodded along for about an hour or so, starting and stopping. Oh yes, and cursing a little. I didn't know who was the more exhausted, me or the dogs. Anyway just about as I was giving up, Larry skied up and said he thought we had better camp and not try to get up to the tractor. I agreed, so he skied up to stop Gil. Toney went back along the trail to join his party. Well, I finally got up to Gil. While we were eating dinner, Perk and the rest pulled into camp. Earl said that their dogs were so pooped that they rested them for about two hours while they listened to the mail bag program.

I held the radio sked tonight. Sent in the weather report for H.H. Got a message from Alda. Clay is sending her news of me. After sked, I fed my dogs and then went and shot the bull with our neighbors. The temperature dropped tonight to $+2$ and is now about 0 at 11 o'clock.

Well, the tractor and Pacific Party made 16 miles. I know one thing, we could have never caught them. They told Pappy R that they lost us in the fog. I forgot but after we had been going this morning about an hour it started to blow a bit so shirts and wind proofs were all put back on and later in the afternoon it clouded up and became hazy and foggy. Anyway the tractor certainly didn't help us any today. All during the trip we have stayed close to it to help in case of a crack. Buck said that if the going got too rough, he would take our sleds back again. Well it got rough all right, but they were well out of sight. In other words they left us in a lurch. Well from now on the Bio Party and our party will travel together.

Twenty-Fourth Day Out – Saturday, November 9

Got up this morning bright and early to a beautiful day—temperature at +16. Our neighbors were up and about. We broke camp at 11 o'clock as usual. I don't think we can get away any earlier. Up at seven away by eleven. The surface today was just about as bad as it could be. The sleds pulled hard and as far as using skis, I almost pulled mine off several times. We were only able to travel 9.1 miles. Gil has been having some trouble with his dogs. Two of his bitches are in heat; hence, they do not pull much. Bill, one of his dogs, has been sick. Then, of course, Molly never pulls anything. In other words, 5 dogs aren't enough to pull a load. If Gil didn't have old Tip, he would be sunk. Long toward late afternoon it got foggy. This is one time I can say I'm riding along in the clouds because we're certainly hitting them. We observed a fog bow, the first I had seen. We had to travel fairly close together because at 100 yards one was out of sight. We got to the 90 mile cache and camped a little beyond that. As usual, just when we are ready to stop for the evening, it starts to blow a little and the temperature drops. Tonight was an exception, o to −2 while we were making camp.

After we left the 90 mile cache, Earl, Tony and Joe and I went ahead. H.H. waited there for Perk and Gil. When they did arrive at the site, we pitched our tents about 4 or 5 tenths beyond 90 mile. Gil was pulling H.H.'s sleds and his and Perk's teams were hitched double and were pulling Gil's sleds and Perk's. Perk said they almost camped back at 90 mile cache, but H.H. talked them into moving on. The dogs were extremely tired, and I know we were all washed up. Radio sked tonight was OK. Clay read a message from folks.

Twenty-Fifth Day Out – Sunday, November 10
Camp No. 20

Made 12 miles today, but from the looks of our start this morning I didn't think we would get anywhere. In fact, we almost camped an hour after we got started. We broke camp at 11 o'clock. The Bio bunch started out first, and then I pulled out with my team.

310

I got about 1/10 of a mile or so when I had to stop so several of my dogs could take their morning constitutional. Well, I can keep going as long as only one feels the urge, but when two or three have to go, that kind of stops progress.

While I was waiting I looked back, and Gil had not left camp yet. He was seemingly having trouble getting started. It's true the two or three good dogs in the outfit (Tip, Yakutz, Grey) were willing, but the deadbeats such as Molly, Bill, and JaJa, as usual, wouldn't budge. He did manage to get up with me, and for the next hour and a half we tried various combinations to get our loads started. We hitched both teams together with Grizzly as lead. I was driving. I pulled back on the gang line and first crack out of the box we got started, but that didn't last long. Gil left Grey, his lead, up front behind Grizzly. Well they were both trying their hand at leading. The only trouble was that Grey was trying to pull the team to one side. We stopped to put her back, and well, we never got started again. My dogs were partly willing at first, but after about a dozen attempts, they kind of gave up. So help me, at every try Molly would fall back on her haunches and pull back, and as for Bill, he wouldn't even bother to get up. Of course, Kodiac would be flirting with a bitch somewhere back in the team. What a mess!

So when finally old Tip and Yakutz gave up, we decided to try the teams separate, but with a line from my trailer sled to Gil's gang line. Well that didn't work. I would get my team started all right, but then the line would tighten up because Gil's team wouldn't have budged. Mine would stop dead. They just couldn't move my load and Gil's too. Gil, by that time, was as exhausted as I was, and, at that point, we almost pitched camp. Well, Gil said he would try his team once more and for me to go on. By that time my dogs were pretty discouraged, and it took some encouragement to get them started. Once they found that they were not jerked to a stop every minute or so, they went along nicely and, of course, we would have a nice grade to climb. Gil, I guess, decided his dogs were going to work or else, and when I looked back he was giving them all a good working over, and I don't blame him.

The Bio Party was waiting for us at the top of the slope. In fact, they were eating lunch, because it was then 1:30. Pretty soon Gil's team came up over the hill with Larry in the lead with a line around his waist tied to the gang line. Gil had Keela as lead dog. We all ate lunch and from then on we didn't have any trouble. We sighted Grace McKinley at that point. The surface improved and sledding was fairly good. We all got in the tractor trail and by three o'clock we came to the point in the trail where it curved into the Mountains. Course N. We held a little pow-wow there, and it was decided to go on for a couple hours or so. Then we would camp for a while, eat and rest the dogs, and then go on until we caught up with the tractor and Pacific Party.

From that point on we ran into a series of hills and steep slopes. On one slope we all had to take off our skis in order to control our sleds. The going was easy though. The surface in the valleys was perfect and by 6 o'clock, we made 12.5 miles. My meter read 318.2. We tethered our dogs, put up a tent and started to prepare food. Well, our plans were certainly nipped in the bud, for no sooner had we started to eat than the wind began to blow. Up to then the weather had been perfect, no wind, +20.5 temperature with a high of 22.4, but the wind got up to 10 miles per hour, started to drift and the temperature dropped to −10.5. After eating we sat in the tent shooting the bull waiting for the weather to clear up. Perk came over and after waiting till after 10 o'clock, it was decided to camp as there didn't seem to be any apparent let up in the wind. We put up our other tent, fed the dogs and secured for the night.

Twenty-Sixth Day Out – Monday, November 11
Camp No. 21

Slept late today as was still drifting; the wind was blowing about 12 or 15 mph. About 2 P.M. it cleared up a bit, and by 4 o'clock we were under way. First crack out of the box I piled my whole team up. Wanda, the left point dog, stumbled, and before I could stop the rest of the dogs, they were all tangled in a heap. I luckily got the sleds stopped so that they didn't run over the other dogs.

We really traveled in the foothills of the Grace McKinley Mountains today, up one and down another. The very first hill we came to, in fact, I will call a cliff; at least it looked that way to me. Anyway, it caught us with our pants down, so to speak. It just sprang up, good and steep too. I happened to come to it first. I tried to stop the team so that I could take my skis off. Just about that time the toes of my skis ran into and through an under cut sastrugi, and I went down. But the team kept going. Luckily, Joe and Tony were skiing ahead. Tony stopped them by throwing himself under the trailer sled. (Joe says he fell.) Anyway, we three thought we could take the sleds down all right, so we started. I zigzagged Grizzley

312

down, but they got to going too fast. The trailer sled tipped over, throwing Tony and Joe to the four winds. I was hanging onto the gee pole and was riding my heels keeping the front sled upright. It cracked all three bridges in the trailer sled. But all we had to do was pull the runners back in place. I set the sled right, and away we went. But not without putting on rope locks.

Before we got to the bottom, Gil and Larry had started down with Larry riding the rear sled and Gil the front. Gil was thrown off a couple of times. Well they tipped their trailer sled over. H.H. did the same. Joe and Toney went up and helped Earl and Perk down. What fun!!! Well, you can bet we were ready for the next ones. We didn't have any more mishaps. The surface in the valleys was bad, deeply undercut. The old trailer sled would whip around and the front sled would pitch and heave.

I forgot to mention the wind, but about 7 o'clock or so, it was blowing pretty hard, drifting. I imagine the velocity got up to 30 or 40 by gusts. The wind was cutting across our trail, and we had a hard time getting the dogs to face into it. I think any one of the valleys we crossed could be called "The Valley of a Thousand Winds." We were all cold and miserable. Joe and I tried to eat our lunch, but couldn't have much luck. The wind blew all of our lemon drink out of the cups.

Late in the afternoon we sighted the camp of the tractor and Survey parties perched high up the slope of Grace McKinley. We couldn't camp anywhere because of the wind and rough surface, so we decided to travel on. In some places it was drifting so badly we had to keep close together as visibility was poor. We made their camp at 9:15 P.M.—cold, tired, and hungry. I had to take off my skis the last mile and help push the sled up the hill. The dogs were pooped. It didn't take us long to put up our tents. We always do it fast when we are particularly tired. After a little food, we didn't feel too badly.

Twenty-Seventh Day Out — Tuesday, November 12
Camped all day at Mt. Grace McKinley

Slept like a log last night. In fact, I didn't get up until noon today. As usual the wind was blowing and a slight ground drift, yet it was clear over head, and the sun was shining like a million. After breakfast I went over to the survey parties' tent and shot the bull with Dick, Len and Jack B. They were just finishing eating, so I got in on a little bacon and coffee. Buck and Phil remade the tractor caboose putting a gable roof on it, making it out of old scraps of plywood and canvas. It's quite an improvement, one can actually stand up in it. Still Buck and Phil stoop when they are inside, by force of habit. Larry, Perk and I went up to the top of Mt. Grace McKinley. A little later on, we skied up to the Cairn which Paul, Al, Corey and Stancliff left on the last expedition. The Survey Party were the first ones there, so they got the note left by Corey and signed by all members. They also got the bottle of Sherry, which we all shared, getting about two or three tablespoons each. Larry and I got some samples of the diabase porphry and also aplite and the gradation of the two. We then skied around trying to reach another outcrop, but when we got to what we thought was the outcrop, we found that only a 1000 foot drop separated us from it. Saw quite a few Snowy Petras, as many as 15 in one flock. They seem to have a rookery somewhere in the outcrop cliff we were trying to reach. They are certainly a beautiful bird, all white except for a black beak. I guess they are about the size of a dove. Perk says he imagines they weigh about 4 oz.

Well, coming down the Mountains was the fun. I took it kind of easy and rather walked down to the smooth slope. Richardson, who later joined us, took right off over the rough sustrugi, tore the seat of his pants out about four times before he finally reached bottom. Perk was also a little careful, but even at that he fell about every 10 feet or so. Earl joined us, but he was afoot so he did not have much trouble. I don't want to brag, but I didn't fall once and I really flew, knees bent, leaning forward, just like a regular expert. Richardson liked it so well he went up a couple or three times. Gil & Joe made several trips up.

While we were up near the cairn, the Survey Party came up and raised the colors. We all signed a poop sheet stating that Mt. Grace McKinley and all land in sight belongs to Uncle Sam. We had another late dinner and had the last of our hamburgers. Quite a treat! While we were eating Phil came with news that the Beechcraft was going to try and land at our camp en route to Mt. Rea. Their purpose was to locate a landing field for the Condor. Al and Pete were in the plane. It's always good to see Al. They brought us some material to repair ski bindings, extra cable etc. Didn't get to bed until about 4 o'clock. Of course, after the plane left I heated up some water and took a spit bath. I at least got my face and hands clean and shaved with the hair clippers. While all that was happening, Gil fried up a little bacon and heated some left over cocoa, and

314

we had a feast. Larry got in on the tail end of it, so he robbed our extra rations of a few Eugenia Biscuits, which prolonged our repast. After I finally got to bed I wrote in my log for awhile. By the way, getting in one's sack out here is a day's work in itself. It takes a good 1/2 hour to get things unzipped, clothes hung up to dry, etc.

Twenty-Eighth Day Out – Wednesday, November 13
Camp No. 22

If I didn't know today was Wednesday the 13th, I'd swear it was Friday the 13th because we certainly have had bad going and lousy luck. We made only 4 miles today. Meter read 328.7. Got up this morning about nine o'clock.

Oh yes, I forgot. Last night I re-arranged my loads, cleaned out my duffel bag and sent some stuff back with Buck. I might say I didn't want to get up this morning. In fact, I think Larry and I were trying to out do one another. Anyway, I lost and finally bailed out. Before I knew it, I was cooking breakfast. Incidently I made oatmeal, bacon, coffee, tea, and a few fried Eugenias. We finally got away from Mt. Grace McKinley about noon after saying goodbye to Buck and Phil. While we were eating, Phil brought over some extra oatmeal, chocolate and milk which they didn't need. We certainly snapped on to it. I gave Phil some messages to send from the mountains to folks and Alda.

Yesterday the tractor took our load of dog food up the trail about a mile. We picked it up there today. After leaving there, we had to climb a fairly long slope. H.H. and then I followed with Earl and Perk. H.H. and I got pretty far ahead. After we got over the top, we noticed that Gil hadn't gotten to the top yet, so we stopped and waited, as did the others. We waited for almost an hour for them. From what Larry said later, the dogs just wouldn't pull. He had to put a line on the gang line, and he and Gil had to pull the dogs and sled up the grade. As soon as they came in sight, H.H. and I started again, stopping at the top of a pretty steep grade down to the barrier. We all had to put on rope locks, and I got the roughest ride I have ever had. The sustrugi was undercut and fairly high, the sleds were tossed around like nothing at all, and, of course, the dogs didn't mind. That was easy going for them, and they really took advantage of it. I thought my sleds were goners a couple of times. What a relief to get to the bottom. I went back to help H.H. and Perk down. Earl also had caught up with us to help Gil. I guess we must have waited a good 45 minutes for them, and when they did finally arrive, they really came down. Well, we re-arranged loads so as to make Gil's lighter. We were carrying each one of the Bio Party's man food. They took that, and I took one of Gil's sacks of dog food and lightened his load by 130 lbs.

But, here is where the trouble began. I relashed my load and was ready to start. I noticed that none of the others were making a move. Gil, Joe, Larry, Perk and Earl were talking in a group. I ambled over to find what the score was, and much to my surprise Larry announced that he thought we had better camp for the night as Gil and Joe didn't want to go on. Gil was fed up, he had enough of dog driving. As for Joe, I don't think he was ever too keen about coming anyway. So we camped. The purpose was so that Gil and Joe could make up their minds before we got too far away from the tractor and Grace McKinley. Well, Joe and Gil talked it over and at our 8 o'clock radio sked we asked for an 11 o'clock sked and in the meantime Larry talked it over with Gil and Joe.

They decided to go as long as they were not a drag on the party. That was an absurd attitude to take, as nothing was ever said by Larry or me. I think Gil just had a tough day and was discouraged, and as for Joe, well, I think he's looking for a graceful way out anyway. At 11 o'clock, we told the base we had solved our own problem and were sorry we kept Paul and Pappy up.

Twenty-Ninth Day Out — Thursday, November 14
Camp No. 23

I am still screwed up on the days. Gil tells me this is our 29th traveling day, and I figured the 28th. Four weeks on the trail today. Got under way at 11 o'clock. While eating breakfast, we heard a couple of shots. I looked out and Perk was shooting at a Skua Gull, the first seen this summer. He took four shots and missed. Earl came out and, as luck would have it, killed him dead with one shot. Perk swears that he killed him and he just happened to drop when Earl shot. The bird wasn't more than 20 feet from Perk. Tony says he was a little blurry eyed as he just got out of his sack.

Made fairly good time today; traveled 11.3 miles. Gil is not driving dogs anymore as that was the change or one thing Larry insisted because the dogs just caused Gil a lot of misery. So Larry is the new dog driver. I gave him Grizzley and started using Myra. She has been doing very nicely, although she will not readily gee or haw. But she will stick to a trail. I took Keela back. Temperature this morning was +20 and now at 10 PM is +9. It is and has been

316

milky out and is now snowing. We got some snow last night and this morning.

Thirty Days Out – Friday, November 15
Camp No. 24

According to Paul and the poop sheets back at Base, we are supposed to be at Mt. Rea today, but I'm afraid we didn't quite make it. We did make 13 miles today and are camping tonight near Garland Hershey ridge. We intend to proceed to there tomorrow and spend a few hours collecting. Got up this morning at 7 A.M. and we actually got away by 10. At 7 o'clock it was milky white, but by the time we were under way, the sun was shining in a clear sky. Temperature about +15; surface today was fair, although we were afraid the 1″ of soft snow would get sticky and make sledding difficult.

Had a pretty rough going as we were doing quite a bit of climbing, plus down fairly steep grades. We had to put rope locks on several times. Earl came on a hill too fast and tipped over his trailer sled. We lost sight of Mt. McKinley about noon, but sighted in ahead Garland Hershey Ridge, Haines Mountains, and Edsel Ford Mountains. We made camp tonight about 6 o'clock. H.H. and Perk's dogs tired out, and I guess mine were plenty glad to stop. We were going to try to make Garland Hershey tonight so we could make one camp do, but it's still a good 3 miles away.

Radio sked tonight was a success. H.H. and Gil got messages. Pappy started to fade out toward the end of sked. I haven't been able to get a time tick for the last week or so. Our course today was about N 45 E. Yesterday, we traveled due N for 10 miles and then started on our present course. Temperature tonight is +12 and wind blowing about 20 miles per hour.

Thirty-First Day Out – Saturday, November 16
Camp No. 25

Didn't sleep very well last night. I had my mind set on waking Larry up at 4:00 A.M. so that he could take a sun shot. Well I woke up every hour or so and looked at my watch and when 4 finally around, the sun wasn't out. Besides it was blowing. Larry did, however, get up at 6. I was going to get up at 7 and get a time tick, but I kind of relaxed. In fact, I relaxed too much and fell asleep and didn't wake up until quarter after. It turned out to be a beautiful day; temperature this morning was +12 with a high of +19. Had a radio sked at 10 o'clock to tell Paul that we had gone by Hershey

Ridge and that what we thought was the Ridge ahead was Haines Mountains. Perk came in last night and told us about it. He had plotted up the course and had a picture from the last expedition. The ridge was the last hill that we had come down. It appeared to be mostly covered, but in looking back this morning, we could see a definite ridge with rocks outcropping in 5 places.

We did not get away from camp till noon as Perk and Larry shot in all of peaks, and I made a sketch of the region using a Bruton compass. The going was pretty tough today.

The dogs weren't as anxious to go as they were at first. I think they were starving on their feet. A one lb. block every 24 hours isn't enough for a dog that has to work as hard as ours, steadily pulling heavy loads for a period of 5 to 6 hours. Several of mine are getting very thin. I don't think old Jad will stand up much longer; I say old, but really he is only two. We made under 10 miles today having come so far, made 38 miles from Grace McKinley.

Our course today was N 45 W, but changed to N 70 W as Survey Party didn't lay trail through pass, and I am glad they didn't. I don't think my dogs could have ever climbed the grade. Instead we went around the N end of the Haines Mountains. Made camp at about 6 o'clock. We found Survey Party cache at 33 miles at foot of pass. Bio Party made cache at 28 miles getting rid of 4 bags of dog food. Their dogs would hardly pull their loads, so it was necessary to make a cache. Earl handled radio sked tonight as he wanted to test his set. They expect to leave us tomorrow sometime and head in a northern direction toward Low Hills. Changed course to N 15 E to skirt W slope of Mountains. When we got around, changed to N 37 E. Distance around slope of mountains was 2.9 miles.

Thirty-Second Day Out – November 17,
Camp No. 26
Thirty-Third Day Out – November 18,
Camp No. 27

Got up bright and early at seven o'clock. It was a perfect day, +14, sun shining. We had our breakfast of oatmeal. I don't know what a fellow would do out here if he didn't like oatmeal and pemmican. The Bio Party was all set to go. Since they were going to leave us anyway in the next hour or so, they went ahead. We all said our goodbyes and good lucks and, of course, took pictures all around. That's a regular ceremony with us. We made a dog food cache, lightening my load 63 lbs. H.H. cut his trailer sled in half, making his load lighter. We got away about 11 o'clock. Surface was pretty good, but I had a hard time getting my dogs started. I bet I stopped 13 times in a half an hour. The mutts didn't seem to be able to get together on their morning's constitutional. We climbed steady for an hour or so, and on top of the hill was the Bio Party just finishing lunch and getting ready to descend down to the John Hayes Hammond Inlet.

It was a beautiful view across the Inlet to Ames glacier and the towering massive Edsel Fords. We saw our destination, Mt. Rea, and next to it, Mt. Cooper with the Bill Board cliff. Also Mt. Saunders to the left and Mt. Donald Woodward almost straight across from us. We stopped and had lunch before going down. Gil and Joe went ahead to see how the Bio Party made out going down.

H.H. tipped his sleds over. We decided to take a different course down and got to the barrier without a mishap. We had rope locks on our sleds. Farther along the trail we came to the point where the Bio Party had turned off to the north. Len had set up three flags so as to line Perk up on his course. He had written in the snow points one way to Mt. Rea and other to Low Hills, which are Perk's first stop. The surface improved as we started to climb up on the barrier ice. We made 11 miles by six o'clock. Since the surface was so good and weather perfect, we decided to rest the dogs and then go on. Had radio sked with Base and listened in on Fitz's sked. At 9 o'clock I contacted Earl. They had made 10 miles on new course. Larry and I sat in the tent looking at maps and pictures of the region we are to cover. Then at midnight we started getting water ready for coffee and a brunch. We got under way by three o'clock with a perfect working temperature of +5 and a clear sky.

It got pretty cold during the night. It must have dropped to zero. The dogs were not overly anxious to get into harness. I had to carry Wanda over. It took quite a bit of encouraging, but finally we were on our way. We stopped at 5:45 after having made 7 miles. Larry took a sun sight, and we had our lunch.

We were then abreast Ames Glacier. We started again, but stopped at 10 o'clock for radio sked with Base as prearranged for time tick. Well we waited for an hour, besides going to all the trouble of setting up. The Base didn't answer my call. I heard Pappy call Phil and sign off with him. I then expected him to call me or call the trail parties. No soap! It kind of annoyed me.

We traveled till noon. The dogs just couldn't go any farther, and I know I was dead—feet hurt and legs ached. My face and neck were burned up. I don't think I have ever had such a sun burn. We camped at the foot of Bill Board, having made 16.8 miles since 3 AM, a total of 27.8 miles for the day.

So far we have sledded 286 miles from LA. We had breakfast as soon as we got the tents up, and, of course, the oatmeal and everything else would taste of kerosene, but I still had 4 bowls. Went to bed at 2 PM.

Thirty-Fourth Day Out – Tuesday, November 19
Camp No. 28

Reached −2.5 during the night. Broke camp at 11:45 and got to Mt. Rea cache at 2:15 PM. Had some trouble finding it. Followed Survey Party tracks which seemed to lead in all directions. They evidently had difficult time in locating it. Report from Base said it was 1/4 mile from North end of Mt. Rea. Larry's bearing found it to be close to 1 mile. Survey party camped here on 16th. They covered 21 miles that day. Surface is fine, rough sastrugi, but hard. Crossed blue water lake at foot of Mt. Rea. Larry and I went over to contact and brought back a few specimens, both sedimentary and igneous. Seems not to be very good metamorphism.

Left plane cache about 3:30 after re-arranging loads, taking 4 man food sacks and kerosene with us. We cached 2 man food sacks, kerosene and some odds and ends of dog repair gear, and 3 radio batteries. Our course from Mt. Rea was N 38 E for 5 miles, where we camped. Radio sked tonight was poor; couldn't hear Base very well, static and weak. Earl did not answer my call. Read a review on Rocks and Rocks Minerals by Pirsson and Knopf. Larry and I talked over plans for tomorrow's work. This starts our field work in the Edsel Ford Mountain Range. Tomorrow when we start our geological study, we will be on territory never before traversed by man. For the next two months we will be looking forward to each new day as we explore and study this magnificent mountain range.

Thirty-Fifth Day Out – Wednesday, November 20
Camp No. 29

Temperature +29.2. Min last night −4, wind 0, clear. Meter reads 402.2 miles. Shots to following peaks from Station C Camp, 28-73A; 231, 247, 245, 244, 237, 25, 200, 27, 21, 185-89. Time

2 o'clock, we spent time shooting in Station C for Base time. Used plane table and transit. Joe took panorama shots of peaks in a complete circle. Departed 2:30 and went 2 miles. We took sights and laid chained base line. Station B meter 404.2 base line bearing from B N 65 W-S 65 E. In laying the base line we used a 100 foot chain.

Made 2 miles today. Camped east of Camp 28. Radio sked was poor tonight. Could hear Base, but not well enough to understand. Pappy then turned to CW, which made it even worse. Had a message from home. I got part of it and rather than have them send it again, they will read it over the first good day we have. Must be having a magnetic storm, as conditions are very poor. I have not been able to get time tick for so long I forgot what one sounds like.

Broke one of my ski bindings today and have been repairing it tonight. It is now midnight and temperature is +5, wind E 3 miles and clear. Larry and Gil did not get to 4500 feet on their part of Base line as after 3500, they could not see the part of Peak 25 Larry wanted to shoot in.

Thirty-Sixth Day Out – Thursday, November 21
Camp No. 30

Minimum last night +28. Temperature +12, no wind, clear meter 404.3. Time 11:15. Made attempt at 9:00 and 11:00 for time tick but failed. It certainly was a job lugging the Alidade, plan table and tripod from Station A to Station B, a distance of 8,000 feet. I first set up at A. So I skied, as it was downhill, but coming back, I wished I had never seen a pair of skis. I walked up slope 3,500 feet to set up at Station B. The wind started to blow as I got halfway up, and it clouded over. It was a cold job setting up and taking sights. I nearly froze to death. My fingers were so stiff I couldn't hang onto a pencil. And wouldn't you know it, the minute I got through the wind stopped. Such is Antarctica.

When I got back to where we had camped, Joe, Larry and Gil were hitching the teams. We moved on to point below Station B and camped. Radio sked tonight was a success, although Pappy Reese burned me up. First thing he hopped on me saying that he noticed that for the past few weeks I had been taking longer than 15 minutes for our sked, and that I was keeping the other parties waiting. So stick to business and make messages short. I sent back saying "Nothing here; all well" and as far as I was concerned that ended the sked. I wasn't going to say our official messages. But

Pappy came back and said he didn't know I was going to take it that way. What way did he expect me to take it? Anyway, he wanted the weather dope and position. So I sent regular poop sheet. He then read a message from folks. The only time I can remember that our sked was overtime was one night Gil had messages from his wife. Conditions were so poor that Pappy had to read it several times. I suppose that overworked him. I can't understand the radio lash up back at Base. Surely the one day contact from the parties isn't killing them. I guess it does cause them to have to get out of bed and throw on a switch. Of course, all we have to do is ring up the set, then turn the hand generator, etc. Well, I guess I had better sleep off my grouch.

Thirty-Seventh Day Out — Friday, November 22
Still in Camp No. 30

Current temperature $+17$. Minimum $+2.8$. Wind o, Milky white. Up at 7:30. Had a wonderful breakfast of oatmeal. I'll say one thing, the Antarctica is the place for a fellow to learn to like things which he would otherwise throw out. It's funny seeing Joe eat graham crackers. He said when he was back in the states he wouldn't ever look one in the face. Well our main topic, of course, is food, what kind and where to get it. Larry and I would like to tangle with a nice head of lettuce and tomato salad and a juicy steak. Joe and Gil go in for the seafood (Mama). Weather has kind of put a cramp in our plans to shoot in peaks, so we will do a little geologizing. After all, that's what we came here for, and not surveying.

Tried for a nine o'clock time tick but failed. Got one last night at 6 o'clock; it came in perfect.

Note—Gil and Joe, while locating Station D, saw 14 snowy petral in one flock   November 21st 3 PM.

Wind started to blow, visibility bad, and driving snow. Almost impossible to escape wind. Larry and I tried to find some shelter while we had a bit of chocolate. Snow made going bad underfoot. I guess maybe I didn't know how to wear crampons, but if I have any wind proofing left after this trip, I'll be lucky.

Joe got breakfast again this morning. Larry and I did not stir till we heard him moving in the galley. Still cloudy after breakfast; sun sure trying hard to break through. Joe thought he would be able to take a circle of pictures, so Larry, he and I went to Station D. We set up the plan table and transit. Joe took the pictures from the plan table. We had quite a time getting the instruments up to a Station D, a climb of 300 feet and straight up. We started right from camp with crampons. Soft snow made going hard. Estimate 6″ of snow fall.

Note: At Station D sighted Pks 18, 73A, 237, 246, 25, 88, 87, 89, and 27. Could not see 21. Have 3 pt Station C. 2 pt A Station D. We had quite some difficulty in operating the board as there was fog in valley making it impossible to see. Marker at Station D. Joe finally spotted it with naked eye. Sun happened to get to it. Larry got it through transit scope, but I buggard around for 1/2 an hour or so before I found it.

After I finished sights I went over to Pk 225 and gave it a final once over. Collected samples ss, sh, and quartz in joints. *Still no fossils.* Saw several snowy petrals flying about.

Note: I saw a dark bird with white v mark on wings. Did not get close enough for further inspection. Thought it was Skua Gull from size.

Larry finished up about 3 o'clock, so we broke camp. We made only 3 miles and are camped E of Pk 25. It took 4 hours to make 3 miles. We had to dump part of load. Larry left one sled but got it before chow. I have to make trip in morning and pick up the rest of my load. Soft snow hot and sticky, not ideal for sledding. I don't think I could have made it back tonight.

Radio sked OK; turned crank myself. I received messages from Alda. She still loves me, which helps, makes me feel better after a hard day. Had late chow tonight, at 9 o'clock. This means we didn't get in camp till late. Zipper on cook fly went hay wire and we couldn't get the stoves started. We had to cook in tent. Didn't have weather dope at regular sked, so we called Pappy at nine and gave him a report. Temperature +6, wind 3 mph, overcast and snowing. If it doesn't stop snowing soon, our whole program will be ruined. We can't travel. We either need a good blow which, of course, will lay us up for a couple of days or a drop in temperature. I guess we are hexed any way we work it.

Note: We are finding that dog food ration does not feed dogs one week as it is supposed to. Gil finished one bag in only six days. I have enough for 5 days left in my 1st bag.

News of other parties: Bio made 5 miles today and will arrive Mt. Ephigene tomorrow. Tractor arriving at Base tonight. Survey party made 20 miles and are at Long 140 25′. Lat. 76 37′

Forgot an important thing. We had our Thanksgiving dinner tonight. Gil and Joe worked on it while Larry and I were in the field. Menu—fried chicken, tomato, lima bean soup with a few onions and strawberries, and fresh frozen ones too. What a feast. I suppose we are the first men on the trail to ever eat strawberries, and I might say I wish we had more. Pappy Grey brought the chicken and strawberries out to 105 in the Condor. The strawberries have had quite a trip, from Pittsburg to Boston by truck, Boston to LA by boat, LA to us by plane, and from 105 to Mt. Rea by dog teams. They are worth it.

Thirty-Eighth Day Out — Saturday, November 23
Still in Camp 30

Regular New England snow storm last night, estimated 4' of snow. I'd still like to know who said it never snowed down at Antarctica and where in the world they thought all of this new snow came from. Larry and I worked last night or rather this morning till 2 AM. We got our samples straightened out and our notes cleaned up. Didn't wake up this morning until I heard some one in the cook fly. Joe was up and starting breakfast at 10:30. Temperature currently +25, minimum +18. Still milky white, ground haze, no wind and light snow. Impossible to see Mt. Rea and Saunder. We are up that well known creek as we cannot inhabit Station D while conditions are such. Hate to spend more time here. Since we have worked geology on this part of Swanson Range, we will probably have to move on and then return to this spot and take shots. Larry has not said as yet.

3 PM Well the weather decided for us. It's still snowing and the only things one can see are the sleds, dogs and Swanson Range. The only reason we can see it is because it's so close. And it won't be long before we miss the dogs, as they are about snowed under. Just finished a very light lunch of tea and Army ration. I have been reading a little Field Geology. I spent the afternoon hoping it would clear up, but no luck. It's a hell of a life being cooped up in these tents. They are about as large as a postage stamp and about as sticky; In fact, they are good and wet now. Had a nice supper of pemmican and a fruit concoction of some kind. Radio sked tonight was a success. Reception was fine. We got ship assignments. I go on Star as well as Larry and Gil. Joe is assigned to Bear; of the survey party, Berlin and Bursey on Star, Dick on Bear. Plane intends to make South flight tonight leaving Base at 2 AM hoping 110 EL Lat 85. Beechcraft will stand by at gas cache.

324

Thirty-Ninth Day Out – Sunday, November 24
Camp No. 31

Elevation, 210 feet

Worked peaks 225, 1025 by collecting rock samples and taking the dips of the beds.

Note: Claimed Claude Swanson Range for U.S. today. Hoisted up the colors on Station D and made a cairn with necessary paper enclosed.

Forty Days Out – Monday, November 25
Still in Camp 31

Overslept this morning. I was rather fatigued last night. Got out of my bunk at nine. Weather bad, milky white, some snow. Larry is out trying to fix the zipper on the cook fly. I don't know why, but all of the bad luck hits one at the same time in this country. Take us for instance. We are snowed in. Then when it's fit to travel, we can't because the surface is too soft and sticky. Then after a hard day when we were tired and hungry, we couldn't get stove started and couldn't get the cook fly zipper on. In fact, things just haven't been going right. Now today, we had plans to split and work the geology in this region, but I don't know now. I don't think the weather is quite safe for such a procedure, especially when we have to go out of sight of camp. We shall have to see.

Note: We left camp at 2 o'clock to study Peak 2025.

Forty-First Day Out – Tuesday, November 26
Camp No. 32

Got to bed fairly late last night as Larry and I talked over the day's work. Joe was the first one up this morning and had breakfast started by 8:30. Since we got to bed so late, we planned on sleeping till 10 or so. Joe and I yesterday covered quite a bit of ground, but not very interesting though. Same old stuff, sandstone, no luck on fossils. Joe left me about seven to return and went to camp to get chow. I went on to Peak 1088, where I met Gil. We got to camp at 9 o'clock P.M. I hurried and set up the radio, and at 9:15 I listened in. No sound from Base. Boy, was I provoked. I was so tired that I had read my watch wrong. I was just an hour off. So I missed the sked. Larry got in at 10. He stopped to visit an igneous contact.

We broke camp about 11 o'clock. We stopped and established Station E and shot in peaks. We then stopped at outcrop 1237, worked it, and made camp tonight about 7 o'clock. Had radio sked OK. After leaving outcrop 1237, we descended through the pass. Gil and Joe went ahead for trail. Everything would have been fine but Grizzley didn't follow. He took off down the hill instead of following trail. Well, Myrna naturally followed Grizzley, and that is where things began to happen. I had no control. In fact, it was all I could do to keep on my feet. Well to make a long story short, before I knew it half of my team was under the front sled. The Saints were good to me, as none of the dogs were injured. Poor Alaska was all the way under and frightened to death. The sled ran up on the gang line and naturally the dogs were held. Jed slipped his collar so he got free. Kusan and Kotik's side stopped the front sled but got hit by the trailer. It took Larry and me some time to untangle the mess.

Forty-Second Day Out – Wednesday, November 27
Still in Camp 32

Time 8:30 AM, Bar. steady 27:30, wind SW, Temperature +17, visibility clear, unlimited. Left camp 11:30 AM to study Peak 231 and several outcrops taking dip strike and collecting samples. Joe and I hunted a shady spot under a nice palm to have lunch. I took some time then to straighten out my collection; my knap sack weighs a ton. Spent considerable time on my fanny due to blue ice, skis plus a slope, none of which go together. Saw Gil and Larry coming from Pk 244. Met them at contact. We skied back to camp, but the day was a heart breaker. I was puffing like an old plow-horse.

Joe had left a little before the rest of us, so when we got back to camp we expected the Pemmican to be hot. But no Joe! He came in about 10 minutes after we got to camp. He had lost his geology hammer and had gone to look for it; no luck. We were late for radio sked but contacted Base at 8:30 and arranged sked for 9 after today.

Pappy gave us the dope on the other parties: Survey 110 miles from Mt. Rea, sighting Mt. Hal Flood; Bio was in big Marujupo Mt, Al Wade was 5 miles from Base doing survey work; Tractor back at Base safe and sound, waiting to go out again. (They hope!) Oh yes, Fitz is still on his Mt.

Used 4 pemmicans tonight and had a nice pudding since tonight's meal is the last of the rations. So we cleaned out the ration box. Starting tomorrow we eat royally at least for a couple of days.

Larry and I checked up on the day's work tonight. It is now 1 A.M. and temperature is −3. It was perfect all day; we could work with gloves off.

Forty-Third Day Out – Thursday, November 28
Camp No. 33

Boy was it ever hot last night, or rather this morning. I actually had to open my sleeping bag. The old sun was really beating down. I did not get to bed last night till about 1 A.M. Larry and I exchanged specimens and checked over our work of the day. We stayed in camp till 4 P.M. Got caught up on a little paper work, plotted in some of the geology structures and indexed specimens. It was a perfect day; in fact, it was too hot to travel, because the dogs wouldn't go so well—too lazy. Local noon comes around about 9 A.M. so naturally that's the hottest part of day. Had quite a steep climb in order to get to the next camp. It took quite a bit of urging (cursing) to get the dogs on the ball.

We made camp at 7 P.M. We had radio sked at nine and heard Base talking to Earl. Then the set went dead. I checked over tubes etc., but all sounded OK. Will try again at 2200 tomorrow. Well old Molly at last met her fate or something. She never has been worth a dime, she was too much a lady, poor soul. The past week she hasn't pulled an ounce; it just wasn't in her heart. Yes, Joe put the final slug smack between her eyes; she never knew what hit her. We are going to let her freeze and then feed her tomorrow night. Speaking of feed, that reminds me today is Thanksgiving. When I think of all the turkeys, chickens, cranberry sauce, etc. that is being eaten all over US, I want to cry. We had our pemmican.

Forty-Fourth Day Out – Friday, November 29
Still in Camp 33

Joe and I left camp at 10:30, but the going is pretty bad, a milky white day. Surface sastrugi is showing no shadow. Joe left me about 3 o'clock when his ski binding gave way. I continued on around PK 245 and crossed the glacier to work Pk 1245. Stopped at Station 1, then continued along ridge to the south end of Pk Station 2. Back to camp at about 5:45. Larry and Gil were not in, so I divided out all the rx and skied over to take a look at Pk 246. By the time I got back, Larry and Gil were in and the pemmican was on. We dressed Molly tonight and fed her to the dogs. All of my dogs but Myra tore right into the meat. I guess she's just too much the lady.

Old Kazan, Kotik and Jad really scoffed it down. I think they were still chewing on the bones. Tongas was not quite sure, but I imagine he will eat his before morning.

Radio sked tonight was OK. We heard Base first and found out that the reason we could not contact them last night and this morning was because conditions were bad and the Base was dead.

Forty-Fifth Day Out – Saturday, November 30
Camp No. 34

Well, we have only 2 weeks to go; then back to Base for us. Got up this morning at 8:30. Didn't sleep very well as my back has been bothering me. I guess I can't get used to sastrugi as a mattress. Had radio sked this morning at 2200—reported clear weather, +15 temperature and a S 7 mile wind. We got under way about 11 AM heading toward Pk 232. Boy what a cold trip. The wind drains off the plateau and sweeps right down the valley we were traveling across. The surface was fine, blue ice. We made 6 miles, then camped. Most of the going was up grade and after about 5 hours of such work, the dogs just gave out. We, however, camped about a 1/2 mile SE of PK 232.

After chow tonight, Larry and I worked Pk 232, getting back to camp about 11:30 PM. It is now 1 AM. Pk 232 is granite with a series of dikes (basalt) running N 70 W, and the north end is all aplite and alaskite. Larry took down the geology. I was just along to observe and lend moral support, and we both needed it. The wind sure blew like hell, say 12 miles per hour. Well, anyway, we had a nice ski back. We just climbed aboard, gave a shove, and the wind did the rest, we almost went by camp. Fed the dogs, then had a snack ourselves. Peak 317 is dark when seen from 232 with glasses.

Forty-Sixth Day Out – Sunday, December 1
Camp 35

There are only 13 more days; then Mt. Read and then Base. I like this life all right, but enough is enough. Joe and I figured that if we get to Base around 1st of January, we will have been on trail exactly 76 days. The thing that gets me is we will have been out 76 days and we are lucky to have 20 days of actual geological work. The rest we have traveled or been snowed in or in a whiteout. We split camp today. Gil and Larry went to 317 and will work toward 307. Joe and I are now camped at 339. We will work 339, 338, 334,

328

337, then go over to 345 where we will meet the others on Wednesday.

Broke camp about 2 o'clock and made 6 miles of about the toughest going I have ever encountered. It was all up grade and easily a 10 or 14% grade. We tried to get up to the table plateau between 339, 334 and 332, but we couldn't make it. So we will work this end of the range from here and then move on. We had to pull one sled up at a time in order to even get as far as we did.

Well you can't expect underfed dogs to work hard, pulling heavy loads. I still don't think that 1 lb per day is enough for the dogs. I can't see how any of them will get fat as claimed. Well one thing I am seeing to is that Tongas is getting plenty to eat. I give him left-over pemmican, etc. Made camp tonight at 6 o'clock. While the region seems to be a series of small cracks, the dogs broke through one on the trip to camp with the trailer sled. I poked around it and found it about 1 foot wide.

Radio sked at 8:15 was OK. They played the "Old Love Song," quite a classic. Joe and I had quite a time cooking our evening chow in the tent. We had to open a new ration, and much to our disgust found no oatmeal, only cerevim. Well it will take a lot of that to fill me. I don't intend to go hungry. Also, I find that there is no tea or coffee in the extra food sack. In other words, we drink cocoa and lemon and like it.

Forty-Seventh Day Out – Monday, December 2
Camp No. 36A

Joe and I left camp at 10:15 and made a steep climb to 329. I know now that we could never have made it with the dogs. This region is certainly different than it looks in pictures; it is not a table top but a steep hill full of cracks.

Joe and I finished Pk 339 and 1339—regret that we were not able to visit 338. I am sure that 339, 337 and 338 are granite. Broke camp about 3 o'clock taking only a limited amount of equipment, also leaving one sled so that we will be able to climb grades in order to camp near 334.

Had radio sked 8:15—OK, and afterwards was going to the top of 1334 in order to take a gander toward 339 and 332. But the wind came up and it clouded over. We had a light snow today and about a 10 mile wind, making work uncomfortable. Joe said that the wind blows on the Mts. just like on a ship, all over and everyplace, which is very true. Hope it clears up by tomorrow.

Forty-eighth Day Out – Tuesday, December 3
Still in Camp 36A

Woke up this morning about 7 o'clock, but the wind was blowing so turned over and went back to sleep. Woke up again at 9:30. It was still blowing but sun was showing and the wind seemed to have let up some. Had breakfast, cerevim, cocoa, bacon and eugenia. Going to Pk 1334 for a look. Visited Pk 334. We left camp about 11 o'clock. The sun was trying to shine but not having much luck. By about noon or 12:30 I had to return to camp and was glad to get back. The wind had picked up to about 20 miles or so. It was overcast and snowing. It was impossible to get to Pk 331 as we couldn't even see it.

So Joe and I spent a miserable afternoon in the tent, half sleeping, half dreaming and wishing that we were anywhere but here. This weather kind of puts a cramp in our work, delaying us a day. I certainly hope tomorrow comes bright and clear.

Radio sked tonight—OK. Pappy read a message from Alda.

This life is all right, I guess, but it's a drag from the minute we get up to the minute we hit the sack at night. Talk about working to survive! We have to work for everything, and the thing that does not make me any too happy is the trip back. I don't think it will be any easier than the one coming out, just plodding along on skis, fighting every inch of the way. It is 10 o'clock. Joe and I just finished our pemmican and washed up dishes. Now for a good night's sleep. Wind still 20 and is driving snow against the tents. Temperature about +10. The poor dogs. Every time I start to bitch or squawk about things, I just think of them. They don't ask for much, just a pound of chow once every twenty-four hours. They work hard and then are chained to a tethering wire at night. I dug them all holes tonight, hoping to make them a little more comfortable.

Forty-ninth Day Out – Wednesday, December 4
Still in Camp 36A

Boy, today is a day for the books. With the exception of about an hour this morning, the wind has blown all the blessed day. Joe and I finished breakfast about nine o'clock and departed for Pk 332. Temperature about +15, cloudy to white, although the sun was trying its best to shine through. The surface was new snow, and you couldn't even drag a ski through it. We had to walk on our skis. By the time we had clipped off the three miles to the peak we

330

were sweaty and hot. So what happens but our friend the wind immediately starts to blow, just a breeze at first but then a 12 mile gale. Boy, there is nothing more miserable than to get hot and wet and have a nice wind to cool you off—I mean freeze you off. Well, I made short work of that Peak. My hands, face, and nose were cold; it was generally miserable.

On the way back to camp, I skied over to Pk 334 and worked it. Joe went back to camp and had some hot water on by the time I got there. We had a spot of lemon. Broke camp about 3 o'clock. The wind was with us all the time, blowing in gusts, as high as 20 to 25 miles per hour. We picked up the trailer sled near Pk 339 and then headed for Pk 345, where we are camped now. Wind still blowing—only a little harder now I think. The wind blows in gusts—it will be dead calm and then all of a sudden you'll think the tents are going to give way. We got here about 8 o'clock and did not bother with radio sked as had hands full making camp. Saw Larry and Gil camped near Pk 207 through the glass—I imagine they will be here tomorrow.

Fiftieth Day Out – Thursday, December 5
Camp 37A

From contact at Pk 2330 to first grandite peak visited is a series of quartz veins dipping steeply to the East. These veins of massive quartz run from 1 1/2 to 2″ or less in thickness. They run unbroken except for numerous East West faults. The whole region seems to be an intricate mass or system of faults. I noticed several clusters of quartz crystals formed in cavity of mass quartz. Mineralization, Cu and Fe. Woke up several times during the night, blowing like hell. I take my hat off to these tents. They certainly can take it although I'll admit I thought a couple of times we were goners. Finally got out of the sack about 10 o'clock and fixed breakfast. What a job to merely heat a pan of water and throw in some powdered milk, and that's all. We have no oatmeal, and all the cerevim needs is milk. We had a little luxury this morning, some leftover apples which were fine with milk. Oh yes, we had our cocoa. What will it be like to sit down to a full meal, from soup to nuts and not have to do anything but eat it?

The wind died down a bit, and we left camp about 11 headed for Pk 330. Sun still trying hard to shine, and it was clearing up in the S East. Surface was slick as ice, and I had only one ski pole. Well, I almost went on my prat a couple of times.

Worked 330 and contact and a couple of peaks on this side. I spotted Larry and Gil coming around the end of 325 and thought they were going to come to our camp, but they stopped and camped near 330. Radio sked tonight was OK. Pemmican chow not so hot. We are getting kind of tired of it; however, it will keep me going. It is now 9:30 PM and time for bed. The sun is still trying to shine and the wind is zero. It is so quiet now you can actually hear it; my ears ring like crazy. Every little noise sounds like it's in the tent. I jump every time one of the dogs move. As for my heart, well, it is in the tent, in fact, is in that sleeping bag with me, I can hear every beat, every thump, the slightest breathing sounds like a snore.

Fifty-first Day Out – Friday, December 6
Camp 38

Up at 8 AM. Ate breakfast and had a 10 AM radio sked. I gave the Base radio report: Barometer 26.25, wind NE 2 miles per hour, temperature +20 and clear. Been getting things squared around a bit—have my sleeping bag out for an airing, etc. Departed from camp 11 AM to Pks 1345, 224. The north end of Pk 1345 is granite. It is even grained then a sudden transition to a very coarse granite with large pieces of feldspar (inch long). Crystals seem to go in all directions. Found one outcrop showing a series of EW faults cutting across the peak. The only indication is a gouged-out place. I also saw a transition of pink granite into gray.

Saw Larry and Gil at contact; evidently Larry wanted to take a look at the contact zone. I worked along the ridge going north from Pk 345. It is a beautiful day with temperature about +20 at noon; the sun is shining brightly. Got back to camp at 4 PM in time for the mail bag program. The first part of the program featured music from St. Louis—very good. Reception was fine I got a letter from the folks and Alda. Boy, I can hardly wait till the ships return so that I can open boxes and read the letters I hope to get.

We expected Larry and Gil to come in before chow, but they didn't so we had our usual pemmican feast. Radio sked was fine. Got the news on all the parties. Survey party has started back to Base. Also Perk's Biology Party is on the way back. That leaves us, the Geological Party, still holding fort, or should I say forth. Still camped at Pk 345, Larry at Pk 330. Turned in about 9 P.M. and for the first time in a couple of days dropped right off to sleep the minute my head hit the pillow. I was awakened by the dogs howling; we had visitors. Larry and Gil arrived. Time about 10:30 P.M.

I got out of my sack and went over to their tent, had a cup of tea and shot the bull till one AM. They were delayed 3 days at Pk 310 because of high winds, 60+ mile per hour, and I thought we had wind.

The 8:15 radio sked OK, Bar 26.30, no wind and temperature +13, overcast.

Fifty-Second Day Out – Saturday, December 7
Camp No. 38

Woke up this morning at 7:30. It is very hot, the sun really drove me out of my sleeping bag. Heard Larry and Gil astir so took over a pan and some food, and we started breakfast. It was wonderful to have a little oatmeal for a change. After breakfast Larry and I worked Pk 345. We then spent the morning getting squared around, drying tents, etc. Broke camp at 2 PM. First pop out of the box we hit a nice downgrade, but rough locks on the sled runners took care of that. I had a fine downhill sled ride out of it. Of course Myra would have to stop right on the slope (for constitutional purposes) and, of course, the rest of the dogs piled up. I was lucky to get the sleds stopped and just when I was enjoying the ride and scenery. (Note: I took panorama shots with my camera of Pk 345 along ridge to 330, 344, 343, 340 etc.) Right at the bottom of the slope we hit blue ice. The going was good except the rear sled whipped about quite a bit. Well I have seen my first crevasses today, and, I hope, my last. Some of them, Gil said, you could throw the city of New York in plus Boston for good measure. We had crossed many places where the crevasse area was small, but this was really scary with some of the crevasses 30' across. Some of them luckily had fairly good bridges so Larry and I used the Passel system of crossing crevasses. We put a long line to the lead dog and then a long line from the team to the sleds. Then we held on to a long line away from the sled and dogs. It works fine. The theory is that if the lead dog goes in a crevasse, the rest of the dogs will pull back naturally, and if the rest of the team falls in, then all we had to do was whip the first sled around, locking the rope, etc. If the two sleds went in, the dogs would be safe and so would we; if the whole business went in, well it didn't much matter. And I would like to say some of those crevasses sounded pretty hollow —like a ripe melon. We went along all right till we found some that were not bridged over, so we detoured in toward Pk 347 hoping to get around the nose of the range. Blue ice and more crevasses at the bottom kind of stopped us. We are camped now near Pk 347 taking a breather. We'll really tackle the situation tomorrow. Radio sked tonight OK.

Fifty-third Day Out – Sunday, December 8
Camp No. 39

Had a 10 A.M. radio sked OK. Sent a long message to Paul telling him about the large crevasse area. Left at 10:30 A.M. to visit Pk 346 and 347. Larry and I worked together while Gil and Joe skied around through a small pass between peaks to see if we could get through with sleds. They reported that there were more crevasses there than in the region we just came through. Got back to camp about 3 P.M. I fixed some cocoa and fried some Eugenias. We had a little snack. It was decided to go around the north end of the range, so we packed up, getting under way about 4 o'clock. Going was pretty rough at first. A slight grade and high sastragi, but when we got to the end of the range and headed south, we hit smooth going. We made 6 miles before time to get 8 P.M. radio sked, so we decided to camp near Pks 203 and 207. We plan to work the Pks tomorrow. Well I finally tried Tongas at the lead, and I think he is going to be all right. I have always wanted to try him out, and I got a little peeved at Myra. It was one of her off days, so feeling a little reckless, I took a chance and put Tongas in, naturally expecting anything to happen. What a surprise to have him start right out and follow the trail.

Larry and I figured out tonight that we have more or less covered 700 square miles since we left Mt. Rea, and that's really something. Well it's 11:15 P.M. and time for bed. When it's light all the time, it's hard to sleep anywhere from 8 P.M. to 3 A.M. Last night I felt kind of like a change, so decided to try sleeping in only my underwear, instead of leaving on my pepper and salt heavy wool suit. It worked fine, and I slept like a log. I still feel pretty brave, so I am going to sleep without my heavy wool socks. I hope I am not going too far.

Fifty-fourth Day Out – Monday, December 9
Camp No. 40

Jumped out of my sack this morning, because thought I heard a plane. Sure enough! The Beechcraft was circling around over camp. Gil, Larry and I waved standing there in our underwear. On about the third trip around they dropped something. We all tore after it.

334

It turned out to be a sack with a loaf of bread in it plus some pictures. They made a couple of more circles and then made a bee line for Mt. Rea and the Base. Boy it certainly ruins our morale to think that in just three hours the plane will be back to Base, whereas we have at least a three weeks' trip ahead of us (if we are lucky). Oh well, such is the life of an explorer.

Well it was 7:30 when they left, so we just stayed up. After breakfast, we left for Pks 203 and 207. Joe and I visited 203; that is, I did. Joe left me after about a 1/2 hour. I got back to the point I started from about 3 P.M., took a look toward camp and saw only one pair of skis sticking up, so I figured the others were still out. I checked another Pk. Well about 4:50 o'clock I was a little tired and very hungry. Since I had no lunch, I figured I might as well go in. I got to camp at 5:30 and the others had been there since 2 o'clock. It kind of got my goat a bit. If Joe had stuck around like he was supposed to, he could have told me that Larry and Gil had gone back. But no, he always leaves either skiing around or goes back to camp. I had a bite to eat, and we broke camp traveling 4 miles to a place north of Pk 202. Made radio sked OK. Paul was on and wanted to know if we got the food they dropped. I told him we had the bread and thanked him for it. He came back saying that they had dropped another package containing a can of meat— well we didn't see that package. It had been originally for the Survey Party, but the Beechcraft couldn't find their camp, so they dropped it off for us rather than take it back. It would be just our luck not to get it. They dropped it a little way from camp, so it wouldn't hit any of us. The sun was right in our faces so we just plain didn't see it. We are tempted to go back and look for it. Maybe Joe will.

Fifty-fifth Day Out – Tuesday, December 10
Camp No. 41

Up this morning bright and early—too hot; couldn't sleep. I crawled out of my sleeping bag for a couple of more winks on top, but Larry was getting up so I did the same. Had breakfast about 8 A.M. and by 9:30 Larry and I had left camp for the saddle near Pk 202.

Incidently, breakfast is getting lean these days. All we have left is cerevim and very little of that. In fact, in a couple of days it will be pemmican twice a day. Well, I suppose I can eat it rather than go hungry, but I don't like it. Larry and I buggered around till

4 o'clock in the afternoon and then went back to camp and had a little lunch. We broke camp and traveled to a site near Pk 201. Radio sked OK tonight. The *North Star* is leaving the States on December 12th for the Antarctic.

Fifty-sixth Day Out – Wednesday, December 11
Camp No. 42

Boy what a day—pea soup fog all day. Larry and I worked blind most of the time. Luckily we didn't have any bad going. We left camp at 9:30 A.M. and returned around 4 in the afternoon. Had lunch, or rather we had pemmican, which I suppose would be called dinner. Anyway, we ate! I had two bowls, crackers and milk (powdered), which isn't much for an all day ski trip, plus a little mountain climbing to boot. We had 8 P.M. radio sked OK.

It was still white milky out, but we decided to travel anyway. We got to Pk 218 about midnight, fed the dogs and then had a midnight snack—Fried Eugenias, cold pemmican, cocoa and anything else we could get our hands on. We got to bed about 2 A.M. —pretty tired. We visited Pk 2205 found interfingering sediments and igneous rock. The sandstone was metamorphosed and very fine grained showing schistoid near contact. It is badly broken up with many stringers of Aplite. Granite north from the sediments was gray acid granite—no dark constituents. Granite on the other side south toward Pk 2205 had biotite and hornblend.

Fifty-seventh Day Out – Thursday, December 12

Larry and I left camp this morning at 10 o'clock. We left Joe and Gil sleeping. The weather cleared up over night, which was a relief to both of us. Breakfast this morning was rather scanty— crackers and milk. We have run out of cerevim and oatmeal long ago. Well, anyway it's better than getting up to a greasy mess of pemmican. Larry and I really woke up bright and early this morning. We didn't get much sleep, but the day was too perfect to linger in our sacks. We had quite a ski trip—visited Pk 718 and then skied what we thought would be a mile, but turned out to be 2 miles to the back range. Got some good pictures of Ames Glacier. Well, all I've got to say is that if they call this stuff around here sediments—then I'll take vanilla (clever, huh). Boy they are certainly buggered up—metamorphosed so that a poor fossil wouldn't stand a chance.

We got back to camp at 4 o'clock, had lunch, and broke camp for Mt. Rea cache. We made 6 miles before we stopped for radio sked. I got a message from Alda. Boy it's wonderful to hear from her. Gil had skied on, and Joe was unable to attract his attention, so he missed chow. He is the darndest guy. He just puts his head down and skis for dear life, not looking right or left. His thoughts are usually miles from this place.

Pappy Reese passed on the dope that the Survey Party was camped near Mt. Rea. We saw their camp at the foot of Swanson Glacier. Gil's tracks were going toward their camp. We had a hard time finding the cache, and was I glad to call it a day.

We made 15 miles, and Wanda pooped out on me today. I had to ride her on the sled a ways till she wiggled loose. Then she followed along behind till I noticed that she was about 1/2 mile back. I stopped for her and tied her on a line to the rear of the sled. Poor little pup. I felt sorry for her, but I am afraid we will have to do away with her. We got to the cache at 1 A.M. We had a few crackers and milk and then turned in. But no sooner did we get settled in our sleeping bags than Gil yelled over to our tent asking if we heard a motor. It was the Beechcraft. She landed with Pete and Paul Siple aboard. Paul is still trying to make a successful flight to and beyond Mt. Hal Flood.

We got all of the Base news. Court and Clay got in a scrap. Court seems to be having trouble all around—Sig, the cook, and Sarg had words with him. Pete said they have some setup at the Base. One meal a day if they are lucky. They cook their own breakfast, and sleep at all hours. I hope they change that when we get back to Base. The plane brought us some oatmeal and ham to share with the Survey Party. We got to bed at 3:30 A.M. after they took off. What a night. No sooner did I get back to sleep again than the Beechcraft was back. Time 9:30. Gil and I got up so as to help them gas up. Pete and Paul took some pictures around our camp. We shot the breeze for a few minutes before they took off for Mt. Grace McKinley. Well I tried to sleep again and finally woke up at noon.

Fifty-eighth Day Out – Friday, December 13
Camp No. 43

I was getting ready to eat breakfast when the dogs started to yowl. The Survey Party pulled in, and that set the dogs off. Boy, it was good to see the fellows again, blistered up face and all. There wasn't much done for the next couple of hours or so except a little first class bull session. I guess they had quite a time coming down

337

the glacier—cracks big enough to throw the city of NY in. They said that the Base didn't say anything about the poop sheet we sent in suggesting a route for them to follow. It's a darn shame, but apparently Paul does not get all the dope we send in.

We finally finished breakfast. They spent the rest of the day getting squared around and visiting in general. I went all through the load on my sleds getting rid of enough junk so that I would not have to haul the trailer sled. Most of the stuff I got rid of was material to repair dog harness, etc. The plane brought a ham and some bread for the Survey Party, so they invited us over for dinner. I even had Dick give me a haircut, and I washed all up for the occasion. I gave Larry a burr head cut; it really is outstanding—his ears stand out anyway. We had dinner about 5 in the afternoon, and what a feast! We started out with cocoa, soup Louise, creamed tomatoes and then the meat course, which was ham and mashed potatoes. A meal fit for a king especially after weeks of pemmican; an explorers delight! I am afraid we all stuffed ourselves—I know I did. Bursey held radio sked, and I cranked for him.

Fifty-ninth Day Out – Saturday, December 14
Camp No. 44

I was disturbed from a peaceful slumber by what sounded like a ladies sewing circle. It was only the Beechcraft again and the fellows were really shooting the breeze. The survey party was up 100%, and Gil finally made his appearance. Larry and Gil got up just in time for the picture taking. Pete and Shirley were in the plane, and naturally, where you have Shirley, you have a camera. We spent about a half hour running around like madmen snapping pictures. They landed here at 7 A.M. and were going to gas up and again attempt to photograph around Mt. Hal Flood. But Berlin noticed that the tail ski was broken, so that nipped that little trip in the bud. Evidently, it happened on the take off from Mt. Grace McKinley as Pete said the sastrugi was very rough and that they had to taxi for about 2 miles.

Well they too were off for the Base, and all is peaceful again. They brought in some fruit and fig bars, so we had fruit for breakfast along with a little cerevim, coffee, bacon and fried eugenias. Broke camp at 10 A.M. It is a perfect day, except it's hotter than Hades. Traveled most of the day with my underwear down to my waist. We made 17 miles by 5 P.M. and decided to camp. I held radio sked tonight—all OK at the Base. One of Jack's dogs, Bo, passed out and he had to be hauled on the sled. Their dogs (Survey Party) are much worse off than our own—in fact, they are very poor. It isn't any wonder, for they traveled 20 to 30 miles a day and on one pound of dog pemmican.

Surface today was fairly good except for patches of soft snow where the dogs would sink in up to their bellies. Was a nice sledding surface, but hard on the dogs. We are homeward bound. We start back to the Base after a successful study of the Edsel Ford Mountains.

Sixtieth Day Out – Sunday, December 15
Camp 45

Up this morning bright and early, 7:30. Joe had breakfast started. It was certainly wonderful having oatmeal for breakfast—I had four bowls. Got under way about 10 A.M. Joe and Len started out on skis going ahead to mark the trail. The rest of us followed and were stretched in a single file over quite a distance. Dick led with his team, then Jack, Larry and Gil and myself. My dogs are usually peppy when we first start out, and I had to stop several times to keep from running past the other teams. It's a shame the way Dick's and Jack's teams are run down. All of us had to slow down to keep from passing them. When they started out they were big, fine look-ing dogs; now they are all skin and bones. Of course, to be fair the Survey Party covered the greater distance, and they had to make maximum mileage each day. We clipped right along today making 7 miles in two hours.

We have started to eat lunch on the fly nowadays. Jack has a large thermos jug on the rear of the sled, and we take turns keeping it full having everything from lemon drink or cocoa to drink plus the always delightful army ration and maybe a Eugenia biscuit or two as our lunch. We separated from the Survey Party when we got near Mt Haines as our dog food cache was at the north end of the mountain. So the Survey Party went through the main pass. We got our dog food and traveled S toward their dog food cache, which is on the W side of the Mt. at the foot N of the pass. They were not there yet so we made camp—time 5 o'clock— after having made 18 miles. They arrived shortly after we had started to get chow. Jack's dogs were a little tired and had trouble making the grade. Dick said he waited at the top for about an hour or so. Bo gave out again, so Jack turned him loose to follow behind the sled. Well, when he got to camp, no Bo. He came in about 9 or

10 P.M. He probably rested up along the way. If he had not shown up in the morning, Jack was going to ski out and get him. He left him about a mile from camp. Radio sked tonight OK. Pappy read me some messages, which are always nice to get. Len and Dick also got messages, so I called them over. After sked Dick brought over some rocks from Mt. Hall Flood for Larry and me to study. He stayed. We shot the bull till 11 o'clock; it's now 11:30 and time for bed. We want to make 20 miles tomorrow.

Sixty-first Day Out – Monday, December 16
Camp No. 46

Woke up this morning about 7:30. Slept like a log last night except I woke up once—a noise like an airplane motor. Guess I am getting airplane conscious because for the past two nights we have been awakened by the Beechcraft. But during breakfast Gil said he had heard a motor and so did Len. We broke camp at 10 A.M., temperature is about 70—a heat wave.

I skied all day in my underwear and wind proof pants. Boy the sun was really hot. My face smarts like crazy. I have never had a sunburn like this one back in the States. I'll have to rig up some sort of protection tomorrow. Well we finally left the Edsel Ford Mountains for good, and we camped tonight in sight of Grace McKinley; that is, we have 16 miles to go. We made 17 miles today, my meter reads 529.8 miles. To date I have skied 418.8 miles, and that doesn't count all the side trips I took around the Mountains. Well, if I ever see a pair of skis again it will be too soon.

Radio sked tonight OK. I am holding the sked for both parties. Pappy gave me a little news from here and there. We did hear the plane as Pete and Paul made a flight to Mt. Maybelle Sidley and vicinity and got back to Base about 11:30. We must have heard them about 2 A.M. Also Perk made 20 miles today. The *Bear of Oakland* is due in Dunedan on the 18th, and the *Star* is well on its way to Honolulu. Jack had to get rid of Bo this morning; he passed out completely. He at least died in his harness—poor Bo! Well I hope we don't lose any more dogs.

Surface was pretty good today—rather rough—and we had to climb a few grades. Outside of that everything was all right.

Sixty-second Day Out – Tuesday, December 17
Camp No. 47

Broke camp this morning at the usual time. We are getting

things down to a system nowadays—each man has his job and does it. While Larry is cooking breakfast, I zip up our sleeping bags and clean the tents. Joe and Gil do the same. Then after breakfast while Larry and I are loading our sleds, Gil carries out the mess gear while Joe starts taking down the tents. Then it's only a matter of a few minutes to harness the dogs and take up the tethering line, and then off we go. Perfect traveling day except hotter than Hades. My face tonight is really burned. Like Len says, he doesn't mind his face being boiled, but when it's parboiled, it's time to quit!

While we were stopping for lunch, a Wilson's petral flew around. Jack took a couple of shots at it, but no luck. It would have been luck because they seem to be about the size of a Robin and fly a rather zigzagging course.

We had nice going all day till we got within about 3 miles of Mt. Grace McKinley. Then we had to tackle the escarpment. Boy what a job! I think I did more work than all the dogs put together. That might stretch it a bit, but I know I pushed and shoved till I was blue in the face. Well there wasn't much to it after we got up on the escarpment, just a 1/2 mile run down to the tractor camp. Phil met us halfway down. It was good to see him. He said cousin Grif had a nice pot of stew on for us, so it didn't take us long to make camp. Although the wind had started to blow some, as it always does when we are near Grace McKinley. (At least the other time it did.) We were able to eat outside. Boy did that stew ever taste good, and there was plenty of it. Grif said Perk's party almost ate them out of house and home. Well, we tried.

Along about radio sked we all gathered in the caboose. It was quite crowded with nine of us. We had a cup of coffee and some cookies, another treat. Oh yes, I forgot the best part, a pudding of some kind for dessert with cold thick milk poured over it—rich, huh! Well that's what drove us inside; it seemed to be colder. We shot the breeze or should I say bull back and forth. Phil held the radio sked giving Pappy the dope on our situation etc.

After the rest of the fellows left, Dick and I stayed on and made a little lemon drink, and we had a big time with more talking. Phil was telling us about the gang at the Rockefeller Seismic Station, that Fitz was a dirty mess, and that the dirt is caked on his face. Well, Fitz was there to run a seismic staton, and he is very dedicated. Even at the Base Fitz was inclined not to wash much. He didn't really care, as he was devoted to his work. I imagine that his partner looks no better. It would be hard to camp in one spot in the mountains for over sixty days. We got to bed about midnight.

Sixty-third Day Out – Wednesday, December 18
In Camp All Day at Mt. Grace McKinley

Got up this morning 9 o'clock, wind blowing, yet a perfect day, clear and sun shining like a million dollars. Went over to the caboose. Phil had already started breakfast. They had invited us all over for ham and eggs. I was Johnny on the spot. Phil tried to keep the 10 A.M. radio sked, but Clay answered everyone's call but his. We did learn that the Condor was up and at that time was circling Mt. June.

We ate breakfast about 11:30: stewed apricots, then ham and eggs, bacon all mixed together, kind of an omelet, and coffee. Well we more or less lingered over breakfast till time for the news— 3 P.M. None of us wanted to move and do any work outside because it was getting too miserable. By that time the wind was blowing strong enough to give us a little ground drift.

Well after the news I ventured out and heated water to clean the dishes. I then spent a couple more hours in the caboose listening to music, Kaye Kaiser etc., reading shoot 'em up stories. What a pleasant way to spend time—nice and warm full of good food, no place to go, just rest. I did manage to get out long enough to dig up our cache and get out the man and dog food. Also I got out the underwear that I cached on our way out. It looked almost good as new, so I changed.

By the time I fed my dogs and got squared around, it was time for the radio sked. Phil told Pappy that he would hold radio sked from now on. Got a short message from Clay saying that my folks would talk on the mail bag program this coming Friday. Grif had already started the evening meal, and what a meal! After we got the radio gear cleared away, we tore into it—Hamburger, mashed potatoes, oh yes, and tomato soup, hot tea—a feast for a king— certainly a change from our pemmican. Oh yes, Paul came on the radio and wanted to know what we thought was the best method to get Fitz and his stuff out of the mountains. We suggested that two of us stay and with one dog team. Well the question is, who should stay? When I left the caboose they were still trying to decide —a big discussion going on. I'm sure Larry will volunteer us. Oh well, I suppose I'll find out in the morning. I imagine Dick will handle the team.

342

Sixty-fourth Day Out – Thursday, December 19
Camp No. 48

Got up at eight this morning—cold as hell and still blowing. What a day to travel. Nothing about Mt. Grace McKinley is good. I don't think the wind ever stops blowing, although Phil and Grif said they had been having good weather. I don't know why it has to get bad the minute we arrive.

We broke camp at 11:30. Had quite a bit of reloading, and we were all a little late in finishing breakfast. I guess none of us wanted to go out and face the wind—and, of course, the wind would be blowing head on. No matter which way we travel, the wind is always right there—right in our face. I left my bags of rocks for the tractor to bring along, much to Larry's discomfort. He is afraid that the tractor will not make it and that the rocks will be lost. Well I am not worried. I know the tractor will come through all right.

Anyway, my load is considerably lighter by about 500 lbs., and the dogs moved right along. They even looked back several times to be sure I was still with them. They are pretty tired by now, and I am sure they appreciated the reduced load. We made 10 miles in the first 2 hours or so. Phil and Grif were not up when we left, but I looked in on them and said farewell and thanked them again for the good chow. The going today was tough as we had all upgrade traveling. Some of the hills or slopes were at least 2 or 3 miles long. We followed the tractor trail, which made good sledding. Joe rigged up a gee pole on his side of the sled, and he hangs on while he skis most of the day. Made 15 miles total and camped at 6 P.M. Pemmican tonight not so hot—I guess the tractor crew kind of spoiled us. Radio sked OK. Len and Dick got Christmas messages. Several of us got messages. Len and Dick stayed after radio sked, and we shot the bull till 10 P.M. Then it was time for bed. The wind is still blowing like mad—my face, I am afraid, will never be the same—burned, blistered and peeling all at once.

Sixty-fifth Day Out – Friday, December 20
Camp No. 49

Up bright and early this morning at 7:30 and no fuel in the stove, which always helps. I dressed (about froze doing it) and filled up our stove. Got the one out of the other tent and started breakfast. Len and Joe were next to appear on the scene. The sun was shining nice and bright, but we still had our friend the wind—not too much, but enough to make me want to stay in the sack. I would have slept later, but I heard a stove go on in the Survey Party tent—so thought it must be time to start the day. We got underway at 9:30—earliest yet—for our party. Made 10 miles by 12:30—going good, but up a little grade.

Being able to go in the tractor trail helps some. We got to the 90 mile cache at 10 miles and had to stop there and wait for Larry and Jack. Up until today I had been following along behind Jack, but he had to stop so much so I passed him and got hot on Dick's trail. I couldn't catch him, though, as he got too much of a head start.

I guess Joe and I arrived at the 90 mile cache about 20 minutes after Len and Dick got there. After we got the dog food, we moved on, making 8 more miles before we stopped for the mail bag program. Dick and I made camp about 3:30. The others got to camp at 4 P.M. or so. We had wonderful going after leaving 90 mile cache and made 5 miles the first hour—all down grade. We hurried and put our tent up as Larry and Gil arrived. We got set up, but no program—the darn set was dead as far as WAEO was concerned. The only station I could get WLWO, and I could hardly hear it. Of all the time not to have the program, is when my folks are going to talk—darn the luck. Also Gil's daughter, Gloria from Lawrenceburg, was to be on the program. Of course, we were both disappointed, but at least we know they got a thrill thinking we heard. The mail bag did come through with about two letters before it completely faded out. We heard Pappy fine tonight on our radio sked. He said they didn't get a signal through well enough to rebroadcast. After I signed off with him, I listened to the rest of the fellows. It appears that Earl had a friend in Indianapolis who was to be on the program. Earl didn't get the program either. Oh well, such is life. I guess Al is the only one of us trail fellows that got it. I am really tired tonight; I guess I'm getting old or something. Anyway, it's 9 P.M. and time to hit the sleeping bag. It's not fitting out, kind of half raining and snowing, and, oh yes, the wind is blowing NE 5 miles per hour. The base reports the temperature of plus 43; our temperature is plus 11.

Sixty-sixth Day Out – Saturday, December 21
Still in Camp 49

Made good time today—spent the day in our sacks and playing poker. Got up this morning, and it was snowing. The wind was blowing, and it was a whiteout; we couldn't even see the trail. In other words, it was no day to travel. After breakfast went over to the Survey tents to see if they planned to travel or what. They were all up biding their time. Dick was just getting breakfast. Well, naturally it was too bad to travel, so we all got together and played poker in our cook fly. First, though, by the time we decided what to do, it appeared time to have a bite to eat. Of course none of us had finished breakfast over an hour ago. That's the way it is though when we don't travel—well, one always has to nibble on something. We played cards till 6 P.M. and then fed the dogs. Had a radio sked OK. We all got Christmas messages, including Joe. Base kept fading out; reception was poor. It's 8:30 and time for bed as we plan to bail out of here early in the morning. Pappy said the tractor will leave tomorrow, so we ought to see them in a day or so.

Sixty-seventh Day Out – Sunday, December 22
Camp No. 50

Well we had no alternative but to travel today. The weather is still bad—snowing, visibility bad, an Antarctic white day. We could have stayed in camp another day, but there is no telling how long the bad weather might last. We might face weeks of it. Our dog food is practically gone; in fact, one party fed the last of their food to the dogs last night. I think, however, that the Survey Party had a little left.

Well, we started out. Luckily the sledding was good and by using a Brunton compass and by keeping a sharp lookout for trail flags, we were able to go along fairly well. At 16 miles Jack wanted to camp because his dogs were tired. Larry was carrying one dog on the sled; Dick and Jack had turned Blackie loose. That left him with 5 dogs. But Dick wanted to push on and so did I because it was almost imperative that we get to the 60 mile cache. I suggested that our party go on and wait for the others the next day since our dogs were in a little better condition. However Jack decided to try to make it.

We pulled into 60 mile cache about 7 P.M. after traveling 22 miles. What a wonderful feeling to know that dog food was on hand. Jack came in without Blackie. He evidently laid down somewhere en route to rest; probably he'll be in in the morning. We put up the tents. They are in a mess; all iced up. One of our tents was all torn. Len was brushing off snow and ice from Dick's tent and put a nice hole in it.

345

Well, radio sked was OK—made it short as we hadn't finished eating. This always seems to come first when you are fighting fatigue. Gil and Joe got messages. We spent most of the evening cleaning the tent.

Sixty-eighth Day Out – Monday, December 23
Camp No. 51

I hated to get up this morning; the sleeping bag was nice and warm. In fact, I slept really well for the first time in a couple of days. Weather still the same, only more of it. After breakfast we were ready to leave when we found that Len had skied back to look for Blackie to bring him back or put him out of his misery. We all stood around waiting; our feet started to get cold since we had put on wet socks, etc., so Jack put up a tent and lit a stove. He, Larry, Gil, and I sat in there and shot the breeze. Joe and Jack had started to ski after Len to keep warm. The rest of us were not that ambitious.

Len got back about noon. He reported no sight of Blackie. Evidently he died and was covered by snow or just wandered off. It's sad when this happens. They are such wonderful dogs and so very important in this early day Antarctic exploration.

We got under way finally and by the time we made 7 miles, all hands were tired. Soft snow made skiing tough. We had to drag one foot after the other. Sledding, however, was not that bad. The sun finally broke through the clouds and haze when we made camp tonight after traveling 15 miles. The sun is really shining bright and it's very clear, so maybe tomorrow we will have a good travel day.

Radio sked tonight OK, got a message from the folks. Len also got Christmas messages. Dick stayed after the radio sked and shot the bull till midnight. Paul gave the dope to Larry on the seismic station and said that he wanted Larry to remain behind and help move the gear down to Pk 105. Oh yes, when Paul talked to Larry, he told him that they planned to fly a seal out to 105. We have about 600 pounds of dog food left, which should be plenty, but the dogs will certainly enjoy the treat and it will revitalize them for the rest of the trip to Base. We could have really used the seal meat at Mt. Rea and Grace McKinley while we were snowed in. Climbing the long slopes in the mountains tired the dogs and they could have used the red meat to pep them up. We radioed in that we were short of dog food at Mt. Rea and if at all possible, send some more with the tractor when it came out to Mt. Grace McKinley. I guess Paul didn't get the message—the tractor arrived at McKinley with no dog food but with plenty of special food for the trail members that weren't dogs.

Sixty-ninth Day Out – Tuesday, December 24
Camp No. 52

Overslept this morning and didn't get up till 9 o'clock—I can't stay up night lifeing and expect to be on the ball early the next morning, so I guess we had better forego the pleasure of shooting the bull and concentrate on getting back to Base. We broke camp at 11 A.M. The weather is about the same, overcast, but the sun is visible. Funny thing, but when we made camp last night it was clear, but when Larry stuck his head out to check the weather for the radio sked, it was overcast. A fog moved in on us and covered us up rather quick like. We made pretty good time today, 4 miles the first hour, completing 16 miles in 5 hours. Dick and I wanted to go on, but we bucked rather strong opposition. Dick says that Jack and Len have to have their 18 hours in the sack.

Surface today was good, good skiing and sledding. Some soft snow about 1/2 inch thick, but not enough to interfere with our traveling. Along toward late afternoon we ran into clear weather again. It is now 10:15 P.M. and the sun is shining like a million bucks. Radio sked tonight was OK. Larry got a message. Dick sent a message to Paul saying we were in good shape as far as dog food is concerned. I added if they wanted to do something really nice, then fly us out a little Christmas chow and cheer. Pappy said if the weather was clear Pete might fly. Here's hoping!

Seventieth Day Out – Wednesday, December 25
Christmas Day   Camp No. 53

Of all the places to be on Christmas day. Oh well, we are having a nice white one anyway. That's something, I guess. Larry and I hung out stockings last night, but no luck. In fact, we had 4 pair hanging just in case. Got up this morning to a perfect day. We got under way about 11 A.M. and before we had gone 5 miles it started to cloud over. The tractor went through camp last night about midnight. I didn't get up, but Gil and Dick did. Gil said they left Grace McKinley last night after the radio sked, so they were traveling right along. We came on the tractor after traveling 10 miles. They were both asleep, but we rooted them out of their

347

sacks. They stopped because of bad visibility. Phil lost the trail. They grabbed a little breakfast and then we got under way.

Traveling was lousy—a typical white day without visibility and on top of that it started to rain a little. Of course, the wind started to blow, which added to our discomfort. The surface was soft and wet making it hard for both sledding and skiing. We got quite a ways ahead of the tractor since they were traveling in reverse. We finally made a temporary camp at 17 miles intending to travel on after a little chow and rest. Joe was with the tractor, and Gil, Larry, and I were in our tent eating our Christmas dinner, which consists of soup and an apple pudding when Joe hailed us and we opened up for him.

He told us the tractor was in a crevasse and done for. After I finished eating I went back to the tractor about a 1/4 mile from our camp—boy she was down pretty bad. Phil sent in a report to Paul saying that he thought the tractor was done for. Naturally Paul got all up in the air, excited like, because they need the tractor to help load the ships when we depart from the Antarctic. The fellows at the Base suggested flying out material to help get the tractor out of the crevasse if the weather would clear. That is a big if, because we haven't had good weather for so long it isn't even funny. Well, at first all dog teams were going on the Pk 105 and then return the following day. Then someone got the bright idea that only one team needed to go. Dick and I said we would make the trip as soon as the wind let up a bit and visibility got a little better. After it was all settled, we put up the other tents. Larry and I tethered our dogs and fed them. I then got my sleeping bag and a little army ration and went over to Dick's tent to wait for it to clear up a bit. We spent the time reading shoot 'em up stories from some magazines borrowed from the tractor. About midnight it acted like it was going to clear up so we fixed a little breakfast of oatmeal, bacon and coffee. There's one thing in this country and that is a man never wants to start anywhere hungry, and we didn't. I can assure you that I ate about 4 bowls of oatmeal.

Seventy-first Day Out — Thursday, December 26
Still Camp 53

We finally got underway about 3 A.M. traveling with only a tent, sleeping bags, a primus stove, and a little grub. We got a tent from the tractor so that we wouldn't have to take one of ours down. Dick has only seven dogs, so I took Toska and wanted

348

Yakutz from Larry's team. I asked Larry, but he did not seem to be too keen about it, although he did say it was OK. However, we didn't bother. Well we hadn't been out more than an hour when we hit a series of crevasses, with very soft bridges. In fact, our sleds sank in up to the bridges and the dogs were in snow up to their bellies. We did not have any trail flags with us, so we decided to mark the crevasses on the way back. The surface was lousy, very soft; and snow stuck to our skis and sled runners. It started to rain and sleet about halfway to Pk 105. Not to add to our comfort, the wind swung around hitting us head on. After about two or three hours, we sighted 105 and were going to ski right on in, but the surface was so bad that we had to take our skis off. We must have walked a mile. Dick said it would probably be easier on the dogs if we would ride. The surface was soft enough so that we sank in over our boot tops. In order to keep with the team, we put quite a pull on the gee poles. So we got on and rode. I don't know if it helped the dogs any, but I was certainly glad for the lift. I was about to call it quits anyway. My legs were about ready to drop off from trying to ski in glue. That's about what it amounted to. Anyway the dogs went right along although they did look back several times—kind of questionable glances—wondering what was going on. We finally made it to 105; as Dick was unharnessing the dogs, I put the tent up. Dick let his dogs run loose—they had a good time running around inspecting this and that. You see, 105 has been the stopping place for all parties and there are some interesting things for dogs, including a trash pile which we will pick up and take back to Base. Well the dogs were doing fine until they started to dig up someone's cache. It had a bag of biscuits, and the dogs made short work of them. Well, Dick collared them and that put a stop to that. We didn't waste much time in getting in our sleeping bags. After having a cup of tea, we hit the hay. We had traveled 30 miles and most of the going was bad. I know I was tired, and even Dick admitted he was.

We arrived at 105 at 6:30 A.M. after traveling 3 1/2 hours. We didn't wake up till around 3 P.M. It took us quite a while to muster up enough courage to get up. Our breakfast, lunch or whatever it was consisted of milk and eugina biscuits. We then loaded on a couple of bags of dog food and broke camp and headed back. We got underway about 5 P.M. We traveled right along, shooting the breeze and every once in a while breaking out into song.

The surface was much better and we were able to at least ski along and keep up with the dogs. We sighted what we thought was camp about 7:30 but could only see the tractor caboose. We knew that our tents were in front of the tractor. It kind of had us baffled, but when we got a little closer it was obvious they had gotten the tractor out of the crevasse and had broken camp. We got to them about 8 o'clock just as Phil was holding radio sked. Incidently they had run and were bogged down in the crevasse that we were going to mark. Oh well, it's a lot of fun anyway. Boy things were really in a mess and Phil was burning up the wire. It seems that Grif wanted to go on but Phil didn't. Phil wanted to wait for clear weather and better visibility, so they each sent a poop sheet to Paul. Paul came back saying that they ought to get to 105 as soon as possible in order to get through the crevasse area. Well, it all ended up that Paul made Len the leader of the whole shebang. Len asked Grif if he would drive. Grif said yes, and Phil said he was through; he would not drive the dang thing again. Dick and I were pretty pooped, so we decided to camp. They wanted to take my team along, but I suggested that they could easy enough put the gear that they needed that was on my sled on the tractor and let my team rest a while.

Well they got under way about 10 P.M. Dick and I fed our dogs, crawled in the tent and took things easy. We had oatmeal again with a few fried euginas. We then did some heavy reading from a few magazines we borrowed from the tractor crew. I got sleepy about 1 A.M. and called it a day. Dick was still reading when I fell asleep.

Seventy-second Day Out — Friday, December 27
In Camp at 105 Mile Cache   Camp No. 54

Woke up this morning about noon or so. I don't know what's the matter with me, but I didn't jump right out of my sleeping bag. In fact, I didn't even budge till 1 or so. Kind of lazy I guess. Well, we had a little breakfast and, of course, that consisted of oatmeal, bacon and coffee. We shot the bull awhile and read a couple more stories, (shoot 'em ups) then broke camp about 3 P.M. We headed straight through, making 105 in 2 1/2 hours, a distance of 10 miles. The boys at 105 were taking it easy. Grif, Phil, Jack and Joe were in the caboose shooting the breeze. Len, Gil and Larry were in Larry's tent doing likewise. Len broke out his Christmas quart of rum, and we all had a sip to celebrate our progress so far. Dick and I tethered our dogs, fed them and set up our tent. Larry, Gil and Joe had eaten, so I ate with the Survey Party—apple pudding, soup and tea with fried euginas, a very good meal. The only trouble was I got sucked in to clear the dishes.

The weather is still overcast, and we are getting a little wind. Radio sked was OK. I got a nice message from Alda, which helps a lot. We discussed what to do about Fitz's gear, and it was decided that all teams would go to his camp in the mountains and bring down all of his gear in one trip. Fitz said he would have everything ready. Well, that simplified everything because Larry would have had a hard time bringing everything down alone. He would have had to make at least three trips, meaning 75 miles, since it is 12 miles up to Fitz's camp. Well it's midnight and a hard day ahead, so time to turn in. Dick just stuck his head in returning clippers and soap. He looks like a new man, face all shining. I was going to wash up too, but I guess I will put it off until tomorrow or maybe till we get back to the Base.

Seventy-third Day Out – Saturday, December 28
Still Camp 105

Radio sked last night cleared up everything concerning Fitz, and we woke up bright and early to go to Fitz's camp. Well, the weather had another idea. As usual, it was snowing, raining or whatever you call it. Anyway we loafed around after breakfast waiting for it to clear up enough to get under way. We couldn't even see the mountains until about noon. We had a light lunch and by 4 o'clock the fog had broken enough to travel. Dick, Larry and I were to make the trip. We hitched up and traveled with empty sleds except for sleeping bags and one tent. I left Kusan behind as he was not feeling well. We made the 12 miles in about 2 1/2 hours. We stopped at Al and Doc's camp before going on up to Franklin Peak. It was certainly good to see Al—he looks fine. We shot the bull there for a little while and then went on up to Fitz's camp, getting there about 7 PM.

Boy what a camp! Phil had told us a little about how the boys were living, but at that he slightly underestimated things. I have never seen such a dirty mess in my life. The tent was a scene of untidiness. In fact, it was just plain dirty. In the center of the tent was a cess pool about 3 sq. ft. in size. They had dug it for their stoves. Well the warm weather took care of that. After they couldn't use it for the stoves, they started using it to dump garbage, etc. The darn thing was right by Ike's bunk, but he didn't seem to mind. He had been in his bunk for days, getting up for only a couple of hours each day. The fellows themselves were not exactly clean. Fitz had scales of dirt hanging to his face. His windproof parka was all torn. In fact, his knees were worn through. His hair was down to his shoulders, and I don't think he ever used a comb. I guess Zeke was the cleanest of all. He at least tried. I think it's all right to be a little lax on the trail, but there is a limit to everything. Of course, we were on the move all the time, but I'll have to admit that when we were weathered in things could get a little messy. I don't know what it would be like to stay in one place for 90 days like the seismic party did. Well, Fitz had a few boxes to bring from his seismic house, so we gave him a hand using Ike's man-hauling sled.

In the mean time Zeke was cooking a meal for us. He asked Dick to pass him a clean pot. Dick checked about 6 pots, but each one had food of some kind left in it—cocoa, oatmeal, pemmican, etc. There happened to be one with eggs in it—that was the clean one. Well the stew was darn good—I ate mine out of a peanut can with my knife. I couldn't quite get the courage to eat using their dishes. They hadn't washed their dishes since they had been in the mountains. I knew the can was clean because I just finished eating the nuts.

Seventy-fourth Day Out – Sunday, December 29
Reunion at 105

I held radio sked, or at least I intended to. I called the Base for about a 1/2 hour, not understanding why I was not getting through. I found that I did not have the generator connected. What a dumb trick. After our coffee we started to break camp and loaded up. We cached a lot of gear—odds and ends up at Franklin Peak. We finally got under way about midnight or so. I had a bad time getting down the glacier. My sled was all over the place, and my dogs couldn't keep their feet. A rough lock didn't do any good. I had Ike's dog Moody hitched in with my team.

We stopped at Al's camp again and he brought out some Park Square toffee—quite a treat. We left there at 1 AM. Our sleds were pretty heavily loaded, having over 1500 pounds between us. We made the first 5 miles to Ike's tent in 1 1/2 hours, all good downhill going. We stopped there for an hour or so while we dug out his tent. We also had a little lunch. We used Ike's stove to cook bacon and fried euginas. We left there about 3:30 A.M. and the going got tough. It started to snow again making it wet and sticky under foot. It was about impossible to ski—so much snow would build up under the ski that it was impossible to move. Ike was traveling with me, and we finally decided to walk a while. We did, and it was tiresome work. The surface was all right for the dogs and despite the heavy load they traveled right along. We did not put on our skis again till we were within about 2 miles of camp and starting across the crevasse area. Boy the crevasses were really open and ready to receive a dog team. We were really very lucky to get through, loaded as we were. Every time we would come to one I would hang on a rope attached to the sled but about 10 feet away from the sled, and hope for the best. The theory behind this was that if the dogs went down, I would be OK, and if I fell in, I would be attached to the sled and then could climb out. In other words we wouldn't all fall in at once. We had one good scare. The largest one we had to cross kind of cracked and creaked as we went across, but the dogs must have sensed the danger because they really pulled. After we crossed the area we took off our skis again and walked the one mile into camp, getting there about 8 A.M. Of course, the whole camp woke up when we arrived. Boy I, for one, was tired, I had been up for 24 hours and had traveled 25 miles under the worse conditions—wet sticky snow.

Well, I tethered my dogs, and as I was feeding them noticed that Kusan was not on the line—I didn't pay much attention till Jack told me he had died. Gosh, I hated that as he was a darn good dog. He had kind of a fit before he died.

Dick said that one of his dogs went the same way—probably worked themselves to death.

I fed my dogs 2 pounds of food, then ate breakfast myself. We had Fitz, Zeke and Ike in to eat. Just before I turned in, I fed the dogs another pound—they had worked pretty hard and certainly deserved that and more. Well I got to bed about 11 A.M., but couldn't sleep. I got up again at 2 P.M. because I smelled bacon frying. Joe and Gil were eating lunch or something, so I joined them. Al and Doc arrived at 105 during the afternoon. I helped them set up camp. I spent most of the afternoon reading shoot 'em ups. After a pemmican dinner, Fitz, Larry and I played a few games of hearts. Then I turned in.

Weather is still the same—we have had about 16 days of wet,

snowy weather. I can't understand it, I have always heard it didn't snow in the Antarctic—yet how did all this snow get here! Something is wrong!

Seventy-fifth Day Out – Monday, December 30
Camp No. 55

Woke up bright and early to take advantage of the good weather we hoped for. Well, that's a laugh because the weather was the same, only worse. Still snowing and wet. Our tents are actually water-soaked, and it's impossible to dry our boots and clothing. My sleeping bed is even getting soaked through. It took us some time to break camp this morning as we had to rearrange loads, etc. We got underway about 11 A.M. The tractor was to follow in an hour or so.

It was good to say goodbye to 105 for the last time. We had quite a caravan—5 dog teams and 9 men plus the tractor and 5 men. The going was pretty bum because snow stuck to our skis. I walked quite a bit but couldn't keep up with the team, so I would hop on the sled. Well, the dogs couldn't pull the additional weight or else they were just drawing the line; they would stop dead and turn around and look at me. We traveled 12 miles and that's far enough under such conditions. The tractor was in sight when we stopped for lunch, but when we made camp they had not come in.

Al held the radio sked, and I cranked the generator for him. It seems that the tractor was stuck 4 miles out of 105. The tractor couldn't move with or without the load because it was sunk clean down to the crank case. Phil wanted the dog teams to come back and pick up the loads they were carrying for us. Well, that was an impossibility because we could just barely pull our present loads. So Paul asked us to try to solve the problem. Oh, yes, Fitz and Zeke wanted to travel with the dog teams; so with their tent, food, etc. we were really loaded. So Al said we would have a conference and let the tractor know in the morning.

So we called Larry and Len over to Al's tent, and the discussion began. Dick, Jack, Doc and I were also there. After much chewing the fat pros and cons, all hands agreed on the following—that Ike, Fitz and Zeke were to join our parties, bringing with them only the bare necessities. Al wrote a note to that effect. Also, two teams would start from camp carrying equipment for 4 men to be a safety factor for Phil and Grif on the tractor. Grif and Phil would wait with the tractor, keep trying to move her, and hoping for a harder

354

surface so that they could get traction. Well, Dick took his team and left about midnight to go back after the other three. He went without a sled; the dogs pulled him on his skis. He made 8 miles in 2 hours. Al stayed up and held radio sked with Phil so that he would know of Dick's safe arrival.

Seventy-sixth Day Out – Tuesday, December 31
Camp No. 56

Well, here it is New Year's Eve. If this isn't a heck of a way to spend such an evening—in a dinky little tent, wet, snowed-in, in the Antarctic. This is the last place on this earth I expected to be. Well, all I can do is snap my fingers a couple of times and call it a celebration.

I got up this morning at 10 A.M. and went over to Al's tent to crank the hand generator for him while he sent news from the trail to the base, including last night's discussion concerning the tractor. Dick came into camp about noon with Ike. The others were just coming into sight. They were going along with packs on their backs. Old Zeke was really bushed when he arrived. They had on clean mitts, shirts, etc., and Fitz had on two suits of underwear, and Ike even had on clean mitt liners. Dick took a little nap. We then broke camp and moved on up to the 90 mile cache.

1941

I can't believe it's a new year, but it is; anyway, everyone is yelling Happy New Year around here. I woke up about 8 A.M. Larry had already started breakfast. After I had finished eating, I went over to help Al hold the morning radio sked, but they were not up. I got them up, started the stove, put on some snow for them and got things straightened around in general. Held the 10 A.M. radio sked—nothing exciting, just a report.

We broke camp at 11 A.M., and traveled 'till 4:30 P.M. making 11 miles. Going was pretty tough because of the soft snow. We could have pushed the dogs another mile or so, but there is no need of it. We hit a little wind just as we were making camp. This ought to improve the surface. If it does, we will try to make the 60 mile cache by tomorrow night.

I helped Al with radio sked tonight by cranking for him. Got a nice message from Alda. Jack was in Al's tent also, and we shot the bull for a while. It is now 10 P.M. and I just finished eating the remains of the apple pudding we had earlier. Oh yes, Al contacted Phil and Grif. They are now at 90 mile cache, and if they get any kind of break, they will join us in the morning. Here's hoping! They are traveling with a full load which sure makes me feel good.

I was awakened this morning about 7 A.M. by a big ruckus outside—the dogs were raising cain. Gil ran outside to find that a penguin had walked into camp just for a visit—an Adalie. Well, Jack skinned him tonight for Gil. I wonder what the little fellow was doing so far from the Bay of Whales. Jack said the only thing he had in his stomach was a couple of rocks.

356

Seventy-eighth Day Out – Thursday, January 2
Camp No. 58

Boy, I didn't want to get up this morning, but I guess there is no way out of it. Joe was up first and had breakfast started. We found a ration cerevim in one of the tractor's rations, so we have had a change the last couple of days. But we were back to oatmeal again this morning. I know that if anyone ever mentions oatmeal to me when I get back to the States—well, I'll be hard to get along with.

We got under way this morning at 11 A.M. as usual. Something new—the sun was shining and it was actually clear. As a result my face burns like mad. We were only able to make 9 miles today; the surface was lousy. It was so soft that the dogs sunk in up to their bellies; of course, our skis iced-up, and we had to stop and scrape them clean. Doc tried walking, but that didn't work. He held on to a line attached to Al's sled, and it took all that he had to keep up. He said he was so exhausted that he didn't have enough strength to yell for Al to stop. He couldn't keep up and if he fell Larry's team would run over him. He was a mess! I guess Al finally looked back and stopped.

Radio sked tonight OK and our last one. Al is lightening his load, so he is dropping off the radio. The tractor made 13 miles using 30 gallons of gas. The Condor is supposed to fly tonight bringing them gas. The Condor might stop at our camp.

Seventy-ninth Day Out – Friday, January 3
Camp No. 59

Well, our sun and clear weather was short lived. The Condor did manage to get in a flight last night to the tractor. But alas! No more Condor as she was forced down 10 miles this side of the tractor—a main bearing burned out or something. Mac, Paul and Walt were in the Condor; they had taken on a load from the tractor and taken off. The motor started to miss, so Walt radioed to the base to send the Beechcraft and Pappy Gray. Well, Pappy said it was a factory repair job, so that took care of the Condor. In the meantime, Paul and Pete flew over to our camp, landed and talked to Al. No one from our party got up—too cold; besides a plane landing is old stuff. I swear I have seen more airplanes since I have been down here than ever before. One is always disturbing our

357

sleep. The Beechcraft brought a couple of sacks of seal meat for the dogs. We made about 12 miles today, and arrived at 60 mile cache. I took on our dog food we had cached there and then pushed on for another mile or so. The surface started out fine, but not for long. After making about 7 miles, the going got tough again. The sleds pulled hard as Hades. I de-iced my sled runners last night, which helped some. We made camp tonight about 3:30 P.M. We got under way this morning about 9:30 AM. The plane saw to that —they paid us a visit around 6 A.M. or so. Al, Dick, Jack and Ike got up, so we decided to leave early. The rest of us were routed out with much grumbling. Paul brought us out a bottle of Scotch, which was our share of the New Year's Party back at the Base. Al gave us each a couple of fingers. I still don't like Scotch, but I drank it. I set up and tried to get the mail bag program but had no luck on the letter part. But the first part, the music portion of the program, came in fine. I just came back from a little session with Al. Boy, it's wonderful to be with him again. He says that Mac and Paul stayed with the Condor while Walt and Pappy went back to Base with Pete. Poor Mac has really had tough luck with the Condor.

Eightieth Day Out – Saturday, January 4
Camp No. 60

I remember waking up at 7 A.M. and yelling at Larry to tell him what time it was. I asked him whether we should get up or just turn over. He said turn over, and evidently we did. But I heard the other parties up and around. I managed to crawl out of my sleeping bed by 7:30 and started breakfast. Dick dropped in as we were eating just for an early morning chat. We got under way at 10 A.M. I cached my radio and lightened my load some. Going was pretty good today in places. In others the surface was like sand. Several times I thought my rough locks had dropped down the sled runners; it pulled that hard. We made a little over 13 miles today. We are camped 46.2 miles from Base. Hope to make it in 3 days. Made camp at 4:30 P.M. After eating, I fed my dogs then and went over to visit Al and Doc and had a cup of tea with them. I shot the breeze over at Al's till Larry and Jack dropped in. Gil is over at the Survey tent talking war and politics with Len, Fitz and Dick. It is now 9:30 and time for bed. We hope to make the 30 mile cache tomorrow. It will depend on the surface of the snow.

358

Eighty-first Day Out – Sunday, January 5
Camp No. 61

Woke up last night about midnight hearing Grif's voice. I thought I must have been dreaming or something. Anyway I went back to sleep—kind of turned over like and slept on. It seemed like I had hardly gotten to sleep again when I heard the motor of the tractor starting up. Well that didn't phase me; I still slept on. I had looked at my watch and it was 4:30 A.M.—too early for me to stir about. Well I finally got up at 7:30 A.M. and started breakfast.

Dick stopped in while we were eating and told us the dope. The tractor had come through camp last night, so I wasn't dreaming. They stopped at Dick's tent, and he cooked them some chow. Al, I guess, came over to visit them. Everyone seemed to hear their conversations but me. Joe said that Grif was really wound up and that he was going to take the tractor back and tell Paul to cram it. I guess both he and Phil had their fill of the tractor, and I don't blame them. I know I did; it's no fun driving that thing backwards making 1 1/2 miles per hour.

We broke camp at 10 A.M. and we got to 30 mile cache about 3 P.M. The surface was good in places. It's hard going for the dogs as they break through the thin crust of the snow. This crust is caused by the snow melting some and then freezing. My sled runners were icing up pretty bad; I had to scrape them several times. I didn't go over to Al's tent to visit tonight, figuring that he and Doc would be pretty tired, since they had their beauty sleep disturbed by the tractor's arrival last night. I started reading a detective magazine, but Fitz dropped in. It is now 10 P.M. We had quite a chat talking about our girls. Fitz hopes to get married when he gets back home. He hopes that he isn't too late. At one time they were to get married, but Fitz said he wasn't quite ready. So now maybe he has lost out. Well, I know one thing, nothing will stop me—I hope. Weather is the same today—white day with a little wind to add to our discomfort.

Eighty-second Day Out – Monday, January 6
Camp No. 62

Joe beat me to the punch this morning; he started breakfast. I wasn't overly anxious to get up, so I kind of waited around until I heard someone up. I imagine he was doing the same thing. It's a wonder we ever get up around here. We broke camp at the usual

359

time. The surface was fairly good, but we still fell through the crust. We made Fort Weiner by 3:30 P.M. It tried to clear a bit but did not meet with much success. The sun did manage to peek through for a second or two, but that was all. We turned in about 5 P.M. and got up at 2 A.M. I woke up at 2 on the dot and started breakfast, and then went around waking the other parties.

Eighty-third Day Out – Tuesday, January 7
Journey's End

We broke camp at 10 till 5 A.M. and had very good going as we traveled in the tractor trail. Made 5 miles the first hour. Well, we made our last camp last night, and what a relief to know that we will not have to eat any more pemmican. I dumped my sleeping bag at Fort Weiner. I was glad to get rid of it. It was kind of rotting away and the eider down was falling out. Well we arrived at Base at 8:30 A.M., and we rather took the place by surprise. Shirley didn't have his cameras set up, so we came in again for his benefit so that history could be recorded. We all made it back to Base safe and sound. We are all happy to be back. We finally made our way into the building for a wild reception from the "stay-at-homes." Gutanko didn't let us down as he soon had a fine meal prepared, and we sat down to a feast, unheard of on the trail— fried steak, eggs, bread, jam and mugs of hot coffee. We had traveled round trip to the Edsel Ford Mountain Range, a distance of 796.2 miles, plus the extra skiing we did in the mountains. I don't think I'll want to get on skis again for a while.

The time between January 7th when we returned to the Base from our summer field work was spent resting, getting our clothes in order and in general, polishing up. With the ships due soon, we had to get ready to break camp, and the items that the Admiral said had to be returned to the States. The Base was to be permanent but when England entered the war in 1939-40 that changed the situation for the Antarctic exploration.

Tuesday, January 14, 1941

Just a week ago today and we were returning to good old Little America. Boy, what a busy week this has been. The *Bear* arrived Friday afternoon about 5:30 and we have been on the go ever since —not working but visiting, etc. Some of the crew have been here every night for a dinner and a show. Some of our fellows have spent the night there. Walter and I went down with my team to meet the *Bear*. Several of the fellows took their teams down also. Dick took Shirley and his camera outfit down but when we all got there the *Bear* was already alongside the ice. Boy, it certainly was exciting to see new faces. Some of the fellows I remembered, but most of them were strangers. It was good to see Frank Pawley, Chief Engineer, again. We had quite a talk and of course he kidded me about my nose. I don't blame him, because it's a sight—all red and peeling. Capt. Crusan remembers me and was very friendly. In fact, he invited me to dinner. Boy, what a meal. He actually had lettuce and tomato salad, which was a real treat.

Talk about mail, wow—there was plenty of it. I took a load on my sled and Frank D. rode back to base with me. Walt tried to hold on the back but the going was too rough down on the pressure bay ice, so he skied alongside till we got to the bottom, then he held on again. Quite a few of the crew came up so we had a show. It was about 10:00 P.M. before we got around to showing it, "Dodge City." Sig did not serve an evening meal but there was plenty of steak cut, so steak sandwiches were very much in evidence. The *Bear* crew really scooped up the coffee. I guess they were kind of tired of Navy coffee, which from what I hear is pretty punk. Well, by the time everyone cleared out of here and it got a little quiet it was about 2:30 A.M. Buck started up the tractor and took the *Bear* fellows down to the edge of the barrier, which saved them some steps.

I hadn't even looked at my mail, so as soon as the lights were low and everyone was re-reading their mail I started on mine. It took a little while to get the letters in order, then picked those I didn't know first. Got a nice letter from Jim S., who also sent me a pipe and tobacco. He said that by now probably my pipe smelled and tasted like hell and also that I might like a change of tobacco. Well, I got a little sidetracked from reading, and decided to open the rest of my packages. Enough funnies to last all the way home, and I certainly appreciate the *Readers Digest*. And of course, food is always tops with me. I was going to put off reading Alda's letter till last but couldn't stand the suspense any longer. She sent three pictures of herself taken at Chatanqua. Mother's letter gave me all the news from home. Well, I kind of spread the letters over four days, just finishing the last news tonight. Didn't do much today, only made two trips to the barrier cache. I intended to go to the *Bear* during the afternoon but she was out in the bay—more ice breaking out. I put Tongas in the tunnel tonight. His eyes seem to be bothering him a bit so I thought a little darkness would help clear them up.

Wednesday, January 15

Was awakened this morning about 6:00 A.M. by hearing Nib cursing at the pups. I found out at breakfast time that Club Foot Lucky jumped up, putting his front feet on Nib's shelf by his bunk. Well, when feet as big as Lucky's are in the near proximity of something, something is bound to happen, and it did. He knocked over Nib's ash can, dumping ashes right in Nib's face. Nib said he didn't know what had happened. Didn't get back to sleep as the two pups played, romping up and down the barracks. Clay got word this morning that the *Bear* was tied up again so I went down taking some mail and odds and ends for various fellows around camp. The ice has gone out of the bay about five hundred yards, beyond our cache of last year. I left the dogs on the barrier and skied down to the ship. Paul, Nib and Pete were there getting ready to climb the Jacob's ladder. The *Bear* was nose in. Wallace was on watch but he opened up the mail room for me. It was just about noon so I stayed for lunch. Spent the afternoon working on my clothing, repacking personal gear, etc. We had a show tonight as quite a few of the fellows from the *Bear* were up. Showed "St. Louis Blues" again.

Thursday, January 16

Red letter day—spent all day in my bunk. Woke up at 5:00 A.M. this morning with cramps in my stomach. I was feeling pretty miserable by 9:00 o'clock so Doc said I had better stay in bed. I slept off and on all day, didn't eat anything all day. I still don't know what the trouble was. Maybe it was my meanness coming out. I am afraid I have acquired quite a few bad habits which I will have to break, such as cursing. I am afraid that my speech has taken a slight trend toward being crude. It will certainly be a pleasure to get back and start associating with ladies and gentlemen again. Not that some of these fellows aren't gentlemen, but some of our topics of conversation aren't exactly parlor-type. And it has been worse since the sailors have been around. They are downright crude and there is no getting around it.

Friday, January 17

Felt much better today. Went down to the *Bear* this morning after Dr. A to Z. He wanted to come up and help Doc Frazier work on Doug's toes, seems like another one has to come off. Took it kind of easy during the afternoon. Packed a little more, then shaved, washed and prepared to spend a nice joyous later afternoon listening to the mail bag. Well, as usual, the thing came in fine—the whole program—till it got to our letters. I think I got three. From whom, I'm not sure. Too much static.

January 18

(*Star* sailed from Dunedin)

January 21

Boy, what a time I am having keeping up in my writing, if one wants to call it writing. Anyway, four days slipped by and I'm trying to think what all happened Saturday. The dog teams hauled down to the barrier, unloading at the cache as the *Bear* was not ready to take our cargo.

Sunday was sort of a holiday—that is, for general work done all hands were to pack their personal gear. The ice in the bay has been going out steadily. Capt. Cruson keeps fifty percent of the crew on hand because the *Bear* has to pull away from ice quite often.

Monday, yesterday, *Bear* sent up a working crew. Mac divided the fellows up into parties. Some worked digging a ramp from the machine shop, others helped pack, etc. Dog teams hauled from the barrier cache to the *Bear*. My dogs were certainly full of pep. I loaded the sled as much as eight hundred or nine hundred pounds, hoping to kind of settle them down. No good. They literally walked away with the load. Tipped over once going down off the barrier onto the bay ice. Myrra saw a seal and went off a little half cocked. Results—I had to unlash and reload. I was kind of angry—in fact, I was plain burned up, but I counted to ten a couple of times and cooled off a bit. Coming back from the ship empty, Pete and I were on the sled, and as luck would have it another seal crossed our path. Before I could do anything about it all my dogs were on the seal. What a mess! Boy, I have never seen a seal move as fast as this one. He scattered the dogs like flies. Poor Kotik got a slap on the side of his head and I guess it's no fun getting slapped by a seal tail, especially an excited seal. Well, I had a hard time keeping them under control the rest of the day. They would want to make for every seal they saw.

We have had movies every night so far, but tonight no soap. Douglas went down to the ship today, excuse: better medical attendance—?? Some of us know better.

Spent all day today packing and working in the clothing cache. I sent down two boxes for the Admiral's personal attention. Pappy Gray worked with me. We finished up in the afternoon and sent all of my clothing boxes down to the barrier by the tractor, therefore closing the clothes cache officially.

The *Star* was seven hundred and thirty-five miles at noon.

Wednesday, January 22

Worked all day packing my gear. The *Bear* crew was not up, so things were practically at a standstill. More ice breaking out, so the *Bear* was out in the bay. The *Star* was five hundred and thirty-five miles today at noon. Made only two hundred miles yesterday, she must be hitting a little pack ice. Tonight worked on my navigation, getting them all ready to go. I developed all of the film I took while on the trail—turned out fine. Phil made some ice cream tonight, a Feranto special, very good, a kind of chocolate vanilla combination.

Thursday, January 23

Yes, sir! Just a year ago tomorrow since the *North Star* sailed, and from latest reports she will be in tomorrow by noon. Boy, I hope I get a lot of mail. We are supposed to start a new ruling today—breakfast at 8:00, lunch at 12:00 and dinner at 6:00 o'clock. But someone slipped up. Sig did not wake up, so we had breakfast and lunch together at noon. I worked all afternoon on my rocks. Al, H.H. and I have been feeding our dogs after dinner—Al and I cut while H.H. wields the axe. Kind of excited, can't believe it possible that the *Star* will be in tomorrow.

Friday, Saturday, and Sunday

I don't seem to be able to keep up with this thing and it would be a shame to stop now as I have written something almost every day. Well, I got up bright and early Friday morning all set to meet the *Star*. First we had reports she would be in at noon, then 3:00, and finally she arrived at 7:00. Well, I guess I entered into the spirit of things a little too much. It seems that Grif had some kind of punch, and I had a few, which kind of put me away. I'd rather not talk about it. Anyway, I was determined to hitch my dogs and meet the ship regardless, so I went out. I got as far as Myrra and that is all I remember—sick. Paul later in the evening returned with two registered letters containing bank drafts. We showed half of the newsreels brought down by the *Star*. Wilkie is a nice-looking fellow, he'll probably be our next president.

Saturday I went down to the *Star* to get my mail. Was surprised at the number of packages, etc. It was good to see all of the fellows, but so many strange faces. Most of the deck crew was new, as was the galley force. Spent the day hauling food from the barrier to the ship. Hard work. I was really tired when the day was done. Ate both meals aboard the *Star*. How nice to sit at a table, a properly set table with cloths and all. I had to stop and think which knives and forks to use. Had a wonderful lettuce and tomato salad. Didn't get a chance to read my letters till night, but I had quite a time. It's so wonderful to hear from Alda, from home, and to get packages. Oh, yes, and Mrs. Sibley wrote a nice letter. Everyone had been so nice to me. I am saving all my eats for on the boat when we sail.

Sunday, but I didn't realize it till just now. It's so hard to keep track of the days. I feel so ashamed—I will have to attend church regularly when I return. Worked all morning getting butter, toweling, matches, etc., out of the caches to be used aboard ship. Got down to the *Star* about 11:30 or so, just in time for lunch. We had chicken and baked ham. I took the ham as I am a little tired of chicken. After dinner went back to base and got another load of butter, ham and frozen eggs, carrying about eight hundred pounds or so on the sled. Spent the rest of the afternoon hauling hydrogen bottles, etc., from the barrier to the *Star*. Ate evening meal aboard the *Star*, then brought Court and Charlie back to the base with the team. Al and I unhitched and fed my dogs. Show tonight for some of the *Bear* fellows and the *Star*. But just as we were getting well along in the second newsreel, Gil interrupted saying that all *North Star* men were wanted aboard. Ice must be getting ready to break out. Main picture was "Ex Champ"—still good. It is now 12:30 and time for bed.

Monday, January 27

Didn't do much today but finish packing personal gear. Both ships were out in the bay. The bay ice is breaking up badly. I went down with Nib on the tractor, taking the last of the clothing boxes. The place had broken out and a high ground swell was working and breaking more out. We had chicken for dinner tonight. I don't know what the occasion was. After dinner who should come into camp but Snooks. And boy, was she glad to get back. Pete and some others immediately took off in the plane following her tracks, hoping to find the rest of the dogs. After an hour's search, no luck. They did land to pick up Bursey, who had skied quite a ways out toward Amundsen's Arm. They found the place where Snooks had spent the night—forty-five miles out. She apparently had chewed through and worked loose from her harness. All she had was the collar. Perk says that he did not use a neck line on her, maybe that accounts for her getting away safely. Anyway, we were all glad to see her, especially Perk, and I know he was happy. I gave her a good feed. Perk's dogs had been gone since Friday (except Snooks). They broke loose while he was fastening his skis prior to going down to meet the ship. Gil just came in, saying the *Star* hopes to be tied alongside early in the morning, so that means work. It is now 12:30 A.M.—time for sleep.

January 28, 29 & 30

Well, I slipped up again. Here I am, three days late again. But we've been pretty busy—that is, a few of us. I swear, I don't know where thirty-three men manage to hide, especially when there is work to be done. Anyway, the same few are doing the work, the dog drivers, and Nib driving the tractor. Petras is very busy taking fellows up in the Beechcraft—hard work. As far as Wells, so far all I have seen him do is ski back and forth from the base to the *Bear*— managing, of course, to hit the *Star* in time for meals. Al is still in bed with his back, kind of a lumbago, while Mac's back still bothers him (he sprained it a few days ago). Well, I've quit trying to figure it out. Just work and say nothing. Got a big surprise Tuesday, I got more mail. Some wonderful sweet letters from Alda.

January 31

This has been our busy day—at least Jack B. and I have been on the go all day. Can't quite get used to hearing a bell in the morning to announce breakfast. Kind of miss the pan the boys used to beat on the back of at base. Jack and I spent the morning working in the forward hold looking for boxes, rearranging, etc. After lunch we put all the dog kennels on the poop deck, getting ready to take the dogs aboard. After that we found out that there was still some radio gear on the barrier edge that hadn't been hauled down. Well, both Jack and I squawked because we were all set to haul it down to the *Bear*, in fact one load did go down, but they said they weren't taking any spare radio parts so we hauled it back. Nevertheless, after much hemming and hawing, Jack and I said we would hitch up and bring the stuff down. Incidentally, today has been a miserable day. Wind blowing like mad, probably only twenty or twenty-five, but still uncomfortable. We no sooner had the radio gear down to the *Bear* when the tractor came from base with a load of personal gear and mattresses, so we hauled that down then we called it a day, our work with the expedition done. We brought our dogs and sleds aboard and we were all set to go. Sent messages to Alda and the folks, as follows: "Letters and pictures wonderful and please send more Valparaiso, arrive by March 15."

Earl also brought his dogs aboard. I guess it won't be long before all hands are aboard. We get underway by noon tomorrow. The Beechcraft does not come aboard till tomorrow morning, so that the boys can get in their February flight pay. Held up the whole expedition just for that. It is now 9:00 o'clock, a little early for bed. Oh, yes, partially heard the mail bag program today, got letters from the folks. Nothing is wrong.

February 1

I just received a message from Alda and she is well. I was a little worried for a while. Then, too, the fellows kidded me, saying that they had heard a mail bag letter from her saying she was getting married. Naturally I didn't believe it, but——. Had quite a bit of excitement last night. Just as the last of the gear from camp was being loaded aboard, the bay ice started to break away and move fast. Dick just got his team across in time. The *Bear* crew let our stern line free as none of the *Star* sailors could get to it. The *Bear* made a turn around the bay while the *Star* stayed nose to. It didn't take long for the ice to clear away so the *Bear* came back in nose to, while the *Star* crew dug more dead men so as to tie alongside again. I got some good shots of the whole thing—I hope. This morning, as usual, up bright and early, 7:00 o'clock. We are on water rations, which means the water is turned on only twice a day, 7:15 A.M. to 7:45 A.M., and 4:30 to 5:00 o'clock P.M. So there is quite a mad scramble to wash. Ten men washing and shaving in a half-hour or so while the rest of the fellows were helping bring down the Beechcraft.

It didn't take long to bring her aboard. Charlie S. (the first mate) certainly knows his stuff. He set her down over the aft well deck hatch just as pretty as you please. Right now she is all secured and the wings are off. We got Dick's, H.H.'s and Larry's dogs aboard and by 11:30 all hands, dogs and gear were aboard, except Paul, who was over at the *Bear*. So the Captain set the sailing time for 1:00 o'clock P.M. and sounded a few blasts just to let Paul know we were getting ready to leave. Well, I still can't believe it, but we actually sailed, saying goodbye to the Bay of Whales and the Antarctic. The *Bear* got away a little before we did, but we soon overtook her. Got some beautiful shots of the *Bear* alongside the barrier, West Cape. As we passed the *Bear* we gave her a three-blast salute, to which she responded in kind. Boy, the cameras were really busy—the U.S. Photographic Expedition. I swear, every member has one camera at least, some have two or three. Well, it is now 10:00 o'clock P.M. and we are nose in at Discovery Inlet. Perk got some penguins and seals. Did not have much luck at West Base, so the Captain and Paul decided to try Discovery Inlet, which is seventy-five miles from Bay of Whales. I think Perk got a dozen penguins or so.

February 4

Missed February 2 and 3, but nothing important really has happened. Got my sea legs surprisingly fast this time. We had our first show in the *Star* theater on the second. I was going to attend, but after taking care of my dogs I climbed up in my bunk and didn't wake up till 9:30 P.M. However, I did make the one last night, "The Awful Truth," which makes about the tenth time I have seen it. Still good, though.

I don't do much during the day but eat and sleep. After breakfast I let my dogs out of their kennels for a little exercise, and water them. That takes me till about 10:00 o'clock A.M., then I crawl in my bunk for a little nap. After lunch usually spend some time shooting the bull in the social hall. Capt. Lysted brought down about a year's supply of *Life* magazines. These have kept us busy for the last two days. Well, it seems that I get a little sleepy about 3:00 P.M. and have to crawl in my bunk till time for dinner. I don't spend all my time sleeping, but read a little, and have started a letter to Alda—a nice fat one. Time 8:00 o'clock P.M. We just passed Scott Island, took several pictures. Our course since leaving Discovery Inlet has been a little N. of N.W., but from Scott Island we are to head east toward East Base.

February 5

Was awakened by the 7:00 A.M. bell. One of the waiters walks around the deck ringing a bell, announcing in a casual voice, "First call for breakfast." That's all I have to hear, I jump right out of bed. After breakfast, let my dogs out for their morning exercise, then watered them and washed down the deck. Oh, I forgot to mention that we have moved all of the dogs from the poop deck to the aft well deck. We have the kennels stacked three high and keep the dogs in their kennels all the time except for twice a day. Morning and night we take them out for exercise and to feed them. The dogs seem much happier in their kennels. It kind of acts as a support when the ship rolls. Then, too, it keeps them dry, and that is the thing they like.

Worked down in the forward hold between decks, moving boxes around, getting things stored. After lunch I shot the bull in the social hall for a while, then spent the afternoon reading in my bunk. Al came in late in the afternoon just before dinner, so we had some of the cookies Howard sent down—darn good. We had very fine lamb chops for dinner. After dinner took care of my dogs, had them all out and was talking with Al. (The engine had stopped while we were eating dinner.) All of a sudden, oil splattered out of an oil jet located on the aft well deck. Boy, we had our hands full the next few minutes getting the dogs in their kennels, oil all over the deck. Luckily I got mine all in okay, but Dick's got fairly much oiled, and I don't mean drunk (clever).

Well, for the next hour or so, Larry, Dick, one of the crew and myself were hosing down the deck, trying to get the oil cleaned up. What a mess. Prior to the stopping of the engines, black smoke was coming from the stack. Later found out from the Chief that the oil was too cold and would burn or something, and the oil that we got on the well deck was thrown out of the engine. Sea is very calm, just a little swell and roll. Makes one very sleepy. Last couple of days we have seen quite a few whales—mammoth things, Blue whales. Also wandering albatross. We have come one thousand and thirty-seven miles since leaving the base. Did not encounter any ice pack. Have seen a few large icebergs. Earl is in the sick bay again with the same trouble he had during the winter nights. Nothing exciting or of interest has happened. Aboard a ship, life is pretty monotonous—just eat and sleep. Gosh, I hate to think that we have two months of this. Well, I'll just take it easy as there is nothing else to do.

February 6

Up bright and early this morning, 7:00 A.M., although when I woke up because of the bell, my watch said 6:00 A.M. It's funny, I didn't realize that they set the time back an hour. Spent most of the day in my bunk. Slept some and read some, a really tough day. Sea is still fairly calm. The sun hasn't been out for four or five days. Show tonight was "St. Louis Blues," which I saw again for the seventh time, still like it.

February 7

Not much happens on board. We did have one fire drill which rather broke the monotony of travel. I'm afraid I'll never make a sailor because I just don't like the do-nothingness of the sea. Everywhere you look there is nothing but water. Perk and Chuck made a tank for Perk's seals. That's exactly what they wanted. They have a great time playing around in the pool. There are six crab eaters and one Ross. The pool is right by H.H.'s porthole, which looks out on the aft well deck. Every once in a while a seal will stick its head in the porthole and sound off. Jack said if he were a drinking man he'd change his brand, at least. After taking care of my dogs this morning I climbed up in my bunk for a slight nap.

The old ship is really making the knots, about twelve plus. We have the steering engine right next to our compartment. It is right noisy and the screw vibrates something terrible. But outside of that, it is nice and quiet down here. It's starting to get dark—gosh, it seems funny to have day and night again. I rather like it. Show tonight was "Holiday," but I didn't go. It is now 12:30, time for bed.

February 8–13

We have all been sick due to taking cold shots, plus bad weather. We've had very heavy seas and the *Star* has been bouncing around like a cork. Roll and pitch, then heave and wiggle. Couldn't keep anything on the tables. Everything that was supposed to be in place just wasn't. Had my fourth shot today and although my arm is a little sore I now feel no other effect. Thank goodness only one more shot to go, then I'm supposed to be immune to any cold. The sea is much calmer today. What a relief to be able to walk without falling all over the place.

We are now getting close to Peter the First Island and will be at East Base by noon Saturday. From what the Captain says, East Base is still iced in and that we will probably have to lay outside till as late as March 1. It is impossible to go farther till Marguerite Bay starts to open up. At present there are thirty miles of sea ice. There has been some talk of putting into the Magallanes before we get to East Base.

Took my last cold shot this morning and it made me sick. I was in my bunk the rest of the day. At midnight we are still traveling toward East Base and should see land by tomorrow noon. I still hope we go to Magallanes. Not much going on our shipboard. Watered and exercised my dogs. They are always glad to get out of their kennels. The rough seas are particularly hard on them.

February 16 (Sunday)
I was awakened this morning about 6:30 when the ship engine was slowed down. There is such a vibration when we go full speed that when the ship runs slow, we all kind of wake up. Looked out the porthole to find that we were entering a light ice pack—hence the reason for slowing down. I washed, dressed and went topside. Saw quite a few seals sleeping on the pancake ice, also a couple of whales. We had fried bread for breakfast.

After lunch it started to rain. It's hard to believe, and it's wonderful. I stood out on the deck for a while and got soaked. Of course, the water's a little cold, but it's still rain and that's something. We have been passing quite a few large icebergs, some of them have the most grotesque shapes. We have been running at half speed all day due to the rain, fog, etc. So we won't get to East Base till in the morning—skipper says about 8:00 o'clock. Have to get up bright and early so I can take some pictures. I have some good shots, and so far I must have at least one thousand five hundred negatives. Fed and exercised my dogs. The show tonight is "Joy of Living." After the show I read a while, not long because the light in the "Glory Hole" is so bad that I always get a headache.

February 17 (Monday)
I am on mess duty today, which means I wait on tables. Since so many fellows are aboard and the galley force is rather small, the expedition personnel have to take one day of washing dishes and one day of waiting tables. Not much work to it and I especially like it because I get seconds on dessert, which happens to be cherry pie. If I only had some ice cream to put on it. Luckily we are not underway or I am afraid that I would have trouble walking and carrying dishes, but we have been standing by since last night at the

371

edge of the sea ice which is around East Base. The Captain said that we are ninety miles from base and I heard him tell one of the other officers that from a plane eight thousand feet over East Base they could see nothing but ice. So I don't know what we will do. What we need is a good east wind to blow the ice out, but at present the sea's as calm as a mill pond. I hope we don't have to lay here for three weeks.

Played hearts most of the afternoon—Larry Warner, myself, Roger Hawthorn (publicity man), Perkins, Al Wade, and Earl Lockhart. Quite an exciting game, but after all, our recreation is limited. I suppose by the end of three weeks we'll all be cutting out paper dolls. I wish we'd get started. The old steering motor noise and the screw motion or vibration was music to my ears, but now silence, and very depressing. There are quite a few icebergs around—all of them so odd-shaped. Our two hundred and twenty-four foot ship seems small by comparison. It's late and time for bed. I have to wash dishes tomorrow.

February 18 (Tuesday)

We are still laying outside the ice, no steering or screw noise, and most of the fellows in the "Glory Hole" are asleep. The ship is rocking gently and all is well. Up to now we do not know exactly where we are. The sun hasn't been out so they could take a sighting. We are somewhere near East Base but seem to be drifting to the southeast.

February 19–21 (Wed., Thurs., Fri.)

I wish the ice would hurry and break out so that we could go in, get the East Base fellows and get sailing again toward home.

The engines just started and the ship is moving. Must have drifted in too close to the ice pack. Boy, are my hands ever clean—washing dishes wasn't so bad. Slept most of the afternoon and tonight played a little rummy till 9:30, then had to go help set out the lunch for the fellows. From 9:30 P.M to 10:30 P.M. is lunch hour and the dishwasher and waiter for the day has to put out food and clean up afterward. I did justice to a couple of roast beef sandwiches and some hot tea. As I was coming back to the "Glory Hole," Keela, one of my dogs, was loose. I had a hard time finding her, but got her back in the kennel again. She was curled up in a dark corner and didn't budge when I called her.

372

February 21 (19th & 20th)

The reason for not writing, for missing a couple of days, was because of rough weather. We have had heavy seas and a forty-five mile wind. It's been so rough you can't sit in a chair, can't walk, stand up or anything. The only safe place is in your bunk, then it is necessary to hold on or be thrown out. We have had the damndest weather—first it rains, then it snows a bit, then, of course, the ever-present wind lends to the discomfort, plus the ship rolling and tossing. It wouldn't be so bad if we were going somewhere, but here we are just going back and forth in slow speed. Waiting, waiting. Boy, I know if we have to wait much longer, a few members of the U.S. Antarctic Service *will* be cutting out paper dolls. I probably won't be far from it. We've been twenty-one days at sea. The irony of it all is that we need a wind to blow the ice out, move it out, but the wind is from the wrong direction. That's fate, I guess.

We have been cruising back and forth trying to find an opening in the ice. One day we will be fifty miles from East Base, then the next, one hundred and seventy miles to the north. Most of the time we are running slow speed, and it's usually snowing. There isn't much to do aboard. We play some cards, ranging from bridge, gin rummy, hearts, and even poker or cribbage. I am afraid I will have to learn a better game of bridge, or else I'm afraid I will have some sore ankles or shins or something.

February 22 (Saturday)

It is 7:30 A.M. and George Washington's birthday. I'd better hurry or I will miss breakfast. We have a bunch of chow hounds aboard this ship and if you're late, no food. After breakfast I took care of my dogs, then played gin till noon. After lunch got caught up in some geology reading, then fell asleep till dinner time (busy, huh!). When I woke up, looked out the porthole—lo and behold, mountains, land ho! We were apparently just cruising around and as the ice would break out we could get a little closer to land. And for some reason the usual haze lifted, the sun came out for a while, and there was land. Beautiful mountains. Adelaide Island, probably. I took a few pictures, then got in an argument as to the height of the mountains and our distance from them. Well, nothing has been settled yet and probably never will be. But the height ranges from four thousand feet to six thousand feet, and the distance from five miles to thirty miles. We even had the high-powered mathematicians working on it. I don't know what was decided. Anyway, it helps pass the time. It's not that any of us really cares too much.

The 9:30 P.M. lunch was a huge success as far as I was concerned. Two cups of tea, roast beef sandwiches, pickles, onions, and oh, yes, two jelly sandwiches. I don't guess I was really hungry.

February 23 (Sunday)

It's now 1:00 o'clock Sunday night. The sun was actually shining this morning when I got up. We are still standing by near Adelaide Island. The mountains show up much better so I took some more pictures, and also of some high bergs. Was surprised to see the *Bear* this morning. I thought they were kidding when they yelled down that the *Bear* was in sight. She came over to us, stood by for about fifteen minutes or so, then sailed away to the east. Going exploring, I suppose. Anyway, she left and nothing was said to any of us as to what was what. Most of us don't know what is going on other than we're waiting. We have no official "poop sheet" which gives us information. Our only source is the "grapevine."

After taking care of my dogs I went down in the hold and got out some clothing which was ordered for use aboard ship. Some khaki shirts and pants, shoes and socks. Gilmour and Richardson helped me and we finished by noon. It did my heart good. Some of the fellows started to squawk on the size they were given, but I broke out my "poop sheet" and showed them that they got the very sizes they asked for. Boy, there was much gnashing and gnawing of teeth, because there wasn't anything they could do. It was all down in black and white, and in their own handwriting.

February 24–25

Up bright and early, after breakfast I exercised and fed my dogs. This chore happens every day, regular as clockwork. At present we are underway. It has been quite foggy and hazy, and I do not think they are quite sure of our position. We left Adelaide Island yesterday after a radio contact with the *Bear* for Port Lockray, where we were supposed to anchor and await favorable ice conditions at East Base. Lockray is about two hundred and fifty miles from Adelaide Island. We got up with the *Bear* last night and stayed alongside in the vicinity of Victor Hugo Island where we saw quite a few rookeries of penguins.

This morning, the twenty-fifth, we must have gotten underway quite early because at breakfast time we were moving at slow speed. The *Bear* was a little ahead of us and she didn't seem to be under-

374

way at all. Apparently a radio contact or something. Sure enough, Paul came in the social hall and told Al that we were going on to Deception Island. Captain Kusan did not want to take a chance on Port Lockray, as there was quite a bit of ice there. He was afraid that we might get stuck there, frozen in. So by the time I was taking care of my dogs at 9:00 A.M. we were underway again full speed for Deception Island, while the *Bear* turned back toward East Base to keep an eye on the ice there. The reason we want to tie up or anchor is so that we can save oil. So far, just messing around starting and stopping, etc., we use a thousand gallons a day. There are only twenty-five thousand gallons aboard. Well, I've just about given up hope of our ever heading north.

After dinner tonight I fed the dogs and watched Perkins try to catch some penguins which were swimming around the ship—no luck. We are now standing by for the night. Where, I don't know. Toward late afternoon it started to get cloudy and foggy, and since they were not exactly sure of the course, they stopped. One would think we were traveling under secret orders. Who knows? Maybe we are. Played a little cribbage tonight, got beat by Richardson. I have just learned how to play the game. It's quite fun but I still am rather slow at it.

I walked around the deck for a while before heading for bed. A most beautiful night, stars and all, but a little cool. Al just informed me that he heard from Washington, and Larry and I will be paid for the summer months upon our return in order to make up our material collected while in the Antarctic. $500.00 for three months—not bad!

Wednesday, February 26

Up for breakfast and then the usual card game in the social hall. Larry Warner, Al Wade, Fitz Simmons and myself have been playing a game called "Sorry." Kind of a screwy card game, but it passes the time. We have had a change of plans. We were going to Deception Island, but we are now anchored in Melchoir Bay. A very beautiful place. It's a natural harbor surrounded by a network of snow-covered islands and mountain peaks. The place is teeming with wildlife—all kinds of birds, gulls, whales, seals, penguins, and even seaweed.

After lunch today took a little excursion in the ship's launch. We visited several of the islands on the pretense of finding, or rather searching for water, which according to the chart is supposed to be found here—fresh water. If we find it we will be able to fill our tanks, then we can all have a good shower. Well, after visiting two islands we are getting ready to go ashore on another island to get some penguins. The third mate, Jack Rattle, jumped from the bow of the boat, and having on rubber boots, slipped and fell in. Outcome and results, a dislocated shoulder. So that put an end to this excursion. Boy, we were certainly scared for a few minutes and it was lucky that a couple of fellows were right there to pull him out because he had on very heavy clothing. You can bet your life we are all going to be more careful.

Just after we left the *Star* it started to snow and get pretty foggy. Not a very good day to look around anyway. I don't think the sun ever shines down in this neck of the woods. Twenty-six days, and the sun has only been seen once. And then for only an hour or so. Spent the rest of the afternoon reviewing a structural geology book. Tonight messed around in general, shooting the bull, playing a little cards, and, of course, eating a bit.

Thursday, February 27

Had a busy day today. After feeding my dogs we departed at 9:00 A.M. for Gallows Point, an island about one-fourth of a mile from the ship, where (so the story goes) a man was hung for mutiny on a whaler. The island was a pretty good place for geologizing. Larry, Al and I got some interesting specimens. Paul collected lichens, algae, plants, etc. Of course, Perkins, our biologist, ran down some more penguins, getting eleven ring-neck penguins. He had a heck of a time getting them, and when he did, several bit him. He also got three or four shats (shot them), a bird which looks something like a goose, plus Antarctic gulls, etc. There are quite a few old rusty barrels on the beach, full of water. The whalers that left them must have gone to a lot of trouble to get them there. Of course, the water was no good, that is, we wouldn't drink it. Yet in an emergency, well, who knows. I did most of my collecting along the shore getting samples of sand, shell, clams, limpets, snails, etc. We had quite a good time. It was wonderful to set foot on good, solid ground. I guess about eight or ten of us went ashore.

After lunch we went to a place where the Captain and Chief Engineer had been in the morning. They found water there, enough so that we could fill the tanks. I have never seen anything quite as scenic and beautiful as the views around these islands. High mountains, rugged peaks, and just about every color imaginable.

We have been doing our traveling around the bay in the motor launch, and while some of the fellows were setting the hose ready and building up a dam so the water would accumulate faster, some of the others took the launch and looked for seals. Al, Larry and I looked over the rock outcrops. We got back to the *Star* about 5:00 o'clock. Had pretty rough going as a little squall had come up and was tossing the launch around like it was a matchbox. Incidentally, I got soaked to the skin.

Saturday, March 1

Listened to the mail bag last night but got no messages. Yesterday we did a little more island-hopping. They moved the *Star* to get it a little closer to the water hole, tying up a stern where a whaler, *Sivilla*, had been tied up at one time. The ship's name is painted on a rock, and the chain they used is still around the rock. The bow of the *Star* is being held by both anchors. While they were moving the ship, I spent the morning working with Larry and Jack Bursey on arranging the dogs. The kennels were too flush with the deck and were not getting the proper drainage, so we had to build a platform, etc. We did quite a good job and can keep the deck much cleaner.

After lunch took the scow and launch over to the water hole for the first load of water. We are carrying the water in an empty lifeboat which will hold about twelve hundred gallons. Quite a few of us went along, spending the afternoon messing around ashore while the ship's crew made several trips with water.

Today we planned to work on an island called Tripod, which is at the entrance of the bay, but it was and is raining, so we called the trip off. Instead, they hauled more water. After lunch, Al, Larry and myself were dropped off at a small island en route to the water hole. He worked the island, finding some sort of iron ore vein, so I got a few samples from the beach. When they brought up the anchors prior to moving to the water hole, I got some bottom samples (mud) and after washing it up hope to find some foraminifera. There is so much to do, it seems like I get to bed later every night.

Sunday, March 2

A gloomy day, it has been raining hard all day, but it's wonderful. Also wonderful—I took my first shower in over a year. A real shower where water runs over you! The Chief Engineer was a man of his word in that if we found fresh water he would keep it on as long as we were anchored and the water could be replaced. Before, he discouraged showers by removing the shower head and the turn-on handle.

We were supposed to go work the island Tripod today, but the rain kind of fixed that up. We were going to stay all day, taking our lunch with us. I spent the morning doing a washing, which I badly needed to do. We are not wearing the heavy winter underwear now, and the lightweight feels funny, like half undressed.

Monday, March 3

We have been out to sea for thirty-one days. Of course, it's not so bad now since we are anchored in a sheltered bay, but still, it's bad enough when one wants to head north. We had our all-day outing today, getting started about 9:00 o'clock. We went to Lambda Island, near the entrance to the bay. The whole bay is very much filled with ice and a big swell made landing rather difficult. Larry, Al and myself worked the geology of the region. Paul and several helpers collected lichens, moss, etc. Nick Moultin and Jack Richardson hunted for birds, penguins, etc. We had quite a lunch and, boy, I ate my share and then some. The ship's launch came for us about 4:30. They had left the ship at 3:00 and were an hour-and-a-half getting over to our island. They had trouble getting us because the bay was almost completely filled with ice. Well, that's the closest I ever came to spending a night on an island in the Antarctic, and if it never comes that close again I'll be plenty happy.

We got the news that the *Bear* sailed into this bay yesterday morning and anchored on the other side of the island. I guess they got tired of bobbing around in rough seas also. If we could only get in and take on the East Base men, all would be well.

Tuesday, March 4

Today we visited several places on Lystad Island. Al, Larry and I worked out the geology and collected specimens. I got a penguin today, cleaned him up and he is now in the freeze room. I'd like to get another if possible. Perkins, our biologist, has been having his hands full. He has about eleven small ring-neck penguins to feed, plus four Emperors. The Emperors are very well-behaved and just stand around the bucket full of fish awaiting their turn. But the smallest ring-neck penguins put up a fight. They are very pugnacious and scrappy. Perk has to catch each one and force-feed them.

378

The crab-eater seals have not eaten a thing since we took them aboard at Discovery Inlet. One died, so Perk put two over the side and skinned out two. Yesterday we got a baby (four hundred pound) Loss Seal. Perk will take back the skinned skeleton.

Everyone aboard manages to keep busy, which helps take our minds off the fact that we are still not heading home. The ship's engineers take turns at running the launch, the ship's crew is busy painting various parts of the ship. The expedition men go on field trips covering biology, geology, etc. Berlin, the surveyor, is taking shots from various stations by the bay to establish positions that are accurate. With feeding and taking care of dogs (forty-three aboard this ship), playing cribbage and rummy, seeing shows and shooting the bull, the days manage to slip by. I still can't believe it's been a month since we left Little America.

Wednesday, March 5

Paul, Al and Capt. Lysted had a meeting today on the *Bear* and it looks like we will be here ten more days at least. The *Bear* is going to leave in a day or so and go over to East Base to look over the situation. The ice is still in the bay at last report. If the ice breaks out by the fifteenth or before, the *Bear* will radio us to come. If by the fifteenth the ice has not moved out then evacuation will be done by plane, taking only the men. That is, we cannot afford to wait any later than the fifteenth for fear of being frozen in ourselves. If only the ice would break out in a day or two everything would be fine.

Friday, March 7 (missed the 6th)

After breakfast we'd planned to go out to work on one of the islands but the launch left before Larry and I were through taking care of our dogs. I then spent the morning washing some clothes and took a shower. I might add that a shower sure beats the bucket which I have been using the past year or so. After lunch we went for a boat ride. It was meant to be a penguin-hunting expedition, so to speak. Some of the fellows the day before had found an island which was literally covered with penguins. Perk wanted to capture some more and the Captain wanted to take some pictures, so we took off. Petras said he knew where the island was so he was pilot. Boy, what a wild goose chase. We messed around for three hours, went clear around Lystad Island probably ten miles or so, but no island that was the right one. We finally ended up on an island about a quarter-mile from the ship and got four penguins.

It got quite chilly late in the afternoon and believe it or not, I was actually cold. I guess I can't take it any longer. Maybe it's the summer shorts. Of course, I haven't got a "T" shirt on so maybe that has something to do with it. Last night I rolled film, which is always quite a job for me. Rolled twelve rolls, finishing up about midnight, then went right to bed.

We did not do any field work today as they used the launch for bottom soundings. It seems that the *Bear* is going to move over here so as to unload some of the expedition men and crew to this ship. This is in case the ice does not break out by the twelfth, the *Bear* is going to try to break through. Because of the risk, etc., I guess they plan on using a skeleton crew. I guess this was all planned in the meeting the other day, but it's just getting down to we nobodies. This afternoon it is now 3:00 o'clock and I am down in the "Glory Hole," just getting ready to take a nap. I put in a hard morning, cleaned up my bunk and around my bunk, took my blankets out for an airing. The show tonight was "Arkansas Traveler," then right to bed.

March 8

Today has been quite a busy day. After breakfast we loaded some dogs (eighteen) on the barge to take over to the *Bear*. The *Bear* earlier in the morning had come into our part of the bay to discharge her expedition members, and last night at a radio conference between Capt. Lystad, Paul and Capt. Crusen, it was decided that two dog teams should remain on, hence changing the original plans that all dogs would come aboard here. So we picked out a few dogs here and there, making up scrub teams, giving them "none too good dogs." From the *Bear* we took all the puppies, seven in all, plus a bitch with three small puppies and one or two of the good dogs that were aboard. I have added one dog to the seven I have, making a total of eight. She belongs to Perkins, name is Snooks. She's a beauty, well-marked. They didn't take any of my dogs because they were too good. Am I proud. There's not much to write about while we're at anchor. When you are confined to a two hundred and twenty-four foot ship, the same people, doing the same things day in and day out—not very exciting. Nothing really happens.

March 9 (Sunday)

Now that we have six more fellows aboard I have to get to the dinner table on time. Big event of my life. I ate at the second mess, so didn't get to take care of my dogs till about 7:00 o'clock and it was dark by then.

Things are pretty crowded aboard with extra men. We all seem to be fitting into the situation well. It is nice, though, to have your own bunk where you can get away from it all—hide out.

Did a little housekeeping today, clean sheets on my bunk, aired my blankets and just did busy work. Our outfits issued by the expedition for the return trip are brown army twill affairs—look quite nice. We had chicken tonight for dinner and I was hungry even though I slept most of the afternoon. Ice cream for dessert and I was able to sneak two dishes. The show tonight was about a Nazi spy and I decided not to go. I read a little geology before I went to bed.

March 10 (Monday)

I was awakened about 6:00 A.M. by dogs barking, growling, and carrying on in general. Kept up for some time so I dressed and went out to put in my two cents worth. Two of the dogs in my team were growling and snarling at each other and the rest of the dogs were kind of kibbitzing. I put a stop to the whole affair and since I was up I decided to stay up since it was only an hour till breakfast. Didn't do much today except care for my dogs. After lunch I did go down in the hold to get out some blue denim work shirts for issue, giving one to each man on the expedition. Show tonight was "It Could Happen To You." I didn't go because I had seen it three times. Got to bed about 10:00 P.M. It seems that we are all hitting the hay earlier than when we were down on the ice.

March 11 (Tuesday)

I was rudely awakened a little before 6:00 and told that I was to wait tables. It was not only a surprise but a shock, as I'd forgotten to look at the "poop sheet" on the bulletin board in the social hall. I'm so ashamed of myself, but I went back to sleep. I guess I wasn't quite convinced. Anyway, they woke me up again and I wasn't really late. The whole day went smoothly as far as waiting tables was concerned. Takes longer now that we have two full messes. After breakfast I fed my dogs. Changed the feeding schedule so that we could worm them the next day. In order to give them the medicine the dogs must not eat for twenty-four hours.

March 12 (Wednesday)

This morning I did not have to get up so early since I was a dishwasher. Just so I ate breakfast by 7:30. Anyway, my hands are clean after an all-day session of washing dishes. I think they have this backward. I think they ought to have us wash dishes first, then the next day wait on tables. It looks to me like it would save soap.

After breakfast I helped Dick Moulton worm the dogs. They didn't like the stuff any too well and besides, they were hungry—poor things. Afterwards Doc Frazier called me in saying he wanted to fill one of my teeth. So far he has successfully filled three. He uses sort of a celluloid material and acetone. It works pretty well and I think I will at least be able to save a few teeth. I have had to have one pulled, but none in the front, thank goodness.

At 11:00 o'clock this morning I gave the dogs a little food—a very watery mixture of dog food. Boy, they ate it up fast, almost before I put it before them. We are still in Melchoir Bay and this is our fortieth day since we left West Base.

March 13 (Thursday)

Stayed up last night till midnight shooting the bull. It's hard to put your finger on any one topic that we talk about. We are all experts on many subjects. Worked in the hold most of the afternoon. The ship's crew was squaring around some of the boxes and gear down there so I had to be on hand to watch where the clothing boxes went.

We had a big meeting tonight concerning Article Nine, the section of the president's "poop sheet" which concerns personal film, drawings, etc. The committee wants us to furnish our film to be checked, looked over so they can have copies or prints of any good shots. There was quite a heated discussion about the matter as most of the fellows don't like it, and I can't say I do. In the first place, the film is personal, bought by individuals, and why should we have to turn it in? Nothing was said about it at the start of the expedition. Besides, we had an official photographer with thousands of dollars worth of equipment. Surely he has better shots than we have as we had to work, and his work was taking pictures. We were all pretty upset at the meeting, but I'm sure something will be worked out.

March 14 (Friday)

Worked down in the hold again today getting everything secured and shipshape. We want to be ready at all times in case we get word to move on to East Base. Well, we got the word that we were going to get underway tomorrow, but where we are going I don't know, and neither does anyone else. Capt. Lystad is noncommittal. All I know is that we aren't heading north. I would assume that we are going to move closer to East Base and stand by while the *Bear* attempts to get in and take the expedition party aboard.

The movie tonight was "Man To Remember." Very fine picture and we all enjoyed it.

March 19 (missed 15, 16, 17, 18)

As promised, we sailed on the fifteenth. When we got out of Melchoir Bay about 8:00 o'clock P.M. I was in my bunk reading. We hit the open seas, and I was thrown out of my bunk. We have never had the seas so rough. They talk about the roaring forties and the howling sixties—well, I believe it. It's very hard to stay secure in your bunk, and also hard to keep from getting hit by everything falling all around you.

We finally got to the pack ice somewhere around Adelaide Island waiting for something to happen. I guess the whole situation is getting pretty critical and at present it doesn't look like we will be able to get the East Base fellows. The ice is still packed in Marguerite Bay and from the latest reports there are one hundred and twenty miles of ice between the base and open sea. I don't know what we're going to do, but we only have about ten more days of fuel left aboard plus a small safety margin. This ship burns one thousand gallons a day just messing around the way we've been doing. For the last couple of days we've been trying to get in close enough to the island to see if there is any chance of setting a land party ashore to look for a landing field. Personally, I don't like the idea of putting men on the ice because if anything should happen so we had to move and couldn't pick them up—well, that would be a fine mess. Besides, there can be cracks and thin ice which makes it hazardous. The fellows would have to wait till at least the first of June for the bay to become solid ice, and then they would have to walk to East Base—one hundred miles or so. Well, so far we haven't had to worry about such a trip because we haven't gotten close enough to attempt a landing party. I think Al, Paul and Dick Moulton would probably make up the party.

Well, we would work our way through the bay ice and get fairly close to the island when a fog would set in, so we'd have to head back to open sea again. We turned around about midnight and tried again. I guess this could keep up indefinitely except for the fuel factor. The Chief Engineer recommended to the Captain that we head for a port no later than the twenty-fourth—he's worried about an oil shortage. He said at cruising speed we burn one thousand eight hundred gallons a day. The East Base fellows face spending another winter if something doesn't break soon. Fortunately, in our plans for the expedition we took extra food, etc., in case we couldn't be picked up for some reason.

They have talked about using the plane but there is a risk there since it has had two crack-ups, and from reports is being held together by the proverbial chicken wire. It, however, may be our best bet. We have another problem in that we have only two months of food supply aboard this ship, and it would be a certain end if we were frozen in and that may happen if we stay in this ice pack too long. The Captain is worried and, of course, doesn't want to take any unnecessary chances. I heard the other day that the East Base is getting short of food and that they have been out of meat for some time. It seems that all of their meat spoiled—they had some unusual hot weather (hot, that is, for Antarctic). Well, the whole thing is a mess.

If we were only getting somewhere, but we're not. Back and forth, go full speed a while, then slow speed, then lay to for a while, then turn around and start all over again. Waiting, waiting—and it wouldn't be so bad if we knew what was going on. No one seems to know, even my source, Al. I understand that they are going to have a radio talk with the *Bear* tonight. Maybe we'll get some dope. I'm beginning to think that the sun never shines in this neck of the woods. I can't believe it, the sun just started to shine through my porthole big as life. Probably made its appearance just to make a fibber out of me. Anyway, it did appear for a few minutes before it set for good.

Earlier in the day we came alongside (that is, within a hundred yards) of the *Bear*. They put a boat over the side and came over to the *Star*. McCoy (pilot) got aboard and went back to the *Bear*. It seems that they upped their radio conference a bit, and McCoy was to be present. He is supposed to put the okay on a landing field if found, which makes sense to me.

The show tonight was "Torchy in China Town," but I can't take it any longer. It will be wonderful to go to a good movie, sit in a soft seat, and maybe eat popcorn.

384

Capt. Cruzan, Capt. Lystad, Paul and Al had another radio conference—a three-way talk with East Base. Out came our orders from Washington for this ship to go to Punta Arenas for food, fuel oil and gasoline for the Beechcraft, and to leave all men, expedition men not necessary to work the ship, etc.

The whole thing came about when we had our big meeting a while back concerning the film. At the meeting Doc Frazier got up and said that he would like to go on record as saying that he did not like the looks of things from the food end, meaning that we had only two months' food supply aboard. He said he thought the ship ought to put into a port and dismiss the expedition personnel and not have them face the risk of being frozen in another winter. Well, the upshot of the whole thing was that this ship should have a year's supply on it left over when the ship brought us down originally, food which was to stay aboard as emergency for when the ship returned to pick us up. A year's supply is a minimum when you are fooling around in these waters—especially in the ice pack. Well, that food isn't aboard and someone has to do some explaining. Anyway, Capt. Lystad sent Cruzan a wire telling him that Doc Frazier and a third of the men from West Base wanted to go to a port. Capt. Cruzan (Navy) wanted to know who the men were. Doc Frazier by that time was sore, so he sent Cruzan a message explaining about the food too, which makes it embarrassing for Lystad, so to speak. Paul also sent one concerning the food. Cruzan forwarded all messages to the committee in Washington, the Admiral (Byrd), and East Base. Hence, the radio contact tonight and our orders to sail.

It's now 1:00 P.M. and I just got back from the social hall. All of the fellows there are talking about what they are going to do in town. I went to the show tonight, "The Mysterious Avenger." A cow picture, two-gun stuff, you know.

March 22 (missed 21st)

We sailed all day yesterday, very heavy seas. We are just about at the tip of the Horn and the seas are something. No wonder so many early sailing ships were lost going around the Horn. Today the seas are heavy. It's really something to be standing on deck looking out at a wall of water at eye level.

I was just thinking how nice it will be to get a good home-cooked meal with fresh fruit and vegetables. Haven't had much of an appetite lately. I guess canned and dehydrated food is finally getting to me. If we had ever lost our can opener during the winter nights we'd have been in trouble.

It's now 8:00 P.M. and we are traveling along about eleven and five tenths knots per hour, seas are fairly calm now, which is a godsend. According to the ship's chart, this stretch along here is always rough with plenty of wind. We will probably sight land late tomorrow afternoon. Everyone is pretty excited. Imagine seeing people, trees, grass and flowers.

By tomorrow night we will be anchored at the mouth of the Straits of Magellan. Will anchor overnight and go into Punta Arenas first thing in the morning. We will all probably check into a hotel and I can't wait to get to a barber shop. I don't know how I am going to tell him what I want as I know no Spanish. Well, we'll have to see.

We have had some good news. They rescued the men from East Base. They completed evacuation of the men, personal gear and most of the scientific data. They used the Condor, making two flights. Now our plans are for the *Star* to stay in Punta Arenas and wait till the *Bear* arrives in port. She has already gotten underway. They will probably change personnel at Punta Arenas as we have some fellows aboard the *Star* that are to return to the States aboard the *Bear*.

March 23

Well, today we sailed around Cape Horn, and as usual it was foggy. But it did clear enough so that with a little imagination I saw the Horn.

It's now 11:00 P.M. and we are really tearing along up the east coast. I thought we would be at anchor tonight, but that's tomorrow night and we get to Punta Arenas on Tuesday.

March 24

It's now 10:00 P.M. and we are anchored in the Straits awaiting daylight so we can continue to Punta Arenas. Civilization at last, just fifty-one days since we sailed from Little America, Antarctic.

AFTERWORD
August 1994

Following his return from Antarctica, Passel returned to graduate school at the University of Indiana to work up his Antarctic materials. He served in World War II in the Pacific with the United States Marine Corps. Eventually he went to work for oil companies until he opened his own geological business, which he continues to this day.

Little America III (as West Base was known) remained on the Ross Ice Shelf, making its way northward, as that ice moved slowly but perceptibly toward the edge of the sea. Eventually the ice containing Little America III calved from the ice shelf and was spotted as an iceberg floating away from Antarctica in February 1963 by a lookout on an icebreaker.

Charles and Alda Passel were married three weeks after he returned from the south polar regions, and fifty-four years later, are living happily ever after.

CONCERNING THE MANUSCRIPT
AND THE NOTES

The diary was kept by Charles Passel on a daily basis at the West Base of the United States Antarctic Service, 1939-41. In Little America III, the writings were made in a large bound book; on the trail, they were drafted in three smaller volumes. The transcribing was supervised by Passel, and as checked by the editor, reflects an accurate reproduction. Before transcribing, Passel chose to strike from the original a few short personal notes about his fiancée Alda and the occasional expletive that found its way to paper. Otherwise, the reader has a true transcription of the actual diary.

End notes rather than footnotes are included; however, the reader should find it easy to use this system as all references are keyed to the page and the line number of text (excluding date entries and blank spaces between days).

1,1.

For an overview of the activities of the United States Antarctic Service Expedition see Kenneth J. Bertrand, *Americans in Antarctica, 1775-1948* (New York: American Geographical Society, 1971), 407-82.

1,2.

The *North Star* sailed from Boston 15 November 1939, and stopped in Philadelphia to pick up the snow cruiser. The *Bear* also departed from Boston leaving on 22 November 1939 and sailed to Norfolk to pick up the Barkley-Grow seaplane and on to Antarctica. The two ships took separate routes across the Pacific to arrive at the Bay of Whales. For further details on the snow cruiser see notes 2,11; 26,13; 46,10; 76,18; and 126,19.

1,3.

Al Wade (1903-1978) should not have a comma between his first and last names. Wade, a veteran of the second Byrd expedition was senior scientist on Passel's expedition. Returning from the Antarctic, he became chairperson of the Geology Department at Texas Tech University and later was in charge of the scientific staff at McMurdo during the International Geophysical Year.

2,11.

The *North Star* put in at Philadelphia to pick up the snow cruiser, a large vehicle designed to take a four-man party to the South Pole. As it turned out, the cruiser was not a success, and instead of reaching the South Pole made it only as far as West Base, seven miles from the sea.

2,18.

Howard Passel, an artist who later taught art at the University of the Pacific, was the older brother of Charles.

2,29.

Ronnie should be spelled Ronne. The decision to leave intact such spelling errors was made to remain faithful to the original text. Although he was excellent and reliable in his duties to the expedition, Finn Ronne (1899-1980) was regarded by some on this expedition as hard-headed and uncooperative. Convinced he was always right—even when he was not—Ronne was not popular. Ronne, Norwegian by birth but who later became a citizen of the United States, was a member of Byrd's second expedition (1933-35) and later returned to the Antarctic in 1947 as the leader of his own expedition, one marked by an absence of great success but remembered as being the first in which women wintered over on the Antarctic continent. The Ronne Ice Shelf in the Weddell Sea, the second largest body of floating ice in the world, is named for him.

4,35.

Paul A. Siple (1908-68) was the Boy Scout chosen to be a member of Byrd's first Antarctic expedition (1928-30). Reestablishing himself in the United States he continued his education and returned as chief biologist on the second Byrd campaign (1933-35). During this endeavor he was in charge of the West Base. Siple was a good leader, allowing his scientists a free hand in their work and managing the affairs of the base in a low-key manner. Siple directed the U. S. scientific work in the International Geophysical Year (1957).

5, 10.

The men made dog sleds en route south, rather than before, to occupy their time during the long ocean voyage.

7, 4.

Smuck (Paul Smucker) was Passel's roommate at Miami University and eventually managed his family's firm, Smuckers.

7, 5.

Passel used the term "poop sheet" for any kind of written memo generated during the expedition.

7, 13.

Alda saved Passel's letters and they have been preserved as part of Passel's Antarctic papers.

8, 6.

Sergeant Asman had been recently released by the doctor and was being relieved by Al Wade and Passel.

10, 24.

Ronnie should be Ronne. See note 2,29 above.

10, 29.

Admiral Richard E. Byrd (1888-1957) was the first person to fly over the North and South poles, although some controversy exists about the North Pole flight. A graduate of the United States Naval Academy (1912), his naval career was cut short owing to an ankle injury. Retiring in 1916, he was called back later that year when the navy began to expand its aerial service. At Pensacola naval station, Byrd was among the first of generations of naval pilots to earn his wings at the west Florida base. He spent World War I in Canada, in charge of a flying squadron. In May 1926, Byrd and his pilot, Floyd Bennett, startled the world by successfully flying over the North Pole, for which Byrd was promoted to commander and awarded the Congressional Medal of Honor. The commander's next exploit was to fly the Atlantic. A crash prevented him from attempting the crossing in May before Charles A. Lindbergh (20-21 May), but the flight was completed in June 1927. With money from major donors, Byrd launched his first Antarctic expedition (1928-30) and returned for a second effort (1933-35). During the latter effort he spent five months alone in an advance base, an action that nearly cost him his life when he suffered from carbon monoxide poisoning. Byrd was a logical choice to head the United States Antarctic Service in 1939, not only for his exploring exploits but also because of his family connections—his brother was a senator from Virginia.

10,40.

In the original text, Passel first wrote "lady" and later crossed it out and wrote "person."

14,4.

Roger Horthorne should be spelled Hawthorne, the press officer of the expedition.

15,14.

The Glory Hole was an area in the aft of the ship, the steerage, where some of the men including Passel, slept. The area also had a open space where the men could meet and talk.

15,15.

The term "post storage" should be "port steerage."

17,16.

E. E. Borchgievick should be C. E. Borchgrevink (1864-1934), the leader of the *Southern Cross* (1898-1900) expedition, the first to overwinter in the Antarctic.

19,13.

Cushman was the author of book on foraminifera (the fossil shell remains of these protozoans are used to identify geologic formations); Passel had brought it with him to review in preparation for his field work.

22,1.

With the outbreak of World War II, few ships came to the island. While the *North Star* was there, the ship's doctors, Geyer and Frazier, performed several operations as well as providing other more general medical services for the islanders.

23,6.

Son of Weiner referred to Murray Weiner, a member of the expedition who was known for his astute trading.

25, 6.

Schuchbent and Dunbart should be Schuchert and Dunbart, a historical geology book Passel brought with him to review.

25, 11.

The "radio mail bag" was a regular broadcast from various stations in the United States to the explorers in Antarctica. Friends and relatives mailed notes to the General Electric Company, which arranged to have them broadcast.

25, 17.

Rapa Island is a crescent-shaped island in French Polynesia.

26, 13.

The Barkley-Grow was a seaplane used by Admiral Byrd for several flights in the Bay of Whales area.

26, 15.

Dick Moulton was in charge of the dogs. Passel met him at Wonalancet, New Hampshire where he learned how to drive dogs.

26, 32.

Admiral Richard E. Byrd dropped by often to check on the recovery of Passel and Dick Moulton.

27, 39.

Little Ellis was a child taken from Pitcairn Island and transported to New Zealand because he needed medical attention.

27, 23.

Malcolm Davis, a biologist, was a member of the ship's company but was not at either base.

32, 30.

No conscious effort was made to keep details such as the ship's schedule from the crew, but by and large, the scientists were more involved with their immediate tasks and were not concerned overly about exact arrival dates.

33, 19.

The dates should read 27 December 1939 to 2 January 1940. Instead of writing in his diary, Passel wrote directly to Alda in a letter.

35,31.

The captain of the *North Star*, Isak Lystad, previously had commanded the ship in Alaska where it was used by the Bureau of Indian Affairs to provide supplies for that northern territory. Lystad regarded this Antarctic venture as an imposition on his ship.

39,8.

The camera that Alda gave Passel was the first camera he ever owned and turned out to be a valuable asset for recording the trip. The photographs in this volume were taken with that camera.

40,35.

The expedition had two tractors. The red one, here referred to as "Dolly" and briefly called "Alda," was a T20 International tractor. A second, faster utility tractor was also used, but could haul less than the International.

41,27.

When traveling through the ice pack, an experienced sailor can determine whether ice or open water is in the distance, even over the horizon, as the sky will appear lighter (ice) or darker (water) because of the surface below.

41,31.

Passel's certificate now hangs in his business office in Abilene, Texas.

45,8.

Apparently no one checked the tractor on ice or snow before sending it to Antarctica. Operating in reverse effectively created front-wheel drive for the vehicle.

46,10.

Although Passel's account downplays the danger of the incident, had the barrels not held up the cruiser, it might have crashed onto the ice where its enormous weight might have broken up or cracked the bay ice, then only about seven feet thick. Many men would have been thrown into the water or found themselves isolated on small floes heading out to sea, a situation that could have resulted in several deaths.

52,1.

The "Jitter Bug" was the smaller utility tractor.

55,34.

Court did marry shortly after he returned from the expedition.

60,17.

Byrd cloth was a windproof cotton used to make windbreakers and pants for the men. Fifty-five years after the expedition, Passel's outfit shows little sign of wear, looking remarkably new and undamaged.

65,33.

"Jake" was a term for "good" used by the naval men and Passel adopted it.

69,27.

Malcolm C. Douglas was a surprise on the expedition because he was a former Boy Scout, extremely wholesome and gentlemanly, and some feared he would not pull his weight. He was the victim of many jokes and much harassing but proved a valuable member of the expedition.

72,34.

Although Passel signed on for one winter, no one knew if the expedition would continue with a second or third winter. As it turned out, Congress did not fund a second year. Wade advised Passel to return after a single year to finish his graduate work.

76,18.

The snow cruiser was unloaded from the ship and driven by Doc Poulter to the West Base where it remained, unable to navigate in the Antarctic conditions. The vehicle was underpowered and could not move across the various surfaces and, although a wonderful idea, was a failure. Passel went to the cruiser to listen to the radio or to spend time visiting Al Wade. The cruiser team slept in the vehicle as the hut was not designed to accommodate them. Originally the group was to proceed to the South Pole and be away for the entire winter season. The men of the cruiser unit took their meals with the others in the hut.

92,22.

Roald Amundsen (1872-1928) was one of the greatest polar explorers of his day. His careful and skilled approach to polar travel allowed him to become the first human at the South Pole in December 1911, one month before Robert Falcon Scott (1868- 1912). In a daring move, Amundsen had established his camp on the ice, affording him a shorter route to the pole, but in doing so he risked having the ice break up, a catastrophe that might have resulted in the deaths of his team.

98,23.

Old Little America where Byrd's earlier expeditions had been based was being crushed by the forces of the ice and the movement of the Ross Ice Shelf and was therefore uninhabitable, forcing Byrd to seek new quarters further from the edge of the ice. West Base was also known as Little America III.

100,33.

A Von Prague was a heater that acted like a blowtorch.

126,19.

The three marines were on the expedition to act as pilots (Theodore Petras and Walter Giles) and navigator (Felix Ferranto) of the snow cruiser.

132,29.

The "temperature freezing test" Passel referred to numerous times in his journal formed the research that led to the development of the Wind Chill Chart, now commonly used in weather reports. The "run" as Passel often described it could take between several minutes and a couple of hours depending on the wind and temperature conditions. For a description of the development of this data, see Paul A. Siple and Charles F. Passel, "Measurements of Dry Atmospheric Cooling in Subfreezing Temperatures," *Proceedings of the American Philosophical Society* 89 (April, 1945): 177-99.

150,12.

Doc Frazier had been a physician with the Anaconda copper mine and thus was familiar with a wide range of medical situations. Having had his diabetes under control before the expedition, he was not disqualified by this illness.

157,38.

Fifty-four years after the event, Passel could not explain the reasons for his sudden illness.

178,22.

"I hurried to know that our promise" was transcribed incorrectly. The text should read, "I hurried and sent Ruth a message. Also I received one from Alda—I am so happy to know that she loves me and

our promise still holds. I know it always will. I love her so dearly."
Ruth was Paul Siple's wife.

214,14.

Had the tractor broken down a day earlier, Passel would have been in
serious danger, exhausted and far from Little America III.

218,6.

A Bruton is a brand-name compass with sights used then and now by
geologists in the field.

227,37.

Fifty years later, Passel surmised that Malcolm became disoriented
while trying to walk back to camp. Because people have a tendency to
walk in the direction of the magnetic pole, Passel belived Malcolm
probably walked away from the direction of the camp.

229,21.

The decision to call off the search must have been a difficult one for
Siple but given conditions that were life-threatening to the searchers
and the extremely small chance that Malcolm would be seen, even by
someone passing quite near to him, the choice to end the search was a
sensible thing to do.

248,1.

Passel's reference to the "Scotts and Shackelford Expeditions" should
read Scott's and Shackleton's expeditions. This referred to Robert Falcon Scott who led two expeditions, the *Discovery* (1901-04) and the
Terra Nova (1910-13) and Sir Ernest Shackleton who led three: *Nimrod*
(1907-09), *Endurance* (1914-17), and the *Quest* (1921-22). Shackleton
died during the last of these three endeavors.

272,2.

Passel's comment on the monotony had been echoed in previous expeditions. Frederick Cook noted during the *Belgica* expedition (1897-
99), "The truth is, that we are at this moment as tired of each other's
company as we are of the cold monotony of the black night and of the
unpalatable sameness of our food." Frederick A. Cook, Through the
First Antarctic Night, 1898-99 (New York: Doubleday & McClure Co.,
1900), 291.

277,18.

Doc Frazier, though not a dentist, had had a good deal of experience in such matters because of his work as a physician in the mining camps.

285,30.

The mist for his teeth was a painkiller; the alternative cure was "straight alky," that is, alcohol.

289,1.

The following list the five parties on the trail while Passel was away from base. The Rockefeller Mountains Seismic Station included: Roy G. Fitzsimmons, Isaac Schlossback, Raymond Butler. The Rockefeller Mountains Geological Party was led by F. Alton Wade with Dr. Russel G. Frazier. The Pacific Coast Survey Party was comprised of: Leonard M. Berlin, Jack Bursey, and Richard S. Moulton. The Ford Ranges Biological Party included: Jack E. Perkins, Ernest E. Lockhart, Louis Colombo, and H. H. Richardson who joined from the Pacific Party at the 105 mile depot. In Passel's group were Lawrence A. Warner, Loran Wells, Harold P. Gilmore, and Passel.

290,23.

The mileages given on the trail were in nautical miles.

289,6.

Given that there were two airplanes with the expedition, one might ask why the trail parties were not taken out by air. The need to spend a good deal of time doing field work and the amount of supplies needed to support such an effort was beyond the air supply capacity of the airplanes. Plus, the use of dogs allowed the men to move more quickly from one site to another while in the field.

291,9.

The destination, 105 camp, was a major cache with food, dog food, and other supplies for the trail parties and fuel for airplanes.

292,31.

A radio sked was a scheduled time for Passel to contact base. They spoke to him and he responded in Morse Code using a hand-cranked generator and sending key.

294,25.

Having someone ski ahead of the dogs gave the animals a point to move toward; otherwise, they would not pull as well. In addition, the danger of crevasses meant that it was better to have Joe ahead scouting for such dangers. During this trip Passel's team found a crevasse despite these precautions and his dogs disappeared into an opening in the ice. Fortunately they were caught by a ledge about twenty feet below the surface and rescued without injury.

294,36.

The phrase "we made Nib and Grif from a couple of cans of soup," means that Passel and his partner talked them out of a couple of cans of soup.

296,31.

Cerevim was a type of cereal that tasted like pabulum. Finer than oatmeal, Cerevim was mixed with water to make a thick cereal with the consistency of porridge.

296,35.

In the end, the scientists and the other expedition members won the argument over keeping their own film. Asked how this victory came about Passel commented, "as per the various bull sessions, everybody was going to quit" and the authorities backed down.

299,3.

Although it appears that the dogs were shunted between the various teams, Passel kept his team intact throughout the trail journey. Passel brought Tongas, his wheel dog (closest to the sled), home with him. Passel had to ride with him in the baggage car back to Indiana as Tongas was quite unhappy when left alone. Departing the station in Indiana, Tongas was afraid to go down the stairs so Passel carried the nearly ninety-pound dog down. Several days passed before Tongas got used to the idea of grass—he would take a step and then look at the bottom of his paw to see if it was all right.

304,4.

Passel's frustration had been reflected in the writings of previous Antarctic heroes. Louis Bernacchi on the Southern Cross expedition (1898-1900) noted in his journal, "Ah well. We are not sorry to leave this gelid desolate spot, our place of abode for so many dreary months! May I never pass such another 12 months, in similar surroundings and conditions." Yet within eighteen months, Bernacchi was en route south again with the Discovery expedition. Similarly, Jean Charcot leader of the Francais (1903-05) and the Pourquoi-Pas? (1908-10) noted in rereading his diary from his first expedition that, "I light on a passage where I assert that, if I ever return to France, I will embark no more on such adventures." Yet he, too, returned within four years. Louis Bernacchi, Journals kept during the British Antarctic expedition, 1898-1900, Scott Polar Research Institute MS 353/1/1-3, 2 February 1900 and Jean Charcot, *The Voyage of the 'Pourquoi-Pas?'* (London: Hodder and Stoughton, 1911), 198.

304,31.

Euginas biscuits were hard, like a ship's biscuit.

310,17.

Passel was describing a rainbow-like phenomenon, only it occurred during fog. A circular arc appears in the direction opposite the sun, usually not as bright as a rainbow because the size of the water droplets are smaller.

312,7.

Going up and down hills with a dog sled is not easy as the sled tends to overtake the dogs or runs over the dog traces, which can upset the course.

313,6.

Rope locks were lines (or ropes) put around the sled runners to act as a brake when going downhill.

314,14.

Snowy Petrels was mistakenly transcribed as Snowy Petras.

316,10.

Gil and Joe were in Passel's party. They wanted to quit and go back because they did not feel they were pulling their own weight. In the end both stayed with the group.

320,2.

Although Passel often indicated that he was tired, he rarely mentioned being hungry, unlike the sledge travelers of the Heroic Era. Two factors contributed to the difference: air resupply allowed Passel's expedition to have more food and they had a much more scientifically balanced diet.

323,13.

Passel was very keen to find fossils but never did on the trail journey in the mountains.

326,35.

Roy G. Fitzsimmons, Fitz, was at his seismic station measuring tremors and doing magnetometer work.

328,18.

By working Pk 232, Passel means that they collected rock specimens from the mountain and did geological investigations at that site to determine the geology of the area.

333,21.

Here Passel's remark is tongue-in-cheek. Although he had encountered crevasses before, these were so large that, by comparison, the others seemed so inconsequential as not to merit being counted.

339,1.

The survey party went much farther than the other parties because their objective was to cover as much ground as possible to widen the area of Antarctica seen by the expedition and to clarify details remaining unclear from the aerial photography. Despite traveling lighter and receiving aerial drops of dog food en route, their dogs became tired because of the great distance traveled.

349,24.

Those interested in the ecology of Antarctica will be pleased to know that Passel's group did remove their trash pile from the area of 105 camp.

356,23.

Adalie should be spelled Adélie.

359,25.

Passel and Alda were married three weeks after he returned from the Antarctic.

363,36.

Douglas was ordered to the ship for other duties.

375,17.

Passel is demonstrating his frustration with the lack of movement; no hint of secret orders was intended.

386,19.

Although the Condor that belonged to the West Base was inoperable, the one at East Base was used to relieve the men at the latter installation.

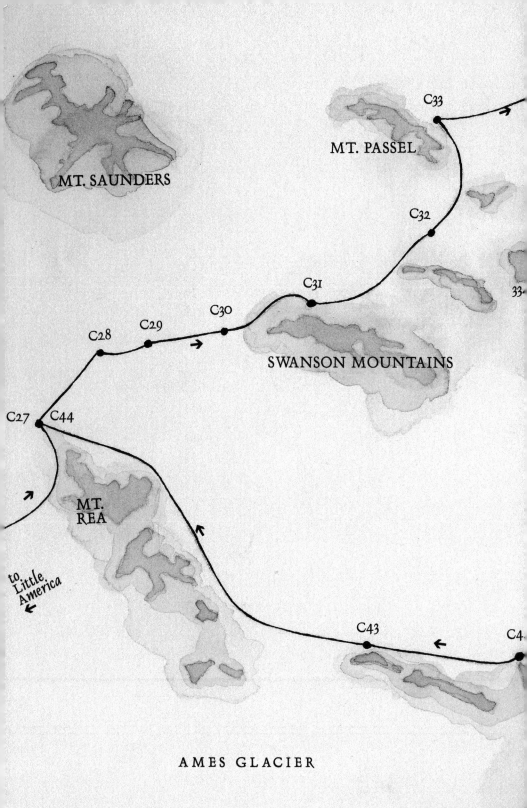

MT. SAUNDERS

MT. PASSEL

C33

C32

C31

C30

C29

C28

SWANSON MOUNTAINS

33·

C27 C44

MT.
REA

to
Little
America

C43

C4

AMES GLACIER